THE PSYCHOLOGY OF RESTORATIVE JUSTICE

Gavrielides' edited collection revolutionizes our understanding of restorative justice through its multidisciplinary, global and comprehensive approach. Despite the volumes written on this topic and billions spent by governments to implement restorative justice programs, the concept remains poorly understood and inconsistently implemented. Through both a theoretical and empirical framework, the authors in this collection discuss critical issues in restorative justice policies and practices and offer a cohesive understanding of the restorative justice movement. I highly recommend this book for academics, practitioners and policy makers alike.

Karen Terry, John Jay College of Criminal Justice, USA

Full of lively chapters that demonstrate that it's not difference that divides practitioners but silence, The Psychology of Restorative Justice *offers a range of multi-disciplinary voices that challenge complacency, invigorate debate and articulate what future next steps might be.*

Lorraine Gamman, University of the Arts London, UK

Justice, in Plato's The Republic, *means harmony, both internal, in the form of the soul, and external, in the form of the state. Restorative Justice, therefore, harmonizing the victim with the offender, is justice* par excellence. *Theo Gavrielides' new collective volume is the epitome of harmony in conflictual situations, in theory and practice, and in psychological perspectives, including the latest research in neuroscience.*

Calliope Spinelli, University of Athens, Greece

Nils Christie invited us to be provocative, creative and critical in seeking justice for those in conflict with the law and each other. He believed that the power of the state, alone, could not deliver justice; he believed in the power within each of us to own our conflicts. This book is a testimonial to that conviction, grounded in the latest praxis across disciplinary domains. It is a must read for anyone interested in the limits and human potential of restorative justice.

Brenda Morrison, Simon Fraser University, Canada

Howard Zehr suggests that 'Restorative Justice is not a map but the principles of restorative justice can be seen as a compass pointing a direction'. With this book the authors point the readers in a new direction, namely to explore restorative justice through a multi-disciplinary lens. By stimulating the discourse about how restorative justice as well as its practices and approaches can bring about justice (restoration) on a deeper level than its current application within a legal paradigm, this book inspires continued debate that transcends the existing boundaries of what we understand restorative justice to be. This is indeed a pioneering and exciting direction.

Marelize Schoeman, University of South Africa, South Africa

Nils Christie (24 February 1928 – 27 May 2015) was a Norwegian criminologist and is considered by many to be one of the founders of the contemporary restorative justice movement. He was a professor of criminology at the Faculty of Law, University of Oslo from 1966. He published 'Conflicts as Property', a paper that is said to have opened the debate on restorative justice. Christie is well known for his long-standing criticism of prisons and industrial society and was often called an abolitionist and a reformist.

Nils Christie was a light on the hill who showed us how to take back our conflicts to transform lives and societies toward paths of social justice. He wrote even in English in a evocatively Norwegian voice that resonated authentically from his roots—John Braithwaite

It is with great humility and honour that I dedicate this volume to Nils Christie who paved the way for contemporary restorative justice. May his vision for returning conflicts and empowering the disempowered be a guiding light for us all—Theo Gavrielides

Nils' provocative work had a significant impact here in North America in the 70s, 80s and beyond. In both form and content they helped shape my own early writing about restorative justice—Howard Zehr

The Psychology of
Restorative Justice
Managing the Power Within

Edited by

THEO GAVRIELIDES
*IARS International Institute, UK and
Restorative Justice for All, UK*

ASHGATE

Published by
Ashgate Publishing Limited
Wey Court East
Union Road
Farnham
Surrey, GU9 7PT
England

Ashgate Publishing Company
110 Cherry Street
Suite 3-1
Burlington, VT 05401-3818
USA

www.ashgate.com

British Library Cataloguing in Publication Data
A catalogue record for this book is available from the British Library

The Library of Congress has cataloged the printed edition as follows:
The psychology of restorative justice : managing the power within / [edited] by Theo Gavrielides.
    pages cm
 Includes bibliographical references and index.
  ISBN 978-1-4724-5530-7 (hardback) -- ISBN 978-1-4724-5531-4 (ebook) -- ISBN 978-1-4724-5532-1 (epub) 1. Restorative justice. 2. Psychology. I. Gavrielides, Theo, editor.
  HV8688.P793 2015
  364.6'8--dc23

                                                                    2015012399

ISBN 9781472455307 (hbk)
ISBN 9781472455314 (ebk – PDF)
ISBN 9781472455321 (ebk – ePUB)

Printed in the United Kingdom by Henry Ling Limited, at the Dorset Press, Dorchester, DT1 1HD

Contents

List of Figures

Notes on Contributors

Dominic Abrams, FAcSS, FBA, is director of the Centre for the Study of Group Processes at the School of Psychology, University of Kent. He is co-chief editor of *Group Processes and Intergroup Relations* and past president of the Society for the Psychological Study of Social Issues. His research interests centre on the social and developmental psychology of social inclusion and exclusion, spanning all forms of intergroup prejudice and discrimination across the lifespan.

Vasso Artinopoulou is professor of criminology in the Sociology Department of Panteion University of Social and Political Sciences (Athens, Greece) and the former vice rector of the university from 2009 to 2011. She is actively participating in many national, European and international organizations, working groups and research projects, and is the co-founder and co-director of the Restorative Justice for All Institute (London, UK). She is also head of the Crime and Criminal Justice Unit and the Gender Issues Unit in the European Public Law Organisation (EPLO, EU) (since 2012); was vice president of the board of the 'Organization against Drugs', Ministry of Health (Greece) (2009–2013); a member of the Empowerment and Equity for Diverse Communities Thematic Working Group of the Global Forum on Law, Justice and Development (GFLJD), The World Bank (Washington, DC, USA) (2012–2013); and is an external expert of the Research Executive Agency (REA) of the European Commission (2014–2020). She is also the scientific head in many European projects on restorative justice, mediation and victims of crime. She is the founder and scientific director of the Hellenic Social Mediation Center; was president of the board at the 'Central Scientific Prison Board', Ministry of Justice, Transparency and Human Rights (2009–2011); a member of Legislative Committee for the assessment and treatment of victims of child sexual abuse, Ministry of Justice, Transparency and Human Rights, Greece (2010); president of the board at the Research Center for Gender Issues (KETHI) (2001–2004); national representative of Greece at the European Observatory for School Violence (founding member) (2000). Vasso has carried out research on human rights and violence (women's and children abuse), victimology, gender equality and sexual harassment in the workplace, juvenile delinquency, restorative justice, social mediation and school violence. She is the author of nine books and almost 70 publications in peer-reviewed journals and collective volumes in English, French and Greek.

Andy Cook qualified in clinical psychology in 2013. Prior to this she worked at the Clermont Child Protection Unit as a senior practitioner consultant undertaking

Court-directed risk assessments, facilitating treatment programmes and working therapeutically. In this context she was concerned with the parents' capacity to change and became interested in the repair of family relational bonds in the aftermath of child protection concerns. When the opportunity arose to research restorative justice interventions within forensic mental health services she was keen to take this on. Her doctoral research was a qualitative exploration of the experience of restorative approaches in a forensic mental health setting. Andy now works as a clinical psychologist within a forensic mental health setting and retains a keen interest in restorative justice.

Gerard Drennan is a consultant clinical psychologist and professional lead for clinical forensic psychology at the South London and Maudsley NHS Foundation Trust. Gerard trained as a clinical psychologist in Cape Town 23 years ago, and has worked in forensic mental health settings in London and Sussex for the past 16 years, while undertaking training as a psychoanalytic psychotherapist and a restorative justice facilitator. Gerard has worked with colleagues across the forensic network in the UK and overseas to articulate the meaning of recovery in settings where mental health difficulties and offending behaviour intersect.

Theo Gavrielides is an international expert in restorative justice, human rights and criminal justice and an advisor and project manager for EU and international programmes. He is the founder and director of the IARS International Institute and the founder and co-director of the Restorative Justice for All Institute (RJ4All). He is also an adjunct professor at the School of Criminology (Centre for Restorative Justice) of Simon Fraser University as well as a visiting professor at Buckinghamshire New University. Theo is the editor-in-chief of the peer-reviewed *International Journal of Human Rights in Healthcare*, as well as the *Youth Voice Journal* and the *Internet Journal of Restorative Justice*. He has published extensively in the areas of restorative justice, human rights, youth justice, equality and criminal justice. Previously, he was the chief executive of Race on the Agenda, as well as the human rights advisor of the UK Ministry of Justice.

Isabel González Ramírez is director of the Centre of Mediation, Negotiation and Arbitration and academic director of the mediation and arbitration Masters programmes, Universidad Central de Chile. Since 2002 she has been professor of criminal law and mediation in the School of Law at the same university. She is a lawyer (Universidad Católica de Chile) and mediator, holds a Masters degree in criminal law (Universidad Central de Chile) and is a graduate student of the doctoral programme in criminal law of the University of Buenos Aires. She directed the Office of Access to Justice, in the Ministry of Justice. She is also the author of various publications in restorative justice.

Ioanna Gouseti is currently a PhD candidate in the Department of Methodology at the London School of Economics and Political Science. Her doctoral research explores people's emotional, cognitive and behavioural reactions to the risk of falling victim of crime, and their interplay with psychological distance from crime and crime-risk construals. Her research is funded by the LSE and the A.G. Leventis Foundation. Ioanna holds a BA (Hons) in sociology and an MSc (Hons) in criminology from the Panteion University of Social and Political Sciences, Athens, Greece. She has taught criminological, sociological and methodological courses in Greece and the UK, and has conducted research in collaboration with the National Centre for Social Research (Greece), the Centre for Penal and Criminological Studies, Law School of the University of Athens, the Restorative Justice for All Institute (RJ4All). She is the (co-)author of criminological articles and book chapters, including 'Psychological Distance and the Fear of Crime' (2015), 'Fear of Crime and the Psychology of Risk' (with J. Jackson, 2014), 'Harmful Traditional Practices against Women and Human Rights' (in Greek, 2011). Ioanna's research interests include fear of crime, public attitudes to crime, risk perception, heuristics, gender issues in criminology, criminal justice practices, experimental criminology and research methodology.

Rina Kashyap is associate professor in the Department of Political Science Lady Shri Ram College, University of Delhi specializing in political theory, international relations, and Indian politics. She also taught courses in the Journalism and Conflict Transformation and Peacebuilding programmes. Her doctoral research on 'responsibility to protect' was funded by Social Sciences and Humanities Research Council of Canada grant. She was a Fulbright Scholar at the Center for Justice and Peacebuilding, Eastern Mennonite University and a Visiting Fellow at Center for International Conflict Resolution, School of International and Public Affairs, Columbia University. Her publications include "Narrative and Truth: A Feminist Critique of the South African Truth and Reconciliation Commission" *Contemporary Justice Review*, *12*(4), 449–467 (2009); "Jihad" in Stout, D. (ed.) *Encyclopedia of Religion, Communication, and Media* (pp. 197–199) New York: Routledge (2006).

Henry Kiernan has been a registered restorative justice facilitator and trainer since 2002, gaining accredited practitioner (RJC) status in 2011. He regularly facilitates and trains staff in education and other organizations including forensic mental health, and is a member of the RJC Standards and Accreditation Practitioner Committee. He was previously a head teacher and education consultant.

Mikhail Lyubansky, PhD, is a member of the Department of Psychology at the University of Illinois, Urbana-Champaign. Among other courses, he teaches an upper-level undergraduate course on the psychology of race and ethnicity and a graduate-level practicum course on restorative justice. Since 2009, Mikhail has been bringing his many years of experience in teaching and writing about racial justice to learning, facilitating, evaluating and supporting others in learning the restorative practice developed in Brazil called Restorative Circles. In addition to multiple book chapters and peer-reviewed articles, Mikhail recently co-edited *Toward a Socially Responsible Psychology for a Global Age* and regularly explores racial justice and restorative justice themes in his *Psychology Today* blog, Between the Lines. Born in the former Soviet Union, Mikhail immigrated with his family to the USA as a child in 1977. He currently lives in Urbana, IL, with his wife and two children.

Giuseppe Maglione is a lecturer in criminology at Edinburgh Napier University, School of Life, Sport and Social Sciences. Giuseppe obtained a PhD in legal theory and history of law from the University of Florence and carried out research on restorative justice at the University of Oslo and at the Max Planck Institute for Foreign and International Criminal Law in Freiburg. Since 2007 he has been lecturing or presenting papers internationally on criminological and socio-legal subjects (Oslo, Oxford, Athens, Dubrovnik, Stockholm, London, Florence, Padua, Rome and so on). In addition to his research activity, Giuseppe has extensively worked as victim–offender mediator for the NGO L'altro diritto in Italy, and as consultant and trainer in mediation/conflict management in Norway. He is currently a member of the Scotland Restorative Justice Exchange Knowledge Group. Among his most recent publications are 'Discursive Fields and Subject Positions: Becoming "Victim", "Offender" and "Community"' in *Restorative Justice, Restorative Justice: An International Journal*, 2(3) (2014); 'Problematizing Restorative Justice: A Foucauldian Perspective' in T. Gavrielides and V. Artinopoulou (eds), *Reconstructing Restorative Justice. Philosophy, Values, Norms and Methods Reconsidered* (pp. 67–89), Farnham: Ashgate Publishing (2013).

Samuel Malamud Herrera is a lecturer in the School of Law, Universidad Central de Chile. He is also a lawyer (Universidad Central de Chile) and holds a Masters degree in criminal law (Universidad de Sevilla). He is currently an assessor in the special unit in Economic Crime, Money Laundering and Organized Crime of the Chilean Public Prosecutor's Office. He is also the author of peer-reviewed papers and book chapters.

Andriana Ntziadima holds a BA in Greek language and linguistics and a BA in communications and mass media, both from the Hellenic Kapodistrian University of Athens, Greece. She also has a Masters degree in international relations from the University of Essex, UK. She is currently working as communications and marketing manager at the IARS International Institute, a non-profit organization with a charitable mission to forge a fairer, safer society. She is also a project officer at the Restorative Justice for All Institute (RJ4All), a UK-based international institute that generates and disseminates knowledge on restorative justice, while providing capacity building, research evaluation and advice to governments, organizations and individuals on restorative justice. Over the past four years Andriana has worked in various European research programmes with a specific focus on justice and human rights including the 'Restorative Justice in Europe: Safeguarding Victims and Empowering Professionals' and the 'Restorative Justice and in Cases of Domestic Violence'. Her research interests include restorative justice, offenders' rehabilitation, impact evaluation, citizenship, participation and youth policy.

Judah Oudshoorn is a professor in the community and criminal justice degree programme at Conestoga College Institute of Technology and Advanced Learning in Kitchener, Canada. He is also a restorative justice mediator in the Canadian federal prison system. Judah's research interests include male violence, the impact of punishment on identity, and trauma-informed restorative justice. He is the author of the books *Trauma-Informed Youth Justice in Canada: A New Framework toward a Kinder Future* and *The Little Book of Restorative Justice for Sexual Abuse: Hope through Trauma.* Judah is grateful to be partners with Cheryl, and proud dad to Emery and Selah.

Nicola Preston has been involved in restorative practices in the UK since 1996 as a founder member of the Restorative Justice Consultancy in Thames Valley Police, where she served for 14 years as a police officer, introducing restorative justice to cautioning as well as the complaints and grievance processes within Thames Valley Police. The work of the Consultancy led to the development of national youth offending services and the spread of restorative justice across the UK. Since that time she has been a trainer, facilitator and researcher in the field, working for 10 years with the International Institute for Restorative Practices (IIRP) in the UK as their assistant director for training. Nicola was involved with the Restorative Justice Council from its establishment and has been part of working groups that have developed national best practice standards and accreditation. She has presented at conferences nationally and internationally on the development of restorative justice and practice. Nicola is currently a primary school teacher and special educational needs co-ordinator at Charles Warren Academy in Milton Keynes, working with 4–11 year olds. She also teaches online courses in restorative practices for the IIRP Graduate School and is a member of the Board of Trustees for IIRP Europe. Nicola works part time as a senior restorative justice practitioner for the Thames Valley Partnership involved with two victim-initiated restorative justice projects funded by the Police and Crime Commissioner. Nicola has a BA (Hons) in psychology from Reading University, an MA in restorative practices and relationships from Chester University and an MA in education from Northampton University. Both Masters degrees involved dissertations focusing on restorative practices.

Daniel Reisel is a research associate at University College London's Institute for Women's Health, where he conducts research in empirical bioethics. He is on the teaching faculty of UCL Medical School and has been involved in curriculum development in medical ethics at UCL and at the national level through Health

Education England. He completed his PhD in behavioural neuroscience at the University of Oxford in 2005, with a focus on the neural basis of learning and memory. As part of a research project funded by the Department of Health, he spent a year working at HM Prison Wormwood Scrubs and, in 2014, trained as a restorative justice facilitator.

Elaine Shpungin, PhD, is the director of the University of Illinois, Urbana-Champaign Psychological Services Center (PSC). She practises, studies, teaches and writes about restorative approaches in families and communities, with particular focus on Dominic Barter's Restorative Circles process. Through the PSC Conflict Clinic and other regional collaborations, she has worked with schools, organizations, justice systems and intentional communities to help strengthen and improve their restorative systems. Her writing focuses on the practical application of restorative justice principles in everyday life, and on improving the outcomes of restorative practices. Her writing appears in academic journals, scholarly books, web magazines, popular books on psychology and her RestorativeRevolution blog.

Matthew Smith holds a BSc (Hons) in applied psychology from Liverpool John Moores University and a PhD in psychology from the University of Hertfordshire. He is currently a senior lecturer in psychology at Buckinghamshire New University where he teaches on the MSc in applied positive psychology. Matthew has previously held posts at Liverpool John Moores University and Liverpool Hope University, and has been a visiting lecturer at Oxford Brookes University and Regent's University, London. His current research interests focus around positive psychology and the psychology of luck.

María Soledad Fuentealba Martínez is a lecturer and researcher in the Centre of Mediation, Negotiation and Arbitration of the School of Law, Universidad Central de Chile. She is also a psychologist (Universidad Central de Chile) and mediator, holds a Masters in mediation and dispute resolution (Universidad Central de Chile), a Postgraduate Certificate in child and youth psychology and is a current student of the doctoral programme in criminal law of the University of Buenos Aires. She is also the author of various papers in penal mediation and restorative justice. She took part in the Chilean mediation programme of criminal conflicts coordinated by the European Union and the Agency for International Cooperation.

Giovanni A. Travaglino, PhD, is a research associate at the Centre for the Study of Group Processes, University of Kent. His research interests include the social psychology of leadership and deviance, collective opposition to organized crime, protest and the epistemology of psychology. He is editor of *Contention: The Multidisciplinary Journal of Social Protest* and founder of the Interdisciplinary Network for Social Protest Research (inspr.eu).

Julie Van de Vyver is a doctoral researcher in the School of Psychology at the University of Kent. She is supported by a CASE PhD studentship from the Economic and Social Research Council in partnership with People United. Her research interests include: moral emotions, prosocial behaviour, equality and human rights, and intergroup and intragroup relations.

Milica Vasiljevic, PhD, is a research associate at the Behaviour and Health Research Unit, University of Cambridge. Her research interests include interethnic conflict and forgiveness, intergroup attitudes and the relationship between inequality and different behaviours. Her current research focuses on the design and implementation of social-cognitive interventions to change people's attitudes and behaviours.

Lorenn Walker, JD, MPH, www.lorennwalker.com, is a public health educator and restorative lawyer who develops, implements, researches and publishes the results of social learning processes using restorative justice and solution-focused approaches. Insoo Kim Berg, co-founder of solution-focused brief therapy, mentored and assisted her in designing programmes for homeless and foster youth, and for imprisoned people. Lorenn and Ben Furman, MD, developed and provide a free online programme for individuals on restorative and solution-focused apology and forgiveness (www.apologyletter.org). She is on the Fulbright Specialist roster until 2018 for international peacemaking training; she administers the Hawai'i Friends of Restorative Justice, a small non-profit; she is on the editorial board for four academic journals; since 1998 she has taught public speaking courses full time every fall semester for the University of Hawai'i Honolulu Community College; she is a former trial lawyer who represented state agencies and employees and prosecuted people for fraud; she later defended people in family court; she has been a member of the Hawai'i state bar since 1983; she received a Juris Doctorate degree from Northeastern University School of Law and a Masters degree in public health from the University of Hawai'i; she is the author of three books and over 40 articles.

Piers Worth holds a BSc (Hons) in psychology and a PhD in developmental psychology. He is a chartered psychologist, and an accredited psychotherapist. He is currently head of the Academic Department of Psychology at Buckinghamshire New University. He introduced the MSc in applied positive psychology. Piers' research interests are focused on expanding the understanding of positive psychology and evidencing its contribution to the community. Prior to this work he spent 30 years in human resources and organizational development, consulting in blue-chip companies in the UK and internationally.

Foreword:
The Psychology of Restorative Justice, Where Have You Been?

The most shocking thing about this important, new book is that it has not existed before now. It is hard to believe that we have had over two decades of sustained insight, excitement and investment in and around restorative justice theory and practice, and yet only in 2015 are we getting a book with the title *The Psychology of Restorative Justice*. What does this say about restorative justice? Equally, what does it say about the field of psychology? How could two such natural bedfellows have so successfully avoided one another the past 20-odd years? As the psychologist Michael McCullough (2008) wrote, '[a]lthough the restorative justice movement was created without reference to the principles of evolutionary psychology, no evolutionary psychologist could do much to improve on this combination of ingredients for making forgiveness happen' (p. 178).

The lack of psychological analyses of restorative justice is especially surprising when one considers that the term 'restorative justice' itself is often attributed to the writings of a psychologist, Albert Eglash (see Van Ness and Strong, 1997). Of course, like the contributors to this fascinating collection, Eglash was hardly a mainstream psychologist, if there is such a thing. Eglash's sparse writings (see, for example, Eglash, 1957, 1959, 1977) were very much based in the 'real world' of correctional practice, not in university psychology labs, and he tended to draw magpie-like from fields as diverse as social work, German theology, Kleinian psychoanalysis and youth studies as much as from psychology proper (see Maruna, 2014, for a review). One might argue that it is only through this diverse, cross-disciplinary engagement that it was possible for him and the other pioneers of restorative justice (who also worked in a wide variety of academic fields or none at all) to build such an original and transformative theory and practice.

Such a hypothesis would certainly receive considerable support from this volume. Contributors, including both practitioners and researchers, here draw eclectically on the vast array of scholarship in the psychological sciences, from neuroscience to script theory to positive psychology, to highlight different aspects of restorative practices. The result is a far richer understanding of restorative justice but also a richer exploration of the potential of psychology for helping us think about criminal justice. Both fields of study – restorative justice and psychology – have adopted their own uniforms over the years, without recognizing that what they were actually fashioning were straightjackets.

Restorative justice is, of course, the newer of the two areas, and has been an interdisciplinary pursuit from the beginning. More importantly, the concept's origins (in founding texts like Christie, 1977) are definitively anarchic and anti-statist in origins. At the heart of the restorative idea has always been a critique of state justice, top-down authority and imposition of justice from above. In recent years, though, the power of restorative ideas has persuaded states to adopt the principles in statutory justice work. Such victories are surely to be celebrated. If restorative justice is going to live up to its revolutionary potential as a new framework for justice, impact on statutory justice practices is absolutely essential. At the same time, there is something worrying about the professionalization of restorative justice efforts. At the very least, the more institutionalized restorative justice becomes, the more genuine the risk that the restorative label might become co-opted by criminal justice agencies who utilize the term to dress up traditional punitive or rehabilitative practices.

In terms of academic work, there is a parallel risk of the emergence of a 'usual suspects' group of 'professional spokespersons' for restorative justice. Restorative justice, as an idea, belongs to all of us, not just a handful of expert 'RJ theorists'. The more scrutiny the concept receives from across the academic spectrum, the better. I hope this book triggers parallel volumes in The Economics of Restorative Justice, The Anthropology of Restorative Justice, The Politics of Restorative Justice and other insights from history, communication studies, law, philosophy, performance studies and more.

Yet, psychology is a perfect place to start – especially since this volume also represents an important new development for psychology itself. Indeed psychological theory may benefit more than restorative justice theory by an engagement with this book. As someone trained and steeped in psychology for much of my career, I have been saddened to see (and experience) the non-sensical efforts to narrow the scope of the psychology of crime. As demonstrated in this book, the field of psychology is a broad, eclectic and endlessly fascinating area of study. Yet, the psychology of crime has been inexplicably limited in scope to include little more than a fixation on risk prediction, structured rehabilitative programming, offender profiling and, of course, eye witness testimony and other forms of courtroom research. This forensic psychology mainstream is of course deeply valuable and has found an important place at the table in the criminal justice system, but it represents only a tiny fraction of what psychology can do and be.

I cannot count the number of times I have been told 'that's not psychology' by psychologists (of all people), because the work is, say, qualitative in nature or because it involves exploring how individuals change on their own instead of how they change in randomized trials, for instance. Whereas other fields (one thinks of economics here) risk being too expansive by trying to colonize every area of enquiry (the economics of crime, the economics of education, the economics of mating and so on). The psychological study of crime appears at times to seek to justify itself by defining itself against criminology: 'If criminologists talk to prisoners, we're not going to talk to prisoners. If criminologists get involved in activism around justice issues, we're not going to get involved in activism. If criminologists get bogged down in theory, then we're not going to do theory.' As a result, we have a psychology of crime that is increasingly free of, well, psychology!

Thankfully, in the present volume (notably, the editor and originator of this volume is not, himself, a forensic psychologist!), we have a chance to see the richness of what real psychology can be – even qualitative, activist and theoretical! This is great news for psychology and great news for justice studies to see what we can learn from the oldest social science. Leave it to restorative justice (again) to lead the way in breaking this important, new ground.

Shadd Maruna
Dean, Rutgers University School of Criminal Justice

Bibliography

Christie, N. (1977). Conflicts as property. *British Journal of Criminology*, *17*(1), 1–15.

Eglash, A. (1957). Creative restitution: a broader meaning for an old term. *Journal of Criminal Law, Criminology, and Police Science*, *48*, 619–622.

Eglash, A. (1959). Creative restitution: its roots in psychiatry, religion and law. *British Journal of Delinquency*, *10*, 114.

Eglash, A. (1977). Beyond restitution: creative restitution. In J. Hudson and B. Galloway (eds), *Restitution in criminal justice* (pp. 91–129). Toronto: Lexington Books.

Maruna, S. (2014). The role of wounded healing in restorative justice: An appreciation of Albert Eglash. *Restorative Justice: an International Journal*, *2*, 9–23.

McCullough, M. (2008). *Beyond revenge: the evolution of the forgiveness instinct*. John Wiley & Sons.

Van Ness, D. and Strong, K. (1997). *Restoring justice: an introduction to restorative justice*. New Providence: Matthew Bender & Co.

Dedicated to my father Constantinos Gavrielides

Acknowledgements

<u>Hopes and Fears of the Unknown</u>

Silence. So quiet in the calm of these sounds around me.
It's been a long time
In the midst of cold and unfulfilled promises
silence takes new dimensions
Extreme dimensions of darkness and light.

And the faces that I know become the saving grace of tomorrow.

So much to look forward to
So much to care for
And so many people to meet and greet
Time goes by and the shadows hide in the corners of my room.

Paths that lead to doors with great promises and fears
Where will this journey end?

Theo. 22 August 2014

The editing of this book felt like a journey into the unknown. Taking a path to new destinations felt both intimidating and exciting. But like all road trips, when taken with good company, they can only lead to exciting adventures. Sometimes, they can even become triggers for life reflection, bringing on new challenges. My poem above captures some of my feelings, hopes and fears while exploring multi-disciplinarity as a tool for constructing a psychological concept for restorative justice. Much has been written on restorative justice. This time I felt compelled to challenge the movement and myself by opening doors into the unknown. Without any background in behavioural sciences and with a natural bias towards normative thinking, I set off editing this volume in the hope that my fellow travellers would guide me through it, while putting up with my legally trained attitude and mind. We are still learning how to do restorative justice well and it is our obligation, as scholars, to provide practitioners with rounded and evidence based arguments about its strengths and weaknesses.

Therefore, I must here acknowledge the support, trust and wisdom of all my contributing authors. Their expertise, time and responsiveness are indeed greatly appreciated. I must also acknowledge the trust and excellent collaboration I had with the publisher, Ashgate, and my commissioning editor, Alison Kirk, as well as her team. This is the third project that we have completed together, and indeed look forward to what is yet to come.

My initial inquiry into the contribution of behavioural sciences to restorative justice theory and practice started with discussions with Dr Piers Worth, head of the Academic Department of Psychology at Buckinghamshire New University, where I serve as a visiting professor. Our debates led to the setting up of a multi-year project focusing on positive psychology and restorative justice. Its first findings were published as T. Gavrielides and P. Worth (2013), 'Another push for restorative justice: Positive psychology and offender rehabilitation' in *Crime: International Perspectives, Socioeconomic Factors and Psychological Implications*, New York: Nova Science Publishers. Chapter 11 in this volume presents the final findings of this programme. I am thus grateful to Dr Worth for his collaboration and indeed friendship. I must also acknowledge the funding that we received from the Research Challenge Fund of Buckinghamshire New University, as it enabled us to complete the research. Many thanks also go to the remaining research team: namely, Dr Matthew Smith (senior lecturer, Bucks New University), Andriana Ntziadima (researcher, the IARS International Institute) and Ioanna Gouseti (PhD candidate, LSE). Despoina Bardosi must also be acknowledged for putting together the index.

Serving the blindfolded Goddess Themis has given me a higher purpose in life and a true direction even in my darkest moments. Thinking about the new avenues that I hope this book will lead us to, I want to dedicate it to my father who passed away suddenly and recently. A servant of justice himself, he inspired me to pursue goals that are larger than my own existence. Here, I must also thank my mother for her continuous support for my decisions. Despite our occasional disagreements, love and by extension trust, have guided us through the years. My gratitude must also be expressed for the friendship and intellectual stimuli that I receive from Professor Vasso Artinopoulou and her family. A true champion of justice, intellect and natural beauty, she always challenges me to be a better writer, a more objective researcher, a richer soul and a better person. Finally, many thanks to you for reading this book. I truly hope that you will enjoy the challenges and knowledge that it promises.

Theo Gavrielides
12 March 2015

Introduction

Theo Gavrielides

Visualizing Justice

Brain specialists and cognitive psychologists claim that the way we create meaning is through a process of visualization of images infused with feelings that lead to connections. The word 'table', for instance, creates a visual image of a surface (most often square) standing on four legs. Conversely, when viewing something resembling this image, our brain labels it as 'table'. Interestingly, online search engines function in a similar way. Try searching for images using the word 'table' and you will most likely get thousands of hits resembling the aforementioned description.

Now, try and visualize the word 'justice' or even 'criminal justice'. When applying the test of using search engines, my hits rendered the same images that were in my mind. These were: the balanced scales of justice, the blindfolded Greek Goddess Themis (again holding the balanced scales of justice and a sword), holding hands or a fist.

Reflecting on the findings of this homemade test, I argue that most of us visualize justice in this way simply because we view it as virtue, a value-based notion, a higher purpose and an honourable goal that can give essence to our life paths and sacrifices. My brain did not visualize justice in the form of prisons, courts, suited white men or ministries and politicians. I believe, that our brains deny diminishing justice to an image anything less than a representation of a higher existence. And yet, when an injustice takes place, we instantly visualize prison bars, tall walls, courtrooms and lawyers.

By extension, this basic test made me think about the essence of restorative justice. Trying to visualize restorative justice, I did not capture any images of suited mediators, signed agreements or formalized registries and structures. I saw holding hands, circles of people deep in their emotions, shaking hands and people hugging. Maybe this is because the goals and processes of restorative justice are found in relations, emotions and shared values. This should explain why many have called it 'relational justice' (Sharpe, 2013). This should also contextualize the word 'ethos' that my research pointed to as the essence of the meaning of restorative justice (that is, not being just a practice, a process or an outcome) (Gavrielides, 2007).

So, if court-based criminal justice refers to the repair of justice through unilateral imposition of state-based forms of punishment, then restorative justice must mean the balancing of an injustice through the reaffirmation of a shared values-consensus in a voluntary, equalitarian and bilateral dialogue.

As a researcher, the value-based identity of restorative justice as relational and as an ethos triggered two opposite feelings. Positive feelings were telling me that an ethos that aims to achieve values consensus and restore broken relationships is much closer to my visualization of justice as a virtue (and not as a 'court' or a 'prison'). This filled me with confidence and hope.

Negative feelings, however, were telling me that such an intense, emotionally driven methodology of justice couldn't serve a higher purpose before it created an understanding of its own emotions and dynamics. I felt that balancing the triggers that could tip these emotions formed part of servicing justice, whether these emotions relate to the parties in conflict, the justice servants, the researchers, the funders or the community within which restorative justice is applied.

To rest my fears, I started looking for writings that would help me understand the humanity and frailty of the restorative justice ethos, including the power structures of its movement. In the rich restorative justice literature, I looked hard to find empirical and theoretical papers that would unravel the very psychology, motivations and emotions of the practitioners who implement it as well as the drivers of its theoreticians and researchers. I also searched for theories that would help me understand the strengths and weaknesses of our communities as these are also called to participate as parties in restorative justice. I felt that I first needed to know their own biases, hunger for power and control, fears and hopes to create an understanding about the context of restorative justice and its purpose. If restorative justice is so relational in nature, then surely also relevant are the psychology and the dynamics between those it aims to reach, especially victims and offenders. Equally important was creating an understanding about those who are funding restorative justice as well as the policy makers and the politicians who have the power to bring it into a system.

My search ended with scant results. Serving objectively the balanced scales of justice and its blindfolded Goddess meant that more knowledge was warranted. Therefore, I felt compelled to start a debate that would establish a psychological concept of restorative justice. I also felt that this concept would have to be grounded in practice and research. My limited knowledge and legal background rendered me sceptical about my approach to answering my objective. I had no training in psychology or any behavioural science. Support from colleagues was, therefore, needed.

To this end, I called for papers that would unravel the dynamics, powers, weaknesses and peculiarities of restorative justice from the perspectives of various disciplines. The response was overwhelming and the selection process hard. As a result, this volume brought together positioning theory (Chapter 1), social psychology (Chapter 2), neuroscience (Chapter 3), affect script psychology (Chapter 4), sociology (Chapter 5), forensic mental health (Chapter 6), political sciences (Chapter 7), psychology (chapters 8, 9 and 10) and positive psychology (chapters 11 and 12).

The Book's Objective and a Word of Caution

It is not an editor's role to praise his/her final output. A key objective of my introduction, however, is to prepare the reader for what is to follow. So far, I hope I have made two things clear: first, the research and practical gap that I have identified in restorative justice; second, the objective of this book to bridge (or start bridging) this gap. Put another way, what is the psychology of restorative justice as relational justice and as an ethos, and how can this volume help us understand it within the context of research, practice and theory?

I also hope I have explained the approach that I wished to adopt for this book. That is a multi-disciplinary methodology of answering its key objective. Despite the intellectual and commercial risks associated with this approach, I wished to test my hypothesis of using interdisciplinarity for the exploration of persistent questions and research gaps.

I now want to articulate a word of caution. The diversity and richness of the arguments that are presented in this volume may overwhelm readers, especially those with trained legal minds. Reading the volume's chapters felt like putting restorative justice in the centre of a carousel. As I stood next to the turning carousel, I tried to catch all the angles of what was in its centre. As the carousel turned, it gave me many views and insights of restorative justice. But it also gave me a headache, often making me feel dizzy.

Therefore, here, I attempt to help you by guiding you through the multi-disciplinary and diverse writings of this volume. As you read the chapters, remember what is in the middle of the carousel. That is the central objective of this volume – understanding the psychology of restorative justice. Then think of how restorative justice is manifested in the real world. To help you achieve this, I attempt a delineation of this manifestation into three levels: micro, meso and macro.

At the micro level, restorative justice is manifested by holding offenders to account and through the reparation of victims' pain, hurt and the harm that the community has experienced. In practice, this means holding meetings such as victim–offender mediation (direct or indirect), circles, conferences and sentencing boards. At the meso level, restorative justice goals are materialized through the restoration of community tensions, intergroup conflicts, society injustices and inequality. In practice, this means holding large group gatherings such as Truth and Reconciliation Commissions, translating restorative justice into local, national and international policy and strategies and using its dialogue-based approaches to build bridges between conflicting values and communities. At the macro level, restorative justice is found within us as it provides a code of conduct and a value system of how we treat each other, our children, friends, enemies, societies, ourselves. In practice, this means the dialogue that we are willing to engage in with our colleagues at work, or with our partner who has just hurt us. It also means all those actions of apology to those we have hurt as well as the very act of forgiving ourselves.

As you read the chapters in this book to understand the psychology of restorative justice, remember this delineation. Some of the chapters deal with restorative justice at the micro level. For example, Drennan's et al. analysis (Chapter 6) of the potential, risks, benefits, caveats, fears, hopes and dangers of pursuing restorative justice goals with parties suffering from mental health problems is at the micro level. Oudshoorn's exposition (Chapter 9) of collective trauma as this is experienced in our communities (for example, through colonialism and inequality) and the potential, weaknesses and promises of restorative justice to restore falls within the meso level. Lyubansky and Shpungin's work (Chapter 10) falls within the macro level of the manifestation of restorative justice goals, as they expand their arguments far beyond the psychology of our surrounding environment to reach deep down into our own overt or hidden biases, our strengths and limitations, value systems and demons.

An Unexpected Challenge

The synthesis of the diverse positions and disciplines in the pursuit of a psychological concept of restorative justice led me to an unexpected question. If we are to study, analyse, improve, criticize and develop restorative justice, who should we be looking at? Sociologists, criminologists, lawyers, psychologists, neuroscientists, educators, philosophers, historians?

Surely, all the aforementioned disciplines (and others) have something to contribute to restorative justice theory and practice. Their methodology and the tools that they make available to us are indeed diverse and complementary. Thus, is this a straw man question?

As many writers in this volume argue, since its inception as a modern (criminal) justice approach, restorative justice has struggled with definitional ambiguity. It has also found it difficult to find a place of belonging in the world of theories. For instance, Artinopoulou (Chapter 5) struggles to place it within the field of criminology as she identifies philosophical and normative aspects that are so important in the application and theoretical development of restorative justice that do not reconcile. Van de Vyver et al. (Chapter 2) strive to understand the manifestation of restorative justice at the meso level while using both social and behavioural sciences.

I dare to argue that what has held back the restorative justice theory is not so much its limited application, but the lack of true ambition by its leaders and movement. While its fathers and grandfathers saw it as a new paradigm, a new way of doing justice and as a movement that could shake the foundations of our society (Barnett, 1977; Christie, 1977; Zehr, 1990; Braithwaite, 1997) our generation of pilots and politics placed restorative justice in a vicious circle of experimentation and justification. I have repeatedly argued that the role of researchers should not be to prove or disprove the superiority of restorative justice (Gavrielides, 2007, 2008). I have also argued that we should stop comparing restorative justice with what it isn't (Gavrielides and Artinopoulou, 2013) and stop obsessing about defining it (Gavrielides and Artinopoulou, 2013a).

Maybe it is now an opportune time to start talking about the restorative justice discipline as an independent, cross-disciplined field of study that starts to understand its own psychology as it manifests itself at the micro, meso and macro level.

In fact, as it will be argued in the volume's chapters, we are now at a point in the development of restorative justice where it must be treated as an autonomous field of study that can be explored through a multi-disciplinary approach. Its strong ethical foundations, as well as the need to use the power within to control and fight the power structures that could bring its demise, are what make it a special field. I welcome this challenge posed by the volume's authors, and call upon the restorative justice movement to focus its energy on developing its emerging, independent field rather than continue to justify it through superiority dialogues and compare it with what isn't. My ambition is that this book helps us start this debate.

Bibliography

Barnett, R. (1977). Restitution: a new paradigm of criminal justice. *Ethics: an International Journal of Social, Political, and Legal Philosophy*, *87*(4), 279–301.

Braithwaite, J. (1997). *Crime, shame and reintegration*. Cambridge: Cambridge University Press.

Christie, N. (1977). Conflicts as property. *British Journal of Criminology*, *17*(1), 1–15.

Gavrielides, T. (2005). Some meta-theoretical questions for restorative justice. *Ratio Juris*, *18*(1), 84–106.

Gavrielides, T. (2007). *Restorative justice theory and practice: addressing the discrepancy*. Helsinki: HEUNI.

Gavrielides, T. (2008). Restorative justice: the perplexing concept. Conceptual fault lines and power battles within the restorative justice movement. *Criminology and Criminal Justice Journal*, *8*(2), 165–183.

Gavrielides, T. (2011a). Restorative practices: from the early societies to the 1970s. *Internet Journal of Criminology*, ISSN 2045-6743.

Gavrielides, T. (2011b). *Restorative justice and the secure estate: alternatives for young people in custody*. London: IARS Publications.

Gavrielides, T. (2013). Restorative pain: a new vision of punishment. In T. Gavrielides and V. Artinopoulou (eds), *Reconstructing restorative justice philosophy* (pp. 311–337). Farnham: Ashgate Publishing.

Gavrielides, T. and Artinopoulou, V. (2013a). Epilogue: reconstructing restorative justice philosophy. In T. Gavrielides and V. Artinopoulou (eds), *Reconstructing restorative justice philosophy* (pp. 337–353). Farnham: Ashgate Publishing.

Gavrielides, T. and Artinopoulou, V. (2013b). *Reconstructing the restorative justice philosophy*. Farnham: Ashgate Publishing.

Gavrielides, T. and Worth, P. (2014). Another push for restorative justice: positive psychology and offender rehabilitation. In M.H. Pearson (ed.), *Crime: international perspectives, socioeconomic factors and psychological implications* (pp. 161–182). New York: Nova Science Publishers.

Sharpe, S. (2013). Relationality in justice and repair: implications for restorative justice. In T. Gavrielides and V. Artinopoulou (eds), *Reconstructing restorative justice philosophy* (pp. 179–197). Farnham: Ashgate Publishing.

Zehr, H. (1990). *Changing lenses: a new focus for crime and justice*. Scottdale, Pennsylvania and Waterloo, Ontario: Herald Press.

PART I:
Developing Theory: Social Sciences Meet Psychology and Neuroscience

Chapter 1

A Micro-Social Psychology of Restorative Justice: The Contribution of Positioning Theory

Giuseppe Maglione

Introduction

Among the diverse developments within social sciences during the past 50 years, one stands out as particularly relevant (Korobov, 2010). This is the analytical endeavour to bridge macro and micro dimensions of social action, focusing on the fluid transactions between small-scale/short-term social practices and long-term/large-scale institutions (Bateson, 1972; Granovetter, 1973; Goffman, 1974, 1981; Bourdieu, 1984). In this perspective, the traditional distinctions between individual and social or agency and structure, have become more blurred, precarious and questionable. The so-called 'discursive turn' in human and social sciences has further fuelled such a transformation, which is at the same time epistemological, methodological and theoretical (Potter and Wetherell, 1987). This work aims at showing the potential contribution of a recent instance of this scholarly development – that is, positioning theory (PT) – to the understanding and the advancement of restorative justice (RJ). The concept of 'positioning' consists in an attempt to challenge the static idea of 'role' within traditional social psychology, in order to articulate both a more interactive and dynamic sense of the multiple 'selves' one 'has', and also how these are actively constructed, in conversations between people or in other discursive contexts (Davies and Harré, 1990; Harré and van Langenhove, 1992, 1999; Harré and Moghaddam, 2003). The positioning's grammar elaborated by Rom Harré and colleagues can be applied as an heuristical tool to develop a specific understanding of RJ practices, focusing on the power dynamics and conversational shaping of the self which might take place within RJ encounters. Moreover, PT can be used as the backdrop for a 'normative' elaboration of RJ. This means that it could help to point out the potential of RJ to redefine the criminal/legal labels which constrain participants' possibilities of doing, being and becoming, offering instead opportunities to rethink themselves, their actions and relationships, in 'restorative' ways. Along these lines it is possible to advocate for a discursive understanding of RJ as an emancipatory and transformative framework for dealing with social conflicts and harms.

The argument of this chapter is established throughout two main sections. First, I provide an introduction to PT, focusing on Harré and colleagues' work, its scholarly underpinnings and recent deployments. In the second section I introduce and discuss the rationale behind the application of PT to RJ, as well as concrete normative and descriptive ways PT can contribute to the development of research and practice of RJ. Some concluding thoughts are finally presented.

Positioning Theory

The concept of 'positioning' is originally known for its use in the marketing of products, services and brands (Trout, 1969). In this context, 'positioning' consists in detecting and trying to occupy a market niche for a brand, product or service by discursively establishing a unique and appealing identity. Within social sciences the first use of 'positioning' was made by Wendy Hollway (1984), who described women's and men's subjectivities as 'the product of their history of positioning in discourses' (p. 228), making reference to the philosophy of Michel Foucault and Louis Althusser. Harré and colleagues, starting from the early 1990s, have further elaborated on Hollway's intuition, offering an articulated theory (i.e. PT) which has gained momentum in the scholarly literature over the past 15 years, mainly due to its contribution to bridge the gap between people, institutions and societies in social analysis (Zelle, 2009, p. 1).

PT emerged in the academic milieu of late 1970s social psychology. Overall, social psychology consists of 'the scientific field that seeks to understand the nature and causes of individual behaviour in social situations' (Baron, Byrne and Suls, 1989, p. 6). Harré, originally a philosopher of science, has contributed to the revision of social psychology through the elaboration of a broad interdisciplinary approach (that is, 'ethogenics'; see below) which combines social psychology with philosophy of language and microsociology (Harré and Secord, 1972; Harré, 1979; Harré and Gillet, 1994). Within this perspective, PT represents the most well-known and widely applied conceptual development. In the following sections, I will focus on the PT's ontological, epistemological and theoretical underpinnings as well as on the possibility of enriching PT by re-elaborating its 'post-structuralist' roots.

Positioning Theory: Positions, Speech Acts and Storylines

As Davies and Harré have openly acknowledged, PT emerged as an attempt to overcome the problems inherent in the use of the concept of role in developing a social psychology of selfhood (Davies and Harré, 1990). They hold that the concept of 'positioning' can be used to facilitate a linguistically orientated thinking of the interplay between individual and social in ways that the use of the concept of 'role' would not permit. 'Positioning', as a methodological tool, is meant to offer a different viewpoint on the dynamic aspects of social encounters, charting their interactive unfolding in everyday life, in contrast to the way in which the use of 'role' serves to highlight static features. More precisely, Harré (2004) describes PT as 'the study of the nature, formation, influence and ways of change of local systems of rights and duties [that is, what you may say/do and what you may not] in small scale social interactions [that is, conversations]', influenced by broader societal discourses (p. 5).

'Positioning' per se is a metaphorical idea that expresses the discursive process by which an individual 'locates' herself/himself (or is located by others) within and through conversation, how speakers' rights and duties, opportunities, obligations and constraints are taken up and laid down, ascribed and appropriated, refused and defended in the fine grain of the encounters of daily lives, within an unfolding storyline (Davies and Harré, 1990; van Langenhove and Harré, 1999). How these speakers' sets of rights and duties (or positions) are shaped and used, within and through conversation, is what a positioning analyst aims to understand (van Langenhove and Harré, 1994). Rights and duties form a sort of 'local moral domain' inserted and gaining meaning within wider storyline(s) developed during an encounter, a dimension usually neglected by psychologists working on conversational interactions (Harré et al., 2009).

The precondition for the positioning is the fact that people's words are provided with 'illocutionary force', the capacity to 'do things with words' in the outer world (Austin, 1962). This is nothing but the social force of discursive acts (also known as speech acts): words do not passively describe the world, but actually shape it, defining our possibilities of doing, being, becoming. It is possible to schematically represent the structure of positioning as the combination of position(s), illocutionary force(s) and story line(s). These three elements and their relationships form a sort of triangle within which it is possible to interpret a wide range of social events (Harré, 2004).

Types and Examples of Positionings

Positioning acts have been described by van Langenhove and Harré (1999) as varying according to 'who positions who' and according to the content of positions. The main way of classifying them is between first-, second- and third-order positioning acts. A 'first-order positioning' takes place when an individual locates herself/himself and others, engages in speech acts and follows a storyline (van Langenhove and Harré, 1999, p. 20). Second-order positioning occurs when the first-order positioning is intentionally challenged by a speaker and has to be then negotiated. This situation might happen when one of the participants in a conversation feels that she/he is being 'wrongly' positioned and thus demands to be repositioned, claiming new rights and duties in the social interaction. Third-order positioning happens when a speaker negotiates a positioning act taking place in a conversation with someone else (van Langenhove and Harré, 1999, p. 21). This occurs when participants in a particular conversation observe another conversation and challenge the positioning happening in this other encounter.

An example can clarify how different forms of positioning actually work. An instance of first-order positioning paradigmatically occurs during criminal justice trials.[1] When a suspected offender tries to challenge the judge or the prosecutor's statements, the judge (or prosecutor) usually authoritatively reminds (that is, discursively positions) the suspected offender that 'it's not his role', that the 'court questions and he answers', that he cannot go 'off topic', that 'we are here to discuss a specific charge' and so on. In this case, we can easily detect a specific institutional storyline (the trial) based on a wider discursive reservoir ('conventional' criminal justice), a certain set of speech acts (questioning, deposition, cross-examination, reprimanding and so on) and one main example of first-order positioning (the authority locates in the conversation the suspected offender, imposing certain rights and duties as a speaker – but also as a legal subject), mobilized within and through a face-to-face interaction.

Let us imagine now, that once the suspected offender has been positioned by the court, he responds saying that the court or the prosecutor has been 'paid' by the victim; for this reason he will not recognize the court/prosecutor's authority, because in short they 'nothing have in common with the really fair justice'. In this way the suspect challenges the first-order positioning enacted and imposed on him in the first instance by the authority, drawing upon a certain discursive field (the 'really fair justice'), performing a certain speech act (public criticism from a moral stand), ultimately repositioning the legal authority and herself/himself.

At this point of the story, the court might consider the suspect's behaviour as contemptuous and then order a police officer to limit the suspect's freedom, scheduling a new hearing. Getting out of the courtroom the suspect might finally shout to the audience, that he was actually allowed as a 'good and abiding citizen' to denounce the court's corruption; it was indeed his 'duty'. In this way we also see a third-order positioning act lastly performed. Two things should be additionally noticed. The first is that the different participants' moral stands anchored in a given societal discursive reservoir ('conventional' criminal justice), create a rigid asymmetry between the participants, enforcing the court's positioning of the suspect. This shows a typical power dynamic taking place when certain positionings are enacted by certain subjects (the court), performing speech acts with different illocutionary force. The second remark is that this kind of process might result in deeply affecting the participants' experience of themselves, even modifying their idea of themselves (understood as social self; see below), especially if repeatedly performed (for example, the suspect's self-image as 'good and abiding citizen' might be weakened or even strengthened by the court's actions).

---

1   This example is drawn from the author's direct experience as audience to a court case held at the Florence Justice of the Peace Courthouse, Italy.

Selves, Others and Power

As already highlighted, PT is originally meant to contribute to a social psychology of selfhood, freed from the objectifying consequences of 'role theory'. Traditionally, within social psychology, the formation of the self in relation to social situations is a crucial topic. The 'role theory', as a specific social-psychological perspective, has typically interpreted the development of self as related to roles (or social positions – for example, husband, student, writer, etc.) tied to statutes (sets of social expectations) rooted in wider social structures (Biddle, 1986). In this way, the self emerges from the individual's strain to conform to social expectations in a broader social context. This perspective helps to describe and explain the self's static features (or fixings), but 'pays the price' to objectify and reduce the individual agency in shaping one's personhood (Davies and Harré, 1990).

In contrast, PT focuses on the formation of self from the specific angle of the local and conversational production of the personhood, as a dynamic and fluid process which involves an agentic role for individuals. On this view, Harré starts from the basic idea that persons 'have' selves (Harré, 2004, p. 3). He identifies four main items in personhood that the word 'self' is currently used to designate. There is the *embodied self*, as the unity and continuity of a person's point of perception and action, a relatively self-identical and fixed self. The *autobiographical self* is the 'character' of the stories we tell about ourselves, a sort of hero or heroine of stories, whose qualities might vary according to within which story the self takes place. The *social self* comprises the personal multiple qualities that an individual expresses in a social encounter. Finally, the idea of *self-concept* refers to what individuals think of themselves, their beliefs, skills, moral qualities, fears and life courses. While the embodied self is invariant under the transformations that occur in everyday life, the autobiographical self, the self-concept and especially the repertoire of social selves (targeted by PT) may and do change and sometimes in fundamental ways (Harré, 2004, p. 4). The positions which individuals create, negotiate, resist and finally adopt contribute to organizing our social selves, understood as dynamic discursive constructs. In this way PT endorses a de-essentialized notion of self, as a 'point of suture' between subject positions (Hall, 1996, p. 5). Positions, in fact, not only 'locate' people within certain 'storylines' (Andreouli, 2010, p. 14.4), but also provide people with ways of making sense of the world. As Davies and Harré (1990) remark, '[o]nce having taken up a particular position as one's own, a person inevitably sees the world from the vantage point of that position and in terms of the particular images, metaphors, storylines and concepts which are made relevant within the particular discursive practice in which they are positioned'.

A relevant issue related to the fashioning of the social self through positioning is the significance and role of the power dynamics entailed in positioning processes. PT conceptualizes power looking at who manages to 'get' the right to position and who does not, but also at the '"moral quality" associated with a set of rights and duties which delimit what can be said or done from a certain position, in a particular context and towards a particular speaker' (Andreouli, 2010, p. 14.5).

In positioning themselves and the other or in being positioned, individuals exert power by initiating, accepting or rejecting positioning acts. The production of 'valid' positions, their social support (that is, illocutionary force), the 'entitlement' to position the other and the condition for 'true' positions are all issues which prominently represent the role of power dynamics within positioning (Andreouli, 2010, p. 14.5).

Ontological, Epistemological and Theoretical Underpinnings

PT is grounded in a wide range of philosophical (Ludwig Wittgenstein and Michel Foucault), sociological (Erving Goffman) and psychological (Lev Vygotsky) concepts and theories. As already stated, the disciplinary framework within which PT emerges is Harré's ethogenic revision of social psychology. Ethogenics is an interdisciplinary approach aiming at understanding social order looking at how individuals attach significance to their actions and form their selves by linking these to the larger structure of rules and cultural resources in society (Harré and Secord, 1972).

Harré's positioning is based on the ethogenic project to identify and understand rules used by people to organize conversations and their social effects. In the ethogenic perspective, positioning is the site as much as the tool to investigate the dynamic and 'ever changing assignment of rule-governed rights and duties (inherent in storylines) among individuals or groups in social encounters' (Korobov and Bamberg, 2006, p. 257). Ethogenics might be considered akin to the more recent discursive turn in psychology, both at theoretical and methodological level (Potter and Wetherell, 1987), as criticism against both the individually orientated behaviouristic psychology and psychodynamic analysis.

Besides ethogenics, as already mentioned, it is possible to identify at least four main thinkers, whose works ontologically, epistemologically and theoretically ground PT: Goffman, Wittgenstein, Foucault and Vygotsky. Goffman's interest in the conversational construction and maintenance of social order led him to develop two analytical concepts very close to positioning: 'frame' and 'footing' (Goffman, 1974, 1981). A frame is a 'scheme of interpretation' that allows individuals or groups 'to locate, perceive, identify, and label' events and occurrences, thus rendering meaning, organizing experiences and guiding actions (Goffman, 1974, p. 21). The concept of footing entails 'the alignment we take up to ourselves and the others present as expressed in the way we manage the production or reception of an utterance' (Goffman, 1981, p. 128). Through the concepts of frame and footing, the notions of speaker and hearer appear as disarticulated into a set of positions or differentiated parts (Marinova, 2004). Both Goffman's analysis and Harré's positioning might be considered close to what Karin Knorr-Cetina (1983) called 'micro-sociological mode(s) for social explanation'. In both cases, in fact, the focus is placed on the pragmatic and performative role that language plays in the production of social reality, re-elaborating the relationship between the individual and the structure, considering the individual as an active hermeneutic being, with agency and engaged in the destruction, reproduction and creation of social order (Tirado and Galvez, 2007).

Looking specifically at the concept of language assumed by PT, different elements can be highlighted. As Davies and Harré (1990) state, 'the view of language in which positioning is to be understood is the immanentist i.e. language exists only as concrete occasions of language in use'. This perspective seems grounded in Wittgenstein's (1958) notion of language as sets of speech acts related and developed through and within actual interaction. Moreover, the notion of positioning triangle is very similar to Wittgenstein's well-known concept of 'language games' (1958, §7). In this perspective, participants in conversation are participating in a kind of game – that is, patterns of language influenced, shaped, defined by and negotiated within the social realm (Ghosten, 2012). Davies and Harré (1990) also emphasize that 'the recognition of the force of "discursive practices", the ways in which people are "positioned" through those practices and the way in which the individual's "subjectivity" is generated through the learning and use of certain discursive practices are commensurate with the "new psycho-socio-linguistics"'.

This idea of language as discursive practice is close to Foucault's view that language is critically important to constructing subjectivity, and social reality at all (Foucault, 1972). Foucault deconstructs the universal and rationalistic 'knowing subject' at the core of the Enlightenment, arguing that situated discursive practices provide subject's positions and that the actions of speaking and acting are necessarily bound to historical discursive practices (Foucault, 1972). In this sense Foucault rethinks the subject's formation as embedded in societal reservoirs of discourses, clearly inspiring PT's claims.

Finally, PT draws upon Vygotsky's view of the individual in 'an ocean of language' (2004) and the idea that certain linguistic and manipulative skills are needed to make sense of cognitive processes and experiences (van Langenhove and Harré, 1999). According to Vygotsky all higher order mental processes exist twice: in the relevant group, influenced by culture and history, and then in the mind of the individual. As Harré (2004) states, in Vygotsky 'the development of a human being is dependent as much on interpersonal relations as it is on individual maturation. The appropriation of public-social practices as personal-individual skills comes about by a kind of psychological symbiosis' (p. 2). This two-dimensional understanding of human development informs Harré's idea of positioning, insofar as the social and the individual development are considered two sides of the same process.

Enriching Positioning

When we try to cast an overall glance over positioning dynamics as described by Harré and colleagues, two main and interlinked issues emerge as recurrent challenges: the agency of subject of and to positioning; the relationships between societal discourses and conversational process.

In the current discussions on positioning and agency, Harré's PT is usually considered as endorsing a 'traditional view' insofar as it explains positions as grounded in societal discourses or master narratives which offer the social locations where subjects are positioned (Bamberg, 2005). In this perspective, subjects maintain a partially agentive status due to the fact that at the same time more, competing and contradictory societal repertoires of positions are available, and that in a same repertoire there might be tensions or incompatibility among different positions. The subject's agency is then related to the fact that in conversations subjects are "forced" to choose among societal discourses and positions. Moreover, the same unforeseeable conversational dynamics might lead participants to negotiate or reshape available positions. As Michael Bamberg (2005) remarks, a different understanding of positioning might be based on Judith Butler's idea of performativity (1990). In this perspective, positioning entails a more agentive subject, because discursive 'repertoires are not always and already given but rather are constructed in a more bottom-up and performative fashion and they can generate counter-narratives' (Bamberg, 2005).

The second issue is related to how we can actually conceptualize the relationship between the macro dimension of societal repertoires of positions and the micro dynamics of conversational positioning. Here the 'choice' has been usually considered between an ethnomethodological bottom-up perspective (from conversations to societal discourses) and a post-structuralist/Foucauldian view (from societal discourses to conversation).

In order to settle these challenges, following Margaret Wetherell (1998), it is possible to argue for a partial synthesis of these different understandings of positioning. This means to integrate performativity in Harré's account and to consider both the bottom-up and top-down approaches, taking into account the possible methodological and conceptual challenges entailed by these combinations. Within this 'synthetic' perspective, the (social) self is discursively produced in conversations anchored in societal discourses which make available a range of positions (Wetherell, 1998). Looking at this process from the perspective of individuals, two different but interwoven phases can be considered. The first stage (*subjection*) results from the ways in which societal discourses 'interpellate' (or define) us, while the second (*self-constitution*) refers to the individual's performative realization of the self (Foucault, 2002) through actual positioning in conversation. People's selves are 'the point of suture' (Hall, 1996, p. 5) between the fluid 'products' of subjection and subjectivation; they result in part assigned and in part actively constructed, contested and negotiated by speakers, through micro-social (bottom-up) practices of self-making inextricably linked to wider (top-down) discursive contexts. A clarification regarding the concept of 'discourse' I use might be useful. Discourse here (following Wetherell) equates with the concept of discursive practice as elaborated by Ernesto Laclau and Chantal Mouffe (1985). Laclau and Mouffe associate discourse with the general social/human meaning-making processes, including both linguistic and non-linguistic elements. In other words, they conceive of the social space as entirely discursive, an open and continuous space of human activity of making meanings. If meanings so produced are never totally fixed but always open to negotiation, it is also possible to obtain some 'discursive articulation' or 'nodal points' – that is, more stable configurations of meanings, more hegemonic and pervasive in a given time/place (that is, authoritative societal discourses).

To sum up, in this view, the idea(s) one 'has' (or better, *does*) of herself/himself is formed by the combination of fluid subject positions made available by hegemonic societal discourses, and enacted, negotiated or rejected at conversational level. 'Selves' are then configured as multiple, contradictory and provisional, temporarily fixed at the intersection of those subject positions and dependent on specific forms of positionings within various discursive contexts (Wetherell, 1998).

Positioning Theory and Restorative Justice

The manner in which a 'synthetic' PT approaches and understands human interactions could prove to be beneficial to the field of RJ theories and practices. Rationales for the application of PT to RJ are numerous. From a normative viewpoint, PT allows for a conceptualization of RJ that eschews some of the theoretical and meta-theoretical limitations that 'mainstream' analyses usually offer: first of all, the problematic relationship between RJ and 'conventional' criminal justice (CJ). From an empirical perspective, PT offers innovative tools to analyse RJ encounters, illuminating the role of meaning-making and its link to behaviours, the functioning of power dynamics, the shaping of participants' selves within RJ processes and the potential of RJ encounters to re-elaborate conflicts. On this view, what usually happens in RJ encounters is understood as relying on discursive processes, such as (re)definition of storylines, production, negotiation, rejection, adoption of positions 'through the speech acts or social forces of discursive manoeuvring' (Zelle, 2009, p. 6). In what follows I try to sketch out the possible use of a 'synthetic' version of PT, distinguishing between 'normative' and 'descriptive' uses. Normative uses entail the contribution of PT to a theoretical characterization of RJ from 'conventional' CJ. 'Descriptive' uses refer to how PT can help to develop an empirical understanding of RJ practices, informing specific ways of researching into the actual application of them. Needless to say, normative and descriptive uses are deeply interlinked, relying on each other from both a theoretical and methodological viewpoint.

Normative Uses: Distinguishing CJ and RJ

Through the lenses provided by PT, RJ and CJ appear as 'discursive fields' – that is, the stratification of societal discourses (some more hegemonic than others), with various cultural, political and social underpinnings, on why and how we should deal with anti-social deeds[2] (Maglione, 2013, 2014). The discursive fields work as repertoires of storylines within which different positions can be created, negotiated, adopted or resisted through various speech acts. They contribute to shape identities, providing certain subject positions, making possible the establishment of specific idea(s) of 'who we are', in a given societal context (Rasmussen, 2006, p. 85). The subject positions of 'victim' and 'offender', for instance, are shaped in these dynamic fields and enacted through actual conversations, where individuals mobilize them, looking at themselves and the world through such positions.

Restorative justice

The RJ field is composed of at least three main 'authoritative' (and empirically overlapping) discursive reservoirs: encounter, reparative and transformative (Johnstone and Van Ness, 2007, p. 1). They offer, in different and sometimes contradictory ways, the 'ground' for positioning acts.

The *encounter* discourse highlights the active participation of relevant stakeholders in order to manage the conflict that ties them together (Strang, 2003; Strang and Sherman, 2003). The restorative encounter makes possible the expression and discussion of the emotional, social, symbolic and material issues at stake, aiming at restoring the relationships among the conflict's stakeholders. The *reparative* discourse refers to an understanding of reparation and prevention of crimes and their consequences, based on the idea of repairing harm. This view discards the retributive idea to coerce the offender to endure pain proportionate to the gravity of the crime committed, emphasizing instead reparation of the crime's consequences. In the *transformative* discourse, RJ is understood as a 'worldview' which can lead us to perceive and act upon the world and ourselves in a 'restorative' way – that is, relying on peacebuilding through dialogue and agreement (Sullivan and Tifft, 2001). The premise of this view is a relational understanding of humans (Johnstone and Van Ness, 2007, p. 17), the 'natural' interconnectedness which can be hindered by destructive and anti-social behaviours.

These three main discourses work as wide-ranging repertoires from which many storylines and positions can be mobilized, adopted or resisted with intersections, combinations and tensions. They also inform different procedures (that is, RJ encounters) composed by various speech acts. The main storylines are that of the crime as censure of communicative channels and interpersonal relationships to be reactivated (encounter); crime as damage/harm to be repaired (reparative); crime as expression of a lack of peace and constructive culture of dealing with conflict (transformative). The key needs of participants are to express and address emotion, to gain a moment of mutual understanding and convergence of interests (encounter); to 'right the wrong' (reparative); to transform themselves, their relationships and their mind-set (transformative). The main positions of 'victim', 'offender' and 'community' involve a diverse distribution of rights and duties in

---

2   This understanding of RJ and CJ is ideal-typical; it is a tool of analysis, not a phenomenon with a 'direct' empirical reference.

the different discourses. In the encounter and transformative, the different positions involve the right to speak out and the duty to hear the other, to understand and to be understood. In the reparative the 'victim' has the right to ask reparation and the 'offender' to 'offer' reparation, emotional, symbolical and material. Finally, in the transformative discourse, 'victim' and 'offender' are positions often not available, because they are considered as objectifying legal labels to be renegotiated, by questioning the asymmetry in the distribution of rights and duties to speak and act that those positions enable.

'Conventional' criminal justice

The first component of the CJ field is the *crime control* discourse (Packer, 1968, p. 158). It underscores increasing police power and criticizes legal interference in law enforcement (Siegel, 2006, p. 476), allowing for harsher and/or stricter punishments for offenders. This perspective seeks to prevent crime through a diffused control and the threat of tough punishments (Davies et al., 2009, p. 23). Another prominent discourse constituting the CJ field is *due process* (Packer, 1968, p. 165). This discourse revolves around the priority of protecting the civil rights of criminals; it advocates an individualized justice and the use of discretion, and emphasizes procedural fairness (Siegel, 2006, p. 478). The *penal welfarism* discourse (Garland, 2001, p. 34) is based on the assumption that criminals are the product of a society that has failed them. What are needed are responses to crime through programmes that empower people, counsel them and teach them to be law-abiding, self-sufficient citizens (Siegel, 2006, p. 479). In the 1970s, penal welfarism was targeted by a powerful and sustained political and theoretical critique associated with the 'justice model'. The *justice model* is a liberal discourse based on a Kantian ground. It criticizes the crime control model for the notion of deterrence and the idea of rehabilitation of offenders for its theoretical faults (Cavadino and Dignan, 2007). It justifies consistent consequences for crimes, proportionate to the seriousness of the offence, promoting the abolishment of discretionary institutions such as parole.

These discourses about understanding and reacting to behaviours assumed to be socially disturbing, through State intervention, inform many possible storylines and acts of positionings. The due process and the justice model both emphasize the role of the legal trial as institutional series of speech acts. The main storyline involves the idea of crime as an offence against the State committed by a free will actor to be retributively punished after a fair process. The crime control discourse and the penal welfarism highlight the role of police and rehabilitation experts, the law enforcement and social/psychological institutions to halt crime. The storyline offered is that of crime as expression of the different criminals' constitution or nature to be alternatively considered as unalterable actor (requiring, then, control over crime more than over criminals) or conversely changeable (requiring rehabilitation). The positions offered by these discourses are many and different, with few but relevant commonalities. In terms of speakers' duties and rights, the 'offender' is characterized as an asymmetric position with respect to the other ones entailed in any CJ storyline. 'Offender' here means to be silenced or entitled to speak only when required according to certain etero-directed scripts (that is, externally imposed), and hardly negotiable. In the crime control and rehabilitative discourses, the offender is actually 'out' of the conversation because radically other or alien, incapable of speaking any 'truth'. A (paradoxically) similar position is that of the material 'victim', also silenced but for different reasons: first of all, because replaced by the State.

Descriptive Uses

The descriptive uses of PT help to explain how these discursive fields are mobilized, from a micro-social point of view, focusing on how stakeholders and practitioner(s) in a specific restorative process, within and through conversation enact, reproduce, negotiate and resist to the positions 'embedded' within discursive fields, positioning themselves and other participants.

Any RJ practice[3] itself forms a structured model of joint interaction involving a range of specific speech acts (exchange of information and eventual apologies, settling a conflict, writing an agreement) and certain positionings dynamics informed by one or more discourses composing the RJ field (Hirvonen, 2013, p. 105). The encounter, as time and space where positioning takes place, can be viewed as consisting of few larger phases (opening statements, storytelling, discussion, drafting of eventual agreement, closing statement) which include different possible 'sub-phases' (Hirvonen, 2013, p. 105). The opening statements comprise the practitioner's and eventually participants' self-introduction as well as the presentation of the case; the storytelling includes both participants' stories; discussing the case involves both a 'confessional' speech toward the practitioner and an exchange with the other participant(s); the agreement includes negotiation and decision making about the case. Within these 'larger' phases based on RJ discourses, participants can draw upon different storylines and negotiate new positions. They can position themselves or the other; they can also question actual or previous positions. The following examples show the possible areas PT can be concretely used to describe such interactions and their benefit to the scholarship and practice of RJ.

Understanding the relationships between practitioners and parties
We can recruit PT into the study of the relationships between the RJ practitioner and stakeholders, focusing on the meanings, themes and behaviours that emerge from moment-to-moment interactions occurring in restorative encounters. Overall this topic is relevant for social psychology, considering the emphasis of this discipline on thoughts, feelings and behaviours within the social context. We can start by investigating the different discursive reservoirs and the ways parties and practitioners draw upon them, the different discursive strategies they utilize and

---

3   I especially think of victim–offender mediation.

the specific positions they choose. Additionally we can focus on the various effects positioning has for the RJ encounter, including the impact on participants' selves. In order to identify the dynamics which conversationally take place, we should pay attention to how practitioners and parties present and describe themselves and others, as well as the specific structure of rights and duties entailed by the positions chosen and eventually negotiated, challenged and adopted (Jarden and Lock, 2004). A set of more specific research targets might be taken into consideration. First, we can inquiry into how parties or practitioners self-position. We should focus on whether parties refer to themselves in terms of, for instance, protagonists and antagonists, passive or active subjects (Jarden and Lock, 2004, p. 3), engaged or detached or as 'offender' and 'victim'. As for the practitioner, for instance, whether she/he explicitly or not positions herself/himself as 'expert' – and what kind of expert (on the content? on the process? both?) – and parties as 'laypeople', and eventually how parties react to such a first-order position.

At this level, it is relevant if the practitioner tries to instruct parties how to handle their emotions, on what is important in terms of restoration/restitution/ reparation, on how to engage in making excuses for actions and on self-blaming. We can also pay attention to the eventual second-order positioning enacted by parties – for example, if they try to challenge the practitioner's position as expert. The analytical focus could be further placed on the common discursive strategies and repertoires they use to enact this particular positioning act. For instance, the way the practitioner justifies her/his position (why she/he is there, what benefit the parties could receive from her/his presence and work, and so on); whether she/he describes herself/himself as drawing upon the typical third-party dispute solving's reservoir (neutrality, impartiality, confidentiality); what kind of discourse on RJ she/he effectively endorses and declares as frame of the encounter. These discursive strategies and repertoires are interesting theoretical targets with relevant practical implications. First of all, they might say something about the power dynamics within RJ encounters between parties and practitioners, and whether they are functional and in what way, to the declared restorative goals. For the practitioner, to adopt a subject position of an 'expert' entails being warranted all the rights and duties, responsibilities and entitlements usually given to or assumed by an expert (Jarden and Lock, 2004, p. 3). This means that by adopting this position the practitioner is provided with credibility, her/his accounts will be validated and various 'powers' achieved, to organize the restorative process. From this 'expert' position, the practitioner might discursively assign parties the opposite subject position of 'laypeople'. As a result, parties might result more passive, lacking knowledge and skill, emotionally 'loaded' and then involving a somewhat diminished capacity to handle the conversation autonomously. This might mean for parties fewer rights to make decisions and have input into and control over the RJ process (Jarden and Lock, 2004, p. 3), or, in other words, 'more' subjection and 'less' self-constitution. Different RJ encounters, based on slightly dissimilar discursive reservoirs, might in different ways enact those or other positions with different effects. To chart, analyse and interpret how diverse reservoirs and positions impact on parties/practitioners' power over the process/ content of the encounter can offer some practical insights in terms of practitioners' trainings, style of work and practical techniques.

To this kind of research, from a methodological viewpoint, it can be suggested a multi-media approach using different types of talk and text from within the RJ domain (Jarden and Lock, 2004, p. 3). For instance, instructional books, demonstration videos and interviews with practising practitioners, as well as video/audio/written records to RJ encounters, all might offer the relevant data with which to build upon the positioning analysis.

Shaping the self and power relationships
A further promising area for the application of PT is the study of how restorative encounters contribute to shape the parties' social selves. PT can help to enable the researcher to investigate how the social self is presented in and formed by positions, how it orientates behaviours, affecting the encounter's outcomes and aftermath (Zelle, 2009). RJ encounters are usually described as allowing and working on demands for sense-making, reinterpretation, reframing and construction of meaning of what happened, why it happened and how to deal with what happened (Johnstone and Van Ness, 2007), all issues which might impact on participants' ideas of themselves.

If we understand RJ as a discursive field composed by many and different discursive reservoirs, some more hegemonic than others, we can easily imagine how from these can be drawn positions impacting on participants' selves. Understandably, the practitioner here plays the role of 'gatekeeper' to access and mobilize those repertoires. The practitioner, in fact, enables or hampers the elaboration of subject positions tentatively performed by participants by offering indications on the content and the form of the encounter, highlighting what is allowed and what is not, framing the encounter from the beginning by indicating goals and rules and/or providing eventual 'scripts' to follow.

The access to (subjugating) discourses which define an ontological difference between 'victim' and 'offender', endorsing legal labels, or, conversely, to reservoirs which allow for reframing the participants' legal statuses, remains tied to the precarious possibility of drawing upon repertoires at least partially 'administered' by the practitioner. Nevertheless, parties are not passive objects, but agentic participants. This is because they have access to reservoirs which have nothing to do with RJ, and actually might be in contrast with the ones made available by the practitioner during an encounter. Parties are then "forced" to choose among eventually contradictory discourses which might offer different and even incompatible positions.

Moreover, they bring to the encounter positions accumulated throughout their lives, the identities so far constituted. In the dynamic interaction between the 'external' pressure to choose positions related to the restorative process and the positions drawn upon personal reservoirs, a further shaping of the self might take place, as a two-way process. In this perspective it is possible to explore opportunities, challenges and constraints that parties experience, what they talk about and how they act with regard to these experiences. Which positions do restorative encounters privilege and which do they silence? What kind of pressure is conversationally placed on parties and which margins and forms of resistance (as effective self-positioning) can be mobilized? Where is the place of emotion (or affect) in this process? Are there among available discourses of RJ some that are more prone to constrain and others that are more inclined to enable self-positioning? Here arises again the crucial issue of power dynamics within RJ encounters. PT helps to identify how power, as capacity to access to discursive reservoirs to self-position, manifests and is handled in discursive encounters. Power expresses itself as the capacity to impose, evade, resist or successfully negotiate such positions through discourse, as the capacity of 'telling the truth' about ourselves and the others. What are the factors which promote or hinder this form of power within restorative encounters? What are the conditions to successfully challenge a position imposed on us by other speakers? Empirical work can illustrate how social self-making, positioning and power are working together in RJ encounters, as faces of the same process, illuminating their complex interrelationships (McKenzie and Carey, 2013).

Re-storying the conflict
If we agree that RJ processes deal with conflict beneath a crime or expressed by a crime, PT can be finally useful to understand (from the scholar's side) and act upon (from the practitioner's side) the conflict dynamics within restorative encounters, focusing on the psycho-social conditions for their emergence, development and maintenance (Kure, 2010). PT offers tools to conceptualize in new ways how conflicts break out and escalate, how cooperation and agreements can be reached, and what it takes to reduce their intensity (Harré, Moghaddam and Lee, 2008). Concretely, the analysis should start from the detection of the different discursive reservoirs that parties draw upon and the positions they create, adopt and resist during a restorative encounter. Next, the analytical focus should be more precisely placed on the specific positions which 'shape' the conflict, intended as a certain distribution of rights and duties on framing reality (for example, interests, needs, resources), in the course of an episode of personal interaction. A conflict might arise because one of the parties is supporting or denying a claim to a right, demanding or rejecting the assignment of a duty or in the case of "forced" positioning of others. To study these dynamics, concentrating on which positions are accessible to participants, may help to provide guidance for practitioners seeking to implement RJ processes. Which discursive reservoirs are potentially exacerbating the conflict or re-traumatizing parties? Which reservoirs and positions can be considered more 'restorative' – that is, allowing parties to reframe their actions and relationship, 're-storying' their conflict? (Rundell, 2007). The reservoirs and positions identified can be considered in terms of their general availability, specific accessibility and effects when mobilized by parties/practitioners (Barnes, 2004, p. 12).

The availability of some positions may depend on contextual factors related to the personal and social characteristics of parties as well as on how the restorative encounter concretely unfolds, or on the different preferences of practitioners in terms of which discursive repertoire to use to justify their task or to self-position (Barnes, 2004, p. 12). The accessibility of positions can also depend on how their interests and capabilities are perceived by other parties in the encounter, and positionings may be contested or resisted on these grounds (Barnes, 2004, p. 3). We might suggest that positionings should be fluid, with parties able to 'move freely in and out of the positions' considering that the 'exclusive occupancy of any position by one individual may have in fact negative consequences' for parties (Barnes, 2004, p. 14).

A participant who is always positioned as overly 'passive' or conversely as 'agentic' may inhibit or stimulate others' positionings, accessing or granting rights and duties in the conversation which might promote or hamper 'restorative' effects. The names and descriptions of positions and patterns of participation provide a language for thinking about and discussing interactions during RJ processes. Practitioners, benefiting from PT insights, can offer a 'third' account of the discursive reservoirs and positions used, showing their momentary and ephemeral nature, challenging specific positioning acts which fuel the conflict. Eventual modifications in positioning 'can change the meanings of the actions people are performing, since beliefs about positions partly determine the illocutionary force of members' actions'; all this 'can consequently modify, sometimes drastically, the story-lines that are taken to be unfolding in an encounter' (Harré et al., 2009, p. 10). Unveiling, challenging, discussing, multiplying discursive reservoirs, positions, broader storylines and speech-acts, might work as a strategy to help parties to rethink their conflict from a different and sometimes alternative perspective.

Conclusions

PT, as social-psychological approach linguistically orientated, can offer a relevant contribution to the understanding and development of RJ, from a normative/ theoretical and descriptive/empirical viewpoint. An understanding of RJ as a discursive field where the conditions for the formation of different subject positions, storylines and speech acts are established, helps to distinguish RJ from CJ by identifying differences, common elements, overlaps and tensions between them. Normatively, RJ is nothing but a range, more or less fluid, of discourses, some of them more pervasive and hegemonic than others, which define a certain reality, making up certain objects (conflict, harm, restoration and so on).

RJ practices are nothing but conversational processes within and through which the 'content' (subject positions, storylines) of those societal discourses is reproduced and reshaped. This happens because 'restorative conversations' are provided with the capacity to produce social effects (illocutionary force), to change or create the reality and to make it available to human beings. In such conversations between practitioners and stakeholders, it is possible to become 'victim', 'offender' or 'community', to 'restore', 'repair' and so on – that is, to adopt or performatively challenge a certain position made available by the societal discourses which 'compose' RJ (sometimes overlapping with those informing the 'conventional' CJ).

The descriptive uses of PT can help to analyse how RJ practices actually work, how they contribute to shape stakeholders' identities, how the relationships between them and RJ practitioners unfold, which power relationships take place and how to handle them. They can help to identify which positions endanger the freedom of parties, which impose limitations of ways of being and doing, which hold a transformative potential. Overall, PT offers a different 'lens' to look at what happens in RJ encounters, apart from the widespread way of researching in the field, too often concerned with the quantitative measuring of performances, taking for granted and 'essentializing' the meanings and features of RJ.

To conclude, the belief which informs the idea of using PT to approach RJ is that a discursive and psycho-socially orientated perspective can help to unveil some problematic overlaps and commonalities between RJ and 'conventional' CJ. One of the main risks I see in advocating for (or inadvertently supporting) a RJ cognate to the 'conventional' CJ, is the etero-direction of positions– that is, the imposition on parties of non-negotiable ideas of 'who they are' from professionals self-positioned as moral and technical experts. Conversely, the transformative potential of RJ could lie in its capacity to offer space and time for interpersonal repositioning (beside or against the CJ im-positions). This means it could provide an opportunity to more freely shape identities and a chance for 're-storying' the narrative of the conflict, its causes and aftermath, toward more peaceful relationships. PT could then help to devise understandings of RJ which aim at unleashing its transformative and inclusive potential, providing awareness of the limitations and risks that restorative discourses and practices might embody.

Bibliography

Andreouli, E. (2010). Identity, positioning and self–other relations. *Papers on Social Representations*, *19*, 14.1–14.13.

Austin, J.L. (1962). *How to do things with words: the William James Lectures delivered at Harvard University in 1955*. Oxford: Clarendon Press.

Bamberg, M. (2005). Positioning. In D. Herman, M. Jahn and M.-L. Ryan (eds), *The Routledge encyclopaedia of narrative theory*. New York: Routledge. Retrieved from http://www.clarku.edu/~mbamberg/encyclopedia_entries.htm.

Barnes, M. (2004). *The use of positioning theory in studying student participation in collaborative learning activities*. Paper presented at the AARE Annual Conference, Melbourne 2004. Retrieved from http://www.aare.edu.au/publica tions-database.php/4082/The-use-of-Positioning-Theory-in-studying-student -participation-in-collaborative-learning-activities.

Baron, R.A., Byrne, D.E. and Suls, J. (1989). *Exploring social psychology*. Boston: Allyn & Bacon.

Bateson, G. (1972). *Steps to an ecology of mind: collected essays in anthropology, psychiatry, evolution, and epistemology*. Chicago: University of Chicago Press.

Biddle, B.J. (1986). Recent development in role theory. *Annual Review of Sociology*, *12*, 1267–1292.

Bourdieu, P. (1984). *Distinction: a social critique of the judgment of taste*. London: Routledge.

Butler, J. (1990). Performative acts and gender constitution: an essay in phenomenology and feminist theory. In S.-E. Case (ed.), *Performing feminisms: feminist critical theory and theatre* (pp. 270–282). Baltimore: The Johns Hopkins University Press.

Cavadino, M. and Dignan, J. (2007). *The penal system: an introduction*. London: SAGE.

Davies, M., Croal, H. and Tyrer, J. (2009). *Criminal justice: an introduction to the criminal justice system in England and Wales*. Dorchester: Pearson.

Davies, B. and Harré R. (1990). Positioning: the discursive production of selves. Retrieved from http://www.massey.ac.nz/~ALock/position/position.htm.

Foucault, M. (1972). *The archaeology of knowledge*. New York: Pantheon Books.

Foucault, M. (2002). The subject and power. In J. Faubion (ed.), *Essential works of Foucault, 1954–1984* (vol. 3, pp. 326–348). London: Penguin.

Garland, D. (2001). *The culture of control: crime and social order in contemporary society*. Oxford: Oxford University Press.

Ghosten, C.D. (2012). *Analyzing conflict in organizations with positioning theory: a narrative inquiry*. PhD dissertation, University of Tennessee. Retrieved from http://trace.tennessee.edu/utk_graddiss/1295.

Goffman, E. (1974). *Frame analysis: an essay on the organization of experience*. London: Harper & Row.

Goffman, E. (1981). *Forms of talk*. Philadelphia: University of Pennsylvania Press.

Granovetter, M. (1973). The strength of weak ties. *American Journal of Sociology*, *78*(6), 1360–1380.

Hall, S. (1996). Introduction: who needs identity? In S. Hall and P. du Gay (eds), *Questions of cultural identity* (pp. 1–17). London: SAGE.

Harré, H.R. (1979). *Social being: a theory for social psychology*. Oxford: Blackwell.

Harré, H.R. (2004). Positioning theory. Retrieved from http://www.massey.ac.nz/~alock/virtual/positioning.doc.

Harré, H.R. and Gillet, G. (1994). *The discursive mind*. London: SAGE.

Harré, H.R. and Moghaddam, F.M. (eds) (2003). *The self and others: positioning individuals and groups in personal, political, and cultural contexts*. Westport: Praeger.

Harré, H.R., Moghaddam, F.M., Cairnie, et al. (2009). Recent advances in positioning theory. *Theory Psychology*, *19*, 5–31.

Harré, H.R., Moghaddam, F.M. and Lee, N.P. (eds) (2008). *Global conflict resolution through positioning analysis*. New York: Springer.

Harré, H.R. and Secord, P.S. (1972). *The explanation of social behaviour*. Oxford: Basil Blackwell.

Harré, H.R. and van Langenhove, L. (1992). Varieties of positioning. *Journal for the Theory of Social Behaviour*, *20*, 393–407.

Hirvonen, P. (2013). Positioning in an inter-professional team meeting: examining positioning theory as a methodological tool for micro-cultural group studies. *Qualitative Sociology Review*, *9*(4), 101–114.

Hollway, W. (1984). Gender difference and the production of subjectivity. In J. Henriques, W. Hollway, C. Urwin, et al. (eds), *Changing the subject: psychology, social regulation and subjectivity* (pp. 227–263). London: Methuen.

Jarden, A. and Lock, A.J. (2004). The expert therapist. *The Bulletin*, *102*, 41–45.

Johnstone, G. and Van Ness, D.W. (2007). *Handbook of restorative justice*. Cullompton: Willan Publishing.

Knorr-Cetina, K. (1983). The ethnographic study of scientific work: towards a constructivist interpretation of science. In K. Knorr-Cetina and M. Mulkay (eds), *Science observed* (pp. 189–204). London: SAGE.

Korobov, N. (2010). A discursive psychological approach to positioning. *Qualitative Research in Psychology*, *7*, 263–277.

Korobov, N. and Bamberg, M. (2006). Strip poker! They don't show nothing! Positioning identities in adolescent male talk about a television game show. In M. Bamberg, A. de Fina and D. Schiffrin (eds), *Narratives in interaction: identities and selves* (pp. 253–271). Amsterdam: John Benjamins. Retrieved from http://www.clarku.edu/~mbamberg/publications.html.

Kure, N. (2010). Narrative mediation and discursive positioning in organisational conflicts. *Explorations: An E-Journal of Narrative Practice*, *2*, 24–35.

Laclau, E. and Mouffe, C. (1985). *Hegemony and the socialist strategy*. London: Verso.

Maglione, G. (2013). Problematizing restorative justice: a Foucauldian perspective. In T. Gavrielides and V. Artinopoulou (eds), *Reconstructing restorative justice: philosophy, values, norms and methods reconsidered* (pp. 67–90). Farnham: Ashgate Publishing.

Maglione, M. (2014). Discursive fields and subject positions: becoming 'victim', 'offender' and 'community' in restorative justice. *Restorative Justice: An International Journal*, *2*(3), 327–348.

Marinova, D. (2004). Two approaches to negotiating positions in interaction: Goffman's (1981) footing and Davies and Harré's (1999) positioning theory. University of Pennsylvania Working Papers in Linguistics, 10, 1, 17. Retrieved from: http://repository.upenn.edu/pwpl/vol10/iss1/17.

McKenzie, P.J. and Carey, R.F. (2000). 'What's wrong with that woman?' – Positioning theory and information-seeking behavior. Retrieved from http://www.slis.ualberta.ca/cais2000/mckenzie.htm.

Packer, H.L. (1968). *The limits of the criminal sanction*. Stanford: Stanford University Press.

Potter, J. and Wetherell, M. (1987). *Discourse and social psychology: beyond attitudes and behaviour*. London: SAGE.

Rasmussen, M.L. (2006). *Becoming subjects: sexualities and secondary schooling*. New York: Routledge.

Rundell, F. (2007). 'Re-story-ing' our restorative practices. *Reclaiming Children and Youth Journal, 16*(2), 52–59.

Siegel, L. (2006). *Criminology: theories, patterns, and typologies*. Belmont: Cengage Learning.

Strang, H. (2003). Justice for victims of young offenders: the centrality of emotional harm and restoration. In G. Johnstone (ed.), *A restorative justice reader: texts, sources, context* (pp. 286–293). Cullompton: Willan Publishing.

Strang, H. and Sherman, L. (2003). Repairing the harm: victims and restorative justice. *Utah Law Review, 1*, 15–42.

Sullivan, D. and Tifft, L. (2001). *Restorative justice: healing the foundations of our everyday lives*. Monsey: Willow Tree Press.

Tirado, F. and Gálvez, A. (2007). Positioning theory and discourse analysis: some tools for social interaction analysis. Forum Qualitative Sozialforschung [Forum: Qualitative Social Research], *8*(2). Retrieved from http://www.qualitative-research.net/index.php/fqs/article/view/248.

Trout, J. (1969), 'Positioning' is a game people play in today's me-too market place. *Industrial Marketing, 54*(6), 51–55.

van Langenhove, L. and Harré, H.R. (1994). Cultural stereotypes and positioning theory. *Journal for the Theory of Social Behaviour, 24*(4), 359–372.

van Langenhove, L. and Harré, H.R. (1999). Introducing Positioning Theory. In H.R. Harré and L. van Langenhove (eds), *Positioning theory: moral contexts of intentional action* (pp. 14–31). Malden: Blackwell.

Vygotsky, L.S. (2004). Imagination and creativity in childhood. *Journal of Russian and East European Psychology, 42*, 7–97.

Wetherell, M. (1998). Positioning and interpretative repertoires: conversation analysis and poststructuralism in dialogue. *Discourse and Society, 9*(3), 387–412.

Wittgenstein, L. (1958). *Philosophical investigation*. Oxford: Basil Blackwell.

Zelle, G. (2009). *Exploring the application of positioning theory to the analysis of organisational change*. Australian and New Zealand Academy of Management Conference, Adelaide. Retrieved from http://ro.uow.edu.au/cgi/viewcontent.cgi?article=1614&context=commpapers.

Chapter 2

The Group and Cultural Context of Restorative Justice: A Social Psychological Perspective

Julie Van de Vyver, Giovanni A. Travaglino,
Milica Vasiljevic and Dominic Abrams

Introduction

Restorative justice (RJ) aims to 'restore harm by including affected parties in a (direct or indirect) encounter and a process of understanding through voluntary and honest dialogue' (Gavrielides, 2007, p. 139). Many different RJ practices exist; however, typically they involve a meeting between the victim and the perpetrator, and perhaps also community representatives. The victim and the perpetrator then discuss, and agree on, the harm done, the values violated, and the compensation, restitution and/or punishment required (Wenzel et al., 2010). There is a large body of literature on RJ (cf. Gavrielides, 2013), which has mostly focused on its effects on victims (for example, mental health) and offenders (for example, repeat offending) (cf. Sherman and Strang, 2007). A considerably smaller body of literature (for example, Gromet and Darley, 2009; Wenzel et al., 2010; van Prooijen and Lam, 2007) has explored when and why individuals or groups (victims, offenders, policy makers, communities, third parties) may support or reject the use of RJ practices. Understanding attitudes towards, and biases during, RJ practices is essential in order to advance and improve its use.

Social psychology provides unique insights into how people respond to their social environment. It thus stands that social psychology enables a richer understanding of when and why people may accept versus reject an RJ (as opposed to a retributive justice – RtJ) approach. This chapter will review this social psychology literature. In particular it will focus on how group processes (intergroup as well as intragroup processes) influence willingness to support an RJ (versus RtJ) approach.

Justice as Forms of Social Inclusion and Exclusion

We conceive of justice as reflecting multiple levels of inclusion and exclusion, based on a relational analysis of social exclusion (Abrams and Christian, 2007;

see also Williams, 2007). This analysis holds that society generally sustains order and meaning by selectively including and excluding people from relationships. Inclusion/exclusion can occur at different levels, from self-determined (for example, a person who lacks the confidence to join a singing group) to interpersonal (for example, relationship breakdown), to intragroup (for example, the application of membership criteria), to intergroup, organizational, political and higher levels. An important insight in this relational analysis is that exclusion at one level does not presuppose, and might even oppose, exclusion at another.

Justice can be seen as the use of methods that signal inclusion or exclusion of another person or group. Sometimes, RJ can be used at the interpersonal level (the criminal must repair the damage to an individual's property), and RtJ (or traditional punishment more generally) at the group level (all members of the criminal's group are banished). In other cases the individual (for example, a phone hacker or rogue trader) can receive a jail sentence (that is, RtJ) while the group or organization can be held liable for reparations for the same offences (that is, RJ). Arguably, these different applications of justice do not just reflect inconsistency but a coherent goal to maintain a social system using different mechanisms of inclusion and exclusion. The jailed phone hacker is excluded from society (for example, by being sent to prison). The heavily fined corporation, however, having made amends, is free to continue its business, maintaining the integrity of the system as a whole. Under other circumstances, an organization or country may be treated to retributive justice (such as military invasion) to eliminate it or destroy its legitimacy, while such justice is delivered in the name of protecting the people who belong to that organization. Ultimately, then, the deployment of retributive rather than restorative justice can be viewed as a psychological and societal vehicle for maintaining systems of authority and control by signalling exclusive or inclusive intent towards the target.

As will be clear from this analysis, a crucial issue for those involved in delivering and receiving justice, is therefore whether the targets of their decisions are defined as (or intended to be) one of 'us' rather than one of 'them'. Theory and evidence reviewed in the remainder of this chapter shows why this is such a powerful axis for justice, and why therefore a social psychological perspective on the group and cultural context of restorative justice can be particularly valuable.

The Group Context

Social Identity Theory

Social identity theory highlights an important distinction between our personal (that is, idiosyncratic personal relationships and traits) and social identities (that is, group memberships) (Hogg and Abrams, 1988, 2003). People's social identities are malleable and dependent on context. For example, in a room among only men, a woman's gender identity might be particularly salient. Similarly, a football player's team identity might be particularly salient during a match, and a person's political identity might be particularly salient while watching a political debate.

Importantly, social identity strongly affects people's thoughts, attitudes and behaviours (Abrams and Hogg, 2004). This is because people are motivated to maintain or achieve a positive social identity, as this boosts their self-esteem (Brown, 2000). To maintain or achieve a positive social identity, comparisons are made between the ingroup (that is, one's own group) and the outgroup (that is, other groups). People may show ingroup favouritism and/or outgroup derogation (Abrams and Hogg, 2004). Indeed, instances of discrimination or bias in society often occur between ingroup and outgroup members (cf. Hewstone et al., 2002). For example, in Britain, the increasingly popular far-right UKIP party propound a political dialogue on increasing resources (or favouritism) for the ingroup and decreasing resources for the outgroup.

Ample empirical support exists for the impact of social identity on attitudes and behaviours (cf. Balliet et al., 2014; Hewstone et al., 2002). Studies have shown that people evaluate ingroup members more favourably than outgroup members (Brewer, 1979; Perdue et al., 1990), are more likely to help ingroup versus outgroup members (Levine et al., 2005), feel more anger at injustices against ingroup than outgroup members (Batson et al., 2009), show more prejudice against outgroup versus ingroup members (Dovidio et al., 2004) and work harder to achieve ingroup goals versus outgroup goals (Ellemers et al., 2004). A recent meta-analytic review of 212 studies in this area showed that people are more willing to incur a personal cost to benefit ingroup members, compared to outgroup members – that is, people show ingroup favouritism (Balliet et al., 2014). This research shows the pervasive effects of social identity and group memberships on people's attitudes and behaviours.

Given this influence of social identity on people's attitudes and behaviours, it seems likely that social identity should also affect people's support for restorative justice. In other words, people's (for example, the victims, the community representatives, society at large, policy makers) support for an RJ approach may depend on whether the perpetrator is an ingroup or outgroup member. This group membership might be based on gender, race, nationality, religion, political orientation or another identity. Similarly, given that people feel less angry about injustices to outgroup than ingroup victims (Batson et al., 2009), it seems likely that people may promote RJ practices differently depending on whether the victim is an outgroup or ingroup member.

Social Identity and Restorative Justice

Subjective group dynamics and the black sheep effect
The research outlined above introducing social identity theory seems to suggest that people may be more lenient when judging transgressions by ingroup (versus outgroup) perpetrators – an ingroup favouritism effect (cf. Gollwitzer and Keller, 2010). However, research on subjective group dynamics (SGD; see Marques et al.,

2001) shows that, under some circumstances, ingroup members who transgress important values or norms are judged more severely than comparable outgroup members. Ingroup members who transgress ingroup values or norms ('ingroup deviants') disrupt the coherence and homogeneity of the group and pose a threat to the subjective validity of the ingroup, in a way that outgroup members do not (see Abrams et al., forthcoming; Abrams et al., 2005). Thus, people are typically more concerned about deviations by other ingroup members than they are about those by outgroup members, a phenomenon known as the 'black sheep effect' (for example, Abrams et al., 2000; Abrams et al., 2014; Abrams et al., 2003; Marques et al., 1998; Marques and Páez, 1994; Travaglino, Abrams, Randsley de Moura, Marques et al., 2014). As we discuss later, however, it is not just the intensity of reaction that might differ when ingroup rather than outgroup members transgress, but also the type of control and justice that people feel is most appropriate in response to the transgressions.

A relatively small, but important, body of literature has directly examined the relationship between social identity, group membership and support for different types of justice (see Gromet and Darley, 2009; Wenzel et al., 2010). This literature shows that rather than solely focusing on the effects of social identity on leniency to transgressors, a more nuanced approach seems necessary. Specifically, the focus must shift away from whether or not ingroup (versus outgroup) perpetrators will receive lenient judgements towards the types of treatment or justice (RJ versus RtJ) that they are likely to receive.

Power, status and values
Wenzel and colleagues suggest that 'the endorsement of a retributive versus restorative justice notion depends on whether or not offender and victim are regarded as sharing membership in the relevant community or inclusive group' (Wenzel et al., 2008, p. 382). Specifically, they propose that when victims and perpetrators share a common identity, support for restorative justice is more likely. In contrast, when victims and perpetrators lack a common identity, support for retributive justice is more likely. This is because when victims and perpetrators do not share a common identity they are more likely to perceive each other as negatively interdependent in terms of status and power. Thus, they will be particularly sensitive to, and focused on, the status and power implications of the offence (for a discussion on how racial power and status differentials impact RJ practices see Gavrielides, 2013). Status and power are particularly important when there is a lack of a common identity because a transgression by an outgroup (versus ingroup) member threatens the ingroup's power and status. The ingroup will then be motivated to remedy this new or increased power/status difference by punishing the outgroup offender (Wenzel et al., 2008).

In contrast, when victims and perpetrators share a social identity they are more likely to see each other as positively interdependent in terms of shared values. Thus, following a transgression by an ingroup member, they will be particularly sensitive to, or focused on, value restoration (Wenzel et al., 2008). Value restoration is only possible when there is a shared social identity because values 'are valid insofar as they are shared within a relevant social category' (Wenzel et al., 2008, p. 383). Indeed the expectation to agree on a shared set of values is grounded in a sense of shared identity (Turner, 1987; cf. Wenzel et al., 2008). In other words, as an outgroup offender is not expected to share the same values as the ingroup victim and community, seeking consensus and the restoration of values is not seen as important or perhaps even possible (the restorative justice approach). In contrast, when the offender is an ingroup member, victims (and community representatives) should be motivated to seek consensus and re-establish shared values in order to maintain ingroup validity.

Two correlational studies provide support for this power/status account (Wenzel and Thielmann, 2006). In their studies, Wenzel and Thielmann (2006) examined reactions to offences (for example, tax evasion and social security fraud) carried out by ingroup members (based on nationality group). They found that agreement with a 'just desert notion of justice' (that is, retributive justice) was a better predictor of sanctioning decisions when participants scored low on social identification (with their nationality group). In contrast, agreement with a 'value reaffirmation notion of justice' (that is, restorative justice) predicted sanctioning decisions only among those who identified strongly with their ingroup.

More recently, Wenzel and colleagues (2010) tested this proposition experimentally. In their first study they randomly allocated Australian students to a social identity (university identity) salient versus non-salient condition. They then measured participants' level of identification with their university. Following this, students were told about a case of academic dishonesty in which one student had taken advantage of another by falsely taking credit for their work. Participants were then shown one of three justice processes that the university had supposedly taken to deal with this issue. In all three cases, the offender was given a punishment in the form of unpaid service to the university. However, the procedures used to arrive at this punishment varied. Specifically, some participants were told that the university chose this punishment and that the offender had no say in the matter (no consensus attempt condition). Other participants were told that the victim and offender were unable to come to an agreement on appropriate punishment and that in the end the university chose the punishment (failed consensus condition). A final group of participants were told that the victim and perpetrator expressed their emotions and views on the incident and were able to come to an agreement on appropriate punishment (consensus condition). The dependent variable in this study was participants' satisfaction with the situation and its resolution. Results showed that the establishment of consensus (that is, RJ) increased a sense of justice particularly among participants who shared identity with the offender (that is, their university identity was salient). Thus, this research suggests that people may be more willing to support RJ (value reinforcing) practices for ingroup deviants and RtJ (intergroup differentiation) practices for outgroup deviants.

Crime severity

According to Gromet and Darley (2009) severity of the crime also affects whether individuals will support RJ versus RtJ practices for ingroup versus outgroup members. Specifically, they suggest that for offences low in severity (for example, petty theft) it is relatively easy to categorize the offender as an ingroup member. However, for serious offences (for example, murder) people may automatically perceive offenders as outgroup members – as 'not one of us' (Gromet and Darley, 2009). If a person does happen to share a social identity with an offender of a serious crime such as murder, they will typically attempt to distance themselves from the offender (for example, Eidelman et al., 2006). One way of doing this is through punishment or retributive justice (Gromet and Darley, 2009).

Summary

In sum, social identity seems to exert a strong influence on people's support for restorative (versus retributive) justice. People are more likely to support a restorative justice approach for ingroup offenders and a retributive justice approach for outgroup offenders (Wenzel et al., 2008, 2010). These differences occur due to concerns around intergroup power and status differences, and intragroup value consensus (Wenzel et al., 2008, 2010). Moreover, such differences between ingroup and outgroup members only occur for minor offences. For major offences, neither ingroup nor outgroup members may receive support for an RJ approach (Gromet and Darley, 2009).

Restorative justice researchers have recently begun to consider how to maximize the effectiveness of RJ practices in the context of multicultural societies (Gavrielides, 2013). In particular, they have highlighted the difficulties that diversity, different communication styles and power imbalances between individuals of different races can present for justice processes. Wenzel and colleagues' (2008, 2010) research shows that difficulties may arise simply because people see others as belonging to a different group from them. In order to maximize the effectiveness of RJ practices, practitioners should collaborate with social psychologists to develop strategies for reducing intergroup salience during RJ processes.

Group stereotypes

While evidence shows that outgroup members are treated differently from ingroup members (Hewstone et al., 2002), research also shows that different outgroups are treated distinctly depending on how they are stereotyped (Fiske et al., 2002). Seminal work on the stereotype content model (Fiske et al., 2002) suggests that groups are evaluated along two primary characteristics: warmth and competence. The combinations of these two characteristics give rise to distinct judgements and behaviours (or forms of discrimination). For example, groups perceived as high in warmth and low in competence are typically viewed with pity and suffer from benevolent (or paternalistic) prejudice (for example, 'the elderly', 'housewives' and 'the disabled'). Groups perceived as low in warmth but high in competence are viewed with envy and suffer from envious prejudice (for example, 'the rich', 'Asians', 'Americans' and 'Jews'). Groups perceived as low in both warmth and competence are viewed with contempt (for example, 'the poor', 'welfare recipients' and 'Hispanics'). Groups perceived as high in both competence and warmth are viewed with admiration. Such groups are usually majority status ingroups and include: 'Christians', 'the middle class', 'white people' and 'students'. There is also a 'middle cluster' eliciting moderate levels of competence and warmth (for example, 'migrant workers', 'gay men', 'Arabs', 'Muslims', 'blue-collar workers' and 'southerners') (Cuddy et al., 2007; Fiske et al., 2002).

Our recent line of research (Abrams et al., 2015) examined whether people assign the human right of equality differently to different status minorities as a function of the evaluative implications of the stereotypes associated with these groups. We hypothesized that status minority groups stereotyped as warmer but less competent (that is, paternalized) would be judged differently from status minorities stereotyped as colder, or potentially more threatening (that is, not paternalized). Data ($N = 2895$) for this study were collected as part of a commissioned representative national survey in Britain in 2005 (see Abrams and Houston, 2006). Participants were asked to rate the extent to which 'there should be equality for all groups in Britain' (equality value). They were also asked to rate their support for group-specific rights and equality. To measure support for group rights participants were told, 'Not all groups in society want the same thing as the majority. How important do you feel it is that the particular wishes of each of the following groups are satisfied?' The groups evaluated in this study were: women, people over 70 and disabled people (that is, the paternalized groups), and Muslims, black people and lesbian women and gay men (that is, the non-paternalized groups). Group equality was measured by asking participants the extent to which 'attempts to give equal employment opportunities to [the relevant minority group] in this country have gone too far or not far enough'.

The goal of this line of research was to understand whether equality hypocrisy exists in British society. Equality hypocrisy occurs 'when people express strong support for equal rights for *all*, but then differentially favour equal rights for some groups above those of others' (Abrams et al., 2015). Our results showed that whereas 84 per cent of respondents claimed they value equality for all groups, fewer than 65 per cent considered it important to satisfy the needs of black people, fewer than 60 per cent considered it important to satisfy the needs of Muslims, and fewer than 50 per cent considered it important to satisfy the needs of homosexual people. Descriptively this equates to an equality hypocrisy gap of between 15 and 30 per cent. Analyses of variance similarly showed that respondents were more willing to support group rights and group equality for paternalized than for non-paternalized groups. This effect persisted even among respondents who reported high support for equal rights (that is, the general equality value). Thus, the results showed strong evidence of equality hypocrisy. People appear less willing to endorse equal rights for specific status minority groups than for all groups in general. This hypocrisy is manifested both at the aggregate level (that is, society as a whole), and within individuals who prioritize equal rights of particular groups over those of others. Note that in this research, equality and human rights are conceptualized in value-based (rather than in legal-based) terms.

Furthermore, a recent theoretical model put forward by Vasiljevic and Viki (2013) proposed that certain social groups may be erroneously associated with criminality more than others, which could explain the higher incarceration rates of ethnic and racial minorities (groups that are commonly not paternalized; cf. Clear, 2007; Mann, 1989; Roberts, 2004; Yeomans, 2010). Examining actual incarceration rates can best show the ubiquity of societal equality hypocrisy. One such study in the state of Florida examined criminal sentencing decisions for black and white defendants who had equivalent criminal histories. Results showed that within each racial group, inmates with more Afrocentric features received harsher sentences than those with less Afrocentric features (Blair et al., 2004). The notions of restorative and retributive justice therefore seem to be intrinsically related to the social identities, group memberships and group stereotypes of the victims and offenders.

Summary

This research has important implications for understanding attitudes towards restorative (versus retributive) justice. The equality hypocrisy phenomenon suggests that not all groups may be accorded restorative justice equally. Combining the equality hypocrisy phenomenon (Abrams et al., 2015) with the social identity research on attitudes to justice (Wenzel et al., 2010), we hypothesize that while people are more likely to support RJ for ingroup offenders, and RtJ for outgroup offenders (cf. Vasiljevic and Viki, 2013; Wenzel et al., 2010), they may be particularly likely to support RtJ for certain (for example, non-paternalized) minority status groups.

Dehumanization

Dehumanization occurs when people perceive another person or group as lacking humanness (Haslam and Loughnan, 2014). According to Haslam (2006) two types of dehumanization exist: animalistic and mechanistic. Animalistic dehumanization refers to the denial of attributes that are uniquely human (for example, civility and moral sensibility). Such a denial results in certain people or social groups being perceived as animal-like. In contrast, mechanistic dehumanization refers to the denial of human nature traits such as interpersonal warmth. This denial results in certain people or social groups being perceived as machine-like. According to Bandura (1990a, 1990b), dehumanization is one of the factors related to moral disengagement, allowing people to justify negative behaviour against particular targets. Such moral exclusion can facilitate aggression because dehumanized targets are viewed as being outside the moral boundaries of society (Opotow, 1990). Consistent with this argument, Baumeister et al. (1994) propose that the dehumanization of victims may inhibit feelings of guilt and distress about any harm inflicted. Recent empirical studies have demonstrated the negative consequences of dehumanization. For example, Cuddy et al. (2007) found that people were less willing to help victims of Hurricane Katrina, to the extent that they perceived them as less human. Taking these findings further, Leidner et al. (2010) found that moral disengagement strategies, which include dehumanization, are used as psychological mechanisms that allow individuals to distance themselves from past ingroup violence. This can lead both to decreased willingness to punish ingroup perpetrators and decreased willingness to offer compensation to ingroup victims. Overall, research demonstrates that dehumanization inhibits the experience of compassionate emotions and increases the likelihood of negative behaviour towards certain groups and individuals (see also Castano and Giner-Sorolla, 2006; Tam et al., 2007; Vaes et al., 2003).

Dehumanization in intergroup contexts and attitudes to justice
Research has shown that people tend to view themselves as possessing more human nature traits than others (for example, Haslam and Bain, 2007). This phenomenon expands outwards so that people have a tendency to view their ingroup as more human than other groups. For example, Leyens and colleagues have shown that people attribute more secondary or uniquely human emotions to their ingroup than they do to relevant outgroups (for example, Demoulin et al., 2004; Leyens et al., 2001; Paladino et al., 2002). Similar findings have been reported by Viki et al. (2006) who asked participants to attribute human words (for example, person and humanity) and animal words (for example, creature and animal) to their ingroup versus an outgroup. The results indicated that human-related words were attributed to the ingroup more than the outgroup (Viki et al., 2006). Certain groups are more at risk than others for being dehumanized. Harris and Fiske (2006) showed that the medial prefrontal cortex, a brain structure crucial for social cognition, was deactivated only when seeing group members stereotyped as low in competence and low in warmth (for example, drug addicts, homeless people).

Importantly, recent research shows that the dehumanization of outgroups is significantly related to people's support for different types of justice. For example, Zebel et al. (2008) found that people were less likely to feel guilty about wrongs perpetrated by their ingroup against an outgroup, if they perceived the outgroup as less human than their ingroup. Similarly, among Protestants and Catholics in Northern Ireland, Tam and colleagues (2007) showed that dehumanization of the other group was related to less forgiveness for past violence. In an interesting line of recent research, Wohl et al. (2012) examined victims' forgiveness following apologies by transgressor outgroups. They found that forgiveness was less likely if the victims dehumanized the transgressor outgroups. Moreover, among these victims, forgiveness was also less likely when the transgressor outgroups expressed secondary (for example, anguish) rather than primary (for example, fear) emotions in their apology. This was because apologies made using secondary emotions (that is, uniquely human emotions) were seen as less genuine.

In another line of research, Viki et al. (2012) examined whether people's dehumanization of sex offenders influenced their attitudes towards their rehabilitation and social exclusion. Their results showed that the more people dehumanized sex offenders, the less they supported their rehabilitation, the longer sentences they recommended, the more likely they were to support their exclusion from society and the more they supported their violent ill-treatment.

Taking this research forward, Bastian et al. (2013) directly examined the relationship between people's dehumanization of offenders and their support for retributive justice. In their studies they asked participants to read an extract that described a crime (for example, child molestation, violence or a white-collar crime) and then measured participants' outrage, dehumanization and the level of punishment severity that they supported. Punishment severity was measured by asking participants: (1) how many years sentence the criminal should receive (maximum 99 years); (2) how harsh the sentence should be; and (3) whether the offender was deemed for a rehabilitation programme. Their results showed that dehumanization (independently of moral outrage) positively predicted length and harshness of sentence, and negatively predicted suitability for the rehabilitation programme. In a similar line of research but with a more applied sample, Leidner et al. (2013) found that the more Palestinian and Jewish Israeli participants dehumanized each other, the more they supported retributive justice (versus restorative justice). This support for retributive justice was associated with support for violence rather than peace deals. Leidner and colleagues (2013) aptly deduced that 'the lower the perceived sentience of the perpetrator, the lower the quest for restorative justice, because a perpetrator lacking sentience is by definition not equipped with the emotional depth that motivates and provides reality to restorative efforts' (p. 185).

Summary
Dehumanization is significantly related to people's support for different types of justice. People who are perceived to belong to outgroups that are stereotyped as having low competence and warmth (for example, drug addicts and homeless people) are particularly vulnerable to dehumanization and thus less likely to receive support for restorative forms of justice.

The Cultural Context

Honour and Justice

As discussed earlier (see also Wenzel et al., 2008), a transgression is likely to have implications for status relationships among individuals and groups. By committing an offence, perpetrators are implicitly communicating their disdain for the victims, as well as claiming a position of superiority relative to the offended and the community (Miller, 2001; Wenzel et al., 2008). The relevance of those implications might be accentuated in honour cultures due to their emphasis on issues of status and public image.

Honour cultures are prevalent in many geographical areas around the globe, including Mediterranean and Middle Eastern countries, south of the USA, and South America (Cohen and Nisbett, 1997; Peristiany, 1966; Pitt-Rivers, 1966; Rodriguez Mosquera, 2013; Travaglino et al., 2015). These cultures tended to emerge among nomadic herding people, in circumstances in which social and topological arrangements did not allow establishment of central institutions for regulating conflicts (Nisbett, 1993).

In honour cultures, individuals' sense of internal worth is strongly affected by how others perceive them (for example, Pitt-Rivers, 1966). Individuals must therefore manage their reputation carefully. This entails different expectations for women and men (Rodriguez Mosquera et al., 2002). Women's reputation in these cultures often revolves around issues of sexual chastity and modesty. In contrast, men are expected to uphold a tough reputation, provide for their families and be able to defend their persona, 'their' women and property from insults and abuses, using violence if necessary (Barnes et al., 2012).

Research has demonstrated a consistent link between honour and aggression, especially among men (Cohen and Nisbett, 1994; Cohen and Vandello, 1998; Nisbett and Cohen, 1996). For example, individuals from the south of the USA are more prone to respond with anger and aggression to offences and insults, compared to individuals from the north (Cohen et al., 1999). Individuals from the south are more likely to express support for retributive brutality in response to external national threats (that is, terrorism; Barnes et al., 2012).

The emphasis on reputation and power may be considered consistent with retributive justice practices (cf. Wenzel et al., 2008). Through coercive punishment and retaliation (Elster, 1990), RtJ may be perceived as being an appropriate mechanism for re-establishing the power balance between society and its enemies, and excluding perpetrators from the social sphere. For example, in southern US states laws are more tolerant of coercive and punitive use of violence, and these states are also more likely to execute criminals (see Cohen and Vandello, 1998).

However, the linkage between honour-related values and justice is complex. There are instances in which these values may be reinterpreted and manipulated to promote inclusion. For example, concerns with the community play an important role in honour cultures (see Guerra et al., 2013). Consequently, ritualized practices aimed at restoring communal harmony in the face of interpersonal conflict may be equally prevalent. These practices promote values akin to those upheld in restorative justice (Umbreit et al., 2005), in that they provide the opportunity to rebuild the relationships between perpetrators and victims, while preserving the honour of the parties involved in front of the community at large.

For instance, in Muslim countries the practice of Sulha (reconciliation in Arabic) provides a culturally acceptable way for interrupting cycles of violence spurring from offences to one's honour (Pely, 2010, 2011). The Sulha, often initiated by the offenders or their clans, involves the intervention of local dignitaries who will guide the reconciliatory process and attempt to reach a settlement between the parties. Similarly, in southern Italy it is common for contenders in a dispute to declare themselves 'sciarriati' (on not-speaking terms, in Sicilian) (Schneider, 1969). This practice ensures a temporary truce, and allows the intervention of mediators who will negotiate an acceptable agreement between the parties involved.

Moreover, at the intergroup level, honour-related values may also promote acceptability of violent, illegal groups. Recently, we (Travaglino, Abrams, and Randsley de Moura, 2014; Travaglino, Abrams, Randsley de Moura and Russo, 2014; Travaglino et al., 2015) examined how young Italians perceive criminal (mafia-style) organizations, and their intentions to engage in collective action to oppose these groups. Italian criminal organizations (COs) manipulate certain facets of honour cultures to sustain their criminal aims (Schneider and Schneider, 2003). They make a strategic use of violence to showcase manliness, and increase reputation. We thus hypothesized that endorsement of honour-related values would be linked to acceptance of these groups.

In line with this hypothesis, we found that young males and females who endorsed the use of male violence in honour-related domains (a 'masculine honour ideology'; see Barnes et al., 2012) also held lower intentions to oppose criminal organizations collectively. This linkage was explained by lower endorsement of the goal of a collective mobilization against COs (Klandermans, 1984), higher perceived threat regarding interacting with police, and more positive attitudes towards COs (Travaglino, Abrams, and Randsley de Moura, 2014). In addition, stronger endorsement of male honour-related values was linked to lower vicarious shame in relation to COs' wrongdoings, suggesting that higher endorsers of masculine honour ideology were less attuned to the implication of COs' actions for the moral self (Travaglino, Abrams, Randsley de Moura, and Russo, 2014). Importantly, these results also held when statistically controlling for the impact of perceived risk about opposing COs, demonstrating that acceptance of COs has more to do with perceived legitimacy than fear.

In sum, while the emphasis upon restoring power and reputation following a transgression present in honour cultures may favour retribution and exclusion, certain facets of these cultures may be reinterpreted to promote inclusion. Honour-related values may allow alternative routes to conflict resolution, or even sustain the power of dominant, illegal groups, to restore harmony and balance in the community.

Social Conditions and Justice Preferences

Preferences for different types of justice are likely to shift depending on other societal changes. Recently, we (Abrams, 2010; Abrams and Vasiljevic, 2014) offered an analysis of how economic downturns affect group identity and intergroup relations. We identified four societal states: harmonious cohesion, rivalrous cohesion, benign indifference and malign antipathy. These states also map onto the relational analysis of social exclusion (Abrams and Christian, 2007) that framed the opening of this chapter. When economic prospects are positive and resources are well shared the conditions seem favourable to advocates of restorative justice. Both groups and individuals are likely to accept or advocate socially inclusive strategies such as multiculturalism, tolerance, forgiveness and equal exchange. However, under conditions of economic malaise individuals may become suspicious and hostile towards all others (malign antipathy), or they may become attracted to social groups that demand change or challenge the status quo, sometimes to the point of hatred and bitter prejudice (rivalrous cohesion). Under these circumstances we would expect greater endorsement of retributive justice, particularly those that help to exclude potentially threatening outsiders. Therefore, quite apart from the actual effectiveness of RJ and RtJ in terms of reducing crime or helping victims, ensuring the wider social acceptability of these strategies is a key task for the legitimacy of the justice system itself. This acceptability is at least as likely to hinge on the implications for group identity as on the practical or moral considerations.

Conclusions

In this chapter we examined the notion of restorative justice through a social psychological lens. We hope to have shown why a social psychologically informed approach should be relevant for future research and policy strategy. These strategies should, at least in part, include effective interventions to overcome group-based biases in the advocacy and use of RJ and RtJ.

Drawing on the psychology of intergroup relations, dehumanization and social exclusion, we highlighted the differential challenges facing people who belong to minority (low status) and those who belong to majority (high status) groups. In particular, our review and conceptual framework identified that society and its agents are likely to be biased and selective in offering restorative justice, thereby limiting its potential to promote constructive change. Empirical evidence shows that people are more willing to support RJ for ingroup members and RtJ for outgroup members. Moreover, people do not apply human rights, justice and fairness equally to all outgroups in society. Majority groups are therefore less likely to offer restorative options to negatively stereotyped outgroups (for example, Muslims in the UK) because they are considered less deserving of equality than other minority groups (for example, disabled people). Recent evidence demonstrates that individuals and groups that are considered as less than human (that is, are dehumanized) are also likely to be denied opportunities for restorative justice. In this chapter we also argued that wider cultural circumstances, such as the honour codes of one's culture, can have a direct effect on how justice and fairness are conceptualized and acted upon, promoting either exclusion and retaliation, or inclusion and acceptance.

The current chapter raises some concerns about RJ practices. Specifically, members of outgroups (particularly negatively stereotyped outgroups) may not receive equal access to RJ opportunities as members of ingroups. This is an important issue that RJ practitioners must strive to overcome. Strategies to overcome this issue may include raising awareness about this bias among practitioners as well as developing social psychological interventions aimed at overcoming such biases in RJ practices. An obvious step forward would be to foster closer collaborations between social scientists and policy makers with a view to addressing the gaps in our knowledge regarding RJ practices. What our chapter shows is that RJ practices that fail to take into account the power and status hierarchies among victims and perpetrators are bound to fail in the long run. In conclusion, we believe that these insights from social psychology show why it is essential for practitioners and policy makers to employ strategies that are sensitive to group and cultural influences on people's support for different types of justice.

Bibliography

Abrams, D. (2010). *Processes of prejudice: theory, evidence and intervention.* Equality and Human Rights Commission. Research Report 56 (118). London: EHRC. ISBN 9781842062708. Retrieved from http://www.equalityhumanrigh ts.com/sites/default/files/documents/research/56_processes_of_prejudice.pdf.

Abrams, D. and Christian, J.N. (2007). A relational analysis of social exclusion. In. D. Abrams, J.N. Christian and D. Gordon (eds), *Multidisciplinary handbook of social exclusion research* (pp. 211–232). Chichester: Wiley.

Abrams, D. and Hogg, M.A. (2004). Metatheory: lessons from social identity research. *Personality and Social Psychology Review, 8*(2), 98–106. doi:10.1207/ s15327957pspr0802_2.

Abrams, D. and Houston, D.M. (2006). *Equality, diversity and prejudice in Britain: results from the 2005 national survey.* Report for the Cabinet Office Equalities Review October 2006. Retrieved from http://kar.kent.ac.uk/4106/1/ Abrams_KentEquality_Oct_2006.pdf.

Abrams, D., Houston, D., Van de Vyver, J. and Vasiljevic, M. (2015). Equality hypocrisy? Equality is a universal human right that we apply unequally. *Peace and Conflict: Journal of Peace Psychology* (Special Issue: Psychologies of Human Rights), *21*, 28–46. doi.org/10.1037/pac0000084.

Abrams, D., Marques, J.M., Bown, N. and Henson, M. (2000). Pro-norm and anti-norm deviance within and between groups. *Journal of Personality and Social Ppsychology, 78*(5), 906–912. doi:10.1037/0022-3514.78.5.906.

Abrams, D., Powell, C., Palmer, S.B. and Van de Vyver, J. (forthcoming). Toward a contextualized social developmental account of children's group-based inclusion and exclusion: the developmental model of subjective group dynamics. In A. Rutland, D. Nesdale and C. Spears Brown (eds), *The Wiley-Blackwell handbook of group processes in children and adolescents.*

Abrams, D., Randsley de Moura, G., Hutchison, P. and Viki, G.T. (2005). When bad becomes good (and vice versa): why social exclusion is not based on difference.

In D. Abrams, M.A. Hogg and J.M. Marques (eds), *The social psychology of inclusion and exclusion* (pp. 161–190). New York: Psychology Press.

Abrams, D., Rutland, A. and Cameron, L. (2003). The development of subjective group dynamics: children's judgments of normative and deviant in-group and out-group individuals. *Child Development, 74*(6), 1840–1856. doi:10.1046/j.1467-8624.2003.00641.x.

Abrams, D., Palmer, S.B., Rutland, A., et al. (2014). Evaluations of and reasoning about normative and deviant ingroup and outgroup members: development of the black sheep effect. *Developmental Psychology, 50*(1), 258–270. doi:10.1037/a0032461.

Abrams, D. and Vasiljevic, M. (2014). How does macroeconomic change affect social identity (and vice versa?): insights from the European context. *Analyses of Social Issues and Public Policy, 14*, 331–338. doi:10.1111/asap.12052.

Balliet, D., Wu, J. and De Dreu, C.K. (2014). Ingroup favoritism in cooperation: a meta-analysis. *Psychological Bulletin, 140*(6), 1556–1581. doi:10.1037/a0037737.

Bandura, A. (1990a). Selective activation and disengagement of moral control. *Journal of Social Issues, 46*, 27–46. doi:10.1111/j.1540-4560.1990.tb00270.x.

Bandura, A. (1990b). Mechanisms of moral disengagement. In W. Reich (ed.), *Origins of terrorism: psychologies, ideologies, theologies, states of mind* (pp. 161–191). Cambridge: Cambridge University Press.

Barnes, C.D., Brown, R.P. and Osterman, L.L. (2012). Don't tread on me: masculine honor ideology in the US and militant responses to terrorism. *Personality and Social Psychology Bulletin, 38*(8), 1018–1029. doi:10.1177/0146167212443383.

Bastian, B., Denson, T.F. and Haslam, N. (2013). The roles of dehumanization and moral outrage in retributive justice. *PloS ONE, 8*(4), e61842. doi:10.1371/journal.pone.0061842.

Batson, C.D., Chao, M.C. and Givens, J.M. (2009). Pursuing moral outrage: anger at torture. *Journal of Experimental Social Psychology, 45*(1), 155–160. doi:10.1016/j.jesp.2008.07.017.

Baumeister, R.F., Stillwell, A.M. and Heatherton, T.F. (1994). Guilt: an interpersonal approach. *Psychological Bulletin, 115*, 243–267. doi:10.1037/0033-2909.115.2.243.

Blair, I., Judd, C.M. and Chapleau, K.M. (2004). The influence of Afrocentric facial features in criminal sentencing. *Psychological Science, 15*, 674–679. doi:10.1111/j.0956-7976.2004.00739.x.

Brewer, M.B. (1979). In-group bias in the minimal intergroup situation: a cognitive-motivational analysis. *Psychological bulletin, 86*(2), 307–324. doi:10.1037/0033-2909.86.2.307.

Brown, R. (2000). Social identity theory: past achievements, current problems and future challenges. *European Journal of Social Psychology, 30*(6), 745–778. doi:10.1002/1099-0992(200011/12)30:6<745::AID-EJSP24>3.0.CO;2-O.

Castano, E. and Giner-Sorolla, R. (2006). Not quite human: infrahumanization in response to collective responsibility for intergroup killing. *Journal of Personality and Social Psychology, 90*, 804–818. doi:10.1037/0022-3514.90.5.804.

Clear, T.R. (2007). *Imprisoning communities: how mass incarceration makes disadvantaged neighborhoods worse.* New York: Oxford University Press.

Cohen, D. and Nisbett, R.E. (1994). Self-protection and the culture of honor: explaining southern violence. *Personality and Social Psychology Bulletin, 20*(5), 551–567. doi:10.1177/0146167294205012.

Cohen, D. and Nisbett, R.E. (1997). Field experiments examining the culture of honor: the role of institutions in perpetuating norms about violence. *Personality and Social Psychology Bulletin, 23*(11), 1188–1199. doi:10.1177/014616729 72311006.

Cohen, D. and Vandello, J. (1998). Meanings of violence. *The Journal of Legal Studies, 27*, 567–584. doi:10.1086/468035.

Cohen, D., Vandello, J., Puente, S. and Rantilla, A. (1999). 'When you call me that, smile!' How norms for politeness, interaction styles, and aggression work together in southern culture. *Social Psychology Quarterly*, 257–275. doi:10.23 07/2695863.

Cuddy, A.J., Fiske, S.T. and Glick, P. (2007). The BIAS map: behaviors from intergroup affect and stereotypes. *Journal of Personality and Social Psychology, 92*(4), 631–648. doi:10.1037/0022-3514.92.4.631.

Cuddy, A.J., Rock, M.S. and Norton, M.I. (2007). Aid in the aftermath of Hurricane Katrina: inferences of secondary emotions and intergroup helping. *Group Processes & Intergroup Relations, 10*, 107–118. doi:10.1177/1368430207071344.

Demoulin, S., Rodriguez, R.T., Rodriguez, A.P., et al. (2004). Emotional prejudice can lead to infra-humanization. In W. Stroebe and M. Hewstone (eds), *European review of social psychology* (vol. 15, pp. 259–296). London: Psychology Press.

Dovidio, J.F., ten Vergert, M., Stewart, T.L., et al. (2004). Perspective and prejudice: antecedents and mediating mechanisms. *Personality and Social Psychology Bulletin, 30*(12), 1537–1549. doi:10.1177/0146167204271177.

Eidelman, S., Silvia, P.J. and Biernat, M. (2006). Responding to deviance: target exclusion and differential devaluation. *Personality and Social Psychology Bulletin, 32*(9), 1153–1164. doi:10.1177/0146167206288720.

Ellemers, N., De Gilder, D. and Haslam, S.A. (2004). Motivating individuals and groups at work: a social identity perspective on leadership and group performance. *Academy of Management Review, 29*(3), 459–478. doi:10.5465/ AMR.2004.13670967.

Elster, J. (1990). Norms of revenge. *Ethics, 100*, 862–885. Retrieved from http:// www.jstor.org/stable/2381783.

Fiske, S.T., Cuddy, A.J., Glick, P. and Xu, J. (2002). A model of (often mixed) stereotype content: competence and warmth respectively follow from perceived status and competition. *Journal of Personality and Social Psychology, 82*(6), 878–902. doi:10.1037/0022-3514.82.6.878.

Gavrielides, T. (2007). *Restorative justice theory and practice: addressing the discrepancy.* Helsinki: HEUNI.

Gavrielides, T. (2013). Where is restorative justice heading? *PROBATION junior*, *4*(2), 79–95. Retrieved from www.ceeol.com.

Gollwitzer, M. and Keller, L. (2010). What you did only matters if you are one of us: offenders' group membership moderates the effect of criminal history on punishment severity. *Social Psychology, 41*(1), 20–26. doi:10.1027/1864-9335/a000004.

Gromet, D. M. and Darley, J.M. (2009). Retributive and restorative justice: importance of crime severity and shared identity in people's justice responses. *Australian Journal of Psychology, 61*(1), 50–57. doi:10.1080/00049530802607662.

Guerra, V.M., Giner-Sorolla, R. and Vasiljevic, M. (2013). The importance of honor concerns across eight countries. *Group Processes & Intergroup Relations, 16*, 298–318. doi:10.1177/1368430212463451.

Harris, L.T. and Fiske, S.T. (2006). Dehumanizing the lowest of the low neuroimaging responses to extreme out-groups. *Psychological Science, 17*(10), 847–853. doi:10.1111/j.1467-9280.2006.01793.x.

Haslam, N. (2006). Dehumanization: an integrative review. *Personality and Social Psychology Review, 10*, 252–264. doi:10.1207/s15327957pspr1003_4.

Haslam, N. and Bain, P. (2007). Humanizing the self: moderators of the attribution of lesser humanness to others. *Personality and Social Psychology Bulletin, 33*, 57–68. doi:10.1177/0146167206293191.

Haslam, N. and Loughnan, S. (2014). Dehumanization and infrahumanization. *Annual Review of Psychology, 65*, 399–423. doi:10.1146/annurev-psych-010 213-115045.

Hewstone, M., Rubin, M. and Willis, H. (2002). Intergroup bias. *Annual Review of Psychology, 53*(1), 575–604. doi:10.1146/annurev.psych.53.100901.135109

Hogg, M.A. and Abrams, D. (1988). *Social identifications: a social psychology of intergroup relations and group processes.* London: Routledge.

Hogg, M.A. and Abrams, D. (2003). Intergroup behavior and social identity. In M.A. Hogg and J. Cooper (eds), *The SAGE handbook of social psychology* (pp. 408–431). Thousand Oaks: SAGE.

Klandermans, B. (1984). Mobilization and participation in a social movement: social psychological expansions of resource mobilization theory. *American Sociological Review, 49*, 583–600.

Leidner, B., Castano, E. and Ginges, J. (2013). Dehumanization, retributive and restorative justice, and aggressive versus diplomatic intergroup conflict resolution strategies. *Personality and Social Psychology Bulletin, 39*(2), 181–192. doi:10.1177/0146167212472208.

Leidner, B., Castano, E., Zaiser, E. and Giner-Sorolla, R. (2010). Ingroup glorification, moral disengagement, and justice in the context of collective violence. *Personality and Social Psychology Bulletin, 36*, 1115–1129. doi:10.11 77/0146167210376391.

Levine, M., Prosser, A., Evans, D. and Reicher, S. (2005). Identity and emergency intervention: how social group membership and inclusiveness of group boundaries shape helping behavior. *Personality and Social Psychology Bulletin*, *31*(4), 443–453. doi:10.1177/0146167204271651.

Leyens, J. Ph., Rodriguez, A.P., Rodriguez, R.T., et al. (2001). Psychological essentialism and the differential attribution of uniquely human emotions to ingroups and outgroups. *European Journal of Social Psychology*, *31*, 395–411. doi:10.1002/ejsp.50.

Mann, C.R. (1989). Minority and female: a criminal justice double bind. *Social Justice*, *16*, 95–114. Retrieved from http://www.jstor.org/stable/29766503.

Marques, J.M., Abrams, D., Paez, D. and Hogg, M.A. (2001). Social categorization, social identification, and rejection of deviant group members. In M.A. Hogg and R.S. Tindale (eds), *Blackwell handbook of social psychology (Vol. 3): group processes* (pp. 400–424). Oxford: Blackwell.

Marques, J.M. and Páez, D. (1994). The 'black sheep effect': social categorization, rejection of ingroup deviates, and perception of group variability. *European Review of Social Psychology*, *5*(1), 37–68. doi:10.1080/14792779543000011.

Marques, J.M., Yzerbyt, V.Y. and Leyens, J.P. (1988). The black sheep effect: judgmental extremity towards ingroup members as a function of group identification. *European Journal of Social Psychology*, *18*, 1–16. doi:10.1002/ejsp.2420180308.

Miller, D.T. (2001). Disrespect and the experience of injustice. *Annual Review of Psychology*, *52*(1), 527–553. doi:10.1146/annurev.psych.52.1.527.

Nisbett, R.E. (1993). Violence and U.S. regional culture. *American Psychologist*, *48*, 441–449. doi:10.1037/0003-066X.48.4.441.

Nisbett, R.E. and Cohen, D. (1996). *Culture of honor: the psychology of violence in the South*. Boulder: Westview Press.

Opotow, S. (1990). Moral exclusion and injustice: an introduction. *Journal of Social Issues*, *46*, 1–20. doi:10.1111/j.1540-4560.1990.tb00268.x.

Paladino, M.P., Leyens, J. Ph., Rodriguez, R.T. and Rodriguez, A.P. (2002). Differential association of uniquely and non-uniquely human emotions with the ingroup and the outgroup. *Group Process and Intergroup Relations*, *5*, 105–117. doi:10.1177/1368430202005002539.

Pely, D. (2010). Honor: the Sulha's main dispute resolution tool. *Conflict Resolution Quarterly*, *28*(1), 67–81. doi:10.1002/crq.20013.

Pely, D. (2011). When honor trumps basic needs: the role of honor in deadly disputes within Israel's Arab community. *Negotiation Journal*, *27*(2), 205–225. doi:10.1111/j.1571-9979.2011.00303.x.

Perdue, C.W., Dovidio, J.F., Gurtman, M.B. and Tyler, R.B. (1990). Us and them: social categorization and the process of intergroup bias. *Journal of Personality and Social Psychology*, *59*(3), 475–486. doi:10.1037/0022-3514.59.3.475.

Peristiany, J.G. (1966). *Honour and shame: the values of Mediterranean society*. London: Weidenfeld & Nicolson.

Pitt-Rivers, J. (1966). Honour and social status. In J.G. Peristiany (ed.), *The nature of human society: honour and shame* (pp. 19–78). London: Weidenfeld & Nicolson.

Roberts, D.E. (2004). The social and moral cost of mass incarceration in African American communities. *Stanford Law Review*, *56*, 1271–1305. Retrieved from http://www.jstor.org/stable/40040178.

Rodriguez Mosquera, P.M. (2013). In the name of honor: on virtue, reputation and violence. *Group Processes & Intergroup Relations*, *16*(3), 271–278. doi:10.1177/1368430212472590.

Rodriguez Mosquera, P.M., Manstead, A.S. and Fischer, A.H. (2002). The role of honour concerns in emotional reactions to offences. *Cognition and Emotion*, *16*(1), 143–163. doi:10.1080/02699930143000167.

Schneider, P. (1969). Honor and conflict in a Sicilian town. *Anthropological Quarterly*, *42*, 130–154. Retrieved from http://www.jstor.org/stable/3317036.

Schneider, J.C. and Schneider, P.T. (2003). *Reversible destiny: mafia, antimafia, and the struggle for Palermo*. Oakland: University of California Press.

Sherman, L.W. and Strang, H. (2007). *Restorative justice: the evidence*. London: Smith Institute.

Tam, T., Hewstone, M., Cairns, E., et al. (2007). The impact of intergroup emotions on forgiveness in Northern Ireland. *Group Processes & Intergroup Relations*, *10*, 119–136. doi:10.1177/1368430207071345.

Travaglino, G.A., Abrams, D. and Randsley de Moura, G. (2014). Men of honor don't talk: the relationship between masculine honor and social activism against criminal organizations in Italy. *Political Psychology*. doi:10.1111/pops.12226.

Travaglino, G.A., Abrams, D., de Moura, G.R. and Russo, G. (2014). Organized crime and group-based ideology: the association between masculine honor and collective opposition against criminal organizations. *Group Processes & Intergroup Relations*, *17*, 799–812. doi:10.1177/1368430214533394.

Travaglino, G.A., Abrams, D., Randsley de Moura, G., and Russo, G. (2015). That is how we do it around here: levels of identification, masculine honor, and social activism against organized crime in the south of Italy. *European Journal of Social Psychology*, *45*, 342–348 doi:10.1002/ejsp.2100.

Travaglino, G.A., Abrams, D., Randsley de Moura, G., et al. (2014). How groups react to disloyalty in the context of intergroup competition: evaluations of group deserters and defectors. *Journal of Experimental Social Psychology*, 54, 178–187. doi:10.1016/j.jesp.2014.05.006.

Turner, J.C. (1987). A self-categorization theory. In J.C. Turner, M.A. Hogg, P.J. Oakes, et al. (eds), *Rediscovering the social group: a self-categorization theory* (pp. 42–67). Oxford: Blackwell.

Umbreit, M.S., Vos, B., Coates, R.B. and Lightfoot, E. (2005). Restorative justice in the twenty-first century: a social movement full of opportunities and pitfalls. *Marquette Law Review*, *89*, 251–304. Retrieved from http://scholarship.law.marquette.edu/mulr/vol89/iss2/3.

Vaes, J., Paladino, M.P., Castelli, L., et al. (2003). On the behavioral consequences of infrahumanization: the implicit role of uniquely human emotions in intergroup relations. *Journal of Personality and Social Psychology*, *85*, 1016–1034. doi:10.1037/0022–3514.85.6.1016.

van Prooijen, J.W. and Lam, J. (2007). Retributive justice and social categorizations: the perceived fairness of punishment depends on intergroup status. *European Journal of Social Psychology*, *37*(6), 1244–1255. doi:10.1002/ejsp.421.

Vasiljevic, M. and Viki, G.T. (2013). Dehumanization, moral disengagement, and public attitudes to crime and punishment. In P.G. Bain, J. Vaes and P. Leyens (eds), *Advances in understanding humanness and dehumanization* (pp. 129–146). New York: Psychology Press.

Viki, G.T., Culmer, M.J., Eller, A. and Abrams, D. (2006) Race and willingness to co-operate with the police: the roles of quality of contact, attitudes towards the behaviour and subjective norms. *British Journal of Social Psychology*, *12*, 285–302. doi:10.1348/014466605X49618.

Viki, G.T., Fullerton, I., Raggett, H., et al. (2012). The role of dehumanization in attitudes toward the social exclusion and rehabilitation of sex offenders. *Journal of Applied Social Psychology*, *42*, 2349–2367. doi:10.1111/j.1559-1816.2012.00944.x

Wenzel, M., Okimoto, T.G., Feather, N.T. and Platow, M.J. (2008). Retributive and restorative justice. *Law and Human Behavior*, *32*(5), 375–389. doi:10.1007/s10979-007-9116-6.

Wenzel, M., Okimoto, T.G., Feather, N.T. and Platow, M.J. (2010). Justice through consensus: shared identity and the preference for a restorative notion of justice. *European Journal of Social Psychology*, *40*(6), 909–930. doi:10.1002/ejsp.657.

Wenzel, M. and Thielmann, I. (2006). Why we punish in the name of justice: just desert versus value restoration and the role of social identity. *Social Justice Research*, *19*(4), 450–470. doi:10.1007/s11211-006-0028-2.

Williams, K.D. (2007). Ostracism. *Annual Review of Psychology*, *58*, 425–452. doi:10.1146/annurev.psych.58.110405.08564.

Wohl, M.J., Hornsey, M.J. and Bennett, S.H. (2012). Why group apologies succeed and fail: intergroup forgiveness and the role of primary and secondary emotions. *Journal of Personality and Social Psychology*, *102*(2), 306–322. doi:10.1037/a0024838.

Yeomans, G.C. (2010). *Justice for all? The disparate impact of mass incarceration on Black communities.* Unpublished Bachelor thesis, Wesleyan University.

Zebel, S., Zimmermann, A., Viki, G.T. and Doosje, B. (2008). Dehumanization and guilt as distinct but related predictors of support for reparation policies. *Political Psychology*, *29*, 193–219. doi:10.1111/j.1467-9221.2008.00623.x

Chapter 3

Towards a Neuroscience of Morality

Daniel Reisel

Introduction

Central to our understanding of the human mind is that its function must be reflected in some way in the neurobiology of the brain. Over the past few decades we have gained a detailed understanding of the neural basis of movement, vision, smell and even higher cognitive functions such as language. Despite these advances, morality as a subject matter and mental activity has so far eluded a convincing neurobiological account.

One reason for this is likely that morality is comprised of several features that combine to inform a person's beliefs and actions. This chapter looks at several foundational aspects of morality, including attachment, empathy and altruism, and attempts to link these concepts to the best available evidence from psychology and cognitive neuroscience.

British psychologist John Bowlby (for example, Bowlby, 1950) first developed of principle of attachment in children while studying a cohort of 44 juvenile delinquents in the late 1940s. He found that many of them had suffered parental deprivation in early childhood as a consequence of the Second World War.

Earlier, animal behaviouralist Konrad Lorenz had demonstrated the principle of imprinting. Lorenz found that young geese had a critical period during which they would become devotedly attached to things in their environment, even inanimate objects like the boots he was wearing. This type of imprinting is thought to be similar to a baby learning to recognize his/her parents. Bowlby ultimately saw the link between Lorenz's animal work and his work with young delinquents, and he began to study these early instinctive processes.

Perhaps it was not strange that Bowlby developed a strong interest in the relationship between caregivers and young children. His own upbringing was marked by repeated traumatic departure of caregivers and mother figures. Bowlby was a member of the English upper class, and both his parents were very distant (his father was a distinguished military surgeon). Bowlby was raised by a nanny until she left the family when he was four years old. Soon after that, the young boy was sent off to boarding school. His godfather, whom he was deeply attached to, died suddenly during a football match when Bowlby was only 12.

So loss of parents loomed large in Bowlby's upbringing. In an article written in 1986, he writes: 'Most of what goes on in the internal world is a more or less accurate reflection of what an individual has experienced in the external world'

(Bowlby et al., 1986, p. 43). In other words, a stable and loving childhood tends to produce a stable and loving mind – and vice versa. This is a crucial tenet of developmental psychology, but before Bowlby we didn't have the language to articulate what happens when it breaks down.

Bowlby's research was mainly focused on the role of mothers and female caregivers, which is unsurprising given the social context he was writing in. But now we have the evidence that a multiplicity of family structures can offer the stability and secure attachment needed by children to succeed in adult life. Recent work on the role of fathers has shown that in families with two parents, children will do best if they have a secure attachment with both. More recent evidence suggests that multiple stable caregivers matter greatly to whether a child will be able to establish emotional security and sound social relations. In a key study, psychologists Mary Main and Donna Weston, at the University of California Berkeley, found that toddlers aged 12–18 months performed best in tests of social responsiveness if they were secure with both primary caregivers (Main and Weston, 1981, see Figure 3.1).

Main and Weston invited each toddler to come for a play session with an adult actor playing a clown. The toddler hadn't met the adult before. They found that social responsiveness (that is, the child's willingness to engage with the stranger) reduced sharply the more insecure his/her attachment was. Instead, insecurely attached children were more likely to exhibit emotional conflict, such as avoiding the actor or engaging with an inanimate object rather than the stranger. The most socially responsive group was the one in which toddlers were secure with both parents. And although maternal attachment made a bigger difference than paternal, the children who were secure with father but not mother were still significantly better at social interactions than those toddlers who were insecure with both parents. This finding reinforces the view that both parents play a key role in early attachment, and that already by the age of 12 months the differences between children living in secure versus insecure environments begin to manifest themselves.

Basic social engagement is, of course, only the beginning. Complex morality grows out of experience. Every time a child feels rewarded for being kind or feels the negative consequences of being uncaring, his/her social brain gets tuned. Through play and countless social interactions, the young person's brain undergoes repeated associative learning, laying down the pathways of empathy in the brain. This occurs in the limbic brain, which comprises the hippocampus, essential for memory formation, the amygdala, likely involved in assigning emotional valence to memories and the cingulate cortex, which is thought to form part of the brain's decision-making ability. All of these structures are co-activated in complex social interactions and their repeated activation is part of the process of laying down the roots of empathy.

Although this process is by nature a social one, it is striking how universal it is. One person who has investigated this is the German psychologist and anthropologist Michael Tomasello. Taking his inspiration from Charles Darwin, who after completing his book on evolution wrote a major scientific work on

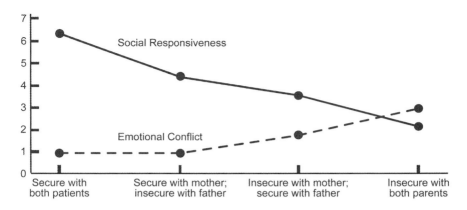

Figure 3.1   Attachment and social responsiveness
Source: Adapted from Main and Weston (1981).

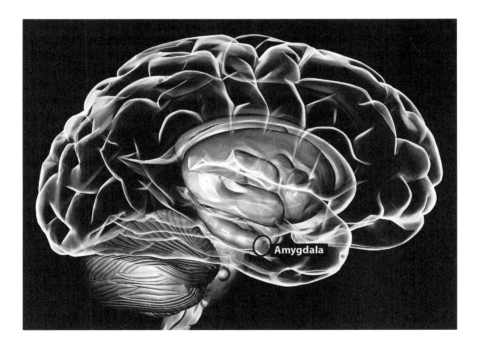

Figure 3.2   The amygdala sits at the base of the brain in each hemisphere
Source: Footage courtesy of Shutterstock, Inc. Used by Permission.

the universality of emotional expressions, he studied toddlers in different places around the world. His subjects were toddlers growing up in very different cultural and socioeconomic settings (Callaghan et al., 2011).

The first group of toddlers were living in the small, rural university town of Antigonish (population 4,235) in Nova Scotia, Canada. Although some parents worked in agriculture, many were professionals such as doctors, lawyers and university staff. The mother's average education level was 15.5 years and literacy was 100 per cent.

The second group of toddlers were from the village of Srikakulam (population 3,200) in the southeastern Indian state of Andhra Pradesh. Most families were poor, supporting themselves by subsistence farming and herding. Maternal education levels were low (4.2 years of schooling, on average) and literacy was at 52 per cent.

The third group of toddlers were recruited in and around the mountain village of San Pedro de Saño (total population of villages 4,183) in the Andean Central Highlands of Peru. Livelihood there is gained through agriculture, traditional crafts, service work or manual labour. Mothers had attended school for 8.6 years, on average, and literacy was at 91 per cent.

Despite these very different backgrounds, the children all began to imitate other people's behaviour around 10 months of age (India 10.8 months, Peru 10.6 months, Canada 10.4 months). At 12 months, children demonstrated early understanding of the intentions and attention of others, by showing caring and helping behaviour and participating in joint attention.

And how about actual empathy? Tomasello and his colleagues tested this by having experimenters appear to need help in a variety of settings. For example, the experimenter would try to reach a number of crumpled balls of paper with a tong, but pretend not to be able to reach them. If the child did not help, the experimenter would state: 'I can't reach'. Researchers looked to see if the child tried to help within 30 seconds.

Between the ages of 18 and 24 months, children from these three different cultural backgrounds all helped approximately three out of five times. Across all cultural settings mothers reported that their infants began to help others between 14 and 17 months of age (India 17.1 months, Peru 15.7 months, Canada 14.9 months). There was no relationship between the mothers' education level and the likelihood of their children offering to help.

What this study suggests – and this has been repeated in numerous similar studies – is that the development of basic empathy and prosocial behaviour is a universal trait that, given sufficiently secure attachment, develops naturally irrespective of cultural beliefs. It is a function of brain development, borne out through the child's interaction with its environment.

And it needs to happen early in life. It is well established that the experience of neglect and abuse has profound consequences for brain development, especially in these early phases. There may well be a window of opportunity, after which learning morality would be akin to learning a second language.

**Figure 3.3   Children in different cultural contexts develop
empathy at similar ages**

Source: Footage courtesy of Shutterstock, Inc. Used by Permission.

Understanding all this as a young researcher, I came to the question that led me to Wormwood Scrubs: how can we see this moral development – or its deficit – reflected in the brain?

Searching for the Neurobiological Basis of Empathy

In order to study the role of empathy in a real-life setting, in 1998 I joined the laboratory of Dr James Blair at the Institute of Cognitive Neuroscience at UCL. Blair had just published a remarkable study in which he used galvanic skin responses to record the physiological expression of emotion in people diagnosed with clinical psychopathy (Blair et al., 1997).

In the study, Blair had recruited 18 psychopathic inmates and 18 inmates without the diagnosis. They wired up each participant to a sensor, like in a lie detector test, that monitored heart rate and skin conductance (increased when stress causes us to sweat imperceptibly). The prisoners viewed three types of images: threatening, like a snake or a gun; neutral, like a chair or a book; or a person in distress, such as a close-up of a crying child's face. The two groups did not differ in terms of their physiological response to the threatening or neutral stimuli. However, the psychopathic men were significantly less responsive to the picture of the child in distress.

Over the course of the year I spent in the Blair group, we got to know the inmates at Wormwood Scrubs well. The Scrubs is an infamous prison in London, and it dominates the local area. Military engineers of the Victorian era designed it, and that shows. The walls are made of fortified red brick and there are barbed wire and metal fences all around. Going in, you have to pass through heavy metal doors.

**Figure 3.4   Children in different parts of the world develop
empathy at similar ages**

A few years ago, a study using MRI brain imaging was able to show this effect
at the level of brain activity (Boccardi et al., 2011). They found that individuals
with a clinical diagnosis of psychopathy had up to 30 per cent tissue reduction
in the basolateral nucleus of the amygdala. These changes were structural
and repeatable across a number of individuals, but not seen in age-matched
schizophrenic controls.

Although the function of each of part of the amygdala is not fully worked
out, this implies that psychopaths may have a specific impairment in picking
up the feelings of others, a kind of blind spot for empathy. Does this mean that
psychopaths were born with an inability to recognize suffering and psychological
pain in other people? Or, conversely, is it a case of the amygdala being akin to a
muscle, so that if you don't use it, you lose it?

To try to answer this question, my colleague at UCL Dr Essi Viding conducted
an intriguing study (Viding et al., 2012). She recruited two groups of 12-year-old
boys. They were recruited following assessment of their behaviour. The groups
were similar in terms of their age, intelligence and socioeconomic background.
However, when teachers and parents assessed their behaviour, one of the groups
scored high callous-unemotional antisocial behaviour. The other group (what in
the lingo is called 'neurotypical') scored average or low on the same scale.

The research team then used MRI to scan the boys while they looked at neutral
or fearful faces. In the group with average behavioural scores, a fearful face created
a powerful amygdala response. However, in the group that scored high in terms
of callous-emotional traits, their right amygdala activity was markedly reduced.

Now, this result does not prove whether the reduced amygdala response is the
cause of the antisocial behaviour or whether it is the lack of emotional behaviour
that over time has caused these young brains to change. However, what the study

does suggest is that it is possible to see precursors of antisocial behaviour in young children, and that their amygdala responses are already at that time similar to the data from adults.

Normally, we learn about the limits of acceptable social behaviour from experience. If a child causes another to cry, it is not uncommon for the parent or the schoolteacher to highlight it, to point out the pain caused. Through numerous such interactions, children fine-tune their behavioural repertoire.

Rewiring Morality in the Adult Brain

However, what happens when there is a failure of associative learning? When there is no connection being made between causing someone else pain and seeing the consequences of that pain? More and more, we are starting to appreciate that there are important individual differences that underlie difference in moral development. However, we are just beginning to understand the mechanisms involved at the brain level.

One way in which social development can fail to develop in a healthy way is through disordered attachment and a chaotic upbringing. In such circumstances, the adult brain has failed to get proper training and, as a result, is unable to correctly link moral behaviour with positive outcomes.

Teaching the adult brain how to unlearn deeply ingrained patterns of behaviour is not an easy task. However, some recent studies have given us some promising places to start. Paradoxically, some of the most interesting work has come from work with the most difficult of all categories of offenders, those who have been classified clinically as psychopaths.

A striking study carried out in 2013 by Christian Keysers at the University of Groningen set out to test the ability of psychopaths to feel empathy (Meffert et al., 2013). His team again showed short video clips to individuals classified as psychopaths and control subjects. The video depicted someone's hand being hit with a hard ruler. As the control subjects looked at the video and winced, their amygdala lit up on the scan. The psychopathic individuals had a lower brain response in several areas, including the amygdala (on both sides).

However, the team added an intriguing second stage to their experiment. After the first part, the subjects were asked to identify with the hand being hit. Remarkably, the empathy regions of the brain lit up, even in the psychopathic individuals. This indicates that the psychopathic individuals were able to recruit these brain areas when they were prompted to do so.

It remains to be seen whether these areas could be recruited in normal social interactions, and whether the brain response would actually translate into empathic behaviour. However, the fact that it was possible to get them to access their empathic brain regions when explicitly asked to do so might mean that there is a basis for future empathy training to strengthen and expand this ability.

Intriguingly, Kent Kiehl, a neuropsychologist at the University of New Mexico, has recently showed that psychopaths do have a reduced response in a circuit of brain regions, including the anterior cingulate, the inferior frontal gyrus and amygdala, when imagining someone being in pain (Decety et al., 2013). However, when the psychopath imagined that they themselves were the recipient of the same bodily harm, the brain response was indistinguishable from non-psychopathic inmates. What this suggests is crucial: psychopaths may have the ability to feel something akin to empathy; however, usually they fail to exercise this ability. The size of their moral circle is only large enough to accommodate themselves.

This has profound implications. It suggests that our task should not be necessarily to teach psychopaths and others how to be empathic. We should take it for granted that they know what it means to imagine and to feel pain. Rather, our interventions should focus on enlarging and expanding their moral circle of concern.

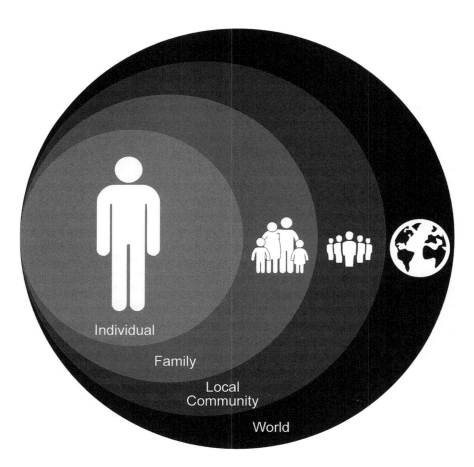

Figure 3.5   The individual sits at the heart of several interlocking circles of moral concern

One way to profoundly challenge one's moral circle of concern is restorative conferencing, where victims and offenders come together face to face. Countless stories tell how, when facing the victim and the victim's story head-on, even hardened criminals may find it impossible not to care. If this emotional trigger is then followed up with rehabilitation and support, some individuals can actually undergo profound change, both behaviourally and on the neurobiological level.

How to Change Your Mind

There are three main strands of research that give us an idea of how we might be able to rewire the adolescent or adult brain through experience. Any or all of these likely play a role in the brain changes that underlie the transformation seen in offenders who take part in restorative processes.

The first is the study of brain plasticity. It looks at how the neurons are able to change their state or shape in order to respond to a stimulus of any kind. Memory is thought to be a product of these molecular changes, though there are still scientific turf wars about the mechanisms that underpin the process.

The second promising area is neurogenesis, meaning the birth of new brain cells. This process is well established in non-human primates, and the most recent research suggests that it occurs in the human brain as well. There is growing evidence that stress has a negative impact on neurogenesis, and the race is on to find out what promotes the right kind of new nerve growth.

The final area of research is on the epigenetics of learning. This is an area of intense activity at the moment, driven in part by better techniques to look at the molecular processes involved. Epigenetics explains how the same DNA codes, subjected to all kinds of natural influences, are expressed differently in different people. And what do you suppose are two prime influences? Environment and experience.

Together, these three mechanisms work in integrated ways to create both stability and change in the human brain. We shall discuss each one in more detail.

Synaptic Plasticity – Cells that Fire Together, Wire Together

In the scope of human history, it's only recently that we've begun to understand the core mechanisms of how the brain learns. The Spanish physiologist Santiago Ramón y Cajal first proposed the modern theory of learning a century ago (Cajal, 1917). He posited that new knowledge is stored through the growth of new nerve connections, or synapses.

Canadian psychologist Donald Hebb advanced that theory in a ground-breaking book (Hebb, 1949), in which he suggested – and other researchers went on to prove – that it's the simultaneous activity of adjacent neurons that prompts new connections, and thus memories, to grow.

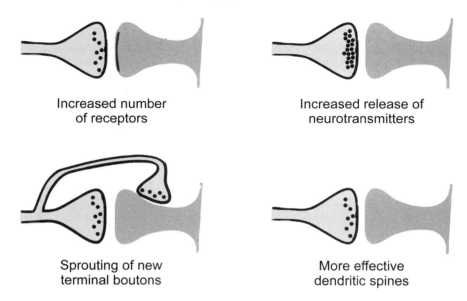

Increased number
of receptors

Increased release of
neurotransmitters

Sprouting of new
terminal boutons

More effective
dendritic spines

Figure 3.6   Four models of neuroplasticity

This is, for instance, precisely how we acquire new fears. Pair a fearful stimulus, such as a loud noise, with a neutral one, such as a light, and pretty soon we'll be flinching at the sight of the light alone. The famous Russian behavioural psychologist Ivan Pavlov (1849–1936) may have showed how this works on the behavioural level, but it was Donald Hebb who laid down the foundations of a neurobiological account of associative learning.

So, learning occurs when there are reliable patterns of stimuli or associations. But what happens when reinforcement of learning is unpredictable, even chaotic?

This kind of chaotic disruption of learning is probably more common than we think. In 1971, psychologists Jean Bresnahan and William Blum at Emory University carried out a landmark study looking at this break between stimulus and response (Bresnahan and Blum, 1971). They presented 60 first-grade children from two different socioeconomic levels with a learning task. However, the reward the children got was unrelated to their performance. Initially, the children from more privileged backgrounds performed better than their poorer counterparts. However, as the number of random reinforcements grew, the behaviour of the privileged children deteriorated to the same level as the children from low-income backgrounds. Although it is of course not the case that all children from low-income backgrounds are necessarily the victims of inconsistent reinforcement, this study does provide compelling evidence that the increased risk that these children face undoubtedly contributes to their relative underperformance in crucial ways. That is not an inherent property in those children. Instead it is a direct consequence of their experience.

This is all the more true for a child who, irrespective of his/her socioeconomic background, grows up in an environment marred by constant chaos and emotional abuse or neglect. His/her brain's normal wiring becomes disrupted and his/her capacity for empathy in many cases may become severely impaired.

In order to understand how this process works, I left the inmates at Wormwood Scrubs and joined a neuroscience laboratory in Oxford specializing in learning and development. There I met Rob Deacon, who has spent a lifetime studying what makes small social animals thrive. For four years, we worked together and he taught me about how to optimize learning in a social animal like a mouse. We built enriched environments for our laboratory animals and were able to show how their changed surroundings dramatically impacted upon their brains.

If a mouse is reared in a standard cage, essentially a shoebox with cotton wool inside, alone and without much stimulation, not only does it not thrive, it will often develop strange, repetitive behaviours. This naturally sociable animal will lose its ability to bond with other mice, even becoming aggressive when introduced to them.

However, mice reared in what we called an enriched environment, a large habitation with other mice with wheels and ladders and areas to explore, demonstrate neurogenesis, the birth of new brain cells. And as we showed, they also perform better on a range of learning and memory tasks. Their improved environment results in healthy, sociable behaviour.

Neurogenesis – How the Brain Renews Itself

One way in which an enriched environment may facilitate brain development could be not only the growth of new synapse connections, but through growth of entire new brain cells. For a long time, this was thought impossible. Santiago Ramón y Cajal, the founder of modern learning theory, was adamant that the adult brain couldn't grow new neurons after childhood (Cajal, 1917). That persistent dogma has now been, quite recently, disproved.

Neurogenesis, meaning the birth of new brain cells, is now one of the most exciting frontiers in neuroscience. From being a controversial notion, adult neurogenesis has now been documented in birds, rats and rabbits, as well as monkeys and humans (Kaplan and Hinds, 1977; Goldman and Nottebohm, 1983; Gould et al., 1997; Eriksson et al., 1998). Elizabeth Gould has done more than anyone to provide compelling evidence that the adult mammalian brain is able to generate new neurons, even in some of its deepest and most primal regions. It is now clear that the amygdala of mammals, including primates like us, can show neurogenesis. In some areas of the brain, more than 20 per cent of cells are newly formed. We're just beginning to understand what exact function these cells have, but what it implies is that the brain is capable of extraordinary change way into adulthood.

However, our brains are also exquisitely sensitive to stress in our environment. Stress hormones, glucocorticoids, released by the brain suppress the growth of new cells. The more stress, the less brain development, which in turn causes less adaptability and higher stress levels. This is the interplay between nature and nurture in real time.

Together with her colleagues, Gould was able to show how this process works at the level of the brain (Gould et al., 1998). By investigating the formation of new cells in adult monkeys, she found that stress stunted the proliferation of brain cells in the hippocampus, a brain area that is thought to be involved in the circuitry that underpins new memories. Even a single exposure to a stressful experience led to a significant reduction (nearly 50 per cent) in the number of new cells in the brain in the immediate period afterwards.

In a paper published in the influential journal *Cell* in 2013, Jonas Frisén and colleagues showed that in the adult human hippocampus, about a third of the cells are capable of neurogenesis (Spalding et al., 2013). With an annual turnover rate of just under 2 per cent, there are approximately 1,400 new neurons added per day. Although the authors found a modest decline of this regeneration rate, it demonstrates that neurogenesis is an integral part of human brain development, occurring throughout life.

Epigenetics – How Our Experience Alters Our Genes

Both synaptic plasticity and neurogenesis can result in semi-stable changes in gene expression. Experience cannot alter the genetic code, but it can alter the way it is read. The study of how the DNA code is read is called epigenetics, and the reading is crucial, because it determines which genes are active and which stay silent. Epigenetics enables temporary change to occur in the expression of genes, and it likely plays a key role in health as well as disease.

Professor Howard Cedar is an American-Israeli molecular biologist, widely regarded as originator of the field of epigenetics. I met him in his office in Jerusalem, which is next to his thriving laboratory. Though he is in his late seventies, he looks like he could run a marathon. When talking about epigenetics, he was exuberant: 'It's not about the book, but rather how that book is read', he said. He underscored what he considered to be the most important feature of epigenetics: that they create transiently stable changes in the way our genes our expressed. This provides for a kind of accelerated evolution, he explained, 'allowing an individual to pick up adaptations without the need for natural selection'.

These adaptations may be useful to a person, such as being able to store more energy in the form of body fat when growing up in an environment of scarcity, or the opposite. Or not so useful: internalized stress is thought to cause epigenetic changes that may play a role in psychiatric conditions including ADHD and depression.

Looking at our central question through this lens, we see that children who are exposed to neglect or abuse may internalize it, causing them to feel overwhelmed and emotionally pressured. This feeling comes with the release of hormones, such as glucocorticoids and adrenaline. Over time, exposure to the hormonal flood can

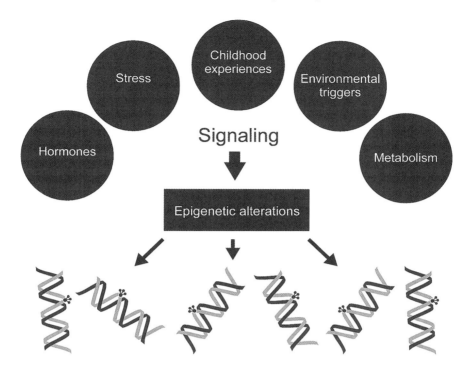

Figure 3.7 Epigenetics alters gene function as a function of experience

change the epigenome, altering the expression of our genes. Among the possible results is low impulse control.

What this suggests is that what happens to a child in the early years, and even before birth, has crucial consequences for his/her later life. It also suggests that change is possible throughout life. Unlike genes, epigenetic mechanisms are potentially reversible. So they might provide a better framework for understanding complex human behaviour than the old, fixed worldview was able to do.

Until recently, different forms of determinism have clouded the study of human behaviour. On the one hand, reductionist scientists claimed that significant aspects of our biology and social functioning are determined by our genes. No less determinist were the psychological theorists who claimed that personality and mood are ordained by one's upbringing and unresolved conflicts from childhood.

Taken together, these three lines of ground-breaking research above represent a paradigm shift in the biology of learning in general and potentially open up opportunities for improvement and intervention. The extent to which different kinds of interventions will work will depend on many factors. Above are three of the most likely conceptual candidates to a better understanding concerning the neurobiology of change that underlies the success of restorative approaches.

Towards a Neuroscience of Restorative Justice?

Practitioners and experienced restorative justice facilitators are convinced of the efficacy of the simple yet powerful methodology of conferencing. However, what is less clear is what the neurobiological basis might be that underlies these changes. The present chapter has outlined three main ways in which these changes might occur in the brain – that is, neuroplasticity, neurogenesis or via epigenetic mechanisms. It is likely that these mechanisms work in parallel and that they support different types of learning.

A deeper understanding of the neuroscience of restorative justice would also be invaluable in helping us design more effective restorative intervention. Since the days of Pavlov, we now have over a century of data on what makes learning more or less efficient. These insights can now be harnessed in helping us understand how to optimize preparatory work prior to conferencing, as well as the importance of follow-up and support.

Finally, it goes without saying but needs to be said nonetheless: it is only through interdisciplinary studies that we will gain a deeper understanding of the compelling ability of the human brain to change. Going forward, joint projects that explore both the neurobiology and the psychology of restorative justice practice are likely to be the ones that succeed.

Bibliography

Blair, R.J.R., Jones, L., Clark, F. and Smith, M. (1997). The psychopathic individual: a lack of responsiveness to distress cues? *Psychophysiology*, *34*, 192–198.

Boccardi, M., Frisoni, G.B., Hare, R.D., et al. (2011). Cortex and amygdala morphology in psychopathy. *Psychiatry Research*, *193*(2), 85–92.

Bowlby, J. (1950). *Maternal care and mental health. The master work series* (2nd edn). Northvale, NJ and London: Jason Aronson.

Bowlby, J., Figlio, K. and Young, R.M. (1986). An interview with John Bowlby on the origins and reception of his work. *Free Associations*, *6*, 36–64.

Bresnahan, J.L. and Blum, W.L. (1971). Chaotic reinforcement: a socioeconomic leveler. *Developmental Psychology*, *4*(1, Pt1).

Cajal, S.R. (1917). *Recuerdos de mi Vida*. Madrid: Madrid Imprenta y Librería de N. Moya.

Callaghan, T.C., Moll, H., Rakoczy, H., et al. (2011). Early social cognition in three cultural contexts. *Monographs of the Society for Research in Child Development*, *76*(2), vii–125.

Decety, J., Chen, C., Harenski, C. and Kiehl, K.A. (2013). An fMRI study of affective perspective taking in individuals with psychopathy: imagining another in pain does not evoke empathy. *Frontiers in Human Neuroscience*, *7*, 489.

Eriksson, P.S., Perfilieva, E., Bjork-Eriksson, T., et al. (1998). Neurogenesis in the adult human hippocampus. *Nature Medicine*, *4*, 1313–1317.

Goldman, S.A. and Nottebohm, F. (1983). Neuronal production, migration, and differentiation in a vocal control nucleus of the adult female canary brain. *Proceedings of the National Academy of Science USA*, *80*, 2390–2394.

Gould, E., McEwen, B.S., Tanapat, P., et al. (1997). Neurogenesis in the dentate gyrus of the adult tree shrew is regulated by psychosocial stress and NMDA receptor activation. *Journal of Neuroscience*, *17*, 2492–2498.

Gould, E., Tanapat. P., McEwen, B.S., et al. (1998). Proliferation of granule cell precursors in the dentate gyrus of adult monkeys is diminished by stress. *PNAS USA*, *95*, 3168–3171.

Hebb, D.O. (1949). *The organization of behavior: a neuropsychological theory.* New York: Wiley.

Kaplan, M.S. and Hinds, J.W. (1977). Neurogenesis in the adult rat: electron microscopic analysis of light radioautographs. *Science*, *197*, 1092–1094.

Main, M. and Weston, D. (1981). The quality of the toddler's relationship to mother and father. *Child Development*, *52*, 932–940.

Meffert, H., Gazzola, V., den Boer, J.A., et al. (2013). Reduced spontaneous but relatively normal deliberate vicarious representations in psychopathy. *Brain*, *136*, 2550–2562.

Spalding, K.L., Bergmann, O., Alkass, K., et al. (2013). Dynamics of hippocampal neurogenesis in adult humans. *Cell*, *153*(6), 1219–1227.

Viding, E., Sebastian, C.L., Dadds, M.R., et al. (2012). Amygdala response to pre-attentive masked fear is associated with callous-unemotional traits in children with conduct problems. *American Journal of Psychiatry*, *169*, 1109–1116.

Chapter 4

Restorative Practices, Affect Script Psychology and the Social and Emotional Aspects of Learning

Nicola Preston

Introduction

Research evidence shows that structured interventions such as social and emotional learning in schools can change brain function *and* structure to promote adaptive emotional and cognitive functioning. Although the emotional environment in early life is central in shaping the circuits of the brain in ways that persist throughout an organism's entire adult lifespan, it is now known that neurogenesis occurs throughout life and, therefore, skills to control and manage negative emotion and reduce stress and anxiety can be taught and can result in positive changes to key areas of the brain. Strategies for emotional regulation are good for the brain and body.

Social-emotional learning is an empirically verified strategy to improve skills of emotion regulation and social adaptation and, as a result, social-emotional learning likely produces beneficial changes in the brain (Davidson, 2008). Education that shapes the child's brain and produces these kinds of alterations lays the foundation for all future learning for emotion regulation, for social functioning and for engagement in learning.

Affect script psychology has played an important role in the field of restorative practices, expanding the understanding of why these approaches are as powerful and effective as they are and how emotions can be effectively regulated. Silvan Tomkins wrote: 'Affect is the bottom line for thought as well as perception and behaviour' (Demos, 1995, p. 51). Models of restorative practices based on affect script psychology provide the opportunity for human beings to be at their healthiest by providing a structured process for the safe expression of emotion, decreasing negative affect and increasing positive affect.

This chapter reviews the multidisciplinary research taking place in neuroscience, education and psychology and identifies the theoretical developments that are helping us to gain a greater understanding of how and why restorative practices can make a difference to social functioning and engagement in learning. The opportunities to teach key social and emotional skills through structured restorative interventions have important implications for cognition, behaviour and learning. Our understanding of the relationship between neuroscience and effective restorative processes is crucial to the ongoing development of restorative justice as a recognized theoretical discipline.

Background

Much has been written on the history and origins of the term restorative justice. Van Ness and Strong (2010) say that the term restorative justice was 'likely coined by Albert Eglash in 1958 when he distinguished between three approaches to justice: (1) retributive justice, based on punishment; (2) distributive justice, involving therapeutic treatment of offenders; and (3) restorative justice, based on restitution with input from victims and offenders' (pp. 21–22). *Changing Lenses – A New Focus for Crime and Justice*, published by Howard Zehr in 1990, is credited with being one of the first to articulate a theory of restorative justice that described an alternative approach to crime and justice. Zehr's restorative justice framework viewed crime as 'a violation of people and relationships'. Zehr refers to the positive results of efforts in the late 1970s and 1980s at victim–offender mediation and develops a model of justice focused on involving those affected by the crime including their communities of care. Work to develop this into theory has continued in many countries around the world since then and the terminology has expanded to include *restorative practices* and *restorative approaches*, which encompass proactive relationship building as well as more reactive processes to address harm. Wachtel (2013b) asserts that restorative practices 'build social capital and have positive implications for all social settings from families to schools to workplaces' (p. 8). He goes further to suggest that 'in restorative practices we have found a unified grand theory that explains how social entities may function best. This theory rests upon a fundamental hypothesis – that people are happier, more cooperative and productive, and more likely to make positive changes when those in positions of authority do things with them, rather than to them or for them' (Wachtel, 2013b, p. 8).

I first became involved in restorative justice and practice as a serving police officer with Thames Valley Police (UK) in 1996 when a model of restorative conferencing was introduced to the UK based on the principles of the New Zealand Family Group Conferencing model and applied to the process of police cautioning (New Zealand Government, 1989; O'Connell, 1998). The implementation of the model led to the development of restorative cautioning and conferencing across Thames Valley and was the catalyst to the growth of restorative justice and practice in the UK. It was also the beginning of my personal journey as a restorative practitioner, teacher and researcher.

Restorative conferences look to bring together all those affected by harm including their supporters and communities of care. The facilitator of these conferences uses a 'script' or 'aide memoire' to lead the discussion. Similar questions are asked of all participants in a particular order. This script is not to be confused with the 'script' in 'affect script psychology' which will be discussed later in this chapter. The reasoning that lies behind the wording of these questions and the order in which they are asked of conference participants has developed over the years into a theoretical framework that I have taken with me as a model for both my personal and professional life and that I am now using both proactively and reactively in my roles as a primary school teacher, special educational needs co-ordinator and senior restorative justice practitioner for victim-initiated restorative justice. As a facilitator of restorative conferences in criminal justice, workplaces and education, I have witnessed the 'power' of the process to deal with harm and conflict and to build or rebuild relationships, providing opportunities for participants to express their emotions in a safe environment and apply the learning to future decision making, communication and relationships.

The advances in our understanding of the psychological and emotional aspects of a restorative process have arguably been the most exciting developments in the past decade and have benefited from a greater understanding of the brain and emotions through the use of functional magnetic resonance imaging (fMRI) techniques and science that measures and maps brain activity. Research evidence from neuroscience, and other psychological theories such as affect script psychology, emotional intelligence, attachment theory, the human givens approach and positive psychology (Reisel, 2013; Chikazoe et al., 2014; Davidson, 2008, 2012; Nathanson, 1992; Kelly and Thorsborne, 2014; Goleman, 1996; Kennedy and Kennedy, 2004; Griffin and Tyrrell, 2013), have all contributed to a greater understanding of why and how restorative processes produce positive outcomes and to the ongoing development of a stronger theoretical model of restorative practice.

The introduction of restorative cautioning into Thames Valley in the late 1990s and the beginning of the development of restorative justice in the UK was evaluated in a three-year action research project. The evaluators produced an interim report with 81 recommendations designed, in their words, to 'close (or at least narrow) the gap detected between the programme's protocols and the behaviour of the facilitators' (Hoyle et al., 2002, p. 10). The facilitators (myself included) were using the scripted model as designed and introduced to Thames Valley by O'Connell (Hoyle et al., 2002, p. 7). The 'script' was a list of questions providing a consistent framework for facilitators to 'focus the encounter' but otherwise 'not actively participate' (Real Justice, n.d.). The key philosophical change was that the participants owned the conflict and resolved their own issues rather than the process being 'stolen' by professionals (Christie, 1977). One of the key findings of the interim study was that 'facilitators tended to dominate the exchanges which took place (accounting, on average, for half of all the words spoken) and some participants, notably offenders' supporters, were side-lined' (Hoyle et al., 2002, p. 13). The recommendations from this interim report, which we as the Restorative Justice Consultancy within Thames Valley Police were charged with implementing, made it clear that there was a link between the actions of the facilitator and the outcomes for participants. The researchers said of the interim report:

> We hoped that this would leave the police in no doubt as to the scale and nature of the deviations from the script and, in this, we were not disappointed. Our 81 recommendations for change were designed above all else to encourage those running cautioning sessions to adopt a more even-handed and genuinely facilitative stance. In other words, we urged facilitators to be more neutral in their facilitation, rather than to align themselves with either the offender or the victim, or, of even more concern, the police organisation. We also urged facilitators to set a clearer focus for these sessions and to adopt a re-integrative rather than deterrent approach to their work. (Hoyle et al., 2002, p. 14)

It was evident to me at this point that the thoughts, feelings and behaviours of those *facilitating* restorative processes were just as important as the thoughts, feelings and behaviours of the participants and that any underlying psychological theory of restorative justice or practice would need to reflect this. There were also implications for commissioners, trainers, leaders, organizations and governments wishing to implement restorative practices relating to their own psychological motivations and understanding of the theory. These motivations and interpretations have continued to influence the way in which the practice has developed, been 'marketed' and how it has been covered by the media. The integrity of what was and is defined as restorative practice continues to be hotly debated and often misunderstood, as evidenced by criticisms of practice ranging from accusations that restorative justice is a soft option through to practice labelled as 'restorative' being blamed for causing further harm to or, in the worst case scenario, the death of a person (Beckford and Taylor, 2014). A clear, explicit underlying psychological theory that underpins successful restorative practice is as important as ever.

Psychological Theories and Restorative Practice

Two key psychological theories supported the development of restorative conferencing at the time it was introduced into Thames Valley – affect script psychology (Tomkins, 1991; Nathanson, 1992) and the theory of reintegrative shaming (Braithwaite, 1989). These theories, based on our neurological hardwiring with nine basic affects, are influenced by our unique life experiences, socialization and learning. Over time these become our individual emotional lives (or scripts).

Braithwaite's separation of the basic affect 'shame' into stigmatizing shame, which rejects and permanently labels the person for their act of 'wrongdoing' and reintegrative shame which only rejects the act of 'wrongdoing' and not the person provides a psychological framework that underpins not only the success of restorative conferences but also the wider and more proactive set of restorative practices that build relationships and community.

These theories have continued to underpin my own practice as practitioner, teacher and researcher, most recently in my role as primary school teacher and special educational needs co-ordinator. How we relate recent developments in neuroscience, neuroplasticity and our understanding of human need, emotion and motivation to restorative practices has powerful implications for the development of the psychology behind the practice and its continued growth as a social science. Most crucial, in my opinion, are the implications that the theory has for the opportunities for social and emotional learning throughout life and the knowledge we are now developing around how to harness the brain's changeable characteristics to create the climate within homes, schools and the workplace to stimulate, shape and change our brain. The psychological theory that has helped us to understand how and why restorative justice works has wider implications for social and emotional learning.

Social and Emotional Learning (SEL)

Proactively, a range of restorative practices such as affective communication and circles (McCold andWachtel, 2001) can help to develop and stimulate those neural circuits that maximize positive affect and we can start from birth with restorative parenting through into early years education and beyond, providing young people with the skills and capacity to manage their emotions effectively and maximize their potential for healthy, happy, productive lives. As Reisel (2014) states, 'if we get the early years right, how to maximize our ability to empathize and reach out to each other, then we will create better, healthier societies and happier communities'. We are then proactively equipping young people with the skills to manage relationships and their emotions during times of stress, anxiety and conflict whatever their background, life experience or socialization.

Social and emotional learning in schools is not a new idea and, as with the origins of restorative justice, has its roots in ancient cultures and with the practices of indigenous people. Plato, in his published works – for example, *The Republic*, written around 360 BC – considered social and emotional education alongside other topics such as the nature of justice. He proposed a curriculum that included a balance of training in physical education, the arts, maths, science, character and moral judgment. 'By maintaining a sound system of education and upbringing, you produce citizens of good character', he argued (Plato, 2000). Preparing our young people to be responsible, productive and caring citizens within our communities has been a timeless pursuit of education and is arguably still the main goal despite the current emphasis on test scores.

Distinct programmes of social and emotional learning are a much more recent introduction to the school curriculum. In 1968, Dr James Comer introduced a school development programme for poor and socially marginalized students to help improve their behaviour, attendance and test scores (Comer, n.d.). The programme used child and adolescent development principles to create interactions and/or relationships that increased the potential for students to learn and to begin to take responsibility for their own learning. Teachers, school staff and administrators were also more able to support student personal development and learning. Comer's team at the Yale Child Study Center created relationship experiences and a culture in school that addressed six developmental pathways – 'social-interactive, psycho-emotional, ethical, cognitive, linguistic and physical'. These curriculum units, which involved students and parents, provided low-income, socially marginalized students 'with the kind of experiences that promote executive function and social skills that many mainstream children acquire in their families' (Comer, n.d.). The initial work with two poor, low-achieving elementary schools in New Haven, Connecticut, changed the schools from having the worst attendance and academic achievement figures in the city to schools that were achieving performance levels that exceeded the national average with significantly lower truancy and behaviour problems.

Many of the programmes introduced since then have been a response to a problem such as the need to reduce truancy, substance abuse, bullying, school drop-out rates, teenage pregnancy or school violence or to address adversity such as poverty or deprivation. It is only in the past decade or so that there has been more widespread acceptance of the need for social and emotional learning to be at the centre of developing school climate and culture rather than as a discrete response to problems. There is now extensive research evidence (Durlak et al., 2011; Zins et al., 2004; Schonert-Reichl et al., 2012) that the key elements or 'active ingredients' in the programmes were largely the same whatever the target problem and that the 'best SEL programs were implemented throughout each year of schooling. They shaped the entire school climate and they used developmentally appropriate lessons' (Zins et al., 2004, p. vii). This evidence has continued to accumulate and become an accepted part of school psychology. As teacher and restorative practitioner, Graeme George highlights: 'the success of specific programmes is most likely dependent upon other issues outside (any) programme such as school climate, pedagogy and the relationships that exist within the school' (George in Kelly and Thorsborne, 2014, p. 209). This is about a whole school experience rather than programmes responding to problems or deficits.

Neuroscience is now also providing us with the evidence that the emotional centres of the brain are intricately linked with the neocortical areas involved with cognition. When a child's learning is caught up by a distressing emotion then the centres within the brain involved in learning can become hampered and the child's attention can become preoccupied with the source of this negative emotion. Learning difficulties, adversity in home life and disadvantage are all recognized as risk factors that impact on the engagement of young people in their learning. For example, there is extensive evidence that young people with speech, language and communication difficulties will have poor conversational skills, poor non-verbal skills and poor social perception which can hinder their ability to form friendships with their peers and may lead to them becoming marginalized (Conti-Ramsden and Botting, 2004). Those young people who become isolated in this way often experience anxiety and depression which can affect their mental health, and research has highlighted that a third of children with developmental language disorders later developed mental health problems sometimes associated with criminal involvement (Linares-Orama, 2005; Clegg et al., 1999). There is also now a strong body of evidence linking speech language and communication disorders with behaviour difficulties and showing the prevalence of speech and language difficulties in the populations of our young offender institutions (Royal College of Speech and Language Therapists, n.d.). When this is combined with the fact that up to 80 per cent of children in some areas of the UK are starting school without these communication skills, it is crucial that educators focus on social and emotional communication and interaction.

Harry and Klingner (2007) look at how schools should focus learning on these so-called 'risk factors' and argue that the perspective should be focused on the strengths rather than on what is lacking:

> If it is evident that students' early home and community experiences have not prepared them well for schooling, what do schools do? Do the schools then provide the students with adequate and appropriate opportunities to learn? Does instruction begin where the students are? Does it move at a pace that enables them to become accustomed to the new norms and expectations? Are the students made to feel that the school values the knowledge they bring from their homes and communities? Do teachers build on these "funds of knowledge" (Moll, 1990), or do they see only deficits in the students? (Harry and Klingner 2007)

What is highlighted as important is meeting students' needs without stigmatizing them with a label. In some communities these 'deficit lenses' can have a profound influence on the educational approach to dealing with difference, whether that difference is a result of environment, culture, race, learning style or biological/psychological limitation. A restorative approach provides the environment in which students and adults can build trusting relationships and get to know each other. It becomes much easier to identify need and differentiate and tailor learning to the individual.

Neuroscience, Affect and Learning

Advances in neuroscientific study have also highlighted the importance of 'affect' to various components of cognition (Davidson, 2000 and 2008; Jensen, 1998). Within the field of neuroscience affect has been defined as a 'non-conscious experience of intensity' (Shouse, 2005). Shouse suggests that it is a 'pre-personal intensity corresponding to the passage from one experiential state of the body to another'. In his opinion, 'feelings are personal and biographical, emotions are social and affects are pre-personal'. Affect is the body's way of preparing itself for action and in the infant is innate. Shouse argues 'every form of communication where facial expressions, respiration, tone of voice, and posture are perceptible can transmit affect'. Affect *theory* is attributed to Silvan Tomkins (1982), who suggests: 'a central characteristic of affects is affective resonance, which refers to a person's tendency to resonate and experience the same affect in response to viewing a display of that affect by another person' (cited in Ekman (ed.), *Emotion in the human face*, pp. 353–95). Importantly for restorative practices and for the psychology that lies behind the process of social and emotional learning, affect is transmittable in ways that emotions and feelings are not and thus has the potential to be a powerful social force.

Over the past 10 to 15 years it has been recognized that the brain circuits for cognition and emotion are not segregated and that the prefrontal cortex is now believed to be an essential convergence zone for cognitive and affective information. The affective neuroscientist Richard Davidson reports that the goal of social and emotional learning is to foster adaptive patterns of emotion so that, 'following a negative event, a child is able to better and more effectively regulate his or her emotions so that they can calm down more quickly permitting a more effective kind of thinking in that situation' ([Davidson, 2008). He identifies through brain imaging research that learning that helps to reduce stress and anxiety reduces the release of the damaging hormone cortisol and improves working memory as well as physical and mental health. Social and emotional learning changes the brain structure and Davidson (2008) claims that these differences can be seen after only an hour of evidence-based SEL training.

This research has important implications for the development of both proactive and reactive restorative processes and strengthens the psychological framework that already underpins the continuum of formal and informal restorative practices (Wachtel, 2013a, p. 4). Empirically verified social and emotional learning that shapes the child's brain can lay the foundations for all future learning, emotion regulation and social functioning. Modern research in neuroplasticity has demonstrated that although there may be key times in the development of the brain when, for example, learning languages or how to play a musical instrument might happen more readily and easily, the brain continues throughout life to create new neural pathways and alter existing ones in order to adapt to new experiences, learn new information and create new memories. You *can* 'teach an old dog new tricks'! Promoting positive brain changes and equipping *young people* with the skills to manage their social and emotional habits must, however, be the priority. Furthermore, evidence that environmental factors (particularly the affective climate) produce experience-dependent changes in the brain structure and function indicates that developing positive school climate from early years onwards is central to developing healthy resilient citizens for the future. Having been involved with restorative practices as a parent, classroom teacher, special educational needs co-ordinator and operational police officer, I have found that the opportunity to offer an explicit framework for learning to manage our emotions in a healthy way that is underpinned by established evidenced-based psychological theory is compelling. Research evidence from work I have been involved in as trainer and practitioner is growing and for schools is clearly demonstrated in an international review of schools programmes (IIRP, 2009).

One of the schools included in this review was Bessels Leigh School, Oxfordshire (a residential school for boys with emotional and behavioural difficulties), which had commissioned restorative practices training with the staff of both the school and residential unit. A punitive approach to discipline up to that point had led to an 'us and them' climate within the school and an increase in vandalism and antisocial behaviour. Staff were suffering from rising levels of stress, resulting in increases in absenteeism and turnover. Teaching staff had very little to do with residential staff even though conflict from one part of the day often spilled over into the other. Following the training of all staff in restorative practices, there were hard data to show a reduction in negative incidents of damage or violence and, more importantly to the school community, a change in school climate. The boys began running their own circles and sorting out their own problems. Circles became embedded in the culture so that all adults and young people were involved. As the head teacher commented, 'I realized that we were moving from a programme of restorative justice to an ethos of restorative practices' (IIRP, 2009).

The Social Discipline Window

A key concept in understanding restorative practices is the social discipline window, as adapted by McCold and Wachtel from the work of Glaser (Wachtel, 2013b). It maintains that by offering high expectations, control or limit-setting alongside high support, encouragement or nurture we are more likely to work 'with' people than do things 'to' them or 'for' them or, worse still, doing nothing at all. During training courses, the International Institute for Restorative Practices will often run an exercise to get students to think about a person who they respected or who had the greatest influence or impact on them. There are consistent qualities that this individual possesses that come up time and time again, such as: 'they listened and empathized', 'they respectfully challenged me', 'they were firm but fair', 'they were interested in me', 'they had high expectations for me and identified my strengths', 'they were consistent and calm'. This person works 'with' others. In my experience as a trainer, this person has often been a teacher and if we consider the amount of time that young people spend in the education system then the opportunities to influence positive change in social and emotional well-being are arguably at their greatest during this time. Developing a school climate with social and emotional learning at its heart is arguably the best way to provide a secure and safe environment in which young people can develop to their full potential, maximizing their own strengths and their ability to make positive contributions to their communities and society.

Saufler (2012) adapts the social discipline window to include research on the brain and school climate and argues that there is a causal relationship between connection to school and a positive life trajectory. He suggests that 'school climate has a direct effect on whether or not a student will develop a positive connection to school, which in turn protects against a wide range of risk factors in students' lives … connection to school is crucial for a safe school environment and positive relationships build this connection' (Saufler, 2012, p. 1). Emotional support within classrooms has a greater impact on academic performance than instructional support. Saufler argues that school climate is a reflection of the 'affective resonance' of a school and that human neurology is set up to respond to this emotional atmosphere. Based on the social discipline window and the research by Diana Baumrind (1968) on parenting styles, Saufler suggests that by providing high nurture/support alongside high boundaries/limits, as well as working with young people in an authoritative style, the brain is also more likely to be in a state of relaxed alertness. Such an environment is more likely to build pro-social, reflective cause–effect thinking and connections (Saufler, 2012, p. 5).

Fundamental to a restorative approach within schools is that relationships are central to learning, addressing issues and development, and *all* members of the school community need to focus on how they foster and maintain these relationships. If the brain is in a state of anxious vigilance due to punitive or stigmatizing responses to wrongdoing or misbehaviour or dealing with other difficulties in life such as poor care and relationships at home, then both memory and cognition will be limited and the opportunities for pro-social changes are diminished. In a class of 25–30 students affective resonance (or the contagion of the prevailing school climate) is heightened and if we also accept that wherever there is 'difficulty' there is likely to be negative affect then the need to approach these negative affects with the brain in a state of relaxed alertness becomes paramount for adults and young people alike. I vividly recall my first class as a newly qualified teacher – 28 Year 3s (seven- and eight–year-old children) including one on the autistic spectrum, one with attention deficit hyperactivity disorder (ADHD) and many living in extreme deprivation. During my first term, one little girl was taken into foster care. I will never forget the morning when she was dropped off at school by her Mum knowing that she would not be going home with her and would also be separated from her three siblings. She would not let go of her Mum and screamed as her Mum prised herself away and walked off across the playground. My planning, differentiation and assessment grids for literacy and numeracy counted for nothing that day. She was distraught and needed the care and understanding of my teaching assistant and myself to give her nurture, comfort and support. She spent much of that day behind a cushion in our book corner crying. She knew we were there for her, she knew she was safe and she trusted us. She would come back to learning when and only when her current anxieties were recognized and addressed.

Strengths or Deficit?

As a special educational needs co-ordinator, I work with many young people who have multiple 'difficulties' that are complex and unstable. The ability to maintain consistent, strong, positive relationships with these young people is challenging, time consuming and requires a multi-agency team approach from the adults involved to ensure they support each other and protect themselves from 'burnout'. These young people and their responses to difficulties and challenge require the support of emotionally literate adults who build school cultures where understanding and compassion thrive and where emotion is considered an integral part of learning.

As previously mentioned, there has been a trend over the past couple of decades to focus on deficit, especially within the field of special education when a child is unable to learn at the same rate or in the same way as their peers and there has been a dramatic increase in the diagnosis of 'difficulties' such as ADHD, autistic spectrum disorders (ASD), neuro-developmental disorders, speech, language and communication difficulties and mental health issues (in the UK currently 850,000 children and young people have a diagnosed mental health condition). Parents and school staff appear to more quickly look to these disorders to help explain a child's inability to concentrate or remain in the classroom, meet age-related expectations in academic subjects or participate in a structured curriculum or abide by school rules in the same way as their peers. Many of these young people may not have been prepared for school within their homes and communities.

> Children who come to school without that preparation, and without the continuing home support of family members who can reinforce the goals of schooling, face expectations that they have not had the opportunity to fulfill. All too quickly the students become candidates for suspected "disability". (Harry and Klingner, 2007)

We should not be separating a student from their social and cultural experiences and thus it would be better to see students' difficulties as 'human variation rather than pathology' (Reid and Valle, 2004, p. 473) and an opportunity for emotional learning. Restorative practices underpinned by affect script psychology, and reintegrative shaming provides the psychological framework in which that learning can take place.

Affect Script Psychology

Affect script psychology describes emotion as the 'scripted outcome of the interaction between social and biological forces in a person's life' (Kelly and Thorsborne, 2014, pp. 34–41). In this context, 'script' relates to the infinite variety of emotional responses that arise in individuals from the nine inborn affects and should not be confused with the 'script' used as an aide memoire in restorative conferences. From birth, an infant learns that the primary caregiver can take away negative affect by feeding, comforting or changing them and that also they can be the source of positive affect – for example, in communication and play. Longitudinal studies are now available to help us understand more about the development of early attachment scripts and how these scripts are constantly updated and influenced by experiences leading to the development of 'self' and the ways in which the child relates to others and deals with negative affect.

This universal biological foundation from which emotion emerges helps us to understand and respond to the interruption of positive affect. The affect 'shame' signals this interruption to positive affect and results in the scripted emotions of shame, guilt, embarrassment, mortification and shyness. These are uncomfortable, often painful, states to be in and can occur to varying degrees. We want them to go away and to return to the biological positive affects of interest–excitement or enjoyment–joy. Kelly provides an in-depth explanation of the theory and how it forms the basis for not only successful restorative practices but also for the development of community and positive social climate (Kelly and Thorsborne, 2014, pp. 26–82).

Kelly also describes the work of Nathanson (1992) to develop a model of how we respond to the negative emotions triggered by the affect shame. Nathanson developed a set of four scripts into which he grouped these defences. The four scripts result in behaviours motivated by the fact that those experiencing them do not know how to manage in any other way. He named his construct the Compass of Shame as he believed the pairs of scripts to be opposites. The four scripts are avoidance, withdrawal, attack self and attack other. These scripts will manifest themselves in various degrees of behaviour intensity depending on how 'painful and enduring the shame is'. The responses will be influenced by the level of shame-inducing experience that the individual has had in their life and thus the frequency with which they have had to call on these defensive responses. Understanding these scripts helps us to understand the intense emotional responses that lead to such negative behaviours as bullying, self-harm, drug and alcohol abuse, violence and suicide. This also becomes crucial in separating the behaviour from the person and being in a position to offer alternative ways in which they can manage negative affect and develop neural pathways and new scripts to increase positive affect and develop healthier responses to shame. Affect script psychology is based on our innate biological affects and we are motivated by what Tomkins called the 'Central Blueprint to:

1. Maximise positive affect
2. Minimise negative affect
3. Minimise the inhibition of affect and
4. Maximise the power to maximise positive affect, minimise negative affect and minimise the inhibition of affect'. (Tomkins cited in Kelly and Thorsborne, 2014, pp. 30–31)

As our understanding of the brain continues to grow and we have a greater understanding of the chemistry, neural pathways and interplay between memory, cognition and emotion then our ability to support others in following the Central Blueprint grows. Restorative practices underpinned by this theoretical framework and facilitated by individuals who have an understanding of their own affective systems and motivations have the potential to support the rewiring of neural pathways. By doing this, they increase the opportunities for individuals to maximize positive affects, increase their sense of well-being, raise levels of self-esteem and maximize learning potential.

Conclusion

This chapter has reviewed the research evidence and underlying theory behind restorative practices and social and emotional learning. This has included an appraisal of developments in neuroscience, education and psychology. Developments across the disciplines are providing us with a greater understanding of the psychological theory that underpins the restorative approach and are helping us to develop a stronger, more explicit framework in which to support people to manage conflict and harm, and build positive affect and healthy relationships.

What we define as restorative and how the theory and practice develop as a social science is the responsibility of all involved and remains of international significance in our approach to developing and maintaining healthy relationships. As highlighted at the beginning of this chapter, restorative practice has implications for all social and emotional learning in the home, school, community and workplace. It presents a different philosophical approach to conflict as compared to the punitive approach that is historically within the cultures of most western criminal justice and education systems.

It is encouraging to see the development of this cross-discipline research which will continue to help us gain a better understanding of how and why restorative practice works. I am excited to be a restorative practitioner, especially in education and especially with young people who, for various reasons, have been identified as having difficulties within the education system and thus almost by default suffer increased levels of negative affect. Working with families and children and building the affective resonance within the school and community remains a challenge. As Graeme George eloquently articulates, 'teaching is emotional labour' and 'moral work that is attempted by fallible and very human people' (George in Kelly and Thorsborne 2014, p. 201). Restorative practices, however, provide that explicit framework that can be used for building relationships, repairing harm and conflict and teaching and reflecting on social and emotional learning.

Many restorative practitioners, myself included, say that 'being restorative' becomes a way of being, a way of managing all relationships rather than a discrete programme or practice to be introduced to an organization by professionals. As a facilitator of restorative conferences, I have come to understand that the greatest compliment I could receive would be that participants couldn't really remember me or what part I took in the conference. It was their conflict or problem and I had just facilitated a safe environment in which they could express their emotions and maximize the opportunity to increase positive emotion and to build or rebuild

The Psychology of Restorative Justice

healthy relationships. In preparation for the conference, I had listened to them, empathized and helped them to identify what they needed. This certainly adds complexity to how we define what is restorative, as we must examine our own motivations and emotional engagement and understand how our own affective scripts influence our engagement in what we call restorative practices. As districts, government departments, public and private sector organizations, local authorities and whole cities identify funding to 'become restorative', the development of an explicit framework underpinned by evidence-based theory is crucial and must continue to develop ethically and with rigour.

Bibliography

Baumrind, D (1968). *Effects of authoritarian parental control on child behavior.* Retrieved from http://persweb.wabash.edu/facstaff/hortonr/articles%20for%20class/baumrind.pdf.

Beckford, M. and Taylor, J. (2014, 28 December). Horrific case sparks crackdown on abusers just saying sorry: wife-beater cheated jail by apologising … then killed her a month later. *Mail Online*. Retrieved from http://www.dailymail.co.uk/news/article-2888755/Horrific-case-sparks-crackdown-abusers-just-saying-sorry-Wife-beater-cheated-jail-apologising-killed-month-later.html#ixzz3NBVd3QIp.

Braithwaite, J. (1989). *Crime shame and reintegration.* New York: Cambridge University Press.

British Psychological Society (n.d.). *The British Psychological Society.* Retrieved from http://www.bps.org.uk/.

Chikazoe, J., Lee, D., Kriegeskorte, N. and Anderson, A. (2014). Population coding of affect across stimuli, modalities and individuals. *Nature Neuroscience, 17,* 1114–1122.

Christie, N. (1977). Conflicts as property. Retrieved from http://static.squarespace.com/static/5033029a84ae7fae2e6a0a98/t/50efa90ae4b02cdfa2b2cfa6/1357883658343/Conflicts-as-Property-by-Nils-Christie.full.pdf.

Clegg, J., Hollis, C. and Rutter, M. (1999, November). Life sentence: what happens to children with developmental language disorders in later life? Retrieved from http://www.rcslt.org/news/docs/ni_dossier_of_evidence.

Comer, J. (n.d.). *School development program.* Retrieved from http://medicine.yale.edu/childstudy/comer/.

Conti-Ramsden, G. and Botting, N. (2004). Social difficulties and victimisation in children with SLI at 11 years of age. *Journal of Speech, Language and Hearing Research, 47,* 145–161.

Currie, L. (2014, October). *Why teaching kindness in schools is essential to reducing bullying.* Retrieved from http://www.edutopia.org/blog/teaching-kindness-essential-reduce-bullying-lisa-currie.

Davidson, R. (2000). Cognitive neuroscience needs affective neuroscience (and vice versa). Retrieved from http://www.investigatinghealthyminds.org/Scien tificPublications/2000/DavidsonCognitiveBrainAndCognition.pdf.

Davidson, R. (2008). *The heart brain connection*. Retrieved from http://www. edutopia.org/richard-davidson-sel-brain-video.

Davidson, R. (2012). *The emotional life of your brain*. London: Hodder & Stoughton.

Demos, E.V. (ed.) (1995). *Exploring affect: the selected writings of Silvan S. Tomkins*. Studies in Emotion and Social Interaction. New York: Cambridge University Press.

Durlak, J.A. Weissberg, R.P., Dymnicki, A.B., et al. (2011), The impact of enhancing students' social and emotional learning: a meta-analysis of school-based universal interventions. Retrieved from http://static.squarespace.com/st atic/513f79f9e4b05ce7b70e9673/t/52e9d8e6e4b001f5c1f6c27d/13910571266 94/meta-analysis-child-development.pdf.

Ekman, P. (1999). Afterword: universality of emotional expression? A personal history of the dispute. In P. Ekman (ed.), *Charles Darwin: the expression of the emotions in man and animals* (3rd edn, pp. 363–393). London: Fontana Press.

Ekman, P. (2004). *Emotions revealed: understanding faces and feelings*. London: Orion Books.

George, G. and Marshall, P. (2014). *The biological bases of our emotions and motivations: why you can't upgrade your firmware but you can change your operating system*. Retrieved from http://www.rpforschools.net/Human%20Mot ivations.pdf.

Goleman, D. (1996). *Emotional intelligence: why it can matter more than IQ*. London: Bloomsbury Publishing.

Griffin, J. and Tyrrell, I. (2013). *Human givens: the new approach to emotional health and clear thinking.* (2nd revised and enlarged edn). Brighton: HG Publishing.

Harry, B. and Klingner, J. (2007). Discarding the deficit model. *Educational Leadership*, *64*(5). Retrieved from http://www.ascd.org/publications/educatio nal-leadership/feb07/vol64/num05/Discarding-the-Deficit-Model.aspx.

Hoyle, C., Young, R. and Hill, R. (2002). *Proceed with caution: an evaluation of the Thames Valley Police initiative in restorative cautioning*. Retrieved from http://www.jrf.org.uk/sites/files/jrf/1859353819.pdf.

IIRP (International Institute for Restorative Practices) (2009). *Improving school climate: findings from schools implementing restorative practices*. Retrieved from http://www.iirp.edu/pdf/IIRP-Improving-School-Climate.pdf.

Jensen, E. (1998). *Teaching with the brain in mind*. Alexandria, VA: Association for Supervision and Curriculum Development.

Johnstone, G. and Van Ness, D.W. (2007). *Handbook of restorative justice*. Cullompton: Willan Publishing.

Kelly, V. and Thorsborne, M. (eds) (2014). *The psychology of emotion in restorative justice*. London: Jessica Kingsley Publishing.

Kennedy, J. and Kennedy, C. (2004). Attachment theory: implications for school psychology. *Psychology in the Schools*, *41*(2), 247–259. Retrieved from http://www.sonoma.edu/users/f/filp/ed420/attachment.pdf.

Linares-Orama, N. (2005). Language-learning disorders and youth incarceration. *Journal of Communication Disorders*, *38*, 311–319.

McCold, P. and Wachtel, T. (2001). Restorative justice in everyday life. In J. Braithwaite and H. Strang (eds), *Restorative justice and civil society* (pp. 114–129). Cambridge: Cambridge University Press.

Nathanson, D. (1992). *Shame and pride: affect, sex and the birth of self*. New York: Norton & Company.

New Zealand Government (1989). *Children, Young Persons, and Their Families Act 1989*. Retrieved from http://www.legislation.govt.nz/act/public/1989/0024/latest/DLM147088.html.

O'Connell, T. (1998). *From Wagga Wagga to Minnesota*. Retrieved from http://www.iirp.edu/article_detail.php?article_id=NDg5.

Plato (2000). *The republic*. [Kindle version]. Trans. Benjamin Jowett. Downloaded from http://www.amazon.co.uk/The-Republic-Dover-Thrift-Editions/dp/0486411214.

Real Justice (n.d.). *Emotion gives the Real Justice conference its power*. Retrieved from http://www.realjustice.org/.

Reid, K. and Valle, J.W. (2004). The discursive practice of learning disability: implications for instruction and parent–school relations. *Journal of Learning Disabilities*, *37*(6), 466–481.

Reisel, D. (2013). *The neuroscience of restorative justice*. TED lecture. Retrieved from http://www.ted.com/talks/daniel_reisel_the_neuroscience_of_restorative_justice?language=en.

Reisel, D. (2014). *Where does morality come from?* Retrieved from http://www.danreisel.com/?p=69.

Royal College of Speech and Language Therapists (n.d.). *Evidence to support speech and language therapy intervention with young offenders*. Retrieved from http://www.rcslt.org/about/campaigns/evidence_for_SLT_for_YOI.pdf.

Saufler, C. (2012, August). School climate, the brain and connection to school. Paper presented at the International Institute for Restorative Practices 15th World Conference, Bethlehem, PA.

Schonert-Reichl, K.A., Smith, V., Zaidman-Zait, A. and Hertzman, C. (2012). Promoting children's prosocial behaviors in school: impact of the "Roots of Empathy" program on the social and emotional competence of school-aged children (abstract). *School Mental Health*, *4*, 1–21

Shouse, E. (2005). Feeling, emotion, affect. *M/C Journal*, *8*(6). Retrieved from http://journal.media-culture.org.au/0512/03-shouse.php.

Tomkins, S. (1962). *Affect imagery consciousness* (Vol. 1). New York: Springer.

Tomkins, S. (1963). *Affect imagery consciousness* (Vol. 2). New York: Springer.

Tomkins, S. (1982). Affect theory. In P. Ekman (ed.), *Emotion in the human face* (2nd edn, pp. 353–395). New York: Cambridge University Press.

Tomkins, S. (1991). *Affect imagery consciousness* (Vol. 3). New York: Springer.

Van Ness, D.W. and Strong, K.H. (2010). *Restoring justice – an introduction to restorative justice* (4th edn). New Province: Matthew Bender & Co.

Wachtel, T. (2009, November). My three decades of using restorative practices with delinquent and at-risk youth: theory, practice and research outcomes. Paper presented at the First World Congress on Restorative Juvenile Justice, Lima, Peru.

Wachtel, T. (2013a). *Defining restorative*. Retrieved from http://www.iirp.edu/pdf/Defining-Restorative.pdf.

Wachtel, T. (2013b). *Dreaming of a new reality: how restorative practices reduce crime and violence, improve relationships and strengthen civil society.* Bethlehem, PA: The Piper's Press.

Zehr, H. (1990). *Changing lenses – a new focus for crime and justice.* Scottsdale: Herald Press.

Zins, J.E., Weissberg, R.P., Wang, M.C. and Walberg. H.J. (eds) (2004). *Building academic success on social and emotional learning: what does the research say?* New York: Teachers College Press.

Chapter 5

Restorative Justice and Psychology: Positivism in Criminology Again? A Few Theoretical Reflections

Vasso Artinopoulou

Introduction

Criminology studies crime and as a discipline is highly dependent upon the findings and methodologies of other related sciences, such as law, sociology, psychology, psychiatry, anthropology and social policy. Criminology, in terms of the interdisciplinarity, needs 'loans' and adopts analytical frameworks, interpretations and methodologies from the related disciplines in order to explain crime, criminality and the criminal justice systems that are complex social phenomena and constructions. Interdisciplinarity in criminology is still an open-ended question that has been addressed through multiple discourses (sociological, legalistic, psychological) from time to time. Between the main discourses, it is the 'Ψ' discourse that appealed to criminology through putting emphasis on the individual, the personality and the behaviour. The letter 'Ψ' (psy) is the symbol representing psychology, psychoanalysis, psychotherapy and psychiatry, and refers to the 'psy-sciences' (Rose, 1998). The 'Ψ' constitutes the 23rd letter of the Greek alphabet and the first letter of the Greek word ψυχή, which translates as mind and soul. Since psychology is the discipline of the mind, and/or the soul, it seems fitting that 'Ψ' represents the psy-sciences. In the framework of positivist criminology the 'Ψ' discourse identified in the psychological explanations of crime and criminal behaviour. It included the etiological explanatory schemes of psychiatrists, psychologists and psychoanalysts, from Lombroso to Freud and Lacan. Nowadays, the 'Ψ' discourse re-enters in criminology as a magnetic pole through restorative justice, positive criminology and neurocriminology.

The aims of this chapter are not only to identify the common ground of restorative justice with psychology in theory, research and policy/practices, but also to explore if there are any possible risks and warnings in adopting the 'Ψ' discourse in restorative justice and criminology. In particular, our main concern is to find out any possible risks while stressing only the individual as the key feature in the crime issue. In other words, to identify the side effects of the 'trendy trends' today, as restorative justice, positive criminology and neurocriminology are.

So, our normative arguments are:

- Restorative justice and psychology have common ground in theory, as they both focus on the individual, responsibility and accountability, the offenders' and the victims' personalities and needs.
- Restorative justice and psychology share common methodologies – namely, qualitative methods, as interviews, narratives and case studies.
- Restorative justice and psychology share common practices focused on the individual, the situation and the dynamics of interpersonal communication. In particular, the victim–offender mediation as restorative justice practice is similar to problem solving and counselling, conferencing, and therapy-practices used by psychologists.
- There are theoretical and methodological links between restorative justice, positive psychology, positive criminology, neurosciences and neurocriminology. Actually, these trends constitute a continuum of theories, researches and practices during the past 30 years and they are based on the inter- and trans-disciplinary character of criminology.
- The warnings and the risks in these trends and in terms of a new 'trendy criminology' are to be found in the individualization and psychologization of procedures. Furthermore, there is a shift from positive to positivism reflected in the neuro-turn and the neurocriminology. This turn leads to a new form of biological determinism and may open the gate to neo-Lombrosian etiological explanations of the criminal behaviour.

There are many terms and concepts used in this chapter that need to be clarified. It is not always easy to give definitions for all of them, either because they include vague and multilevel approaches –terms as interdisciplinarity and trans-disciplinarity fall into this category- or they refer to rather complex social phenomena, as crime and criminality are. I try to address the issues where needed in a descriptive way. Furthermore, I have already argued that "we live the end of definitions" (Gavrielides and Artinopoulou, 2013b, p. 348) and restorative justice definitions do not necessary reflect their multiple conceptions and reflections. Based on Giddens' (1990) perspective on historical, social and cultural continuities of criminological theory, research and action, I then argue that 'the restorative justice movement reflects the continuum in the criminological thought' (Artinopoulou and Gavrielides, 2013, p. 37). Thus, in this chapter I place criminology, restorative justice, positive psychology, positive criminology and neurocriminology in the continuum of the criminological thought.

The chapter includes three main parts. In the first part the relations between restorative justice and psychology are identified in the levels of theory, research and practice. In the second part, I try to describe the links and the continuum between restorative justice, positive psychology and positive criminology in the prevention of reoffending, through the concepts of individualization and psychologization. In the last part, the new trend of neurocriminology is analysed while I explore the possible risks for biological positivism in explaining criminal behaviour. I then conclude with certain recommendations for restorative justice to avoid any identification with the risks of the neuro-turn, the individualization and the psychologization procedures; and to recognize the social and power structures that are reflected in the restorative discourse.

The 'Ψ' Aspects of Restorative Justice

The debate on restorative justice has continued for almost 30 years now (Gavrielides, 2011). Theory, research and practice on restorative justice are becoming more and more integrated, putting restorative justice practices either at the core or on the periphery of the criminal justice systems. The 2012/29/EU Directive on Establishing the Minimum Standards on the Rights, Support and Protection of Victims of Crime in the criminal justice procedure reinforces the victim's rights and calls for restorative justice schemes to be implemented safely. In our book, entitled *Reconstructing Restorative Justice Philosophy* (2013b), Gavrielides and I argue that restorative justice is a different Zeitgeist. It relates to how you and I view, pursue, achieve and indeed want to experience justice at the interpersonal, intercommunity and interstate levels (Gavrielides and Artinopoulou, 2013b). So, restorative justice is more than a trend in criminology, even if it reflects the continuum in criminological thinking. Restorative justice lays on abolitionism and victimology (Artinopoulou, 2010) and focuses on the individual (offender/ victim) and the micro and meso level of analysis. According to Gavrielides' definition, 'restorative justice is an ethos with practical goals, among which to restore harm by including affected parties in a (direct or indirect) encounter and a process of understanding through voluntary and honest dialogue' (Gavrielides, 2007, p. 139). Restorative justice perceives crime as a violation of interpersonal relations that reflects the broken social and community bonds. It also introduces practices such as victim–offender mediation and conferences, aiming to give voice to the victims and the offenders and restoring relations through forgiveness and healing (micro and meso level in case of community involvement). Restorative justice's key concepts are the accountability and the responsibility of the offender, the reparation of the damage done to the victim, the active participation of community, and healing through the process of catharsis (Artinopoulou, 2010). Restorative justice aims to repair the harmful effects of crime and advocates for the offender to have the opportunity to repair the harm and the implications caused by his/her actions (Eglash, 1977; Gavrielides and Artinopoulou, 2013b). It also stresses the importance of repairing the relationships between the offender and the victim, as well the offender's relationship to society, aiming finally at his/her re-integration into the community. At the same time, it also calls for an active participation in the restoration process of all the members involved or affected by the crime (Artinopoulou, 2010; Marshall, 1996). Conferences and victim–offender mediation are a few of the practices encompassed by restorative justice that offer the opportunity to all the involved parties to come together in a safe context and resolve the issues or damages caused by the offender's actions (Artinopoulou, 2010). Finally, a 2005 meta-analytic study examining the effectiveness of restorative justice practices found that restorative programmes were significantly more effective in recidivism reduction compared to traditional approaches (Latimer et al., 2005).

Because restorative justice focuses on the micro and meso level of analysis, meaning the individual and the community respectively, I argue that restorative justice provides a link between the macro and micro levels in the criminological thinking. Restorative justice has certain psychological aspects as it deals with the offender, victim, trauma, healing, emotions, process and dynamics, and transformation, and uses the methodologies, techniques and practices of psychology, as conferencing – group therapy, counselling, catharsis, transformation, healing and restoration. Restorative justice is the *arena* in which psychology and criminology meet. Both restorative justice and 'Ψ' focus on individual/micro-level analysis and share commonalities in the concepts and perspectives. They both also deal with emotions, processes, dynamics and transformation. I argue that restorative justice includes the 'Ψ', and the 'Ψ' includes restorative justice, in a mutual and interactive relationship. In their article Cremin et al. (2012) examine restorative justice from an interdisciplinary perspective and discuss its effectiveness in educational contexts. Following a series of seminars on restorative justice held at the University of Cambridge by experts from different disciplines, the authors examine both the challenges and benefits of restorative justice and its roots in different disciplines. More specifically, the article introduces the interdisciplinary roots of restorative justice and presents the papers of international experts that examine restorative justice from different perspectives: namely, psychology, criminology, philosophy, peace studies and conflict theory, sociology and education.

Cremin et al. (2012) take interdisciplinarity a step further and suggest that restorative justice is fundamentally related to all three of Klein's (2010) concepts:

> it lists multidisciplinary perspectives on the phenomenon of restorative justice; it discusses the ways in which concepts re-emerge and inter-relate across disciplinary boundaries; and it begins to suggest ways in which transdisciplinary approaches can be drawn upon to transgress, transcend and transform, with particular relevance for those non-academic actors who are charged with implementing strategies for more just and equal social relations through education and schooling. (Cremin et al., 2012, p. 422)

From a psychological perspective, the foundations of restorative justice in social psychology are already explored in the literature (Johnson, 2010). Cremin et al. also emphasize the importance of examining criminal acts as a result of dysfunctional social contexts and relations, and not solely as individual behaviour (Morrison, 2010). Additionally, the links between restorative justice and humanitarian psychology (especially Carl Roger's theory on the assumption that humans, if properly enabled and facilitated, will self-regulate and self-actualize and attempt to restore the negative consequences of criminal acts), are also addressed Cowie, 2010). When considering the philosophical input in restorative justice, the article focuses on the term 'transformative restorative justice' and the paradox between the two words (MacAllister, 2010). According to the Oxford English Dictionary (1991 version) *restorative* means to bring back to the original state, whereas *transform* refers to changing into something completely different. Additionally, a second paradox in the restorative approaches in educational settings is emphasized: restorative justice in schools should have a preventative scope for the general population, not only focus on those involved in some kind of dispute. However, once restorative justice becomes proactive then it basically loses its restorative notion. Thus, the examination of restorative justice from diverse perspectives and disciplines suggests that restorative approaches should include all three conceptions of restorative justice: repair of harm, encounter of the affected parties and transformation of relationships and culture (Cremin, et al., 2012, p. 434). The need for the combination of addressing harmful behaviours along with proactive changes in the cultural environment remains evident if restorative justice is to be 'both remedial and preventative' (p. 434).

For analytical reasons only, I identify the 'Ψ' aspects of restorative justice in theory, research and practices in Table 5.1 (overleaf).

Research-based evidence justifies the interrelations between restorative justice and 'Ψ'. Recall that the term 'restorative justice' was first used by A. Eglash, a psychologist. Pioneers in the field of restorative justice are also psychologists (social, clinical, cognitive). Excluding mental illness from the scope of their research, restorative justice and psychology both develop interdisciplinarity. Furthermore, psychology was always very close to crime issues. In the history of criminology there is a symbiotic relation between the two disciplines. We find 'Ψ' in the criminal justice systems through criminal profiling, expert witness testimonies and forensic psychiatry. We also find 'Ψ' in corrections and prisons, through counselling and support services, and the therapeutic treatment of convicted offenders as well. In communities, 'Ψ' is also found in crime prevention programmes and in support services for victims. And in other social institutions that deal with juvenile delinquency, bullying, excessive alcohol consumption and other deviant behaviours, the 'Ψ' is always present, either as explanatory to the behaviour scheme or as support to the parts involved in the offence/crime. 'Ψ' stresses the etiology, causalities, prediction, treatment and therapy in the individual micro level of analysis. A continuous, vague and ambiguous relation between criminology and psychology existed from the very beginning, while the explaining of the criminal behaviour was the shared object of analysis for both of them. The key questions of who becomes delinquent and why are now reflected in the criminal profiling and the predictability of risk factors of reoffending.

Table 5.1   The 'Ψ' aspects of restorative justice:
Where psychology and restorative justice meet

Theoretical level (focus on micro and meso level)
<ul><li>individual (micro level): offender/victim</li><li>community (meso level)</li><li>crime as violation of interpersonal relations and social bonds (micro and meso)</li><li>accountability (micro): offender-cognitive</li><li>responsibility (micro and meso)</li><li>empathy (micro and meso)</li><li>relational and transformative process – psychological dynamics – social psychology (meso)</li></ul>
Empirical research
<ul><li>qualitative methodologies (interviews, narratives, case studies, focus groups)</li></ul>
Policy level/practices
<ul><li>victim–offender mediation</li><li>counselling</li><li>conferencing</li><li>therapy</li><li>healing, catharsis</li></ul>
Fields of implementation
<ul><li>criminal justice systems</li><li>community</li><li>schools</li><li>corrections: prisons</li><li>juveniles</li><li>conflict resolution</li><li>workplaces</li></ul>

Historically, the 'Ψ' discourse in criminology was a positivist discourse. Psychology and psychiatry tried to find the psychological factors to explain criminal behaviour. Criminology as a discipline was established through positivism, indeed. It was the Italian physician and psychiatrist Cesare Lombroso who believed that criminals are a special kind of people and they were born to be criminals (Bosworth and Hoyle, 2011). Psychiatrists then tried to explain criminal behaviour through mental illness (phrenology) and in the 1960s the criminological etiological research focused once more on the chromosomes to explain the criminal personality. Sigmund Freud, John Bowlby, Hans Eysenck and many others focused on one-dimensional psychological explanations for the personality of the criminal. Biological, psychological and social positivism were the three main categories of the etiological factors that explain the criminal personality and/or behaviour (Jeffery, 1959). In other words, positivist criminology assumed that there are differences between criminals and non-criminals and attempted to find these differences in a set of etiological factors, biological, psychological and social. The causality in terms of cause – result/effect – is inherent in the positivist approach. Psychology as a discipline was always very close to the issues of crime and justice (Furby, 1986; Lerner, 1974). From the early etiological approaches to crime and criminal behaviour until the recent 'Ψ' discourse in restorative justice, I address an established trend of psychologization of the crime issue. Psychologization attempts to explain human behaviour in psychological terms. In social psychology, psychologization is perceived in terms of categorization, stereotypes, naturalization and stigmatization of the otherness (Fernandez, 2010). Jan De Vos (2013) brings us into the heart of psychologization, perceived as

> the fact of the knowledge of psychology having become central in mediating the presence of the human being with himself, the others and the world … this is my central argument, it is precisely here that psychology is inextricably linked to psychologization: psychologization is psychology's very paradigm through which to connect ontology to knowledge. Again, the issue is not to construct a meta-theory – taking the quest for being as a point of departure for a psychology without psychologization – but, rather, to fully value the fundamental disparity between *being* and *knowledge*. Or in other words: if you want to know something about mankind, don't study the human, don't study psychology, study psychologization, and, above all, study how psychology and psychologization are so inseparable that they have to be understood as each other's doubles. (De Vos, 2013, p. 5)

There are many reasons for that expansion of psychology in the object(s) and fields of criminology. First of all it's the interdisciplinary character of criminology itself that facilitates the development/expansion of other disciplines within the scope of criminology. Furthermore, since criminology hasn't a unique, separate and discrete subject of analysis (because crime is a complex social phenomenon) its methodologies and policies/and or practices are 'loans' from other related disciplines, such as law, sociology, psychology and social policy. Criminological research is mainly social research; criminal justice policies and crime prevention policies are public/social policies including social design, implementation, evaluation and impact assessment. Another possible reason for the expansion of psychology in crime issues is that criminology – in order to escape 'legacy' of the etiology of crime, and following the Second World War – shifted to the study of the criminal justice systems, structures and functions, and to the macro-level issues. The micro level of analysis, which traditionally focused on the offender as individual, now was operationalized in theory, research and practice through the criminal justice system approach. Psychology gained that ground left behind by criminology. The more criminology focused on the criminal justice systems (policing and corrections), the more psychology intervened in explaining the criminal behaviour before, during and after committing a crime.

Thus, the links between psychology, criminology and restorative justice are very strong and closely interrelated. Sometimes it appears as if psychology is a branch of criminology and vice versa. Restorative justice is the arena in which all these aspects meet and are transformed into practice, in a symbiotic, long and complex relationship of mutual interdependency. However, in this symbiotic relationship a few side effects appear, such as the individualization and psychologization of restorative justice. The warning here for restorative justice is not to become trapped in the 'Ψ' discourse, adopting the individualization and psychologization processes while addressing the crime, the criminal behaviour and the restoration procedures. Restorative justice has to keep its integrating, comprehensive and inclusive character and not identify either with the individualization or the psychologization approaches. I try to explain why these processes risk and signal a striking comeback of positivism.

Restorative Justice and the Individualization of Crime

I use the term 'individualization' according to the original theory of Ulrich Beck (1992) – namely, that the individual is becoming the central unit of social life. Individualization is mostly a sociological concept. In criminology the concept is used to describe sentencing procedures and the imposition of the punishment (Saleilles, 1911; Packer, 1964). Marvin Wolfgang introduced the concept of 'victim individualization' at the Third International Symposium of Victimology in 1979 (Wolfgang, 1982). Errez and Sebba (2102) conceptualize individualization both for the victim and the offender within the criminal justice systems. Individualization as a concept has also been used in forensic psychology to identify the offender (Champod, 2009). I agree that individualization is more than subjectivity and recognition of the key role of the individual. I argue that individualization is, rather, the process of constructing and conceptualizing the individual as the fundamental subject in terms of an explanatory framework. Individualization is differentiated from individualistic as the latter means just putting emphasis on the individual. I also relate individualization to restorative justice, because emphasis is put on the accountability and the individual responsibility of the wrongdoer. Restorative justice recognizes the wrongdoer as the 'fundamental subject' who acts under rational choices in committing the offence/crime; and it also puts the wrongdoer in the centre of reintegration approaches (Artinopoulou, 2010). Individualization in restorative justice is aligned with the psychological, psychiatric and psychoanalytical approaches that try to explain the individual criminal behaviour, and the personality factors and traits that lead to offending and reoffending.

Therefore, and through putting emphasis on the individual, other social, cultural, economic etiological aspects are obviously neglected. Stressing the individual as the only one responsible for offending and reoffending mostly undermines the role and the impact of the structural victimization (Artinopoulou and Maganas, 1996). Furthermore, by defining crime as a violation of interpersonal relations and by stressing apology and healing as reintegration procedures, restorative justice is sought to adopt an individualistic perspective, without taking into consideration the wider social inequalities and the power structures. Not surprisingly, those are the key points of criticism in restorative justice (Artinopoulou, 2014). There are numerous theories, explanations, methodological choices and interpretations of the multiple and complex facets of the social and structural inequalities that originally or secondarily lead to and reproduce crime, offending and reoffending. Crime is related to injustice and the multi-faceted inequalities within families, communities and societies. Justice in societies and in social institutions is a wide, abstract and complex concept that derives its meaning only from its opposite – that is, social injustice and inequality. The history of social revolutions and social uprisings is the history of the realization of the struggle for justice and equality. Despite the ambivalence of the concept as an ideological and social construction, the 'value of justice' is a fundamental principle of the socialization and foundation of democratic social formations. It is noteworthy that the values of justice and the rule of law in the context of the current financial crisis environment are under question in everyday life. Values such as equality, fairness, equity and respect are becoming more and more ambiguous, in the frustrating context of crisis that has faced the countries of Southern Europe and Greece during the first decade of the twenty-first century. The recession became an alibi and an excuse to cut social benefits and to place blame and responsibility on to the individual (Artinopoulou, 2013).

David Garland (1985, p. 122) agrees that 'the individual is assumed to be similarly constituted – as a free, rational, human subject' and while individualization in restorative justice relates to the individual responsibility of the offender, it includes the logic of the absolute accountability of committing the crime. George Pavlich (2005) argues that 'though there may be differences in understanding, restorative governmentalities replicate a criminal justice emphasis on the individual (as opposed to, say, systemic) responsibility' (p. 74). There are similar warnings about the failure of restorative justice to address the economic inequalities, and more research-based evidence is needed (Roche, 2007). Wallace and Wylie (2013) stress that 'restorative justice cannot be seen in isolation, but must be underscored by considerations of the relationships between poverty, inequality and offending and the cycles of crime these perpetuate' (p. 61) and Gavrielides (2014) argues in favour of bringing the issue of race into the restorative justice debate. Just such a reflection of individualization in restorative justice is the debate on the appropriateness of restorative justice in cases of domestic violence cases/and or interpersonal violence. Feminists argue that the gender powers and patriarchal structures that pass through the interpersonal violence are so powerful that may cancel any attempt of mediating between the victim and the offender; and moreover, all these inherent power imbalances may affect the victim's safety within the restorative justice procedures (Gavrielides and Artinopoulou, 2013a). Individualization in that case has a twofold meaning: not only does it perceive the problem of interpersonal/domestic violence as a private problem of the individuals (offender/victim) engaged in the violent relationship and not as a social and complex phenomenon, but it also reflects a shift in doing the public issue of structural victimization a private/ personal problem. Thus, I use the term 're-privatization' for interpersonal/domestic violence to define the process of doing private –again- an issue that is really social by its nature and public (Artinopoulou, 2000). The feminist movement struggled to recognize as public issues the 'private troubles' of domestic and interpersonal violence through the disclosure of similar cases and incidents (Daly and Stubbs, 2006; Stubbs, 2004).

Thus, the loss of the 'social' is the main risk in the individualization perspective of restorative justice. John Muncie (2005), while trying to explain the globalization of crime, addresses the homogenization of criminal justice policies. He argues that 'this homogenization, it is contended, is underpinned by a fundamental shift in state/market relations. A loss (or at least a major reconfiguration) of "the social" is evidenced in the processes whereby neo-liberal conceptions of the market and international capital encourage the formulation of policies based less on principles of social inclusion and more on social inequality, deregulation, privatization, penal expansionism and welfare residualism' (Muncie, 2005, pp. 36–37).

From 'Ψ' to the 'N' Discourse: The Shift from Positive to Positivism

Restorative justice, positive psychology and positive criminology share common aspects and perspectives in the field of reoffending prevention. Gavrielides and Worth (2014) argue that positive psychology is another push for restorative justice. Reviewing the criminological, sociological and psychological theories that encompass the use of positive, strength-based elements, instead of punitive sanctions, Ronel and Elisha (2011) attempt to identify theories, some well established and others new, that could be implemented in the correctional field. Bringing together strength-based theories and applications, the authors reintroduce Gottfredson and Hirschi's (1987) term of 'positive criminology' with a different meaning. Recognizing the current debate in offender rehabilitation literature between the Risk–Need–Responsivity (RNR) model[1] (Andrews and Bonta, 2010) and the Good Lives Model (GLM)[2] (Ward, 2002; Ward and Stewart, 2003), the authors stress the fact that positive criminology is not a singular approach (Ronel et al., 2013, p. 136): it "is not a theory but rather a broad perspective encompassing diverse models and theories" (Ronel and Elisha, 2011, p. 306). This perspective emphasizes the individual's strengths and supports interventions, both formal and informal, that focus on humanistic strengths (Elisha et al., 2013, pp. 67–68). The definition of the term positive criminology refers to:

---

1 Risk–Need–Responsivity (RNR) model attempts to ensure public safety by managing (re)offending risk. It calls for a constructive and collaborative way of working with offenders by promoting the *goods*, the offenders' strengths, in order to enhance treatment effectiveness.

2 The GLM is based on the principle that offenders, as with all human beings, seek certain states of mind, personal characteristics, experiences and activities, which are referred to as *primary human goods*.

a focus on the encounter with significant forces and effects that are experienced positively and that distance the individual from deviance and crime whether by means of formal and informal therapy programs and interventions (such as self-help organizations), through emphasis on positive social elements (such as reintegrative shaming, human kindness, or social acceptance), or based on positive personal factors (such as factors of protection and resilience, positive emotions and subjective attitudes, coherence, faith, and morality). (Ronel and Elisha, 2011, p. 307)

Thus, the current trend in restorative justice uses terms such as 'positive' and 'restorative' to describe the variables that have a positive relation to the reintegration and rehabilitation of offenders. 'Positive' comes to describe the directions of policy and stresses what to do and what to avoid doing. It includes a kind of certainty and reflects the normative argument, without any doubt or inherent relativism. 'Positive' reflects the affirmative and optimist discourse in criminology currently, focused on the individual and the micro-climate of the rehabilitation procedure. It is noteworthy that the focus on rehabilitation is at the micro and meso level – once again – and the individualization perspective is also present. On the contrary, the need for public policies on rehabilitation and for structural changes that may facilitate the reintegration procedures, are – not surprisingly – missing.

The newcomers to that scene are neurocriminology, in particular, and neurosciences, in general. Given the continuum in the discourses on crime, criminal behaviour, restorative justice, positive psychology and positive criminology, nowadays neurocriminology enters to examine not only how the criminal personality is constructed, but also how the prevention of the reoffending could also be achieved. Controversial enough, neurocriminology, the new branch of neurosciences, tries to explain the criminal personality through the criminal brain, using the new knowledge of the brain construction, functions and internal architecture of the neurones. The emerging field, which has evolved over the past two decades, draws on principals and techniques from neurosciences in an effort to explain, but also predict and eventually prevent, criminal behaviour (Glenn and Raine, 2014). Proposing a biopsychosocial model, stressing the importance of both factors, and emphasizing the gene–environment interactions, this branch is attempting to examine how antisocial behaviour is produced (Nordstrom et al., 2010). As Nordstrom and colleagues (2010) suggest:

Human beings are biological creatures. Whatever the truest essence of our souls may be, our subjective mental lives are mediated by and expressed through a system that is undeniably biological. This biological self exists in a specific social reality, which, in turn, shapes and alters the biological self in ways that will find some biological expression. (p. 274)

Genetics and the influence of specific genes or combinations of genes, prenatal and perinatal influences, hormones and neurotransmitters, psychophysiology, braining image and neurology are few of the fields in which associations or even possibly causal relations with crime have been identified. Furthermore, similarly to positive criminology, neurocriminological models for successful re-entry and desistance of chronically incarcerated offenders have been also proposed (Hilborn, 2011). The past failures of treatment and prevention programmes could also be potentially attributed to the failure of recognizing and tackling both social and biological deficits at the same time (Raine and Liu, 1998, p. 122). From a methodological standpoint, although several studies have identified potential associations, the vast majority of them implement correlation and cross-sectional designs, which cannot prove causal associations (see Glenn and Raine, 2014, for a review). Additionally, a major methodological limitation lies in the operationalization of the variables examined. As Glenn and Raine (2014) mention, most of the relevant studies use rather broad definitions of antisocial behaviour and crime (p. 54). Their findings therefore refer to a 'broad propensity to crime', antisocial and aggressive behaviour in general and not to criminal activity per se. Further research into longitudinal prospective studies, implementing biosocial designs, is necessary in order to fully evaluate the significance of these factors in criminal behaviour (Rocque et al., 2013). Apart from the evident fact that further research is required before neurocriminology can be more widely accepted in the criminological field, even by those that are currently lees dismissive and more open to considering the effects of 'neuro' in crime prevention/prediction/perception, other significant issues arise as well. One of the pioneers and best-known researchers and academics in the field of neurocriminology, Adrian Raine has been providing expert witness testimonies in criminal cases in the USA. In one particular case, Raine found that the offender's brain exhibited dysfunctions in the prefrontal cortex. This finding, in addition to poverty and adverse childhood events, was the basis of Raine's argument that was taken into consideration, eventually leading to life imprisonment instead of the death penalty for the accused (Raine, 2013).

Neuroscientific evidence appears to have significant influence in the determination of punishment in criminal cases. A relevant study found that when such evidence is presented both judges and juries tend to find the defendant not guilty based on reasons of insanity (Gurley and Marcus, 2008). Similarly relevant findings suggest that there has been a significant increase in criminal cases presenting neuroimaging evidence on behalf of the defence during the sentencing phase (Hughes, 2010). Assuming that the neurocriminological research continues to progress, what would be the implications of their findings in cases such as the one mentioned above? Combining responsibility and accountability of the offender with the kind of punishment is one of the first evident implications. Neurocriminologists suggest and anticipate that the emerging finds of this new field will eventually result in a broader conceptualization of responsibility (Glenn and Raine, 2014). Similarly, prediction of violent behaviour and the inclusion of neurobiological factors in the current risk prediction models could also present with rather negative implications, referring to possible violation of the fundamental/constitutional human rights – namely, the rights to human dignity and civil liberty. Any possible generalizations and comparisons between offenders and non-offenders for the sake of prediction and prevention of crime behaviour are extremely risky. The question is not only how to tackle crime and criminality, but how to tackle them within a human rights approach. The biological background on the etiology of crime and criminal behaviour is a determinist, positivist and neo-Darwinian approach, which is so risky for the protection of human rights. Most importantly, though, prevention and, thus control, of criminal behaviour appear to be the most significant concerns, as moral, legal and policy implications of neurocriminology knowledge.

Farah (2012) refers to "neuroethics", to stress the importance of considering the ethical implication stemming from the application of the findings of neurosciences to offenders, among others. For instance, involuntary enhancement of offenders, through the use of relevant drugs (such as SSRIs of oxytocin), can potentially improve mood, self-control and empathy.

> Similarly, involuntary enhancement of criminal offenders to improve their personality, mood, and self-control (with SSRIs) or to promote trust and empathy for others (oxytocin) presents us with another set of tradeoffs between potentially desirable outcomes and troubling infringement of personhood. If these treatments can enable offenders to live outside of prison and can protect society against crime, then the "benefit" side of the equation is substantial. However, state-imposed psychopharmacology poses a relatively new kind of limitation on offenders' autonomy and privacy. In contrast to the restrictions on autonomy and privacy imposed by incarceration, which mainly concern physical restrictions, brain interventions would restrict offenders' abilities to think, feel, and react as they normally would. (Farah, 2012, p. 585)

Concluding with Warnings and Recommendations

It is obvious that neurosciences overlap with criminology through positive psychology, positive criminology and restorative justice (Reisel, 2013). The warning is reflected in the potential revival of positivism and biology determinism through the prediction of criminal behaviour and reoffending. The neuro-turn in criminology – and other fields – has emerged at a critical time. The deadlocks of the criminal justice systems and the overpopulation of prisons are the key features in not doing justice. The multi-faceted inequalities (gender, financial, cultural and so on) are reproduced within families, communities, the economy and other social structures and institutions. It is quite concerning that the rule of law and the values of justice, as equality, fairness, equity and respect are becoming more and more ambiguous in the current financial crisis environment; and they are coming into question in everyday life (Artinopoulou 2013). Furthermore, citizens no longer trust their criminal justice systems (Maffei and Markopoulou, 2014).

So, can we argue further about justice as value or the values of justice today? In the USA and Europe during the past decade we have faced an increase in penal populism and in punitive attitudes. Research findings highlight that criminal penal attitudes and prison populations are increasing more and more. In this context, the concepts of doing justice, equity, restoration, transformation, punishment and crime prevention are redefined and reorientated. Neuro-turn in this context is critical for imposing – through the neo-Darwinianism – an a-moral, a-historical and a-cultural perspective in explaining the human/social/criminal behaviour. Restorative justice has to include the multiple social and structural inequalities in its debate and not focus only on individuals per se. Roger Cooter describes the current neuro-turn as mind parasites and criticizes the wide neurobiological acceptance of our times (Cooter, 2014). He says about today's neuro-turn in popular and academic culture:

> If it isn't exactly a repeat performance of nineteenth-century phrenology, with its reductions of mind, ethics, and character to cerebral biology, it's surely much the same old story of lighting up parts of the brain to rationalize and naturalize compulsions to social justice, "bad" parenting, artistic creativity, and so on. "Human nature" once again innate, is made historically transcendent. (Cooter, 2014, p. 145)

Thus, the possible warning for restorative justice is not the 'Ψ' discourse itself and what it represents. It is rather the individualization that leads to the neglection of structures and the marginalization of social policies. Furthermore, it is the risk of restorative justice to lose its democratic character and its 'ethos', according to Gavrielides' (2007) definition, and to align with neoliberal ideologies.

Last but not least, and as advised above, restorative justice must keep its theoretical and methodological distance from the causalities and prediction of criminal behaviour and reoffending. Since 'Ψ' stresses such causalities and etiologies, the possible risk for restorative justice is to open the doors to determinism through the trendy neurosciences and neurobiology. If 'Ψ' becomes the dominant discourse in restorative justice – through the individualization of crime and the offender's accountability – then a new form of positivism comes back. Unfortunately, if this is the case, then the vision of social change, social justice, equity and fairness may have been lost.

Bibliography

Andrews, D.A. and Bonta, J. (2010). *The psychology of criminal conduct* (5th edn). Albany: Lexis Nexis/Anderson Publishers.

Artinopoulou, V. (1995). *Incest: theoretical perspectives and research findings*. Athens, Greece: Nomiki Bibliothiki (in Greek).

Artinopoulou, V. (2000). *New Social Movements: A criminological perspective*. Athens, Greece: Nomiki Bibliothiki (in Greek).

Artinopoulou, V. (2010). *Restorative justice: a challenge for the current justice systems*. Athens, Greece: Nomiki Bibliothiki (in Greek).

Artinopoulou, V. (2013). The values of restorative justice. In A. Pitsela and E. Symeonidou-Kastanidou (eds), *Restorative justice in criminal matters: towards a new European perspective* (pp. 263–272). Athens and Thessaloniki: Sakkoulas Publications.

Artinopoulou, V. (2014). Race, power and restorative justice: theoretical implications. Paper presented at the 2nd International Symposium on Restorative justice, RJ4ALL Institute, Skopelos island, June.

Artinopoulou, V. and Gavrielides, Th. (2013). Aristotle on Restorative Justice: where the Restorative Justice and Human Rights Movement meet [κοινοί τόποι]. In Gavrielides and Artinopoulou (eds), *Reconstructing Restorative Justice philosophy*. Farnham: Ashgate Publishing, pp. 25–45.

Artinopoulou, V. and Maganas, A. (1996). *Victimimology and aspects of victimization*. Athens, Greece: Nomiki Bibliothiki (in Greek).

Beck, U. (1992). *The risk society*. London: SAGE.

Binder, A. (1987). Criminology: discipline or an interdiscipline? *Issues in Intergrative Studies*, *5*, 41–67.

Bosworth, M. and Hoyle, C. (eds) (2011). *What is criminology?* Oxford Scholarship Online, doi:10.1093/acprof:oso/9780199571826.001.0001.

Champod, C. (2009). Identification and individualization. *Wiley Encyclopedia of Forensic Science*.

Cooter, R. (2014). Neural veils and the will to historical critique: why historians of sciences need to take the neuro-turn seriously. *Isis*, *105*(1), 145–154.

Cowie, H. (2010). Restorative practice in school: a psychological perspective. Paper presented as part of the Restorative Approaches to Conflict in Schools seminar series, Nottingham, September. Retrieved from http://www.notting ham.ac.uk/EducationResearchProjects/ConflictinSchools/RestorativeApproa chestoConflictinSchools.aspx.

Cremin, H., Sellman, E. and McCluskey, G. (2012). Interdisciplinary perspectives on restorative justice: developing insights for education. *British Journal of Educational Studies*, *60*(4), 421–437. doi:10.1080/00071005.2012.738290.

Daly, K. and Stubbs, J. (2006). Feminist engagement with restorative justice. *Theoretical Criminology*, *10*(1), 9–28.

De Vos, J. (2013). *Psychologization and the subject of late modernity*. Basingstoke: Palgrave Macmillan.

Eglash, A. (1977). Beyond restitution: creative restitution. In J. Hudson and B. Galaway (eds), *Restitution in criminal justice*. Lexington: DC Heath and Company.

Elisha, E., Idisis, Y. and Ronel, N. (2013). Positive criminology and imprisoned sex offenders: demonstration of a way out from a criminal spin through acceptance relationships. *Journal of Sexual Aggression*, *19*(1), 66–80. doi: 10.1080/1355 2600.2011.638145.

Errez, E. and Sebba, L. (2012). From individualization of the Offender to the individualization of the Victim: an assessment of Wolfgang's conceptualization of a Victim Oriented Criminal Justice System. In F. Adler and S.W. Laufer, *The criminology of the criminal law* (pp. 171–198). New Brunswick, NJ: Transaction Publishers.

Farah, M.J. (2012). Neuroethics: the ethical, legal, and societal impact of neuroscience. *Annual Review of Psychology*, *63*, 571–591.

Fernandez, R.G. (2010). Beyond psychologization: individual and collective naturalizing stigmatizations. *Annual Review of Critical Psychology*, *8*, 81–95.

Furby, L. (1986). Psychology and justice. In R.L. Cohen (ed.), *Justice* (pp. 153–203). New York: Springer Science and Business Media.

Garland, D. (1985). The criminal and his science: a critical account of the formation of criminology at the end of the nineteenth century. *The British Journal of Criminology*, *25*(2), 109–137.

Gavrielides, T. (2007). *Restorative justice theory and practice: addressing the discrepancy*. Helsinki: HEUNI.

Gavrielides, T. (2011). Restorative practices: from the early societies to the '70s. *Internet Journal of Criminology*. ISSN 2045-6743 [Online].

Gavrielides T. (2014). Bringing race relations into the restorative justice debate. *Journal of Black Studies*, *45*(3), 216–246.

Gavrielides, T. and Artinopoulou, V. (2013a). Restorative justice and family violence. *Asian Journal of Criminology*, *8*(1), 25–40.

Gavrielides, T. and Artinopoulou, V. (eds) (2013b). *Reconstructing restorative justice philosophy*. Farnham: Ashgate Publishing.

Gavrielides, T. and Worth, P. (eds) (2014). Another push for restorative justice: positive psychology and offender rehabilitation. In *Crime: international perspectives, socioeconomic factors and psychological implications*. New York: Nova Science Publishers.

Giddens, A. (1990). *The consequences of modernity*. Stanford: Stanford University Press.

Glenn, A.L. and Raine, A. (2014). Neurocriminology: implications for the punishment, prediction and prevention of criminal behaviour. *Nature Reviews Neuroscience*, *15*(1), 54–63.

Gottfredson, M.A. and Hirschi, T. (eds) (1987). *Positive criminology*. Newbury Park: SAGE.

Gurley, J.R. and Marcus, D.K. (2008). The effects of neuroimaging and brain injury on insanity defenses. *Behavioral Sciences & the Law*, *26*, 85–97.

Hilborn, J. (2011). SEL SID SON: a neurocriminology model of the re-entry and desistance process. In I. Ekunwe and R. Jones (eds), *Global perspectives on re-entry* (pp. 21–57). Finland: Tampere University Press.

Hughes, V. (2010). Science in court: head case. *Nature*, *464*(7287), 340–342.

Jeffery, C.R. (1959). The historical development of criminology. *Journal of Criminal Law and Criminology*, *50*(1), 3–19.

Jeffery, C.R. (1978). Criminology as an interdisciplinary behavioral science. *Criminology*, *16*(2), 149–169. doi:10.1111/j.1745-9125.1978.tb00085.x.

Johnson, R.W. (2010). Restorative conflict in schools: necessary roles of cooperative learning and constructive conflict. Paper presented as part of the Restorative Approaches to Conflict in Schools seminar series, Nottingham, September. Retrieved from http://www.nottingham.ac.uk/EducationResearchProjects/Con flictinSchools/RestorativeApproachestoConflictinSchools.aspx.

Klein, T.J. (1990). *Interdisciplinarity: history, theory, and practice*. Detroit: Wayne State University Press.

Klein, T.J. (2010). A taxonomy of interdisciplinarity. In R. Frodeman (ed.), *The Oxford handbook of interdisciplinarity* (pp. 15–31). Oxford: Oxford University Press.

Latimer, J., Craig, D. and Muise, D. (2005). The effectiveness of restorative justice practices: a meta-analysis. *The Prison Journal*, June 2005, *85*, 127–144.

Lerner, M. (1974). Social psychology of justice and interpersonal attraction. In T.L. Huston (ed.), *Foundations of interpersonal attraction* (pp. 331–355). London: Academic Press.

MacAllister, J. (2010). Restoration, transformation or education? A philosophical critique of restorative practices in schools. Paper presented as part of the Restorative Approaches to Conflict in Schools seminar series, Nottingham, September. Retrieved from http://www.nottingham.ac.uk/EducationResearchProjects/Con flictinSchools/RestorativeApproachestoConflictinSchools.aspx.

Maffei, S. and Markopoulou, L. (eds) (2014). *Fiducia. Research project for new European crimes and trust-based policy* (Vol. 2). http://www.fiduciaproject.eu/ media/publications/12/FiduciaV2_web.pdf.

Marshall, T.F. (1996). The evolution of restorative justice in Britain. *European Journal on Criminal Policy and Research*, *4*(4), 21–43.

Moran, J. (2010). *Interdisciplinarity* (2nd edn). London and New York: Routledge.

Morrison, B. (2010). Beyond the bad apple: analytical and theoretical perspectives on the development of restorative approaches in schools. Paper presented as part of the Restorative Approaches to Conflict in Schools seminar series, London, February. Retrieved from http://www.educ.cam.ac.uk/research/proje cts/restorativeapproaches/seminarone/.

Muncie, J. (2005). The globalization of crime control – the case of youth and juvenile justice: neo-liberalism, policy convergence and international conventions. *Theoretical Criminology*, *9*(1), 35–64.

Nissani, M. (1997). Ten cheers for interdisciplinarity: the case for interdisciplinary knowledge and research. *The Social Science Journal*, *34*(2), 201–216. doi:http:// dx.doi.org/10.1016/S0362-3319(97)90051-3.

Nordstrom, B.R., Gao, Y., Glenn, A.L., et al. (2010). Neurocriminology. *Advances in Genetics*, *75*, 255–283.

Osgood, W.D. (1998). Interdisciplinary integration; building criminology by stealing from our friends. *The Criminologist*, *23*(4), 1, 3, 4, 41.

Packer, H.L. (1964). Making the punishment fit the crime. *Harvard Law Review*, *77*(6), 1071–1082.

Pavlich, G. (2005). *Governing paradoxes of restorative justice*. London/Sydney/ Portland, Oregon: GlassHouse Press.

Raine, A. and Liu, J.H. (1998). Biological predispositions to violence and their implications for biosocial treatment and prevention. *Psychology, Crime and Law*, *4*(2), 107–125.

Raine, A. (2013). The criminal mind. *The World Street Journal*, April 26, 2013. Retrieved from http://www.wsj.com/articles/SB10001424127887323335404578444682892520530.

Reisel, D. (2013). *The neuroscience of restorative justice*. TED2013. Filmed February 2013.

Repko, A.F. (2011). *Interdisciplinary research: process and theory* (2nd edn). Thousand Oaks: SAGE.

Roche, D. (2007). Retributive and restorative justice. In G. Johnstone and D.W. Van Ness (eds), *Handbook of restorative justice* (pp 75–91). London: Routledge.

Rocque, M., Raine, A. and M'Elsh, B.C. (2013). Experimental neurocriminology etiology and treatment. In B.C. Welsh, A.A. Braga, G.J.N. Bruinsma (eds), *Experimental criminology: prospects for advancing science and public policy* (pp. 43–64). Cambridge: Cambridge University Press.

Ronel, N. and Elisha, E. (2011). A different perspective: introducing positive criminology. *International Journal of Offender Therapy and Comparative Criminology*, *55*(2), 305–325. doi:10.1177/0306624x0935777.

Ronel, N., Frid, N. and Timor, U. (2013). The practice of positive criminology: a Vipassana course in prison. *International Journal of Offender Therapy and Comparative Criminology*, *57*(2), 133–153. doi:10.1177/0306624x11427664.

Rose, N. (1998). *Investing ourselves, psychology, power and personhood*. Cambridge: Cambridge University Press.

Saleilles, R. (1911). *The individualization of punishment* (Vol. 4). Boston: Little, Brown & Company.

Schmidl, F. (1946). Psychological and psychiatric concepts in criminology. *Journal of Criminal Law and Criminology*, *37*(1), article 3, 37–48.

Stubbs, J. (2004). Restorative justice, domestic violence and family violence. *Australian Domestic and Family Violence*. Clearinghouse, UNSW, 1–24.

Wallace, R. and Wylie, K. (2013). Changing on the inside: restorative justice in prisons: a literature review. *The International Journal of Bahamian Studies*, 19, 57–69.

Ward, T. (2002). Good lives and the rehabilitation of offenders: promises and problems. *Aggression and Violent Behavior*, *7*(5), 513–528. doi:http://dx.doi.org/10.1016/S1359-1789(01)00076-3.

Ward, T. and Stewart, C. (2003). Criminogenic needs and human needs: a theoretical model. *Psychology, Crime and Law*, *9*(2), 125–143. doi:10.1080/1068316031000116247.

Wellford, C. (2007). Crime, justice and criminology education: the importance of disciplinary foundations. *Journal of Criminal Justice Education*, *18*(1), 2–5. doi:10.1080/10511250601144191.

Wolfgang, M.E. (1982). Basic concepts in victimological theory: individualization of the victim. In H.J. Schneider (ed.), *The victim in international perspective* (pp. 47–58). Berlin: De Gruyter.

Wolfgang, M.E. and Ferracuti, F. (1967). *The subculture of violence: towards an integrated theory in criminology.* London: Tavistock.

PART II:
Critical Issues

Chapter 6

The Psychology of Restorative Practice in Forensic Mental Health Recovery

Gerard Drennan, Andy Cook and Henry Kiernan

Introduction

Restorative justice (RJ) has found almost no traction in forensic mental health services. Certainly not in the UK, and there is no evidence that it has yet found a foothold anywhere else. This is in spite of the strong tradition of restorative justice in many of the countries where links have been made with the practices of First Nation peoples and where forensic mental health services are well developed, such as New Zealand, Canada and Australia. The UK has seen a significant rise in the funding for restorative justice initiatives within criminal justice settings across many police authority regions, and yet there has not been a corresponding rise in investment in mental health initiatives. For anyone who has worked in forensic mental health, or indeed in mental health settings generally, this is counterintuitive. There are many clear parallels between the principles of restorative justice applied to criminal justice settings and the principles of treatment in the therapeutic milieu (Drennan, 2014). Community meetings, where all members of a residential community sit together once or more times a week, and where conflict and transgressions are negotiated and challenged, and individual members are held accountable for the effect of their actions on other individuals and on the wider community, are ubiquitous in mental health settings around the world (see Lees et al. (2004) for a description of the culture of therapeutic communities). Informal face-to-face meetings between patients in conflict or between staff and patients in conflict are also commonplace and have been the staple of maintaining what has come to be referred to as 'relational security' (DoH, 2010). Perhaps even more compelling is the range of therapeutic techniques employed in restorative justice conferencing that are clearly visible to anyone with training in psychological therapies and who undertakes training as a restorative justice facilitator. However, restorative justice training manuals and published guidance (RJC, 2011) explicitly disavow that conferencing is a type of therapy. And herein lies the rub. For a range of reasons that we will return to below, the restorative justice intervention and the therapeutic intervention have been kept at arms' length from each other, and this we will argue has inhibited the development of restorative justice interventions in forensic mental health settings.

This chapter will make an attempt at a rapprochement between the rehabilitation of offenders with mental health difficulties and restorative justice practices. We will do this by setting out the psychological underpinnings of approaches to offender rehabilitation and contrasting this with the available psychological models of the action of restorative justice interventions. Through this 'compare and contrast' exercise, we hope to begin to articulate the common ground, and the potential for developing better psychological models of change and restitution, that is enabled by a closer alignment of both traditions. However, we will begin with a discussion of clinical experience with restorative interventions in forensic mental health settings. This will set the scene for a selective analysis of why forensic mental health settings have to date proven to be 'stony ground' for the seeding of restorative justice approaches.

The Texture of Restorative Interventions in Forensic Mental Health Settings

It was our hope to include in our account here clinical cases in which formal restorative interventions have been employed. As we highlight below, such case descriptions would be unique in the existing literature on restorative justice and compelling practice-based evidence of what is possible, even when patients have severe illnesses that include the symptoms of psychosis, such as hearing voices or having held false beliefs (referred to as delusions). Indeed, an early draft of this chapter included detailed case material to illustrate the successful participation in a restorative intervention of a patient with a diagnosis of paranoid schizophrenia who had committed a serious offence in an acutely psychotic state, but who had recovered sufficiently well within a relatively short period of months to engage in a mutually beneficial restorative meeting with the victim. However, inclusion of this material became untenable for clinical and ethical reasons that are common features of the landscape.

Restorative interventions, when used properly, are going to address deeply personal and potentially shame and guilt-inducing situations and events. Often the psychological treatments for people with severe and enduring mental health problems are long-term and sensitive. It may not be possible for protracted periods of time to broach the subject of consenting to the experience of a restorative intervention being allowed into a public domain through publication. This may be the case when simply considering the perspective of the patient who has harmed someone. When a restorative intervention is included as part of the mental health and offender recovery work, there is also the perspective of the victim to consider. Often there is not only one victim of an offence. The well-worn phrase of the 'ripple effect' of crime means that the circle of harm can extend to the circle of people who are close to the victim, either as family or friends. When restorative conferences are held that include the family members of victims, sometimes as supporters or as a family group, their consent to the release of case material in a professional publication is also necessary. This may itself provoke a 'ripple effect' or raise the possibility of unintended consequences for people who are not in receipt of care from the mental health institution. Approaching all of the participants in a restorative conference conducted on purely clinical and needs-led grounds, to revisit their experience of the conference and it's after effects may re-evoke feelings that are unwelcome. There is the question of who is approached first. The fundamentally important ethos of restorative conferencing being victim-led can be thrown into question if the offender patient has the first refusal on whether a clinical team can approach a victim for what might be yet another intrusion. It has been our experience that when dealing with restorative interventions for offences committed within family groups, that the level of distress in the wider family members can be quite concealed until a conference brings everyone's experiences to the fore. When each family member involved has the opportunity to answer the set of six questions that form the backbone of restorative conferencing (assuming the practice guidelines adopted in the United Kingdom are employed), unexpected vulnerability can emerge. When family groups are involved, the anguish and psychological pain that has resulted from an offence may be just as intense in someone who cares very deeply for the victim. This can have an added layer of poignancy when the wrong-doer is also a family member.

It has also been our experience that restorative interventions with victims who are external to the mental health service are most likely to be raised as a possibility, most likely to develop even if they subsequently do not proceed, and most likely to take place, if the harm that resulted from offending is some form of direct relational harm. In other words, when the ties that bind families or close associates are the ones that are damaged. So-called 'stranger offences' are very much less likely to be raised or to develop, often because of complex layering of ambivalence about the viability of intervening with restorative justice when the wrong-doer suffers from a mental illness. We have also seen anecdotally that prison-based substance mis-use services are drawing on restorative conferencing and restorative justice groupwork programmes to develop the recovery capital they provide.

The family members of patients who have offended in the family will be more likely to recognise that dialogue and change are possible with their ill family member, and that it is possible and desirable to repair relational harm in the interests of recovering relationships. This can produce unexpected results. Our experience has been that some situations can progress from the germ of an idea to overcome the fear and upset caused by an offence to a full restorative conference in a matter of days and with relatively brief preparation of the participants. The speed of response and progress is in no small measure contributed to by the fact that the health service has a duty of care towards family members, and where a restorative intervention can be seen as simply a special type of family intervention, over which the service has legitimate governance. When other agencies are involved because the victim is outside of a family, progress can be slow and faltering. Of course, it is also the case that when family members are involved, the progress towards conferencing can be slow too, for factors to do with the dynamics of the family relationships or the harm caused.

Restorative interventions that are aimed at addressing the relational harm between two or more patients in the same facility can also produce surprising and rapid results. It is not uncommon when violence erupts between patients that they have to be housed in separate wards for their own safety. Strict guidelines to manage their 'incompatibility' are instituted. This may have a significant knock-on effect for their access to group treatments, ward transfers that would signal progression, and even simple hospital shop access can become fraught. Before restorative interventions were available, this 'incompatibility' could be seen as a static status and which would then paralyse the system for long periods of time. Such 'incompatibilities' also tend to multiply across the patient population. The capacity to offer restorative conferencing as a remedy to such stale-mates has had a profoundly beneficial impact on the patients and the institution when relations can be normalised once more. This is clearly a cost effective and efficient use of hospital resources.

Restorative Justice Practice: Challenges for Forensic Mental Health Applications

Moral Responsibility and Mental Capacity

Arguably, the single most significant obstacle to introducing restorative justice practices in forensic mental health settings is the widely held view that the patients involved would not have the mental capacity for moral responsibility and accountability. The scepticism that psychiatric patients who have offended are capable of accounting for their actions or of contributing meaningfully to the restorative process exists outside formal mental health settings (see Liebmann (2007) for a rare mental health case example in the restorative justice literature in which this issue is touched upon). Even within the mental health community, there can be an assumption that a patient who has experienced a psychotic illness cannot take responsibility or be held to account. This is curious given that only a very small fraction of offenders in the UK are found not guilty by reason of insanity in any given year. A trial has an implicit assumption that there is a person who can reasonably be held responsible for their actions. The vast majority of mental health patients who have offended are found guilty and sentenced, even if the mental health condition is taken into account in mitigation. A substantial majority of patients with mental illness who commit offences are not directed to hospital on sentencing and serve their sentence in prisons. Those that are directed towards hospital are required to engage in treatment and undergo rehabilitation in which they should demonstrate victim empathy and develop a relapse prevention plan that addresses taking responsibility for avoiding a repeat of the circumstances that resulted in offending. Only a small number of patients will be considered to be so impaired by their illness that they will be discharged from hospital without demonstrating some evidence of remorse and victim empathy. Garner and Hafemeister (2003) and Hafemeister et al. (2012) have set out the theoretical case for why there are no conceptual or in principle reasons why restorative justice should not also be suitable for a mentally disordered population. It is perhaps telling that almost a decade after Hafemeister first published this argument, the case is yet to be made on the basis of empirical evidence. Cook et al. (2015) have made a small-scale contribution to the evidence base through a qualitative study of institutional mental health practice. Data were drawn from the early stages of a project to introduce restorative justice and no victims of index offences were included in the study. The case description above illustrates that a patient with a diagnosis of paranoid schizophrenia, who experienced delusions, ideas of reference and auditory hallucinations, can plausibly recover sufficiently to meaningfully participate in a restorative encounter. Not only may this have contributed to his future mental health stability, but most importantly, he was able to participate to the extent that the victim of his attack could experience the documented psychological benefits of RJ in her recovery (Poulson, 2003) and in the restoration of the familial network of which the victim was a part.

Three Possible Inhibitors to Progress

We suggest that there are three principle factors that come together to inhibit the implementation of restorative justice interventions in forensic mental health contexts. First, a systematic conceptualization of the psychology of shame, guilt and remorse within forensic mental health rehabilitation is at a relatively under-developed stage. While these concepts have always had a role in psychotherapeutic practice on a one-to-one basis (Cox, 1978), they have only recently been articulated in therapeutic group settings for offenders (Adshead, 2014; Ferrito et al., 2012; Adshead et al., 2015). This has led to our second point – it is the sin qua non of mental health rehabilitation that long-term goals are broken down into progressive steps. To be successful, mental health rehabilitation has always depended upon supporting a patient through a defined set of step-wise movements towards a relatively defined end goal. The possible steps towards being prepared for a restorative justice encounter have never been developed or articulated for a mental health offender population. This is to a large extent true of mainstream restorative justice or RJ. The change processes that prepare for a meaningful encounter are largely left to the capacity of the individual to enter into a 'stage of contemplation' (Prochaska and DiClemente, 1983) about facing something of their wrongdoing through RJ. As RJ as a rehabilitation process for the wrongdoer is highly controversial, only group interventions that include proxy victim testimonies, such as the Sycamore Tree Project (Feasey and Williams, 2009), approximate restorative situations. And a final point in relation to this, is the relative under-theorization of the psychological mechanisms that are mutative, or change-inducing, in RJ. More of this below. Next we will deepen the discussion about the place of rehabilitation in what may appear to be a 'single event' transformation.

Emotion and Skills-Based Rehabilitation in Desistance Processes

Tony Ward and colleagues working in New Zealand have critiqued the place of restorative justice in offender rehabilitation. Ward and Langlands (2008, 2009) raise questions about the ethical standing of RJ in offender rehabilitation and the role of the offender's human rights. They also caution against what they see as the sweeping claims of efficacy for RJ reducing reoffending, when their experience would suggest that offenders 'go straight' or 'desist' only after just the sort of step-wise rehabilitative programme referred to above. They accept that RJ may have a place for some offenders as an additional and complementary rehabilitative intervention, but argue that RJ should not be seen as a panacea that will remove the need for the primarily skills-based, cognitive behavioural programmes that characterize offender rehabilitation for high risk individuals. As a foil to the claims of efficacy of RJ, they suggest that an offender who agrees to an RJ intervention would almost by definition not be in a high risk group.

Ward et al. (2014) have paid restorative justice interventions the complement of rigorously cross-examining the model in terms of offender rehabilitation models. The critique of restorative justice practices takes issue with RJ programmes as a 'patchwork of loosely connected ideas and practices' and 'messy' (p. 24). More telling is the challenge that restorative values do not constitute an etiological (causal) model of human behaviour and crime, and hence an incomplete theory of how change comes about. Also exposing is the challenge that restorative justice practices are not framed as '*therapeutic*' in the conventional sense of that term. In fact, practitioner and facilitator training avowedly avoids explicit links with therapy because of the implications for who could practice. Police officers, victim support officers and volunteers cannot claim to provide a form of therapy by virtue of their restorative justice training. The restorative encounter may be a one-off event and hence Ward et al. argue that it is unlikely to make a dramatic impact on offender goals and orientations. The focus on victims' needs for restitution prompts Ward et al. to suggest that RJ's links with '*offender rehabilitation theory and practices is weak, contingent and unsystematic*' (p. 33).

Our response to the Ward et al. critique is that it appears to be based on a conceptual analysis and may lack the grounding of experiential insight. It is suggested that RJ would need to consider dismantling the polarized distinction between offenders and victims, as many offenders have also been victims. However, the lived experience of RJ is that it creates a space in which the subjectivity of the wrongdoer is given a place. It is only because the process validates the human experience of the wrongdoer that it has the moral authority to enable the wrongdoer to see that a victim mentality cannot justify or excuse the creation of another victim. It is the very awareness of the wrongdoer's own victimhood that can give rise to the psychological conditions in which it is possible for the transferring of that empathy onto the victim of the offence. In this way the '*victim in the mind*' can enter into a dialogue with the '*victim in the room*' and a rapprochement becomes possible.[1] Our view is that one of the strongest arguments for the efficacy of RJ is that it creates an immediate experience in which the victim is not an abstract entity, but a real, three-dimensional person. When confronted by

---

1 We are grateful to Dr Cleo van Velsen for suggesting the importance of the '*victim in the mind*' in restorative processes.

a flesh and blood victim, one who talks back, the idea of the victim in the mind of the offender is less likely to be subject to all the cognitive distortions that an offender may use to diminish the significance of the victim. Rather, the victim is a real presence who can challenge and intrude upon a set of rationalizations, in a sincere manner, with all of the moral authority that comes from having been wronged and yet acknowledge the humanity of the other. This real presence in an encounter can leapfrog the long and painstaking efforts of rehabilitation to invoke, in spite of the array of psychological defences at work, the idea of a 'victim in the mind' of the offender.

Our own reading of the Ward et al. critique of restorative justice is that the conceptualization of the process by which offenders reform is somewhat mechanistic and suffers from the elision of the role of emotion. The neglect of the role of emotion has been identified as a shortcoming in criminological theory, in contrast to the central role that emotion plays in the theories underpinning restorative justice (Rossner, 2014). There is little appreciation of the power of a single encounter between two human beings, when one sentient human being, the wrongdoer, has a 'Eureka moment', or a 'Road to Damascus' experience, in which they achieve an insight that will result in them choosing to change the course of their lives. In what may appears to be a single truncated moment, a vista of new possibility can open up. What can get lost in the idea of a single-event restorative justice encounter is the fact that the process may have started many months or even years before, either through formal preparatory steps, or through the accumulation of experiences that have not yet created a paradigm shift, but which have in some way aligned the elements of a shift, or what Foucault (1970) called the *episteme*, the 'ground for thought'. There are powerful accounts of how restorative justice experiences have been watershed moments in the lives of prolific offenders, or offenders who have committed very serious crimes (for example, Woolf, 2008; see also http://www.chrisdonovantrust.org/). While Ward et al. are strong advocates for promoting the agency of offenders (see Ward and Maruna (2007) for an account of the Good Lives Model), it is perhaps in the area of agency that they may most underestimate the effect of restorative processes. It is in the nature of the academic and scholarly literature that the signifiers of the potential of restorative justice can be characterized as 'anecdotal' until there is a body of research that meets the required evidential standards. For Ward et al. (2014) the lack of a '*cogent psychological theory of change*', in which the '*cognitive, emotional, social and behavioural mechanisms involved*' (p. 37) are systematically set out in the form of an overarching theory, is a significant limiting factor in the development of restorative practice as form of offender rehabilitation.

In spite of their critique of RJ, Ward et al. (2014) do recognize helpful links between RJ, rehabilitation and desistance processes. However, rather than suggesting that a rehabilitation approach be built around the practice of RJ, they suggest that RJ could form an '*overarching ethical umbrella*' (p. 39) under which the established interventions continue. This would appear to relegate the practices arising out of RJ principles, such as conferencing, to the sidelines. Our position would be to argue that the practices of offender rehabilitation could usefully align themselves with broadening out of restorative justice practices such that the 'ethical framework' they provide is operationalized in multiple and systemized formats. This would create various forms of conferencing as integral to rehabilitation and desistance processes in offenders.

Psychological Models of Efficacy in Restorative Justice – A Broad Church?

Given the setting of our contribution here within the domain of mental health practice, we will touch upon the psychological models available to inform practice. Clearly, the contribution of Nathanson (1994) and Braithwaite (1989) are seminal. Nathanson's (1994) work on emotion, and shame in particular, owed much to the work of an American psychologist, Silvan. S. Tomkins, who first published in the early 1960s. Building on this work, Braithewaite's (1989) concept of 'reintegrative shaming' as an alternative to 'stigmatizing shaming' has been a cornerstone of the development of theory underpinning practice. Increasingly, Tomkins' Affect Script Psychology (ASP) (see Chapter 4 for a fuller account of this theory) has come to occupy a key position in the literature on restorative practice. A recent publication has argued for the potential that ASP has to conceptualize and structure restorative practice (Kelly and Thorsborne, 2014). Vernon Kelly and Donald Nathanson co-founded the Silvan. S. Tomkins Institute to promote the understanding and development of Tomkins' ideas and their prominence is attested to in this collection. However, Nathanson (1994) laments the neglect of Tomkins' genius in the wider field of psychology and mental health, and certainly the first and second authors of this chapter are examples of this, as both are practising clinical psychologists who did not encounter ASP to any significant extent in their training or at any other time in their post-qualification continuing professional development. This, at least anecdotally, suggests that ASP has had little penetration in academic psychology or the praxis of psychology. Proeve and Tudor (2010) have made a significant contribution to the literature underpinning restorative justice through their comprehensive review the literature on remorse, from both psychological and philosophical perspectives, and made no reference to ASP or Tomkins. In a recent publication, Rossner (2014) describes a study that analysed restorative justice conferences, making the novel contribution of focusing on the ritual elements of the interactions as markers of success or failure, in the moment and over time in reducing reoffending. While Braithewaite's contributions to the debate on the 'effective ingredients' of restorative justice are well considered, Nathanson, and the derivation from Tomkins of his work, no longer merited explicit consideration. The notion of the 'successful ritual' is an important addition to the conceptualization of how restorative justice 'works', even with offenders or victims who were not 'ready' before a face-to-face encounter, endorsed by both Proeve and Tudor (2010) and Rossner (2014).

Rossner (2014) highlights the competition from the emotions of guilt, remorse and empathy as alternative explanations to shaming in the efficacy or otherwise of restorative justice interventions. Rossner refers to the work of Van Stokkom (2002, in Rossner, 2014), Harris, Walgrave and Braithewaite (2004, in Rossner, 2014) and Tangney (Tangney and Dearing, 2002) to give more prominence to guilt as the emotional mechanism by which empathy, forgiveness and repaired social bonds develop. Proeve and Tudor (2010), while acknowledging 'it is no doubt mis-conceived to present remorse, guilt and shame as stark, mutually exclusive alternatives' (p. 197), make a strong case for the need to deepen our understanding of the relatively neglected area of remorse, arguing that the compassion that flows from remorse – a form of suffering – is more instrumental than either guilt or shame. Later in the text, Proeve and Tudor (2010) comment that 'remorse is related to the theme of human redemption and renewal, and so is ultimately an emotion of hope, despite its darkness and pain' (pp. 207–208). This pithy formulation captures the links between restorative justice practice and the desistance literature in an offender context (Maruna, 2005) and the recovery literature in a mental health context (Shepherd et al., 2008).

The history of the development of psychological therapies is one of a multitude of competing theories contesting roughly the same territory. Far from being a weakness, the richness and diversity of these perspectives have driven innovations in technique and practice. The same should be true for restorative justice practice. At this early stage of the development and understanding of this powerful and potentially transformative experience for victim and offender, a 'monotheistic' approach would foreclose on the articulation of links with a host of models of human relatedness and mechanisms of human growth and development. Indeed, even contributions that overtly include religious and spiritual considerations (Randall, 2012) argue for an eclectic approach.

Psychological Dimensions of Restorative Practice in Mental Health Settings

Some four years ago the first author initiated a project to introduce restorative justice practice in a forensic mental health service in Sussex. The second author took on the task of the research evaluation as part of doctoral studies in clinical psychology and the third author provided restorative conferencing facilitator training to a number of staff across a range of disciplines and one peer support worker and then continued in a consultative and supervisory role as the project developed. The evaluative study took place at a stage of the project where work towards conferencing with offender patients and the victims of the offences that brought them to a secure hospital had not yet led to a conference. However, a key feature of the learning process for the project was the importance of situating restorative justice within the wider context of institutional practice and mental health offender rehabilitation. This led to an early emergence of the role of restorative practices in the institution as providing an underpinning for restorative justice practices per se. In other words, the grounding for restorative justice lay in the way in which restorative practice began to form a component of the wider rehabilitative environment. The way in which this happened was through the introduction of restorative practice to address conflict and harm as it arose in the everyday care of patients. To anyone familiar with the development of restorative practice across educational (Williams, 2014), prison (Barabas et al., 2012) and community settings (Gavrielides, 2007) this will not come as a surprise. However, the particular character of this development, being for the first time in a secure forensic mental health setting, was highly instructive. The difference between the 'map' and the 'terrain' is always something to hold in mind.

The possibility of using restorative meetings between a harmed person and a harm-causing person became a legitimate question for the organization in relation to a wide range of circumstances. The most prominent of these was assaults by patients on members of staff, but also included conflict between patients resident on the same ward; complaints about care from patients; patient behaviour that put staff at risk; sexualized harassment of staff by patients; instances of absence without leave by patients escorted by staff members; instances of staff restraint on a patient; the impact of self-harm by patients on staff and other residents; using and supplying illicit substances on the unit; and so on. Any institutional infraction or behaviour that could have resulted in a negative impact on another member of that community could be considered for a restorative intervention. When examples of these situations arose and a restorative intervention was considered, the wheels of pursuing this were set in motion and preparation work began. As is the case for the vast majority of cases identified for RJ in criminal justice settings, more often than not a restorative meeting did not take place. However, it became clear that the process of considering this with the parties, initiating preparation and the decision to proceed or not proceed, became part of the rich tapestry of rehabilitative activity, and at another level, part of the learning process in the organization becoming a restorative environment.

The data for the evaluation study of the project were derived from precisely the type of learning experiences within the institution described above. Interviews were conducted with patients and staff on both sides of the victim/perpetrator dyad, and facilitators who prepared for or who conducted restorative meetings. The findings of these interviews were analysed using a constructivist grounded theory methodology (Charmaz, 2006) and used to generate a model of the psychological processes underpinning this work. For our purposes here we will highlight a selection of key features identified in Cook et al. (2015).

Psychological Containment as a Primary Task

It should not be taken for granted that high levels of satisfaction were expressed by both victims and wrongdoers, whether staff or offender patients in their experience of restorative practices. The next most important finding was that patient participation was possible across a wide range of diagnostic categories and clinical presentations, and it was only during the acute phase of illness or relapse that participation became contra-indicated. The importance of immediacy in the organizational response to situations that lent themselves to restorative approaches was another key element of the emotional, and hence therapeutic, efficacy of the interventions. However, a cornerstone aspect of the psychological model developed within the grounded theory methodology was that of the psychological containment needed for all concerned.

The implementation of restorative practice depended upon developing protocols and guidance for all potential participants to create psychological containment for an anxiety-inducing intervention. Staff in particular were found to need clear information to inform decisions and to dispel fears about participation. There were implications for staff of the psychological vulnerability they felt when using restorative meetings to address the harm caused to them by patients. Staff in such units are trained to maintain boundaries with patients that restrict self-disclosure to a minimum. Staff needed support to recognize when a philosophy of face-to-face conciliation could be useful, in an organizational culture where the type of psychological contact required in an encounter in which the victim/staff member's experience of harm is critical to the power and efficacy of the intervention, is seen as risky and potentially destabilizing. Staff needed and wanted reassurance that facilitators would have the necessary skills to maintain safety. Trust in the facilitator, who could be a colleague, was key. It was imperative that the technical skills to prepare participants and to manage the process of the interaction in a face-to-face meeting, which included the skilled use of the structure of a conference but also the containment of strong emotions as manifested in the preparation phase and the meeting itself, were convincingly held. This was challenging given that the introduction of restorative interventions was new to the service and the staff members recently trained, at the same time as all cases were immediately in the category of 'complex and sensitive' as defined by the RJC (2011).

To illustrate this, there was one instance of a face-to-face meeting between a staff member returning to work after a period of time off recovering from an assault by a female patient. The patient suffered from depression, chronic post-traumatic stress disorder and had been diagnosed as meeting the criteria for a Borderline Personality Disorder. The patient had an established pattern of assaulting staff members while at the same time being highly dependent, and of using self-harm behaviours, including cutting and tying ligatures in response to distress. The outcome of the conference on the day the staff member returned to work was considered to be successful by both the staff member and the patient. The staff member felt acknowledged and less vulnerable after the process, and the patient demonstrated a protracted period without assaultative behaviour towards staff. However, the narrative of the intervention would be incomplete if it were not acknowledged that the patient had left the face-to-face meeting and proceeded to tie a ligature. This was detected by staff on the ward and the situation was de-escalated successfully. This was an almost daily occurrence with the service user at the time and so was in some respects unremarkable. However, had there been a very negative outcome on this occasion for the service user, there would have been enormous implications for the staff member who had challenged the patient within the conference meeting and the staff member who had assessed the risk and elected to progress with the intervention.

Examples such as this notwithstanding, Cook et al. (2015) conclude that '[t]here was agreement across all participant groups that the components of RJ interventions provided a safe structure within which to have a psychologically meaningful encounter that seemed to bring with it an experience of being positively affected and motivation to reduce repeating the harmful behaviours'.

The Limits of Containment

In spite of the challenge of containment for processes and participants within the institutional setting, containment for victims external to the service was to prove even more difficult. If the victim was a stranger victim, scoping the possibility of conferencing depended upon third party agencies, such as probation, being actively involved and resourced to progress this. Our experience was that they were often not resourced for this work. It was not only a question of resources. Conversations with criminal justice agencies regarding partnerships to work together to bringing a forensic mental health patient together with the victim of the 'index offence' often begin with a question about the type of offence. The best criminal justice agencies will publish a list of the offences that are permitted to be considered for restorative justice, and even within that there is likely to be a hierarchy of which offences will receive an allocation of limited resources. This is challenging in mental health settings where the index offence is not the primary defining characteristic of the offender, but the presumption that all patients, no matter what their illness or their offence, have equal legitimacy of access to the technologies of recovery.

What emerged in the mental health project was that, when victims of offences were family members, the clinical governance of processes of reconciliation properly sat with the social care staff of the mental health institution, and in this way they were more likely to be enabled.

'New' Technologies in 'Old' Resources

Here in the UK, many restorative justice projects in criminal justice services have benefited at the outset from the magisterial document Wait 'til Eight (Thames Valley Partnership Associates, 2013). This guide to setting up projects arose out of 12 years of experience of implementing RJ within the Thames Valley region and recommends that eight key elements are in place before training staff and beginning to offer restorative justice interventions. These criteria include the resourcing of dedicated project staff such as project managers, dedicated RJ workers and administrators. Our experience has been that it was necessary to start with a project leader, with some degree of organizational approval and flexibility to respond to emerging need, and a small number of motivated staff (and where possible peer workers or volunteers) who received training as conference facilitators. It was not until undertaking training that the technical nature of the intervention was understood, along with enough theoretical understanding to make links with an existing knowledge-base in mental health and offender interventions, that there was a platform for the psychological containment necessary to proceed within the organization.

The absence at the present time of an evidence-base within mental health for restorative interventions means that dedicated resources are unlikely to be budgeted for by mental health service commissioners or allocated by already pressured hospital managers in a time of austerity in health funding. So we have a 'new' intervention that is not specifically commissioned or accommodated in job planning, but which requires detailed preparation, perhaps over a protracted period of time, where there is a unique pattern of readiness in each case, that is not routine or manualized, and which requires careful and ongoing co-ordination with clinical teams responsible for the care of offenders. A challenging set of circumstances indeed. It is our hope that encouragement can be drawn from our experience nevertheless. Even on a small sample of limited experiences, restorative practices made a contribution to the overall therapeutic goals of the service, through helping to address offence paralleling behaviour as manifested during institutional care (Daffern et al., 2010). These practices also increased empathy for others, and the self, which in turn led to increasing victim empathy, preparing for discharge into the community, repairing family relationships and generally contributing towards offender and mental health recovery. All of this suggests that treatment plans could usefully incorporate restorative practices as a supplemental approach that adds value to other aspects of rehabilitation and recovery.

It is important nevertheless that the restorative intervention is not seen in isolation, as simply an idealized moment that is abstracted from the setting of its practice, as if it is simply a discrete or even surgical intervention that sits in isolation from the domain of institutional praxis. Focusing our psychological understanding on the moment of interaction between the victim and the wrongdoer within a conferencing setting is to miss the psychological factors at work in the wider context. As in the Gestalt Laws of Closure, figure and ground each play their part. At this early stage of the development of restorative practice in institutional settings, and in mental health institutional settings in particular, attention needs to be paid to the wider context of application, as a necessary step towards making such interventions possible to conduct in a safe and sustainable way.

The Place of Restorative Justice in Offender Recovery

Murray Cox, a renowned psychoanalytic psychotherapist who practised at Broadmoor High Secure Hospital in England for many years, is quoted as describing the pathway for offender recovery in the following simple terms:

I didn't do it.

I might have done it but they made me do it.

I did it but I was helpless in the circumstances.

I did it.

I did it and I don't want to do it again. (Buckley et al., 2014, p. 585)

This describes in essence the narrative journey that mentally disordered offenders would undertake in the course of their recovery, if the journey is to include mental health recovery and offender recovery (Adshead et al., 2015; Cox, 1978; Drennan and Alred, 2012; Drennan et al., 2014). Or as Buckley et al. (2014) put it, '[t]he change must be in health certainly, but also in ownership of behaviour' (p. 585). Our view is that restorative practices could make a powerful contribution to the development of insight and emotional understanding in offenders with serious mental health challenges. However, we are at a beginning in understanding the psychological processes that are operative in a restorative process that is transformative. Our brief review of the literature above suggests that this is something that remains true of the field of restorative justice in general. We are therefore also only beginning to consider how mental health factors mediate the mutative (change-inducing) aspects of the intervention across a range of diagnostic and subjective dimensions and the organizational factors that are needed to create the necessary and sufficient conditions for a patient to experience an adequately successful restorative event. At the same time it is crucial to avoid the trap of prioritizing the recovery needs of the wrongdoer, while neglecting the primary moral and ethical requirement to prioritize the restoration of the victim. However, the restoration of the victim could mark an important step towards the restoration of the 'victim in the mind' of the offender who is afflicted with neurotic, psychotic, or indeed, criminal motivations that lead to offending.

Bibliography

Adshead, G. (2014). Safety in numbers: group therapy-based index offence work in secure psychiatric care. *Psychoanalytic Psychotherapy, 28*(4), 1–16.

Adshead, G., Ferrito, M. and Bose, S. (2015). Recovery after homicide: narrative shifts in therapy with homicide perpetrators. *Criminal Justice and Behaviour, 42*, 70–81.

Barabas, T., Fellegi, B. and Windt, S. (2012). *Responsibility-taking, relationship-building and restoration in prisons.* Budapest: Foresee Research Group.

Braithwaite, J. (1989). *Crime, shame and reintegration.* Cambridge: Cambridge University Press.

Buckley, P.F., McGauley, G., Clarke, J., et al. (2014). Principles of treatment for the mentally disordered offender. In J. Gunn and P.J. Taylor (eds), *Forensic psychiatry: clinical, legal and ethical issues* (2nd edn, pp. 551–579). Boca Raton: CRC Press.

Charmaz, K. (2006). *Constructing grounded theory: a practical guide through qualitative analysis.* London: SAGE.

Cook, A., Drennan, G. and Callanan, M.M. (2015). A qualitative exploration of the experience of restorative approaches in a forensic mental health setting. *Journal of Forensic Psychiatry and Psychology*, 26(4), 510–531.

Cox, M. (1978). *Structuring the therapeutic process: compromise with chaos.* Oxford: Pergamon Press.

Daffern, M., Jones, L. and Shine, J. (2010). *Offence paralleling behaviour: a case formulation approach to offender assessment and intervention.* Chichester: Wiley-Blackwell.

DoH (Department of Health) (2010). *See, think, act: your guide to relational security.* London: Government Publications. Retrieved from https://www.rcpsych.ac.uk/pdf/Relational%20Security%20Handbook.pdf.

Drennan, G. and Alred, D. (2012). Recovery in forensic mental health settings: from alienation to integration. In G. Drennan and D. Alred (eds), *Secure recovery* (pp. 1–22). Abingdon: Routledge.

Drennan, G. (2014). Restorative practice in forensic mental health. *Resolution*, *51*(Spring), 10–11.

Drennan, G., Wooldridge, J., Aiyegbusi, A., et al. (2014). *Making recovery a reality in forensic settings.* London: Centre for Mental Health. Retrieved from http://www.imroc.org/wp-content/uploads/ImROC-briefing-10-Making-Recovery-a-Reality-in-Forensic-Settings-final-for-web.pdf.

Feasey, S. and Williams, P. (2009). *An evaluation of the Sycamore Tree programme: based on an analysis of Crime Pics II data.* Project Report. Sheffield: Sheffield Hallam University.

Ferrito, M., Vetere, A., Adshead, G. and Moore, E. (2012). Life after homicide: accounts of recovery and redemption of offender patients in a high security hospital – A qualitative study. *Journal of Forensic Psychiatry and Psychology*, *23*, 327–344.

Foucault, M. (1970). *The order of things: an archaeology of the human sciences.* New York: Vintage Books.

Garner, S.G. and Hafemeister, T.L. (2003). Restorative justice, therapeutic juriprudence and mental health courts: finding a better means to respond to offenders with a mental disorder. *Mental Health Law*, *22*, 1–15.

Gavrielides, T. (2007). *Restorative justice theory and practice: addressing the discrepancy.* Helsinki: Hakapaino Oy.

Hafemeister, T.L., Garner, S.G. and Bath, V.E. (2012). Forging links and renewing ties: applying the principles of restorative and procedural justice to better respond to criminals with a mental disorder. *Buffalo Law Review*, *60*, 147–223.

Kelly, V.C. and Thorsborne, M. (2014). *The psychology of emotion in restorative practice: how Affect Script Psychology explains how and why restorative practice works.* London: Jessica Kingsley Publishers.

Lees, J., Manning, N, Menzies, D. and Morant, N. (2004). *A culture of inquiry: research evidence and the therapeutic community*. London: Jessica Kingsley Publishers.

Liebmann, M. (2007). *Restorative justice: how it works*. London: Jessica Kingsley Publishers.

Maruna, S. (2005). *Making good: how ex-convicts reform and rebuild their lives*. Washington: American Psychological Association.

Nathanson, D.L. (1994). *Shame and pride: affect, sex, and the birth of the self: affect, sex and the birth of self*. New York: W.W. Norton & Company.

Poulson, B. (2003). Third voice: a review of empirical research on the psychological outcomes of restorative justice. *Utah Law Review*, *1*, 167–203.

Prochaska, J.O. and DiClemente, C.C. (1983). Stages and processes of self-change of smoking: toward an integrative model of change. *Journal of Consulting and Clinical Psychology*, *51*, 390–395.

Proeve, M. and Tudor, S. (2010). *Remorse: psychological and jurisprudential perspectives*. Farnham: Ashgate Publishing.

Randall, P. (2012). *The psychology of feeling sorry: the weight of the soul*. Abingdon: Routledge.

RJC (Restorative Justice Council) (2011). *Best practice guidance for restorative practice*. London: Author.

Rossner, M. (2014). *Just emotions: rituals of restorative justice*. Oxford: Oxford University Press.

Shepherd, G., Boardman, J. and Slade, M. (2008). *Making recovery a reality*. London: Sainsbury Centre for Mental Health.

Tangney, J.P. and Dearing, R.L. (2002). *Shame and guilt*. New York: Guilford Press.

Thames Valley Partnership Associates. (2013). *Wait 'til eight*. London: NOMS.

Ward, T., Fox, K.J. and Garber, M. (2014). Restorative justice, offender rehabilitation and desistance. *Restorative Justice*, *2*(1), 24–42.

Ward, T. and Langlands, R. (2008). Restorative justice and the human rights of offenders: convergences and divergences. *Aggression and Violent Behavior*, *13*, 355–372.

Ward, T. and Langlands, R. (2009). Repairing the rupture: restorative justice and rehabilitation of offenders. *Aggression and Violent Behavior*, *14*, 205–214.

Ward, T. and Maruna, S. (2007). *Rehabilitation*. Abingdon: Routledge.

Williams, S. (2014). Keep calm and carry on: from fear and fun in over two years in a British Youth Arts organisation. In V. Kelly and M. Thorsborne (eds), *The psychology of emotion in restorative practice* (pp. 158–178). London: Jessica Kingsley Publishers.

Woolf, P. (2008). *The damage done*. London: Bantam Books.

Chapter 7

The Concept of Humiliation as a Critical Issue in Restorative Justice: An Exploration

Rina Kashyap[1]

Introduction

Described as 'one of the worst evils' (Statman, 2000, p. 536) and a 'potential nuclear bomb' (Lindner, 2009, p. 167), humiliation is increasingly being seen as a social and political problem that requires urgent attention in our violent conflict punctuated times. Since humiliation creates vicious cycles of violence, which involve the categories of the offender/perpetrator and victim, humiliation must be a concern of justice. In this chapter, I discuss humiliation as a critical issue of restorative justice and argue that it is a useful guide to explore possible solutions for this problem.

The phenomenon of humiliation has long been the subject of many a literary work – the oeuvre includes works of Homer (Cairns, 1993; Holway, 2012; Lateiner, 2007), Shakespeare, Dodie Bellamy and Elfriede Jelinek (Koestenbaum, 2011), Fyodor M. Dostoevsky, Leo Tolstoy and Anton Chekov (Lapidus, 2008) and John M. Coetzee (Nashef, 2009), Mahashweta Devi and Saddat Hussain Manto (Baxi, 2007). However, some of its aspects in the guise of justice, freedom, exploitation, equality and alienation have also been the subject matter of the social science disciplines. In recent times this euphemistic pursuit has given way to a more open, direct and clearly articulated research interest on the subject of humiliation (Guillermo, 2013; Guru, 2011; Kelly and Thorsborne, 2014; Klaassen and Klaassen, 2008; Lindner, 2010; Luban, 2009; Mansfield, 1995; Miller, 1993; O'Neill, 2005; Silver et al., 1986; Statman, 2000; Steinberg, 1996; Wyatt-Brown, 2014).

The dynamics of humiliation, depending upon the historical circumstances, can victimize both the powerless and the powerful (see Held, 2003). The negative spiralling of humiliation has destructive social and political repercussions: 'far

---

1 I am grateful to Howard Zehr and Theo Gavrielides for their valuable comments on the chapter and for drawing my attention to the new literature on the subject. I also thank Aseema Sinha, Anjali Bhatia, Anil Hira and Denis Dogah for their suggestions and review of the chapter.

from inspiring ethical subjects, humiliation merely cultivates *ressentiment*-filled beings who seek to pull down all those around them' (Spinoza paraphrased in Saurette, 2005b, p. 5). Humiliation is a problem because an inhumane and unjust practice more often than not creates unending cycles of conflict and violence; these cycles make yesterday's victims become today's offenders (see Mamdani, 2001). Research in 'psychotherapeutic work with violent criminals' demonstrates that most assaults and killings are attempts to 'eliminate the feelings of shame and humiliation' (Gilligan, 2001, p. 29). Acts of violence are acts of offence that create categories of offender/perpetrator and victim but conventional accounts of justice do not speak of humiliation. In this chapter I argue that restorative justice takes cognizance of the problem of humiliation as it recognizes it as one of the major hurdles in: (a) meeting the needs of the victim; (b) ensuring that the offender fulfils his/her obligations even as his/her needs are met. I further propose that since restorative justice as a perspective, movement and 'way of life' is premised on the 'promise' to *not humiliate* it focuses on humiliation's *other*. This other resides in the philosophy and practice of restorative justice under many aliases, most prominent of which are respect, empathy and dignity: 'Restorative justice, in a word, is about respect' (Zehr and Toews, 2004, p. 408; also see Zehr, 1998). I contend that the restorative justice practice intuitively and quietly jettisons acts of humiliation in its process. I must clarify that I do not use the word intuitively, to impute magical powers or some otherworldly grasp of sixth sense to restorative justice. I do so only to emphasize that the privileging of respect and rejection of humiliation are integral and organic features of restorative justice. Restorative justice's stance vis-à-vis respect and humiliation as emotions/attitudes emerges from its understanding and belief in the interconnectedness of life – that is, the relationship among human beings *and* between them and their social environment. It is my contention that restorative justice does not treat respect and humiliation as emotions *only* but also as phenomena that are enabled or disabled by structures such as those of patriarchy, racism, colonialism and market economies that are characterized by wide gaps between the rich and the poor. Some of the rich and evocative writings on the restorative justice philosophy of interconnectedness draw from indigenous traditions (in small-scale societies and tribal communities) and emphasize the need for harmony between human beings and nature (see Pranis, 2005; Ross, 1996). These learnings enrich restorative justice understanding of the values of empathy and respect. While these values remain relevant and crucial today, their operationalization is rendered difficult due to the increasing complexity of contemporary political, social and economic structures. Therefore, I propose that restorative justice must engage with not just the disciplines of social sciences, but also those of psychology, and neurosciences to understand the changing forms and sources of what are identified as problems of our times; this is crucial for formulating a relevant restorative response.

This chapter is divided into three sections. In the first, 'The Concept of Humiliation', I problematize the concept of humiliation as a cluster concept since most of the conceptualizations of humiliation use the binary trope. I underline that an examination of humiliation as an emotion must be supplemented by a study of humiliation as a social and political practice that is embedded in social, political and economic structures. The contextualizing of restorative justice concerns requires quarrying of the social science disciplines to understand the changed and changing structures of our times. In the second section, 'The Problem of Humiliation and Restorative Justice', I discuss certain features of restorative justice that demonstrate that a weltanschauung rooted in an ethic of respect is obviously premised on non-humiliation. I conclude this section with a discussion of how storytelling in restorative justice is *not* the reliving of the trauma for the victim and the offender but a 'gift of pain' (Gavrielides, 2013) for the stakeholders including the community. This pain is cathartic precisely because it is experienced in and through the restorative justice process. This catharsis is a way for parties to break out of the vicious cycle of violence and revenge; the pain endured in the process is thus a gift. In the third section, 'Restorative Justice and Humiliation: Learning from New Research in Social Sciences, Psychology, and Neurosciences', I discuss the reasons why restorative justice's concerns with the psychological and structural dimensions of humiliation make it necessary for it to quarry the latest relevant research in social sciences, psychology and neurosciences. In my conclusion, I reiterate that although restorative justice views humiliation as both a psychological phenomenon and a social practice, restorative justice must learn from research in the other disciplines to better engage with these problems. This is also important because restorative justice itself has to function within the existing structural constraints.

The Concept of Humiliation

Some of the prominent scholarship on the concept of humiliation makes a distinction between shame and humiliation (Callahan, 2004; Miller, 1993). The view that shame and humiliation are distinct concepts emerges primarily from research in the disciplines of psychology, sociology and more recently in the field of neuroscience where they have been studied as emotions: humiliation is a 'combination of three innate affects' which include shame alongside disgust and dissmell (Nathanson in Lindner, 2006, p. 45), shame is 'some felt deficiency in oneself' and humiliation is disrespect of the self by another (Held, 2003, p. 75), shame is part of a 'triad' that includes embarrassment and humiliation (Erving Goffman in Scheff, 2004, p. 237), humiliation has *only* a negative connotation, while shame is *multicoded* – that is, it can be 'both a virtue and a problem' (Callahan, 2004, p. 200). The last nuance echoes an influential (and subsequently controversial) articulation of John Braithwaite's (1989) theory about stigmatizing shame and reintegrative shame that I discuss in the section on restorative justice.

I do not challenge the merit in these distinctions but note that even those who spell out the differences do not deny the interrelatedness between the two – that is, shame and humiliation. Before going further I must point out that following Zehr

(2011), I use the words shame and humiliation interchangeably in this chapter. I do so because treating shame and humiliation as discrete phenomena is a handicap while addressing issues of justice, as they are likely to occur simultaneously in the experiences of the victim and the offender. Thus the role of consciousness is important in the concept of humiliation. An act of humiliation becomes *useful* for the humiliator only when the humiliated perceives it as so. As perception is contingent on consciousness, a person with no sense of self will not perceive its violation. If not a hubristic consciousness there has to be in the individual a certain degree of recognition of his/her ego in order to feel humiliated. Immanuel Kant in a similar strain says that the self-consciousness of being humiliated triggers one's self respect and dignity. Kant thus also reveals humiliation like dignity as 'not a metaphysical property of individual human beings, but rather a property of relations between human beings – between, so to speak, the dignifier and the dignified', between the humiliator and the humiliated (Luban, 2009, p. 214). Karl Marx (1963) viewed the historic moment of working-class consciousness, 'when a class in itself becomes a class for itself', as a prerequisite for a successful proletariat revolution. Awareness sows the seeds of rebellion or revolt, which then may lead to endless cycles of violence and humiliation.

However, some argue that laying too much weight on the individual's subjective consciousness is wrong when the humiliation is not intentional; therefore, in such situations the 'normative strength of claims about hurt feelings' of the humiliated is weakened (Statman, 2000, p. 536). The role of consciousness is also downplayed to make a contrary argument that humiliation exists irrespective of the intention of the humiliator (Margalit, 1996, p. 10). We can, therefore, conclude that consciousness is crucial to confront and end humiliation, but its absence does not take away from the illegitimacy of the structures of humiliation that are discussed next.

Two observations emerge from the above. The first is that humiliation is not a 'stand-alone' but a 'cluster' concept – that is, it becomes meaningful by aligning with other concepts. Several studies on humiliation, therefore, view it in terms of binaries: humiliation and decency (Margalit, 1996); humiliation and dignity (Hornle and Kremnitzer, 2011 Kleinig, 2012; Lindner, 2006; Luban, 2009; Saurette, 2005a); humiliation and honour (Nisbet and Cohen, 1996). I read these several 'others' in these binaries as synonyms of respect. The second observation is that the significant insights from the lens of psychology should not be used to reduce the concept of humiliation *only* to a subjective experience. The individual's subjective experience is no doubt important and therefore restorative justice privileges this, and so does not just prioritize the needs of the victims but also emphasizes their articulation by the victims themselves. Having said this we cannot deny that even though meaning-making by an individual may appear a solitary exercise, it is influenced by a host of social, political, cultural and economic forces. We must be alert to the potential trap whereby society can absolve itself of responsibility by designating humiliation as the problem of a weak, overly sensitive individual who is prone to imagining slights. After all, the tactical deployment of humiliation by the humiliator is intended for some social and political gains; also, the structures of power (for example, caste, gender, class and race) make some of us more susceptible (because of our location in those structures) to humiliation.

Structures of Humiliation

Humiliation is a means to maintain 'social order and hierarchy' (Saurette, 2005b, p. 5). In the following paragraphs I discuss through examples how structures that are marked by inequality – for example, patriarchy, colonialism, racism and the market economy – use humiliation as a mechanism to control and maintain order. Power is an essential dimension in these practices of humiliation, which often manifest in social pathologies. As I argued in another chapter:

> Humiliation is a strategy to mask the unjust and exploitative nature of an oppressive activity. It seeks to dis-empower and disable its victim. It assumes many forms – verbal and nonverbal, manifests in myriad arena – social, cultural, economic and political. It is most powerful in the realm of ideas where it discourses itself as legitimate. This strategy makes humiliation appear as a just desert, thereby making opposition to it illegitimate. (Kashyap, 2005, p. 3)

Operationalization of humiliation in power structures involves dehumanization of the other. For instance, gender inequality of patriarchal structures was justified by some political philosophers on the grounds that a woman is less of a human: Aristotle described woman as a 'deformed man' (MacLehose, 2006, p. 35), Kant saw women as incapable of reason and principles (Schott, 2004, p. 102), and women were not signatories in Hobbesian and Lockean social contracts because they were deemed to be devoid of rationality. Despite the formal equality between sexes today patriarchal control of women through the dehumanization of their mind and body continues through various modes – for example, propagation of the beauty myth (Wolf, 1992) and rape as a weapon of war (Tickner, 2001).

The structural dimensions of humiliation are emphasized by Avishai Margalit's work, in which he contrasts the concept of humiliation with that of decency. He puts the burden of decency on the society's institutions that must be characterized by 'non-humiliating' practices. In this regard, he sees the institution of the state as best equipped, because of its immense resources, to eliminate humiliation (Margalit, 1996, p. 4). His emphasis is on the structural dimensions of the practices of humiliation whereby the role of intention (to humiliate) and perception (of being humiliated) is not significant, since humiliation for him is a normative not a psychological concept (Lukes, 1997, p. 41). Therefore, he characterizes poverty as a condition that humiliates since it closes 'off possibilities of living that are worthwhile in the eyes of the poor themselves' (Margalit, 1996, pp. 230–231).

Indeed there is a growing literature in development economics in which the structural links between shame/humiliation and poverty are identified (Chase and

Walker, 2012; Reyles, 2007; Sen, 1983, 1993; Sutton et al., 2014; Vorbruggen and Baer, 2007). This corpus researches shame and humiliation – as indicators to understand and measure poverty (Reyles, 2007, p. 419), as factors that adversely impact 'social solidarity', and as both consequences and factors 'in the increasing persistence of poverty' (Chase and Walker, 2012, p. 752). This insight puts the shame/humiliation and poverty linkage in the same template as that of the vicious cycle of shame/humiliation and violence. This is yet another example of the fact that humiliation resides not just at the psychological realm of the individual but in the social, economic and political domains.

The vicious cycle argument is significant as it reveals that in addition to being an inhumane practice humiliation adversely impacts social, economic and political goals. Therefore, marginalization and exclusionary consequences of the market economy that lead to 'alienation' (Marx, 1964) and loss of self-esteem (see Tangney and Dearing, 2002; Sen, 1993) should be a concern for the society at large and not just for the economically impoverished. Humiliation is not a surprising facet of a system where the pursuit of profit not only justifies but also glorifies the dehumanization of nature – for example, the aggressive masculine metaphor of 'conquest' is part of the romanticized lore of the entrepreneurial spirit of capitalism. Restorative justice advocates see this as a key problem and contrast it with the aboriginal communities' empathetic relationship with nature (see Ross, 1996).

Humiliation was an important aspect of the colonial strategy to maintain order and control in colonies; therefore, colonial discourse and policies infantilized, effeminized and racialized the colonized. These were tactics to shame them and construct them as inadequate human beings (see Nandy, 1983; Spivak, 1988). In addition to economic exploitation, therefore, the colonized were victims of cultural imperialism, a form of ascriptive humiliation, which denied to the oppressed the right to develop their own culture and way of life (Lukes, 1997, p. 46).

To sum up, humiliation occurs in hierarchical structures and relationships and when this hierarchy is questioned, some its acts and practices are exposed as unjust and humiliating. This exposure could be used as an exhortation to march on a path of violent revenge thereby continuing the vicious cycle of violence. Restorative justice philosophy offers an alternative route.

The Problem of Humiliation and Restorative Justice

I propose that the malaise of humiliation (in its various forms and synonyms) that afflicts our times can be treated with the prescription of restorative justice. Restorative justice, I argue, has an intuitive understanding of the problem even though it may not be specifically discussed by its theorists. While conventional accounts of justice do not emphasize the concept of humiliation, restorative justice regards respect and humility as its underlying values (Zehr and Toews, 2004, pp. 403–404). In the following paragraphs, I discuss why I lean on restorative justice for a remedy to the problem of humiliation.

The Humble and Respectful Travellers in the Journey of a New Paradigm

Though restorative justice draws from ancient traditions, it is primarily a new paradigm and movement;[2] indeed, a significant corpus of the literature in the field is a result of 'thinking on one's feet' by practitioners as they respond to local problems. This improvisation and praxis impart the field with a fluidity and dynamism that allow it to question orthodoxies with sensitivity and look at problems including that of humiliation through a 'changed lens' (Zehr, 2005). Significant in this regard is the metaphor of journey that we often encounter in restorative justice writings. Howard Zehr (2011) writes about the exploration of the 'journey to belonging' of the victim and the offender (p. 21). Theo Gavrielides and Vasso Artinopoulou speak about the 'egalitarian dialogue' and 'value-based methodology' that they adopted for their edited volume on the subject. It is a testimony to the field's philosophy that even an intellectual exercise of writing a book becomes a journey of discovery for the authors who want to share with readers their 'learning, successes and failures' (Gavrielides and Artinopoulou, 2013, p. 4). This embarking on a journey of discovery can be a source of worry as it implies that, unlike the certainty of answers/solutions that the mainstream criminal justice system has, restorative justice is not yet equipped to take up complex issues. However, the profession of 'enlightened ignorance' by one does not necessarily mean the omniscience of the other. I read the above assertions by the authors, practitioners and advocates as an affirmation of restorative justice's core values of humility and respect. Therefore, my contention is that restorative justice has an intuitive grasp of the problem of humiliation.

The Contrasting Premises of Retributive Justice and Restorative Justice

Restorative justice is contextual and is characterized by a humanist worldview while retributive justice is informed by an alienating bureaucratic-rationality approach in which the specifics of the case get lost in the maze of general rules. Also, retributive justice focuses more on punishment than on justice (Braithwaite and Pettit, 1990; Quinney and Wildeman, 1991, pp. 40–41). Nowhere is this more evident than in the prison system. The harshness and humiliating environment of prison culture is antithetical to the very idea of prison term becoming an occasion to reflect and reform. The prison experience only hardens the offender (Cayley, 1998). There have been some successful attempts to do restorative work in the prison in which the prisoners are provided with a range of opportunities to make

---

2   Some fear that the mainstreaming of restorative justice will embark it on the road to institutionalization and disable it as a movement (Masters, 2004).

amends.[3] Incarcerated men and women who have engaged with restorative justice observe that it makes them reflective and positive about their lives. They acquire a respectful perspective about themselves and others. This sense of empowerment is not at the cost of abdication of responsibility of the offence; in fact they consciously seek 'ways to make amends to their victims' (Toews, 2006, p. 8). Shaming and humiliating the offender may be counterproductive to the restorative justice goal of ensuring offender accountability and responsibility since 'shame is known to reduce human agency' (Walker et al., 2013, p. 217).

Restorative justice looks beyond the 'here and now' of the justice verdict binary of innocent or guilty and takes into account both the *process* of justice and the consequences of the verdict. It tests justice by its fruits not by its intent; it is dialogic not 'adversarial'; 'searches for commonalities' instead of emphasizing differences; it is marked by 'rituals of lament and reordering' and not those of 'personal denunciation and exclusion'; it follows Mahatma Gandhi's dictum, 'hate the sin not the sinner'; the focus is on 'right relationships' and not just 'right rules' (Zehr, 2005, pp. 211–213). Therefore, as a process and as an approach, restorative justice is characterized by respect and this provides a congenial context to deal with the problem of humiliation. The restorative justice ethos privileges the idea of human relationships, respects the innate humanity and dignity of all and is 'premised on the assumption that we as individuals are interconnected, and what we do matters to others and vice versa' (Zehr and Toews, 2004, p. 407). A crime in the restorative justice lens is a violation of relationships (Zehr, 2005, p. 11; Toews, 2006, p. 6).

The Belief in the Interconnectedness of Life and the Erasure of Humiliation

The belief in interconnectedness is the restorative justice rationale for enlarging the circle of stakeholders beyond the victim and the offender to include the community. This aims to ensure that the process and space of justice are non-humiliating for both the victim and the offender. But we may note that even with the entry of the community, the victims and offenders continue to have central roles. Participation of the community ensures that it does not slip into the roles of the vicarious public or the neutral detached observer. The acknowledgement of the community as a victim does not trivialize the experience of *the* victim; rather it attempts to draw the victim in an empathetic embrace and help end the isolation into which victims tend to withdraw. Isolation could be a result of a hostile or indifferent community, but it can often be self-imposed by the victim because she/he may feel shame and guilt for what has happened to her/him.

---

3   I had the opportunity to observe this at close quarters. As a student in the Conflict Transformation Programme at the Center for Justice and Peacebuilding, Eastern Mennonite University, I along with other students in Howard Zehr's course on restorative justice interacted with some of the women lifers who were part of Barb Toews' restorative justice work in the Pennsylvania Prison Society.

In Jeffrey Kauffman's view most victims are in need of restorative justice as they are likely to experience not just shame, but a 'shame-guilt' complex where 'the primary object of attack is oneself, more than one's deeds' (2006, p. 228). Therefore, making the victim not feel alone is a prerequisite for giving her/him the confidence to shun the feelings of shame, humiliation and self-blame. Reaching this state of being cannot be possible overnight; therefore, the accent of restorative justice advocates is on the *process*. Importantly, as a stakeholder the community also tacitly admits to its role as an offender because the offence happened *in* it. This admission is important as it prevents further othering or demonization of the offender and helps in the reintegration of the offender into the community; the goal is reconciliation and not alienation (Zehr, 2005, p. 213).

It is this goal of reconciliation that is the rationale of the theory of reintegrative shame (Braithwaite, 1989; also see Braithwaite and Braithwaite, 2001). Inspired by the practices of the aboriginal communities, John Braithwaite proposed that while shame that ostracizes and stigmatizes the offender must be avoided, there is positive value in a shaming that compels the offender to recognize and take ownership and responsibility for the wrong done. But this shaming comes with a qualification – it should happen in a manner that does not alienate the offender from the community whose norms and rules he/she has violated. The community must assume an active role and responsibility to shepherd the offender back into its fold. Needless to say, this reintegration of the offender into the community must not compromise the needs of the victim. Research shows that participants in victim–offender conferences 'perceived others to be more disapproving, yet more reintegrative and less stigmatizing, than participants who attended court cases' (Harris in Harris and Maruna, 2006, p. 460). This argument about the restorative consequences of reintegrative shame also finds support in the works of Kauffman (2006) and Retzinger and Scheff (1996). However, there are others who view the use of shaming techniques in restorative justice as 'both risky and potentially counter-productive' (Maxwell and Morris, 2004, p. 139).[4]

Most importantly, restorative justice recognizes shame as an emotion that should not be ignored because unacknowledged shame gets 'projected on to others in a scapegoat fashion' (Harris and Maruna, p. 460). Therefore, restorative justice mechanisms – victim–offender mediation, group conferencing and circles – are particular in ensuring that the space and process are shame- and humiliation-free. A reference to the circle process is insightful as it helps us appreciate how the emphasis on restorative justice as *process* helps it to jettison humiliation from its practice. In addition to healing, the circle process is said to be a transformative experience for the participants – victims, offenders and community. Sentencing

---

4   Subsequently, reintegrative theory of shame was revised by replacing the word 'shaming' with 'shame management' (Braithwaite and Braithwaite, 2001). However, we must note that the concept of 'shame management' continues to echo the earlier premise that if assured of reintegration individuals can better manage 'feelings of shame' (Harris and Maruna, 2006, p. 460).

and peacemaking circles ensure that participants feel safe in talking about issues of 'conflict, pain, and anger' (Pranis, 2005, p. 6). Rituals play an important role here: for example, the ritual of the 'talking piece allows full expression of emotions, deeper listening, thoughtful reflection, at an unrushed pace' (Stuart and Pranis, 2006, p. 127). Promotion of mutual responsibility among the circle participants puts on them the onus to guarantee that disagreements do not close a conversation. Respect as the underlying value of the circle process ensures that participants be treated with dignity and their right to be different is honoured (Pranis et al., 2003, pp. 34–35). The tool of storytelling is crucial in this regard; therefore, it occupies a significant space in the circle process and other restorative justice mechanisms.

Storytelling as a Tool to Heal the Trauma of Humiliation

Storytelling is a 'quintessential feature' of restorative justice, a crucial tool that heals and liberates (Kay, 2006, pp. 231–232). Restorative justice recognizes that an act of crime and its consequences create contexts of humiliation for both the victim and the offender. Medical experts argue that the victims of torture and humiliation undergo similar experiences of traumatic stress (Bacoglu et al. in Luban, 2009, pp. 222–223). The restorative justice lens seeks to extricate both the victim and the offender from consequences of their respective tragedies – the vicious circle of continued victimhood or recidivism. The restorative justice 'therapy' first and foremost consists of acknowledging that the act has resulted in humiliation of the victim and the offender too experiences trauma either as a precursor to the offence or as a consequence of his/her experience with the criminal justice system (Zehr, 2011, p. 22).

This storytelling in restorative justice is different from the testimonies of witnesses, victim and offender in a retributive justice or mainstream criminal justice system. In the latter the aim is to furnish evidence, whereby the 'storyteller' is likely to be asked tough and uncomfortable questions. Recounting the event(s) in the courtroom setting often results in the victim reliving the trauma of the crime. Also, revenge is smuggled in when the prosecutor appropriates the storytelling to get a tougher sentence for the offender, so the priority in the criminal justice system is not the healing of the victim (Sarat in Kay, 2006, p. 239).

Restorative justice, on the other hand, strives to ensure that stories are not just heard but *listened* to – that is, the audience has the responsibility to set aside voyeuristic temptations and instead listen empathetically to the storyteller. Therefore, listening is not a passive act but one that requires active engagement (Kashyap, 2009, p. 456). Very often the stories need to be told and listened to several times (this is why restorative justice is a process, whose duration is contingent upon the needs of the victim and the needs and obligations of the offender). This re-storying leads to the possible transformation of the 'stories of humiliation and shame into that of stories of dignity and courage' (Zehr, 2011, p. 25).

An important aspect of this transformation is that it is usually a cathartic experience for all the restorative justice stakeholders. Theo Gavrielides terms it as 'restorative catharsis' triggered by the gift of 'restorative pain' (2013, p. 313). This pain is a gift because it is a result of 'self-reflection' and is not imposed by the state but made possible by the restorative justice nurturing of a safe space for storytelling and story-listening (p. 321). This perspective of catharsis brings to light a key strength of restorative justice. It problematizes the haloed privileging of the principle of objectivity or detached persona stance taken by the mainstream criminal justice system. The emotional experience of pain and catharsis serve to acknowledge the fact that the offence was possible because of: (a) our individual complicities; and (b) structures created or endorsed by us actively or through our silence. Therefore, the offence is not a breach of structures by an enemy from the outside but from one who is within. Thus this is an admission that the community is not just a victim but also bears the responsibility as an offender to make amends and repair broken relationships. This gift of pain is a restorative justice rite of passage that also unfreezes the stakeholders from the emotion of immobilizing guilt so that they can act upon acknowledged and informed responsibilities.

Restorative Justice and Humiliation: Learnings from New Research in Social Sciences, Psychology and Neurosciences

In this section I argue that in order to avoid a possible blurred vision, the 'changed lenses' (restorative justice) must be cleaned by new learnings (about issues like shame and humiliation) that are emerging from the fields of social sciences, psychology and neurosciences. The encouraging news is that researchers in psychology and applied sciences have of recent shown keen interest in the study of the restorative justice values (Gavrielides, 2015).

This interface helps us understand the changing nature, form and sources of social and political problems (including that of humiliation) in our rapidly changing times, where in addition to new problems there is also the persistence and repackaging of the old ones. Restorative justice must undertake this exercise for a self-evident reason, which is that understanding a problem is a prerequisite for its solution. Also, an interdisciplinary dialogue will help us understand better the strengths and limitations of restorative justice in relation to humiliation.[5]

The engagement between restorative justice and the disciplines of social science, psychology and neurosciences is crucial for three reasons. First, the social, political and economic structures of our times are growing rapidly in both complexity and scale. Restorative justice is not a quarantined practice, and the contextualizing of its concerns requires quarrying of the social science disciplines to explain the changed and changing structures. Second, restorative justice's recognition of both the psychological and structural dimensions of humiliation (and also the needs of victims and offenders) necessitate that restorative justice scholars do a critical reading of the relevant literature in the diverse fields of social sciences,

---

5   I thank Theo Gavrielides for this insight.

psychology and neurosciences. We may note that the latter two are dominated by the positivist approaches, which do not sit well with the epistemology of narratives and interpretation that is favoured by the restorative justice philosophy. However, restorative justice scholars are not averse to quantitative methods and often employ them to supplement qualitative studies (see Davies, 2008; Jahic and Kalem, 2008; Littlechild and Sender, 2010; Rossner, 2013). Third, such an engagement is a prompt for restorative justice to introspect and develop its philosophical foundations. Theo Gavrielides (2013), citing the concerns of Liz Elliot and Sir Anthony Mason among others, underlines the need for a philosophical grounding of restorative justice's normative framework (p. 313).

The reassuring insight from neurosciences and psychology is the malleability of the human mind and nature: research on brain development has led to the proposed 'cognitive behavioral treatment' to change the 'offenders' brain functioning' and 'reduce recidivism' (Vaske et al., p. 96). However, we need to be alert to the limitations of an approach that gives ontological priority to the neurobiological entity in a human being over her/his 'psychological, social and ethical' being (Kelly and Thorsborne in Gavrielides 2015). Therefore, while welcoming such research, we must note that in such arguments there is the implied denial or neglect of the key restorative justice insight and premise about the spiritual interconnectedness of human life. Therefore, the findings of approaches like affect script psychology (ASP) must not be applied discretely; ASP 'should work alongside other normative, spiritual and philosophical understandings of restorative justice' (Gavrielides, 2015). Also, in the context of restorative justice, advances in neurosciences will be useful only if the latter are open to observations and findings that emerge from social sciences. For example, social sciences can help us understand and overcome the cultural, political and social barriers/gatekeepers to the successful implementation of the 'cognitive behavioral treatment' programme.

Similarly, restorative justice cannot rely solely on its commitment and zeal to change existing mindsets and structures that inhibit its functioning. It must access the knowledge from social sciences about how these structures work in order to change them or work within them or despite them. Without this, restorative justice will remain only a palliative measure that inadvertently performs the role of co-option of dissent by bringing in the much needed restorative relief to a retributive saturated system. Successful individual instances of restorative justice inadvertently provide legitimacy to the existing system by preventing *an* offence from becoming the last straw.[6] This is not to suggest that restorative justice make the replacement of the existing criminal justice system its agenda, but restorative justice must guard against its possible (mis)appropriation.

Restorative justice scholarship's intellectual engagement with other knowledges must be a dexterous exercise so as to avoid compromise of its key philosophical principles. That is, restorative justice must retain an autonomous critical stance

---

6   I view such a role of restorative justice as akin to that of the welfare state measures in capitalist democracies.

and avoid the perils of embedded scholarship. Understanding the social context should not mean its endorsement, especially if the same has been exposed as unjust. After all, the whole point of changing lenses is to bring about a change, a restorative premised change.

Conclusion

Even though this study is still in its exploratory stages, I think it makes a confident gesture towards the claim that humiliation is a critical issue in restorative justice. Indeed the latter also has the appropriate 'mechanisms' and tools (for example, empathy, humility and respect) to deal with the problem.

Though humiliation impacts the individual's mental and emotional states of being, it should not be *reduced* to a psychological phenomenon since it is also an important instrument for maintaining order in hierarchized structures. Power is an important element in the relationship between the humiliated and the humiliator; therefore, the act of humiliation is pregnant with possibilities of resistance. History is replete with examples of how the humiliator's act results in a subsequent response by the humiliated to avenge and subvert their victimhood through acts of violence. Therefore, humiliation is not merely an emotion but a 'social practice' that is embedded in national and political discourses (Callahan, 2004, p. 201). This awareness about the individual and structural dimensions of humiliation and offence is a key strength of the restorative justice perspective.

This awareness is also a reminder that the restorative justice practice itself functions within structural constraints. Therefore, in restorative justice participating in a victim–offender conference or a circle process is not the end goal or the end of the story; it is only a stop that enables one to move forward based on reflections informed by certain ethics – the negative of a 'do no harm' and the positive of an 'empowerment'. A paradigm shift is a success only if it is reflected in both discourse and practice, but paradigm shifts are not easy, as they have to contend with vested interests (Zehr, 2005, p. 222). This is not a pessimistic or fatalistic but a pragmatic outlook that encourages one to move forward strategically and not naively. I underscore this point only to iterate the fact that the idealism of restorative justice should not be mistaken as auguring an impending doom or failure of restorative justice.

Bibliography

Baxi, U. (2007). Humiliation and justice. Retrieved from http://www.academia.edu/8155271/U._Baxi_Humiliation_and_Justice_Contribution_to_Seminar_on_Humiliation_Centre_for_the_Study_of_Developing_Societies_September_6_2002_revised_May19_2007.

Braithwaite, J. (1989). *Crime, shame and reintegration.* Cambridge: Cambridge University Press.

Braithwaite, J. and Braithwaite, V. (2001). Shame, shame management and regulation. In E. Ahmed, N. Harris, J. Braithwaite and V. Braithwaite (eds), *Shame management through reintegration* (pp. 3–70). Cambridge: Cambridge University Press.

Braithwaite, J. and Pettit, P. (1990). *Not just deserts: a republican theory of criminal justice.* Oxford: Clarendon Press.

Cairns, D.L. (1993). *Aidos: the psychology and ethics of honour and shame in ancient Greek literature.* Oxford: Clarendon Press.

Callahan, W.A. (2004). National insecurities: humiliation, salvation, and Chinese nationalism. *Alternatives*, *29*, 199–218.

Cayley, D. (1998). *The expanding prison.* Toronto: Anansi Press.

Chase, E. and Walker, R. (2012). The co-construction of shame in the context of poverty: beyond a threat of the social bond. *Sociology*, *47*(4), 739–754.

Davies, M. (2008). Monitoring and evaluation – practice and research working together: a national model. *Report of the fifth conference of the European Forum for Restorative Justice, Building restorative justice in Europe: cooperation between the public, policy makers, practitioners and researchers, Verona.* Retrieved from http://www.euforumrj.org/assets/upload/Verona_Research.pdf.

Gavrielides, T. (2013). Restorative pain: a new vision of punishment. In T. Gavrielides and V. Artinopoulou (eds), *Reconstructing restorative justice philosophy* (pp. 311–337). Burlington: Ashgate.

Gavrielides, T. (2015). Book review of Vernon C. Kelly and Margaret Thorsborne, *The Psychology of Emotion in Restorative Practice. Internet Journal of Restorative Justice.*

Gavrielides, T. and Artinopoulou, V. (2013). Prolegomena: restorative justice philosophy through a value-based methodology. In T. Gavrielides and V. Artinopoulou (eds), *Reconstructing restorative justice philosophy* (pp. 3–24). Burlington: Ashgate.

Gill, C. (2007). Achilles' swelling heart. In H. Bloom (ed.), *Homer's The Illiad* (pp. 95–108). New York: Infobase Publishing.

Gilligan, J. (2001). *Preventing violence.* London: Thames & Hudson.

Guillermo, B.C. (2013). *Shame and humiliation: a dialogue between psychoanalytic and systemic approaches.* London: Karmac Books.

Guru, G. (ed.) (2011). *Humiliation: claims and context.* Delhi: Oxford University Press.

Harris, N. and Maruna, S. (2006). Shame, shaming and restorative justice: a critical appraisal. In D. Sullivan and L. Tifft (eds), *Handbook of restorative justice: a global perspective* (pp. 452–462). New York: Routledge.

Held, V. (2003). Terrorism and war. *The Journal of Ethics 8*(1), 59–75.

Holway, R. (2012). *Becoming Achilles: child-sacrifice, war, and misrule in the Illiad and beyond.* Lanham: Lexington Books.

Hornle, T. and Kremnitzer, M. (2011). Human dignity as a protected interest in criminal law. *Israel Law Review*, *44*, 143–167.

Jahic, G. and Kalem, S. (2008). Researching attitudes towards restorative justice and VOM: comparing qualitative and quantitative approaches. *Report of the fifth conference of the European Forum for Restorative Justice, Building restorative justice in Europe: Cooperation between the public, policy makers, practitioners and researchers, Verona.* Retrieved from http://www.euforumrj.org/assets/upload/Verona_Research.pdf.

Kashyap, R. (2005). The subversion of the colonial system of humiliation: a case study of the Gandhian strategy. *Human Dignity and Humiliation Studies Conference.* Columbia University, New York.

Kashyap, R. (2009). Narrative and truth: a feminist critique of the South African Truth and Reconciliation Commission. *Contemporary Justice Review*, *12*(4), 449–467.

Kauffman, J. (2006). Restoration of an assumptive world as an act of justice. In D. Sullivan and L. Tifft (eds), *Handbook of restorative justice: a global perspective* (pp. 221–229). New York: Routledge.

Kay, J.W. (2006). Murder victims' families for reconciliation: story-telling for healing, as witness, and in public policy. In D. Sullivan and L. Tifft (eds), *Handbook of restorative justice: a global perspective* (pp. 230–245). New York: Routledge.

Kelly, V.C. and Thorsborne, M. (2014). *The psychology of emotion in restorative practice.* London: Jessica Kingsley Publishers.

Klaassen, J.A. and Klaassen, M.-G. (2008). Humiliation and discrimination. *Social Philosophy Today*, *24*, 121–129.

Kleinig, J. (2012). Humiliation, degradation, and moral capacity: a response to Hornle and Kremnitzer. *Israeli Law Review*, *44*, 169–183.

Koestenbaum, W. (2011) *Humiliation.* New York: Picador.

Lapidus, R. (2008). *Passion, humiliation, revenge: hatred in man-woman relationships in the 19th and 20th century Russian novel.* Lanham: Lexington Books.

Lateiner, D. (2007) Probe and survey: nonverbal behaviors in Illiad 24. In H. Bloom (ed.), *Homer's The Illiad* (pp. 65–94). New York: Infobase Publishing.

Lindner, E. (2006). *Making enemies: humiliation and international conflict.* New York: Greenwood Press and Praeger Publishers.

Lindner, E.G. (2009). The relevance of humiliation studies in the prevention of terrorism. In T.M. Pick, A. Speckhard and B. Jacuch (eds), *Home grown terrorism* (pp. 163–188). Amsterdam: IOS Press.

Lindner, E.G. (2010). *Gender, humiliation, and global security: dignifying relationships from love, sex, and parenthood to world affairs.* Santa Barbara: Praeger.

Littlechild, B. and Sender, H. (2010). The introduction of restorative justice approaches in young people's residential units: a critical study. Retrieved from www.nspcc.org.uk/inform.

Luban, D. (2009). Human dignity, humiliations, and torture. *Kennedy Institute of Ethics Journal, 19*(3), 211–230.

Lukes, S. (1997). Humiliation and the politics of identity. *Social Research, 64*, 36–51.

Maclehose, W.F. (2006). Aristotelian concepts of women and gender. In M. Schaus (ed.), *Women and gender in medieval Europe: an encyclopedia.* (pp. 35–36). New York: Routledge.

Mamdani, M. (2001). *When victims become killers: colonialism, nativism, and the genocide in Rwanda.* Princeton: Princeton University Press.

Mansfield, M.C. (1995). *The humiliation of sinners: public penance in thirteenth-century France.* Ithaca: Cornell University Press.

Margalit, A. (1996). *The decent society.* Cambridge, MA: Harvard University Press.

Marx, K. (1963). *The poverty of philosophy.* New York: International Publishers.

Marx, K. (1964). *Economic and philosophical manuscript.* Ed. D.J. Struik and trans. M. Milligan. New York: International Publishers.

Masters, G. (2004). What happens when restorative justice is enabled, encouraged and/or guided by legislation? In H. Zehr, and B. Toews (eds), *Critical issues in restorative justice* (pp. 227–238). New York: Criminal Justice Process.

Maxwell, G. and Morris, A. (2004). What is the place of shame in restorative justice? In H. Zehr and B. Toews (eds), *Critical issues in restorative justice* (pp. 133–142). New York: Criminal Justice Process.

Miller, W.I. (1993). *Humiliation and other essays on honor, social discomfort, and violence.* Ithaca: Cornell University Press.

Nandy, A. (1983). *The intimate enemy: loss and recovery of self under colonialism.* Delhi: Oxford.

Nashef, H.A.M. (2009) *The politics of humiliation in the novels of J.M. Coetzee.* New York: Routledge.

Nisbett, R.E. and Cohen, D. (1996).*Culture of honor: the psychology of the violent South.* Boulder: Westview Press.

O'Neill, J. (2005). Need, humiliation and independence. *Royal Institute of Philosophy Supplement, 80*(57), 73–98.

Pranis, K. (2005). *The little book of circle processes: a new/old approach to peacemaking.* Intercourse, PA: Good Books.

Pranis, K., Stuart, B. and Wedge, M. (2003). *Peacemaking circles: from crime to community.* St Paul: Living Justice Press.

Quinney, R. and Wildeman, J. (1991). *The problem of crime: a peace and social justice perspective.* Bloomington: Indiana University Press.

Retzinger, S. and Scheff, T. (1996). Strategy for community conferences: emotions and social bonds. In B. Galaway and J. Hudson (eds), *Restorative justice: international perspectives* (pp. 315–336). Monsey: Criminal Justice Press.

Reyles, D.Z. (2007). The ability to go without shame: a proposal for internationally comparable indicators of shame and humiliation. *Oxford Development Studies, 35*(4), 405–430.

Ross, R. (1996). *Returning to the teaching: exploring aboriginal justice.* Toronto: Penguin.

Rossner, M. (2013). *Just Emotions: rituals of restorative justice.* Clarendon Studies in Criminology. Oxford: Oxford University Press.

Saurette, P. (2005a). Humiliation and the global war on terror. *Peace Review: A Journal of Social Justice, 17*(1), 47–54.

Saurette, P. (2005b). *The Kantian imperative: humiliation, common sense, politics.* Toronto: University of Toronto.

Scheff, T. (2004). Elias, Freud and Goffman: shame as the master emotion. In S. Loyal and S. Quilley (eds), *The sociology of Norbert Elias* (pp. 229–242). Cambridge: Cambridge University Press.

Schott, R. (2004). Feminist rationality debates: rereading Kant. In L. Alanen and C. Witt (eds), *Feminist reflections on the history of philosophy* (pp. 101–116). Dordrecht: Kluwer Academic Publishers.

Sen, A.K. (1983). Poor relatively speaking. *Economic Articles, 35*(2), 160–175.

Sen, A.K. (1993). Capability and well-being. In A.K. Sen and M. Nussbaum (eds), *The quality of life* (pp. 30–53). Oxford: Clarendon Press.

Silver, M., Conte, R., Miceli, M. and Poggi. I. (1986). Humiliation: feeling, social control and the construction of identity. *Journal for the Theory of Social Behavior, 16*(3), 269–283.

Spivak, G. (1988). Can the subaltern speak? In C. Nelson and L. Grossberg (eds), *Marxism and the interpretation of culture* (pp. 271–313). Urbana: University of Illinois Press.

Statman, D. (2000). Humiliation, dignity and self-respect. *Philosophical Psychology, 13*(4), 523–540.

Steinberg, B.S. (1996). *Shame and humiliation: presidential decision making on Vietnam.* Montreal: McGill–Queens University Press.

Stuart, B. and Pranis, K. (2006). Peacemaking circles: reflections on principal features and primary outcomes. In D. Sullivan and L. Tifft (eds), *Handbook of restorative justice: a global perspective* (pp. 121–133). New York: Routledge.

Sutton, E., Pemberton, S., Fahmy, E. and Tamiya, Y. (2014). Stigma, shame and the experience of poverty in Japan and the United Kingdom. *Social Policy, 13*, 143–154.

Tangney, J.P. and Dearing, R.L. (2002). *Shame and guilt.* New York: Guilford Press.

Tickner, J.A. (2001). *Gendering world politics: issues and approaches in the post-cold war era.* New York: Columbia University Press.

Toews, B. (2006). *Restorative justice for people in prison: rebuilding the web of relationships.* Intercourse, PA: Good Books.

Vaske, J., Galyean, K. and Cullen, F.T. (2011). Towards a biosocial theory of offender rehabilitation: why does cognitive-behavioral therapy work? *Journal of Criminal Justice, 39*, 90–102.

Vorbruggen, M. and Baer, H.U. (2007). Humiliation: the lasting effects of torture. *Military Medicine, 172*(December Supplement), 29–33.

Walker, R., Kyomuhendo, G.D., Chase, E., et al. (2013). Poverty in global perspective: is shame a common denominator? *Journal of Social Policy*, *42*(20), 215–233.

Wolf, N. (1992). *The beauty myth: how images of beauty are used against women.* New York: Anchor Books.

Wyatt-Brown, B. (2014). *A warring nation: honor, race, and humiliation in America and abroad.* Charlottesville: University of Virginia.

Zehr, H. (1998). Justice as restoration, justice as respect. *The Justice Professional*, *11*, 71–87.

Zehr, H. (2005). *Changing lenses.* Herald Press: Scotdale.

Zehr, H. (2011). Journey to belonging. In E.G.M. Weitekamp and H-J. Kerner (eds), *Restorative justice: theoretical foundations* (pp. 21–31). New York: Routledge.

Zehr, H. and Toews, B. (2004). Closing reflections. In H. Zehr and B. Toews (eds), *Critical issues in restorative justice* (pp. 401–404). New York: Criminal Justice Process.

Chapter 8

Re-Entry Circles for the Innocent: The Psychological Benefits of Restorative Justice and Taking Responsibility in Response to Injustice

Lorenn Walker[1]

Introduction

'I heard about the circles and want to try an have one. I want to make amends with my kids. I haven't seen them for 20 years. I was a drug addict. My kids grew up in foster care. I wanna apologize to them for feeling abandoned. I was young. I got convicted for crimes I didn't commit. The judge gave me life terms with no parole', says the woman.

She smells like soap and looks like she just took a shower. Her wet dark hair is combed neatly behind her ears. She has soft brown eyes and a friendly smile. She is dressed in the prison uniform of bright orange surgical scrubs.

The woman is meeting with two facilitators[2] from Hawai'i Friends of Restorative Justice (formerly Hawai'i Friends of Justice and Civic Education), a small Hawai'i based non-profit (NGO) that developed the re-entry circle process discussed here.

The facilitators have arranged to interview Alice,[3] who is from Hawai'i and has Puerto Rican and Native American heritage. She is 37 years old in February 2010 when she is interviewed about an application she filled out several months earlier requesting a Huikahi re-entry circle.

The re-entry circle application asked her 'Expected release date', to which she replied, '(N/A – life)'. During the interview Alice explains that she has been incarcerated since she was 19 years old for alleged child abuse. She is the mother of four children. She has only seen two of them once in the past 20 years. Alice

---

1   I extend my appreciation to Paul McCold for his helpful comments on a draft of this chapter.

2   I was one of the facilitators and all references to the cases studied here concern my personal observations with the subjects' permission.

3   Alice is a pseudonym for the woman who gave her permission to write about her case. Her identity is not being revealed to protect her and her children.

would have been 17 and 18 years old during the time the offences were committed. The case against her hinged on the testimony of two of her children who would have been between the ages of 23 months and four years old when the crimes occurred, and who were ages five and six when they testified. The trial and investigation also took place shortly after the notorious Mary McMartin preschool case involving alleged sex assaults by preschool teachers in Manhattan Beach, California. The McMartin 1980s era of child abuse investigations are known for 'highly suggestive' questioning by authorities, with much learned since then about the necessary standards for questioning children (Schreiber et al., 2006, p. 35). These standards were not in place when Alice was convicted and was sentenced to over 100 years in prison.

Alice has adamantly maintained her innocence since she was charged with the offences. 'I am guilty of being a drug addict. I neglected my kids, but I didn't do the crimes', she says.

Before her trial Alice refused the prosecutor's plea bargain. The plea would have required her to spend one year in prison (of which she had already spent over six months incarcerated for the charges) and five more years on probation. She refused the plea bargain because 'I didn't do it', she says. After being found guilty by a jury, the judge sentenced her to multiple life sentences to be served consecutively as recommended by the prosecutor.

Alice lived in foster care for much of her childhood. Her mother suffered mental health and substance abuse problems. When Alice was five years old, her mother tried to kill her and her siblings. All the children were put into foster care for several years. They were reunited with their mother when Alice was about 10 years old, but their mother relapsed. After that Alice began spending time in Honolulu pool halls. When she was 12 years old she started free basing crack cocaine. When she was 13 she had her first baby, and by the time she was 17 years old she had three more children.

Twenty-two years after her conviction, Alice's public defender[4] remains 'deeply troubled' over what she believes was a 'terrible injustice'.

> Alice was in foster care. She had her first baby at age 13 and second one at 14. She was the victim of statutory rape. The system failed her. At the beginning of the case, the prosecutors offered her a plea bargain. One year in prison and five years probation. When she didn't accept it, and they got a conviction, they wanted her to spend the rest of her life in prison – like she was some kind of super predator. I still can't believe the jury convicted her and anyone wants her in prison forever. (Personal conversation, 6 January 2015, and email correspondence 12 January 2015).

---

4   Her public defender's identity is also not being revealed to protect Alice and her children's identity.

After all her legal appeals were exhausted, and there remained no hope that her conviction could be overturned, her public defender referred her case to The Hawai'i Innocence Project.

The Hawai'i Innocence Project is part of the national Innocence Project (Innocence Project, 2015). The Innocence Project works to:

> exonerate wrongfully convicted individuals through DNA and reforming the criminal justice system ... We gather extensive information about each case application, and our intake and evaluation staff researches each potential case thoroughly – and, along with our legal staff, ultimately determines whether DNA testing can be conducted and, if so, whether favourable results can prove innocence. (Innocence Project, 2015)

The Hawai'i Innocence Project accepted Alice's case and represented her. Alice's innocence, however, was not something that could be proved by DNA evidence. While her conviction remains, her sentence was eventually reduced. It is expected that she will be released from prison by 2017, after having been incarcerated for almost 25 years for crimes she insists she did not commit.

Despite Alice's experiences, she has maintained an optimistic attitude about her situation. 'I grew up in prison. I'm not afraid. I find the most out of what I have', she says (personal conversation, 17 February 2010). Alice adopted the motto of a fellow incarcerated friend: 'I may be in prison, but prison is not in me' (personal discussion during a restorative justice cognitive course conducted in the Hawai'i women's prison, 12 November 2010).

When Alice heard about the re-entry circle programme being offered at her prison, she was one of the first applicants. The circles help individual imprisoned people meet with loved ones to plan for a successful life, including finding ways to repair the harm resulting from wrongful behaviour and from their imprisonment (Walker and Greening, 2013).

Re-Entry Circles

Purposes

The re-entry circle programme in Hawai'i provides a facilitated group planning process for individual incarcerated people who meet with their invited loved ones, a prison staff member and other community or professional supporters (Walker and Greening, 2013). The re-entry circle model is being replicated in Rochester, New York (Dougherty et al., 2014), and in Santa Cruz, California (Conflict Resolution Center of Santa Cruz County, 2015).

The circle's main purposes are to assist the incarcerated person in making a detailed written plan that addresses his/her needs for a successful life in prison and after release in the community. These needs include the need for reconciliation.

Equally important, the circles are designed to help loved ones heal from any harm caused by the imprisoned person's criminal behaviour and his/her incarceration.

Description of Re-Entry Circle Process

Trained facilitators convene and conduct the circles using solution-focused language (Walker, 2013), which is goal-orientated and strength-based. Instead of focusing on problems, the solution-focused language is used to find out what people want and identifies their resources and when there are exceptions to their problems.

The primary circle recipients are the imprisoned individual and their loved ones. Secondary beneficiaries are prison staff, fellow incarcerated individuals and the community at large. Circles are held in prison or in a programme under court, prison or parole jurisdiction (for example, parole, furlough or drug treatment). A comprehensive written transition plan, which the incarcerated person chooses to follow while confined and after release, is prepared and given to the participants after the circle. Circles are ideally held early after imprisonment to begin reconciliation and to help rebuild family ties and promote healing and desistance from crime.

After the prison programme staff and incarcerated people are educated on the circle purposes, and interested incarcerated people submit a one-page application, which is given to Hawai'i Friends of Restorative Justice, an assigned facilitator contacts the prison to schedule an interview with the incarcerated circle applicant. Using solution-focused language, which invites people to take responsibility for finding solutions to their problems, and for repairing the harm caused by their criminal behaviour, the facilitator interviews the applicant (Walker, 2013). A brochure describing the process is also provided to the applicant.

A circle takes about three hours to complete and has two phases. Phase 1 focuses on the need for reconciliation, and normally addresses the harm that the confined person's criminal behaviour and incarceration have caused. Loved ones say how they were affected and what the incarcerated person might do to repair the harm. Plans for how the harm might be repaired are made. Reconciliation does not necessarily mean a repaired and restored relationship, although this often results from the circles.

Phase 2 addresses the imprisoned person's other basic needs for a positive life including identifying potential housing, transportation, employment, obtaining any necessary documents, how to spend leisure time, and maintaining good emotional and physical health. Collaboratively the group offers suggestions for how these needs might be met. Additionally, incarcerated individuals identify the specific steps that they will take in prison and back in the community to achieve their goals. A follow-up *re-circle* is also scheduled. A printed transition plan, usually about six pages, is provided to the incarcerated person and other participants several days after the circle.

Alice's re-entry circle included her sister whom she had not seen in over 10 years; the input of three of her four children (who the facilitator interviewed by telephone prior to the circle for their responses to questions, which were printed out and held on an empty chair during the circle); her stepfather's input also held on an empty chair; and a prison employee. While the author facilitated the circle, a recorder kept written notes of the group's discussion on large sheets of paper, and this information later became part of Alice's written transition plan.

Theoretical Basis for the Re-Entry Circle Planning Process

John Braithwaite's work suggested the idea for the re-entry circle (Braithwaite, 2004a), and the late Insoo Kim Berg, co-founder of solution-focused brief therapy, helped develop the process (Walker, 2010).

The re-entry circle applies public health learning principles that are inherent in both restorative justice and solution-focused brief therapy (Walker and Greening, 2013). Public health learning principles include the assumptions that '[a]ll through their life-span, individuals can learn and change their behaviour to ways more satisfactory to themselves' (World Health Organization, 1954, p. 8). These priniciples are optimistic by recognizing that people have the strength to learn 'all through their life spans'. Additionally, the public health perspective of the learning process is based on social interactions, and the 'Chinese aphorism' that individuals learn best by being actively engaged in experiences with other people and not simply by being told what they should do. Public health too recognizes that people are motivated by their goals (World Health Organization, 1954, p. 8). The effectiveness of these learning principles is well established (Bandura, 1977).

Public health learning principles are inherent in restorative justice. First, restorative justice is optimistic in terms of recognizing that individuals have the strength to actively engage in, and create the outcomes of, restorative processes. Professionals do not determine outcomes or participate for individuals in restorative practices. Professionals do not determine what individuals need, unlike other processes (for example, in legal processes where lawyers speak for clients, and judges and juries determine outcomes). Second, restorative processes are about people interacting to 'collectively identify and address harms, needs and obligations, in order to heal and put things as right as possible' (Zehr, 2002, p. 57). Finally, the goal of restorative processes is to learn and find what might help people 'heal and put things as right as possible that people learn best through their participation and personal engagement (this idea is also attributed to a 'Native American saying'; De Jong and Berg, 2013, p. 59). In solution-focused brief therapy the clients are considered to be 'the experts about their own lives' (De Jong and Berg, 2013, p. 19), not the therapists who instead are considered to be more like facilitators than counsellors. Finally, the solution-focused approach is based on social constructionism, which assumes that people construct reality in relationship to each other, and that language 'plays a central role' (Bannink, 2007,

p. 89). The solution-focused approach assumes relationships between people are key to their well-being.

There is no universally accepted definition of restorative justice (Gavrielides, 2007), but Howard Zehr's definition, which he says is 'an adaptation of Tony Marshall's definition' (Zehr, 2002, p. 71), is quoted by some of the field's most respected leaders including John Braithwaite:

> Restorative justice is a process to involve, to the extent possible, those who have a stake in a specific offense and to collectively identify and address harms, needs, and obligations, in order to heal and put things as right as possible (Zehr, 2002, p. 37). (Braithwaite, 2006, p. 2)

Zehr's notion that restorative justice practices are provided on a scale or a 'continuum' (Zehr, 2002 p. 54) explains the first clause in his restorative justice definition 'to involve, to the extent possible' (something Zehr added to Marshall's definition).

Heather Strang et al. reference Braithwaite's definition:

> "Restorative justice" is a concept denoting a wide range of justice practices with common values, but widely varying procedures (Braithwaite, 2002). These values encourage offenders to take responsibility for their actions and to repair the harms they have caused, usually (although not always) in communication with their personal victims. (Strang et al., 2013 p. 3)

Strang et al. recognize that restorative justice is provided by a 'range' of practices and that communication between parties is 'not always' a part of restorative practices.

Restorative justice is driven by values, which is reflected in the way restorative practices are applied (van Wormer and Walker, 2013). Zehr (2002) believes that '[t]he value respect underlies restorative justice principles and must guide and shape their application' (p. 36).

Two important ways in which restorative practices respect people is that individual participants speak for themselves, without professional representation, and restorative encounters are conducted privately. While restorative participants may agree to allow observers, and even have their meetings filmed for the public, restorative practices are privately, not publicly, held. Allowing restorative process participants to share in their own words and, in private, their personal information about how they have suffered harm is respectful.

Zehr references Paul McCold's (2000) continuum of restorative practices from 'fully restorative' to 'non-restorative' (Zehr, 2002, p. 55). The quintessential group participating in a 'fully restorative practice' includes the person who caused harm, the person who directly suffered the harm, each party's supporters and any other affected community stakeholders. 'Mostly' and 'partially restorative practices', may not include meetings between key stakeholders, yet these practices benefit participants, including helping harmed people to heal (Walker, 2004), and helping people who have caused harm to desist from wrongdoing (Walker, 2009).

Much of my work for almost 20 years, designing, providing and researching the outcomes of restorative practices, has been on the continuum of 'mostly restorative' practices, which do not include face-to-face meetings with unrelated 'victims' and 'offenders'[5] of specific incidents of wrongdoing.

Restorative Practices for Victims without Offender Participation

Restorative practices have been successfully provided for people harmed directly by crime who never meet with the people who committed the crimes. In 2002 the Hawai'i Friends of Restorative Justice and I collaborated with a number of state and federal agencies and NGOs to develop, provide and evaluate a restorative practice for victims who never met with offenders (Walker, 2004). The victims did not meet with those who had perpetrated crimes against them for three general reasons. One, they did not know who the perpetrators were. Most reported crimes do not result in anyone ever being arrested (United States Department of Justice, 2009. Two, sometimes victims simply do not want to meet with the offenders. Research shows between 40 and 60 per cent of victims want to meet with offenders (Umbreit et al., 2003). Finally, some offenders deny that they committed the offences, making a meeting with the victims problematic (Braithwaite, 2004b). If a victim believes an offender harmed him/her, and the offender denies it, a meeting is likely to be heated and could possibly cause re-victimization.

Restorative Practices for the Imprisoned without Victim Participation

Just as many victims do not know who committed the crimes that harmed them, many people who have committed crimes often cannot identify the victims of their crimes. Property crimes are the most frequent crimes in the USA (United States Department of Justice, 2012). Offenders commonly commit property crimes without knowing who the victims are – for example, resident of the house they burgled; owner of car they stole and so on.

Whether they know who their victims are or not, restorative practices for people in prison are beneficial. The circles provide the imprisoned with the opportunity to take responsibility for their lives, and to seek ways to reconcile and make amends with the community. Often too victims are not interested in meeting

---

5   Every effort is made to not use the labels victim and offender, which can be limiting. People are always more than what has happened to them and what they have done in their lives. The terms are only used here for clarity and simplicity.

with offenders, or no mechanisms exist for them to personally meet. Yet offenders can benefit from restorative processes and the re-entry circles.[6]

Reconciliation for the Re-Entry Circle Process

The re-entry circle process includes addressing an incarcerated person's need for reconciliation, housing and other basic needs for a successful life. For the purposes of the re-entry circle process, reconciliation does not require nor necessarily include a reconciled relationship with another person. Reconciliation for the circle participants can simply be 'the state of being reconciled, as when someone becomes resigned to something not desired' and 'the process of making consistent or compatible' (Dictionary.com, 2015).

An individual can have 'internal reconciliation'. Individuals can internally reconcile in dealing with trauma and injustices that they cannot control (Morrison, 2007, p. 94). Professor Brenda Morrison is Director of the Centre for Restorative Justice at Simon Fraser University. She says:

> I have been reflecting on the dimensions of relationships in the context of restorative justice and reconciliation for a number of years now through my PhD work (re-defining the self in self-interest) and then through my work at the Centre for Restorative Justice at the Australian National University. The Aboriginal People of the Land in Australia taught me a lot and it really struck home when I walked in the first national day of reconciliation in Australia. It was an emotionally powerful day on many levels.
>
> Now living in Canada, the work of the Truth and Reconciliation Commission and Reconciliation Canada again brought that message home to me. It really does begin with me. How am I going to show up in the world? How am I contributing (or not) to creating a world where everyone belongs, everyone feels valuable powerful and needed.
>
> We give so much of our power away in a state based society. We let our social institutions (justice, education) take care of the problems and set the direction. This breeds passive bystanders not active citizenship.
>
> So the internal work, reconciling with our own past, and who we are, and what we bring to the world, is central to this vision. (Personal email correspondence, 29 January 2015)

---

6 Another type of re-entry circle for incarcerated individuals is the *modified re-entry circle*. It is for a detained person whose loved ones do not attend, but other incarcerated supporters participate instead (Walker, 2009).

No one should resign themselves to wrongdoing and stop working for justice, but in Alice's case she had vigorously pursued and exhausted all of her legal appeals. The criminal justice system applied the rule of law, she was found guilty and her efforts to overturn the conviction were unsuccessful. Alice needed to deal with her loss and suffering, which is what restorative justice is about. It is about healing for people who have been affected by wrongdoing. No one can change the fact that they were harmed or that they harmed others. No one can wish away loss, but people can engage in restorative processes to help them deal with the suffering and pain that results from injustice.

The re-entry circle can help imprisoned people find reconciliation internally for themselves, or with others, and help them make plans for a successful life despite their imprisonment. This kind of reconciliation is proactive and solution-focused (De Jong and Berg, 2013).

The re-entry circle focuses on what to do about problems instead of focusing on why the problems exist or who is to blame for causing the problems. Solution-focused reconciliation is healing. It is consistent with Peter Block's understanding: 'Reconciliation is for me the possibility of the end of unnecessary suffering' (Block, 2008, p. 163). A person has healed when his/her suffering has ended.

By the time Alice applied for a re-entry circle, she had already spent almost 20 years in prison and had largely reconciled with the injustice of her imprisonment. When interviewed for the circle, she indicated she had reconciled with her imprisonment when she said, 'I grew up in prison. I'm not afraid. I find the most out of what I have'.

Alice said she wanted a circle in order to apologize and make amends to her children. She wanted to reconcile with them, not for the crimes that she was convicted for, but for being 'a drug addict' and neglecting them.[7] Alice recognized and wanted to reconcile with how her imprisonment harmed her children by keeping their mother out of their lives. She wanted them to know that she was sorry for any hardships and feelings of abandonment they might have suffered.

In another case, a woman's unjust imprisonment for approximately 18 months in a European immigration detention centre was addressed during a re-entry circle held there. Marie[8] was in her late twenties. She had been sex trafficked to Europe from a different continent. After several years she escaped to another country with her new spouse and their two-month-old infant. Marie and her spouse were incarcerated in immigration detention centres upon their arrival in the country because they entered without the required visas. The baby was taken away from Marie and placed in foster care while she was incarcerated. When she had her re-entry circle she was awaiting the decision of an immigration tribunal on the

---

7   Considering Alice's life course as a child, including having a mentally ill mother, being in foster care, being sexually abused and impregnated four times by age 17, her having the capacity as a teenager to be responsible for her substance abuse and child neglect is questionable.

8   Marie is a pseudonym for the woman whose identity is being protected.

family's request for asylum in the country. Marie wanted the circle to help her make a plan for her future and to address the injustice she suffered at being incarcerated and separated from her baby.

Marie had a re-entry circle with her spouse and her therapist about a year after being released from the detention centre. She described the hardship she suffered being incarcerated, including not seeing her baby who she was nursing when taken away from her, and who did not remember her by the time they were reunited.

During her circle Marie and the group openly discussed what she might do to help repair the harm she suffered. She decided it would help her to 'live a life following the advice my mother gave me' (personal conversation, 12 September 2011). Marie said that following her mother's advice is how she coped with the difficulties of being incarcerated. Her mother's advice was to 'live for someone'. At her circle, Marie decided that she would apply this advice to her daily life and continue being a good mother to her child. She also said she would continue working hard in all areas, including trying to gain asylum to stay in the country that had imprisoned her, which would help make things right for herself and for her harmed family.

Vicki Assegued, who provides re-entry circles in California, suggests that '[i]f clients have been wrongly accused, and incarcerated for a crime they are not guilty of, it could be very beneficial for someone representing the system to listen to the experience of the clients and to apologize on behalf of the system. If that is not possible, clients can still develop a plan for their future success' (personal email correspondence and conversation, 28 January 2015).

Despite not having a representative of 'the system' apologize to her, Marie said the circle process helped her deal with the suffering of having been imprisoned, and in setting her goals and making a plan. About six months after she had her re-entry circle, Marie was granted a residency permit and was living legally in the country she escaped to.

Everyone who engages in restorative practices has unique needs. What is required to make things right for some people may not be helpful for others. The circles are an example of what McCold (2004) discusses as the 'needs-based' perspective of restorative justice for both individuals and their communities of care and the community at large.

In Alice's case, her main need and focus for reconciliation concerned her children. She wanted them to know that she was sorry for not being a better parent. She was not taking the blame for the crimes she was imprisoned for, but she was taking responsibility for the problems her youthful choices caused her children. Alice wanted her children to know that she was wholeheartedly sorry that as a teenager she was not the parent she grew up to value as an adult. Instead of focusing on blame, and finding whose fault it was for her youthful decisions, the circle gave Alice, her children and everyone participating the opportunity to consider healing and how things might be made right, which is a goal of restorative justice (Zehr, 2002).

In Marie's case she needed reconciliation to deal with the injustice of having been the victim of sex trafficking and trying to reach safety in the country she fled to, but that instead imprisoned her. The harm from this included the loss of her freedom, fear of losing her family and having the bonding process with her baby disrupted (to abruptly stop nursing a baby is also physically very painful). She wanted a circle to find ways to deal with the injustice she suffered. She could not change the fact she was imprisoned, which was over, but her pain and suffering from the injustice remained. The circle gave her the opportunity to tell people what had happened – to share her pain with them – and it helped her find what she might do to end her suffering and heal.

The re-entry circle model promotes 'active responsibility', which John Braithwaite says is 'a more meaningful jurisprudence of responsibility' (Braithwaite, 2006, p. 7). 'Active responsibility means *taking* responsibility for putting something right into the future. One can be actively responsible for righting a wrong in the future without being causally responsible for the wrong in the past' (Braithwaite, 2006, p. 15; emphasis in the original).

The other important purpose of the circle is for the loved ones of the incarcerated individual to explore and discuss their needs for healing, and what their imprisoned loved one might do to help repair the harm they have suffered. Quantitative research on the outcomes of the circles for children of incarcerated parents shows that the process helps them increase healing. Healing was operationalized as the ability to move past the trauma of losing their parent and letting go of painful memories, which can be defined as forgiveness (decrease in ruminations of past trauma; Luskin, 2002) and increased optimism about the future (Walker et al., 2015).

Alice's children did not attend the circle. The three youngest children would have attended, but were unable to. All three of the children, however, were able to partially participate in their mother's circle through telephone calls with the facilitator who asked them the same questions they would have been asked had they attended. Their answers were printed out and placed in an empty chair during the circle and read aloud as the questions were asked throughout the circle process.

Alice's children all wanted her to do similar things to help them address the harm they suffered by not having her in their lives growing up. They mainly wanted her to stay connected to them, get out of prison, work and be independent after her release. Alice agreed to do these things and has continued to write them and has plans to see them after she is released from prison.

While a reconciled relationship is not always the result of the circles, the process can help people find reconciliation to address their suffering (Block, 2008). In another circle a daughter in her early twenties met with her mother, who was a substance abuser throughout the daughter's childhood. The daughter discussed how the circle helped her reconcile her pain and loss not having a mother growing up. After participating in a circle, she discussed her mother: 'I expect her to stay sober, and I now realize she may not grow as a person and she may stay selfish. So even though she's sober she hasn't really changed. So I learned that and that's all I expect. I don't expect her to be the mother I missed out on in my life and I'm okay with that now' (Walker et al., 2015, p. 344). The circle helped the daughter learn that she could expect her mother to stay sober, but she could stop expecting her mother to be more than that, and she was 'okay with that now'. Reconciliation, like the concept of forgiveness, can simply mean no longer wishing or hoping for a different past (Luskin, 2002), which can be healing and help end suffering like it did for the daughter.

Finally, the circles also provide the opportunity for incarcerated people and their supporters to consider how unrelated people, including the community at large, may have been harmed by the imprisoned person's past behaviour and imprisonment. Unrelated and unknown victims do not participate in the circles, but circles address and promote collaboration on developing ideas for what an incarcerated person could do to make amends while still imprisoned and after release. Commonly, being a law-abiding citizen and staying clean and sober are parts of the plan to reconcile and make amends with the community at large including unknown victims.

Unrelated victims do not participate in the re-entry circles, and sometimes the circle group determines there were none. If there are unrelated victims (for example, cashier who the imprisoned person pointed a gun at during a robbery), how the incarcerated person might make things right while in prison and after release is discussed and determined (for example, it was decided the imprisoned person would write an apology letter to the company that employed the cashier and that he would also stay clean and sober and law abiding, no longer robbing stores for money to buy drugs).

While the circle process was not originally designed to deal with cases like Alice's and Marie's, where incarcerated people maintain innocence and are not accountable for crimes for which they were imprisoned, these cases show that the process can provide a meaningful opportunity for people to cope with injustice.

Restorative Justice, Responsibility and Accountability

Taking Responsibility for the Future and Solutions

It is commonly said that restorative justice 'requires offenders to take responsibility for their actions and for the harm they have caused' (Van Ness and Strong, 2002, p. 50). According to John Braithwaite (2006), '[r]estorative justice as an accountability innovation has developed mostly as an experiment in re-democratising criminal law' (p. 2).

Taking responsibility in the re-entry circle process can include past behaviour, which it normally does, but always it is solution-focused, and prospective. The re-entry circles give incarcerated individuals the opportunity to be responsible for determining their goals and plans for the future with a group of their invited supporters. This future-orientated concept of taking responsibility is supported by

Brickman et al. (1982), and referred to as 'a compensatory model of responsibility, [where] individuals do not blame themselves for their problems, but hold themselves responsible for the solution to the problems' (Maruna and Mann, 2006, p. 167). Stepleman et al. (2005) conducted research to design and evaluate a measure that operationalized Brickman et al.'s (1982), compensatory model of responsibility, which supported its use as a new and effective attributional structure. The research found that there is a difference between focusing on solutions to problems and focusing on the causes of problems. What people take responsibility for (future versus past) affects their ability to cope with difficulties (Stepleman et al., 2005).

A future-orientated approach to taking responsibility is also supported by Maruna's 'desistance research' (Maruna and Mann, 2006 p. 167), which found that successful desisters' self-narratives concerned taking responsibility for solving problems, and not for past causation. Gavrielides and Worth (2014) recognize too the value of restorative justice processes for supporting desistance.

Shadd Maruna has studied how people desist from crime for his entire career. Maruna's *Making Good: How Ex-Convicts Reform and Rebuild Their Lives* (2001) is a seminal guidebook for designing effective rehabilitation programmes. Like Maruna, Insoo Kim Berg also distinguished the important difference in taking responsibility for solutions and being responsible for problems (Berg, 1998). She believed it was more helpful for people to be responsible for finding the solutions to their problems instead of insisting that they take responsibility for causing them.

Psychological Benefits of Taking Responsibility

Psychology has a long history of encouraging individuals to take responsibility for finding solutions to their problems. America's foremost psychologist, William James, 'belonged to an era that needed a more optimistic philosophy than was found in the period's social Darwinism and scientific positivism; his radical empiricism provided an ethics grounded in understanding reality as a complex of interconnected systems, founded on individual responsibility to larger communities, whether in the natural world or a global community' (Hawkins, 2011, p. 19). James believed individual cognition created reality: 'Be not afraid of life. Believe that life is worth living, and your belief will help create the fact' (James, 1912, p. 62).

William James's optimistic ideas about individuals being able to create better lives by taking responsibility for their thoughts was demonstrated by Viennese psychiatrist Viktor Frankl, who took responsibility for dealing with his unjust and highly immoral imprisonment. The Nazis imprisoned Frankl for being Jewish and he spent several years in concentration camps where members of his immediate family died (Frankl, 1997).

In recounting his concentration camp experience in *Man's Search for Meaning*, Frankl described how he and other prisoners coped with their suffering:

We needed to stop asking about the meaning of life, and instead think of ourselves as those who were being questioned by life – daily and hourly. Our answer must consist not in talk and meditation, but in right action and in right conduct. Life ultimately means taking responsibility to find the right answer to its problems and to fulfil the tasks, which it constantly sets for each individual. (Frankl, 2006, p. 77)

Frankl also said, 'those who were oriented toward the future, toward a meaning that waited to be fulfilled – these persons were more likely to survive' (Frankl, 1997, p. 97).

Frankl did not take responsibility for causing his imprisonment, but he took responsibility to find the best solutions he could to the problems his imprisonment presented. For him it was to find meaning in his experience. 'I am convinced that, in the final analysis, there is no situation that does not contain the seed of a meaning' (Frankl, 1997, p. 53).

Viktor Frankl was part of the first wave of positive psychologists, along with Maslow, Rogers and May, who believed in the human potential for personal growth. (Wong, 2014, p. 150)

Alice also never accepted responsibility for committing the crimes for which she was imprisoned, but she has taken responsibility to make amends with her children and to make a re-entry plan. She also found meaning in her prison experience. She plans to use what she learned in prison by becoming a counsellor and helping youth and others facing difficulties.

About three and a half years after she had her re-entry circle, Alice said that the process gave her hope. She said the circle helped her because 'it made me realize no matter what I choose to do, it's always a choice to make amends with myself and others, and to heal from the hurt so we can move forward in life' (personal conversation, 26 November 2014). It was in her taking responsibility to deal with the problems her children suffered due to her imprisonment that helped her cope and heal.

Frankl believed so strongly that taking responsibility for life's problems was vital for health and survival that he suggested a Statue of Responsibility be erected in the USA. He thought that it should be placed in the Pacific Ocean along the West Coast juxtaposed to the Statue of Liberty in New York (The Responsibility Foundation, 2015). According to Frankl:

Freedom is only part of the story and half of the truth. Freedom is but the negative aspect of the whole phenomenon whose positive aspect is responsibleness. In fact, freedom is in danger of degenerating into mere arbitrariness unless it is lived in terms of responsibleness. That is why I recommend that the Statue of Liberty on the East Coast be supplemented by a Statue of Responsibility on the West Coast. (The Responsibility Foundation, 2015)

There is an ongoing effort to erect the 300-foot statute along the coast of San Diego (Rodriquez, 2010; The Responsibility Foundation, 2015).

Conclusion

People imprisoned for crimes they did not commit, along with their loved ones and communities, can benefit from re-entry circles. The circles, which apply a multi-disciplinary approach using solution-focused brief therapy and public health, can help innocent incarcerated people take responsibility for finding solutions to their problems and to reconcile with the harm they have suffered.

The circles give incarcerated people an opportunity to articulate a positive self-narrative, which is important for desistance (Maruna, 2001). Additionally, research shows that desistance is more likely when two vital elements in one's life are achieved: relationships are maintained with law-abiding others, and meaningful work and activities are engaged in (Shover, 1996). Positive psychology and positive criminology (Ronel and Segev, 2015) are disciplines that can also support rehabilitation and complement restorative interventions.

An incarcerated person's loved ones too can benefit. The circles can help them find healing for their suffering caused both by any harmful behaviour, and from the loss of their loved one to prison and their absence in their daily lives.

The community additionally benefits from the re-entry circles that are likely to generate 'collective efficacy, defined as social cohesion among neighbours combined with their willingness to intervene on behalf of the common good, [which] is linked to reduced violence' (Sampson et al., 1997 p. 918). Even the most disadvantaged communities benefit when there is increased social capital, which the circles generate by bringing people together to find solutions and plan for the future:

> Communities are human systems given form by conversations that build relatedness. The conversations that build relatedness most often occur through associational life, where citizens unpaid show up by choice, rather than in large systems where professionals are paid and show up by contractual agreement. The future hinges on the accountability that citizens choose and their willingness to connect with each other around promises they make to each other. (Block, 2008, p. 178)

People who participate in circles may not gain restored relationships, but the process generates internal reconciliation and connections between people. For example, four years after contributing information for Alice's circle, one of her children, at age 25, said that the circle '[m]ade me a better person. It made me realize I play a big part in my brother and sister's lives. I have to be there for them' (personal telephone conversation, 18 January 2015).

Social growth comes with healing and with people caring about each other. The community is better off with members who plan for the future, and who reconcile with injustice. Restorative justice is recognized as a strategy to build collective efficacy in communities (Block, 2008; Bazemore, 2000), and, as John Braithwaite (2006) urges, 'we must understand that restorative justice is a wider strategy of confronting injustice in any arena where injustice occurs' (p. 2).

Restorative justice is more than only taking responsibility for past behaviours, it is also about taking active responsibility for solutions to problems. Restorative justice is a solution-focused approach. It developed in response to the failure of mainstream justice systems to deal with injustice (Zehr, 1990).

People in prison should be encouraged to take responsibility for their futures and to find solutions to their problems, which benefits everyone. More research and opportunities to study internal reconciliation, the application of mostly and partially restorative processes and how they promote desistance, and multi-disciplinary approaches with restorative justice, should be undertaken.

Bibliography

Bandura, A. (1977). *Social learning theory*. Englewood Cliffs: Prentice-Hall.

Bannink, F. (2007). Solution-focused brief therapy. *Journal of Contemporary Psychotherapy*, *37*, 87–94.

Bazemore, G. (2000). Community justice and a vision of collective efficacy: the case of restorative conferencing. In *Policies, Processes, and Decisions of the Criminal Justice System*. United States Department of Justice, Justice Programs. Retrieved from https://www.ncjrs.gov/criminal_justice2000/vol3_2000.html.

Berg, I. (1998). Dusseldorf, Germany conference workshop on *Weltkongress für Familientherapie*. Retrieved from https://www.youtube.com/watch?v=cQioE Q0tM-k.

Block, P. (2008). *Community: the structure of belonging*. San Francisco: Berrett-Koehler Publishers.

Braithwaite, J. (2004a). Emancipation and hope. *The Annals of the American Academy of Political and Social Science*, *592*(March), 79–99. Retrieved from http://www.anu.edu.au/fellows/jbraithwaite/_documents/Articles/Emancipation_Hope_2004.pdf.

Braithwaite, J. (2004b). *Restorative justice: theories and worries*. Visiting Experts' Papers, 123rd International Senior Seminar, Resource Material Series, No. 63, pp. 47–56. Tokyo: United Nations Asia and Far East Institute for the Prevention of Crime and the Treatment of Offenders. Retrieved from http://www.unafei.or.jp/english/pdf/PDF_rms/no63/ch05.pdf.

Braithwaite, J. (2006). Accountability and responsibility through restorative justice. In M. Dowdle (ed.), *Rethinking public accountability*. Cambridge: Cambridge University Press. Retrieved from http://www.anu.edu.au/fellows/jbraithwaite/_documents/Articles/Accountability_Responsibilty_2006.pdf.

Brickman, P., Rabinowitz, V.C., Karuza, J., et al. (1982). Models of helping and coping. *American Psychologist*, *37*, 368–384.

Conflict Resolution Center of Santa Cruz County (2015). Retrieved from http://www.crcsantacruz.org/restorative-justice.html#R5.

De Jong, P. and Berg, I. (2013). *Interviewing for solutions*. Belmont: Brooks/Cole.

Dictionary.com (2015). Retrieved from http://dictionary.reference.com/browse/reconciliation.

Dougherty, J., Duda, J. and Klofas, J. (2014). Evaluation of Step by Step's Restorative Transition Circles Program. Center for Public Safety Initiatives, Rochester Institute of Technology.

Frankl, V. (1997). *Viktor Frankl recollections: an autobiography*. Reading, MA: Perseus Books.

Frankl, V. (2006). *Man's search for meaning*. Boston: Beacon Press.

Gavrielides, T. (2007). *Restorative justice theory and practice: addressing the discrepancy*. Helsinki: HEUNI. Retrieved from http://www.heuni.fi/material/attachments/heuni/reports/6KkomcSdr/Hakapainoon2.pdf.

Gavrielides, T. and Worth, P. (2014). Another push for restorative justice: positive psychology and offender rehabilitation. In M.H. Pearson (ed.), *Crime: international perspectives, socioeconomic factors and psychological implications* (pp. 161–182). New York: Nova Science Publishers.

Hawkins, S. (2011). William James, Gustav Fechner, and early psychophysics. *Frontiers in Physiology*, *2*, 68. US National Library of Medicine, National Institutes of Health. Retrieved from http://www.ncbi.nlm.nih.gov/pmc/articles/PMC3185290/.

Innocence Project (2015). Retrieved from http://www.innocenceproject.org/about-innocence-project.

James, W. (1912). *The will to believe and other essays in popular philosophy*. New York: Longmans, Green, and Co. Retrieved from http://www.gutenberg.org/files/26659/26659-h/26659-h.htm.

Luskin, F. (2002). *Forgive for good: a proven prescription for health and happiness*. New York: HarperCollins.

Maruna, S. (2001). *Making good: how ex-convicts reform and rebuild their lives*. American Psychological Association: Washington.

Maruna, S. and Mann, R. (2006). A fundamental attribution error? Rethinking cognitive distortions. *The British Psychological Society*, *11*, 155–177.

McCold, P. (2000). Toward a holistic vision of restorative juvenile justice: a reply to the maximalist model. *Contemporary Justice Review*, *3*, 357–414.

McCold, P. (2004). The role of community in restorative justice practice and theory. In H. Zehr and B. Toews (eds), *Critical issues in restorative justice* (pp. 155–171). Monsey: Criminal Justice Press.

Morrison, B. (2007). *Restoring safe school communities*. Leichhardt: The Federation Press.

Responsibility Foundation, The (2015). Retrieved from http://statueofresponsibility.com/story/.

Rodriguez, A. (2010). 300-foot-tall statue in San Diego's future? Foundation seeks West Coast site for its responsibility project. *U-T San Diego.* Retrieved from http://www.utsandiego.com/news/2010/aug/26/300-foot-tall-statue-in-sa n-diegos-future/.

Ronel, N. and Segev, D. (2015). Introduction: 'the good' can overcome 'the bad'. In N. Ronel and D. Segev (eds), *Positive criminology: the good can overcome the bad* (pp. 3–12). London: Routledge.

Sampson, R., Raudenbush, S. and Earls, F. (1997). Neighborhoods and violent crime: a multilevel study of collective efficacy. *Science, 277*, 918–924.

Schreiber, N., Belllah, L., Mrtinez, et al. (2006). Suggestive interviewing in the McMartin Preschool and Kelly Michaels daycare abuse cases: a case study. *Psychology Press, 1*(1), 17–47.

Shover, N. (1996). *The great pretenders: pursuits and careers of persistent thieves.* Boulder: Westview Press.

Stepleman, L., Darcy, M. and Tracy, T. (2005). Helping and coping attributions: development of the Attribution of Problem Cause and Solution Scale. *Educational and Psychological Measurement, 65*, 525–540.

Strang, H., Sherman, L., Mayo-Wilson, E., et al. (2013). Restorative Justice Conferencing (RJC) using face-to-face meetings of offenders and victims: effects on offender recidivism and victim satisfaction. A systematic review. *Campbell Systematic Reviews, 9*(12). Retrieved from http://www.campbellcollaboration. org/lib/project/63/.

United States Department of Justice (2009). Table 25: Per cent of offenses cleared by arrest or exceptional means. Federal Bureau of Investigation, Criminal Justice Information Services Division, Crime in the United States. Retrieved from http://www2.fbi.gov/ucr/cius2009/data/table_25.html.

United States Department of Justice (2012). Property crime. Federal Bureau of Investigation, Criminal Justice Information Services Division, Crime in the United States 2012. Retrieved from http://www.fbi.gov/about-us/cjis/ucr/cri me-in-the-u.s/2012/crime-in-the-u.s.-2012/property-crime/property-crime.

Umbreit, M., Vos, B., Coates, R. and Brown, K. (2003). *Facing violence: the path of restorative justice and dialogue.* Monsey: Criminal Justice Press.

Van Ness, D. and Strong, K. (2002). *Restoring justice.* Cincinnati: Anderson Publishing.

van Wormer, K. and Walker, L. (2013). *Restorative justice today: practical applications.* Thousand Oaks: SAGE.

Walker, L. (2004). Restorative justice without offender participation: a pilot program for victims. International Institute for Restorative Practices. Retrieved from http://www.iirp.org/library/lwalker04.html.

Walker, L. (2009). Modified restorative circles: a reintegration group planning process that promotes desistance. *Contemporary Justice Review, 12*(4), 419–431. Retrieved from http://lorennwalker.com/articles/Modifiedrestorative circles12-2009.pdf.

Walker, L. (2010). Huikahi restorative circles: group process for self-directed reentry planning and family healing. *European Journal of Probation*, *2*(2), 76–95. Retrieved from http://lorennwalker.com/articles/0624C44Bd01.pdf.

Walker, L. (2013). Solution-focused reentry and transition planning for imprisoned people. In P. De Jong and I.K. Berg (eds), *Interviewing for solutions* (pp. 318–328). Belmont: Brooks/Cole.

Walker, L. (2015). Applied positive criminology: restorative re-entry and transition planning circles for incarcerated people and their loved ones. In N. Ronel and D. Segev (eds), *Positive criminology: the good can overcome the bad* (pp. 128–139). London: Routledge.

Walker, L. and Greening, R. (2013). *Reentry and transition planning circles for incarcerated people*. Honolulu: Hawai'i Friends of Civic and Law Related Education.

Walker, L., Tarutani, C. and McKibben, D. (2015). Benefits of restorative reentry circles for children of incarcerated parents in Hawai'i. In T. Gal and B.F. Duramy (eds), *Promoting the participation of children across the globe: from social exclusion to child-inclusive policies*. London: Oxford University Press.

Wong, P.T.P. (2014). Viktor Frankl's meaning seeking model and positive psychology. In A. Batthyany and P. Russo-Netzer (eds), *Meaning in existential and positive psychology* (pp. 149–184). New York: Springer. Retrieved from http://www.drpaulwong.com/viktor-frankls-meaning-seeking-model-and-positive-psychology/.

World Health Organization (1954). *Expert Committee on Health Education of the Public*. Report Technical Report Series, No. 89.

Zehr, H. (1990). *Changing lenses: a new focus for crime*. Scottdale: Herald Press.

Zehr, H. (2002). *The little book of restorative justice*. Intercourse, PA: Good Books.

Chapter 9

Trauma-Informed Rehabilitation and Restorative Justice

Judah Oudshoorn

Introduction

Even though trauma affects many prisoners, correctional processes in North America largely ignore its impact, choosing instead to overemphasize the individual psychology of offender conduct in the rehabilitative process. However, if offenders are in fact to desist from crime more attention must shift towards the healing of trauma. There is a significant body of evidence indicating that most people behind bars have experienced *individual trauma* like family violence, sexual abuse and/or poverty. Individual traumas have roots in structural or collective violence. A capitalistic economy concentrates wealth in the hands of few, giving rise to poverty for others. Patriarchal structures give permission for family violence and sexual abuse, as men are allowed to dominate women and children. Indeed, men are much more likely to be perpetrators of violence than women. Giving rise to the individual traumas in Indigenous Communities in North America are the *collective traumas* of settler colonialism: physical and cultural genocide; stolen lands and resources; and forced assimilation, which has caused a loss of languages and cultures. Indigenous offenders in Canada make up almost one quarter of the prison population, in spite of being only 3 per cent of the overall population (Sapers, 2013). Native Americans enter prisons at four times the rates of white Americans (Hartney and Vuong, 2009). The psychology of criminal conduct misses both individually and collectively caused traumas.

Conversely, trauma-informed rehabilitative approaches work towards addressing and healing individual and collective trauma. Why is healing trauma important for desistance, for ceasing criminal behaviour? Trauma is a primary cause for why offenders end up in conflict with the law in the first place. At the individual level, offenders must be accountable for their actions. Healing individual trauma helps with accountability. At the level of society, there is a need for collective responsibility to dismantle structures of violence. Nineteenth-century anarchist Emma Goldman famously said: 'Every society has the criminals it deserves'. Likewise, my former supervisor in an offender reintegration programme, 'Offenders cannot reintegrate when they were never integrated to start with'. Healing collective trauma helps create safer communities.

This chapter argues in favour of trauma-informed practices to support offender rehabilitation or desistance. To be trauma-informed means that practitioners in the field of rehabilitation: (1) understand trauma, especially how it affects a person's behaviour; (2) work towards helping people and communities heal; and (3) try to do no further harm. The chapter is divided into three parts. The first exposes some of the current problems with using a psychology of criminal conduct perspective with offender rehabilitation practices. I describe two main critiques: (1) the limits of risk assessment tools; and (2) the failure of the psychology of criminal conduct to consider the prior trauma of offenders, as well as the trauma of incarceration. In the second section I discuss some impacts of individual and collective trauma, and how trauma is a central influencing factor of offending behaviour. The third section describes trauma-informed rehabilitation. The best framework for doing rehabilitation work is by an interdisciplinary melding of restorative justice with psychological, trauma-informed perspectives.

The Psychology of Criminal Conduct: From 'Nothing Works' to … Measuring Risk

When I first heard about the plan for this book – bringing psychology and restorative justice into dialogue for the purposes of rehabilitation – I was somewhat tepid. Not quite apathetic, but lukewarm. The disciplines of criminology, which restorative justice is often placed within, and psychology already have a long disciplinary partnership. Although fruitful in some areas, rich in ideas and theory development, it has largely been impotent in correctional practice, making only a mildly positive difference in the lives of victims, offenders and others affected by crime. Somehow, in practice, it has become a rather reductionist exercise. Instead of mobilizing a broader framework, a one-size-fits-all mechanism is being used – an understanding of the psychological nature of criminal conduct for the purposes of rehabilitation.

The psychological risk assessment tool is *the* tool for this. Employed by criminal justice professionals, at least in Canada, at most phases – entry to exit – of the correctional process, its actuarial outputs shape everything about an offender's experience. Imagine an inmate named John, convicted of beating his children while drunk. A risk assessment produces the following correctional plan: family violence and substance abuse education to offset his erroneous thinking, and a maximum-security penitentiary regime to counter his long history of violence. In Canada, the Statistical Information on Recidivism (SIR) itemizes an offender's risk of reoffending, which in turn shapes the application of correctional programming, as well as the inmate's security classification (maximum, medium or minimum). In correctional literature, across North America, this is known as the 'what works' approach to offender rehabilitation, intended to counter a 'nothing works' – that offenders are incorrigible – attitude.

The 'what works' model is based on four principles: risk, needs, responsivity and professional judgement. The first says that the higher the risk, the more service an offender should receive; the second, that programming should target needs specific to an offender; the third, that the capacity of the offender to learn and to understand should be considered. Finally, some professional consideration, or override, is important when considering the above three principles. It all sounds logical. The problem is that the tools for measuring risk have very low predictive accuracy for whether an offender will commit another crime, or recidivism. Numerous meta-analyses, or studies of groups of studies, demonstrate that only 6 to 10 per cent of the variance in recidivism can be accounted for by risk assessment models (Olver et al., 2009). However, in spite of this, there is a correlation between principles of classification, determining whether an offender is low, medium or high risk, and reductions in recidivism (Andrews et al., 1990). For example, in 1990 researchers Andrews, Bonta and Hoge published an article called 'Classification for Effective Rehabilitation: Rediscovering Psychology'. In it they track a number of studies that are able to link risk categories (low, medium, high) with effective prediction of recidivism; that is, those assigned a low risk label were in fact much less likely to reoffend, while the opposite held true for the high risk. Notice, though, the shift from predicting future *individual* behaviour (that is, one offender) to *group* behaviour (that is, high risk offenders). Sociologists Eric Silver and Lisa L. Miller (2002) clarify this:

> By focusing on the aggregate probability of failure [recidivism] associated with more or less homogenous population subgroups, the actuarial model avoids the pitfall of attempting to predict the actual behavior of any one individual. Rather, the model estimates the probability that individuals with a certain configuration of risk markers will engage in the outcome behavior. (p. 143)

Over the past few decades the psychology of criminal conduct proponents, especially Donald A. Andrews and James Bonta in Canada, have contributed an impressive body of work (see, for example, Andrews and Dowden, 2008; Andrews and Bonta, 2010). The value of this research has been in matching programming with those most in need of it. Unfortunately, while not surprising, human behaviour is rather unpredictable. There are two problems with why a psychology of criminal conduct approach does not work: first, it fails to capture the complexity of human identity, and how it is shaped by social context, particularly traumas experienced by offenders; second, it fails to account for its own context – that is, risk assessment approaches, although bent towards rehabilitation, are actually fulfilled in a punishment context, the prison.

Risk Assessment Misses Offender Trauma(s)

The research on prior trauma in offender populations is fairly consistent: many people who end up in conflict with the law do so because of trauma. Trauma is any experience that overwhelms a person's ability to cope. Typically, in the moment and beyond, the person believes that his/her life is over. Although certain experiences are more likely than others to cause trauma, like instances of domestic violence and sexual abuse, or large-scale situations like settler colonialism, slavery, war and natural disasters, it really is the person's experience of the event that will determine whether he/she is traumatized. In the words of trauma expert Judith Herman (1997), '[a]t the moment of trauma, the victim is rendered helpless ... traumatic events overwhelm the ordinary systems of care that give people a sense of control, connection, and meaning' (p. 33). Studies of young offenders consistently show that close to 90 per cent of young offenders have experienced at least one trauma; most commonly, domestic violence, neglect and sexual abuse are cited as the causes of trauma (Ford et al., 2012). Both adult male and female offenders are twice as likely as the general population to have suffered physical or sexual abuse growing up (Bureau of Justice Statistics, 1999). On this topic, researchers Natalie Anumba, David DeMatteo and Kirk Heilbrun (2012) say, '[b]oth male and female inmates commonly experience violent victimization such as physical and sexual assault, but more males report being physically assaulted by strangers. Females have reported higher rates of sexual assault by relatives and strangers, physical assault by intimate partners, and emotional abuse' (p. 1205). Another large study of over 300 adult male inmates in a medium-security facility in New York, USA, found that almost 70 per cent had experienced some form of childhood victimization before the age of 12 (Weeks and Widom, 1998).

Furthermore, traumas imposed by the structures of settler colonialism on Indigenous Societies in North America have created large-scale intergenerational traumas. In Canada, for example, the toxic combination of many factors rooted in settler colonialism have contributed to collective trauma: widespread cultural and some physical genocide; stolen land; treaties not honoured by settlers; residential schools that sought to destroy Indigenous languages, cultures and family systems; a reserve system that corralled Indigenous Communities from traditional lands into small mostly unusable plots; the forcible removal of a high percentage of Indigenous children into foster care; colonial laws like the Indian Act that in the past kept Indigenous Peoples captive to reserves, and banned traditional practices, and still today control most aspects of their lives (Anaya, 2014). Although Indigenous Peoples have survived – and in many ways, thrive – rates of poverty and poor health outcomes among this group are high. Today, Indigenous Peoples are dramatically overrepresented in Canadian and American prisons.

Similar overrepresentations apply to other marginalized groups. It applies to black Canadians, especially those from neighbourhoods identified as at-risk (Sapers, 2013). Furthermore, one cannot talk about incarceration in the USA without speaking to mass incarceration of African American and Latino people. The Sentencing Project in the United States reports that while being 30 per cent of the overall population, people of colour represent close to 60 per cent of prison inmates (The Sentencing Project, 2014). One in three black men will likely serve time behind bars at some point in their lifetime (Bonczar, 2003). None of this can be divorced from a history of slavery, Jim Crow laws and racism in the USA – the structural violence of yesterday, carries on in a different form today (Alexander, 2010). Canada and the USA were founded on beliefs of white supremacy, which still reverberate today.

Overrepresentation also applies to people with mental illness, and people living in poverty (Shields, 2013). Citing the work of the Office of the Correctional Investigator in Canada, policy analyst Roslyn Shields (2013) from the Centre for Addiction and Mental Health in Toronto says, '36% of federal offenders were identified at admission as requiring psychiatric or psychological follow-up, and 45% of male inmates and 69% of female inmates received institutional mental health care services … the overrepresentation of people with mental illness in the criminal justice system is often referred to as the "criminalization" of mental illness' (p. 2). Whether trauma is individually or socially caused, whether it affects a single person or an entire group, offenders' lives are ripe with trauma.

How does a psychology of criminal conduct deal with trauma? It doesn't. When a male (non-Indigenous) inmate enters the correctional system in Canada the SIR is used to classify his risk category. It measures 15 items – for example, previous incarceration, age at first adult conviction and marital status at most recent admission (Nafekh and Motiuk, 2002). None of the 15 items accounts for the trauma. Rehabilitative programmes then use information from the SIR to direct an offender along a correctional plan, or to formulate what work they need to do while they are being monitored. There are many criticisms of a psychology of criminal conduct approach: how it individualizes responsibility and ignores social influences (Chancer and Donovan, 1994; Jenkins, 2009); how it ignores racism and other disparities in the justice system; that risk assessment might be a tool for politically motivated control of disadvantaged populations (Chan and Rigakos, 2002; Pratt, 2001; Robert, 2001; Zinger, 2004); or, as stated earlier, whether risk assessment tools are valid or accurate enough (Olver et al., 2009; Baird, 2009). Although statistically significant, risk assessment models are only able to capture a small amount of the variance in why offenders reoffend. Fundamentally, risk assessment is only a partial diagnosis of the problem of crime and fairly inadequate at pointing in the direction of a cure. Back in 1980, David Rothman in *Conscience and Convenience: The Asylum and Its Alternatives in Progressive America* warned about the limitations of psychological models in relation to the work of corrections: 'In the prison, as in probation and in the mental hospital, most attention went to diagnosis because psychiatrists remained uncertain of how to translate their understanding of the deviant into specific recommendations for cure. For all their allegiance to a medical model, they had no medicine to prescribe' (p. 125).

Risk Assessment Misses the Trauma(s) of Incarceration

The second major critique of risk assessment is that it fails to account for its own context; that is, risk assessment happens within a punitive, carceral environment. More awareness – or acknowledgement – of this must be incorporated into correctional practices. Why? Incarceration damages human beings. It is trauma-inducing. Mika'il DeVeaux, himself a former inmate, now a professor and researcher, highlights the harmful effects of prison in an article titled 'The Trauma of the Incarceration Experience' (2013). He says, '[t]he experience of being locked in a cage has a psychological effect upon everyone made to endure it. No one leaves unscarred ... some literature suggests that people in prison experience mental deterioration and apathy, endure personality changes, and become uncertain about their identities' (pp. 257, 259). DeVeaux goes further to describe the incredible difficulty offenders have in trying to reintegrate, to desist and to be rehabilitated after prison because of this scarring.

The result is that prison is criminogenic, or crime causing. Lynne Vieraitis and Tomislav Kovandzic from the University of Texas, along with Thomas Marvell of Justec Research (Vieraitis et al., 2007), tracked 28 years (1974–2002) of data across 46 States in the USA to determine whether prison had a criminogenic effect. In discussing their findings they say: 'our analyses indicate that increases in the number of prisoners released from prison seem to be significantly associated with increases in crime. Because we control for changes in prison population levels, we attribute the apparent positive influences on crime that seem to follow prison releases to the criminogenic effects of prison' (Vieraitis et al., 2007: p. 614). The obvious question is 'why' – why would prison make things worse? The theory put forward by these researchers is that prison life causes trauma because it 'interferes with inmates' capacity for power and control over their lives', making the transition to life on the outside difficult. In a poem that I often cite on topic of incarceration and trauma, written by retired Judge Dennis Challeen (1986), he captures the topic like this: 'We want prisoners to be responsible, so we take away all their responsibilities ... We want them to take control of their lives, own their problems and quit being a parasite, so we make them totally dependent on us'. Vieraitis et al. also suggest that incarceration stigmatizes offenders, impacting their abilities to secure future housing and employment. Other researchers have taken this discussion further, exploring other traumatic components of incarceration on people.

In a book titled *The Effects of Imprisonment*, edited by criminologists Alison Liebling and Shadd Maruna (2005), psychologist Craig Haney argues that individual human behaviour is dramatically shaped by social contexts, and therefore the powerful, negative effects of incarceration must be taken more seriously. In his words:

> [t]he problems of crime and violence – formerly viewed in almost exclusively individualistic terms – are now understood through multi-level analyses that grant equal if not primary significance to situational, community and structural variables ... Prison behaviour, including the way we understand the effects of incarceration, must be understood through the lens of this new conceptual framework ... Prisons environments are themselves powerful and potentially damaging ... The long-term effects of exposure to powerful and destructive

situations, contexts and structures means that prisons themselves can act as criminogenic agents – in both their primary effects on prisoners and secondary effects on the lives of persons connected to them. (Haney in Liebling and Maruna, 2005, pp. 77–78)

The first prison in the USA was built in the 1770s, while in Canada the first one opened in 1835. Although intended to be more humane than the pillory or public hanging (Johnston, 2004), prisons were anchored in a retributive worldview. Incarceration was and is primarily about punishment. Philosophers – among others in society – have long argued in favour of the moral worthiness of punishment. For example, Immanuel Kant proposed that for the sake of freedom, the guilty must be punished (Rauscher, 2012). However, since the days of Kant other justifications for prison have emerged, like deterrence and rehabilitation. Prisons are intended to provide the right amount of punishment to specifically deter offenders from future behaviour, and generally deter others from committing crime. Prisons are to be places of reform, doing the work of rehabilitating criminals. Today, there are multiple paradigms at work in the correctional system.

I would argue that punishment dominates, if not overwhelms, the perspectives of deterrence and rehabilitation. Correctional systems are really about punishment, about inflicting pain on offenders. Even where the correctional approach is community-based, research shows that punishment often trumps rehabilitative intentions. For example, a study of offender experience in community-based batterer programmes by Buchbinder and Eisikovits (2008) found that offenders experience them as part of the punishment for their wrongdoing. This led the researchers to postulate that whatever paradigm dominates also overpowers. Punishment of guilt is determined to be the one – usually unquestioned – moral obligation of society (Brodeur, 1992). A psychology of criminal conduct perspective fails to recognize the harms of incarceration – how a retributive approach undermines offenders' capacities for rehabilitation.

In the next section I will discuss the impacts of trauma and how it influences offending behaviour. The purpose is to demonstrate why rehabilitative practices must be trauma-informed.

Impacts of Trauma

Asking For It
by Judah Oudshoorn

marching. ten to two, or is two past ten.
onwards.
from the curb and back.

it's not a drop, nor a precipice, an edge, even a cliff.
but a step. take it.

whirls around, wind like extinguished candles.
hope like thunder, rumbling on.

heartbeat is a flush.
all spades.
but not for digging, for building.

this is it.
one foot in front of the other. go.

but the moment has passed.
tick.

but the feelings have not.
tock.

life moves.
it packs its things. constantly.

"that child, he never listens"
"why won't he clean his room, do his homework, get off the computer!"
"he's doing it on purpose, those looks, those glares, those sighs"
"he's trying to provoke me"
"his shoes in the hall, his bag on the table, the C's on his report"

"you're a slob!"

"fuck you dad!"

"what's THAT?"

it's over.
a long sleeve shirt won't cover bruised eyes.
face a flush. it's clubs.
with broken hearts.
it's over.

but the feelings are not.

inside, cauldrons brew.
from mind, to gut, to gut, to mind. and back.

a volcanic mix.
the kind that extinguishes civilizations.

next eruption will be the end.
or will it be the first?

cry for help.

it's not a drop, nor a precipice, an edge, even a cliff.
but a step. take it.

In order to understand the importance of a trauma-informed perspective to desistance, it is necessary to grasp the impacts of trauma. The poem that I wrote is meant to highlight how traumatic parts of a person's past tend to catch up with him/her in a way that impacts the present day. To sketch out the impacts of trauma I'd like to expand on the fictitious story of John from the section above, 'The Psychology of Criminal Conduct'. Although I am making it up, the story is representative of research evidence, as well as my personal experience counselling men who have used violence. By examining John's life history I am not minimizing harmful behaviours, nor avoiding the need for people who use violence to take responsibility. I am trying to explain why men use violence, so as to stop cycles of abuse.

For the following scenario, imagine that you are a counsellor, working with John and other men who are mandated to attend a group for men who have used violence. During the group, John shares parts of his childhood. He recalls – in bits and pieces – some instances of physical violence directed towards him. He shares physical pain: about being five years old, accidentally waking his dad up from a hangover sleep on the basement couch; his dad reacting by knocking him over and dragging him upstairs by his feet. John explains that after that time he was very, very careful not to disturb his dad, in any way, in the future. He shares emotional pain: his embarrassment of having a friend over as a preteen and his dad stumbling in from work, drunk, yelling at his mom for some food. Another time, rather many times, he talks about sitting alone, waiting after school for his dad to pick him up. Teachers would wave goodbye, until the schoolyard and building were abandoned. Eventually, John would walk home, alone. He shares more stories of feeling alone: his dad never came to parent–teacher interviews at school and rarely observed any of his extracurricular activities. He shares watching how other children interact with their dads. His surprise that they would talk to their children – even hug them – things John's dad never really did. He shares observing intimate partner violence between his parents: his dad once held his mom by the throat after a particularly heated argument; another time, his dad put out a cigarette on his mom's leg, after she called him 'good for nothing'. He shares his dad's version of tough 'love': a belt that he kept in his workshop to teach Johnny 'respect'. Usually the days after he was taught this 'respect' he had to wear long clothes to school to cover up cuts and bruises. On days after beatings, he was either completely lost in space, in his own mind, or would get into fights with anyone and everyone, teachers, other students, even the hapless crossing guard. The stories go on. He shares his confusion: trying to make sense of it. He can't. John doesn't characterize what happened to him as violence, or even wrong, more matter-of-fact, as 'the way it was back then'.

Understanding Trauma

It is likely that John has been traumatized by his father's violence. Howard Zehr (2001), a restorative justice professor who has worked for many decades with victims of serious crime, explains that the experience of trauma fundamentally undercuts a person's capacity to feel safe, to feel a sense of control and to feel like life has meaning: 'The experience of violence, then, calls into question our most fundamental assumptions about who we are, whom we can trust, and what kind of world we live in. The core trauma of victimization can be called the "three d's": disorder, disempowerment, disconnection' (p. 189). Witnessing the abuse from John's dad towards his mom would be enough to cause trauma, let alone all his other experiences of his dad's abuse.

The core impacts of trauma are multiple: problems regulating emotion and arousal; alterations in consciousness and memory; damage to self-concept, disruptions in cognitive capacities; mental health challenges like anxiety, depression and post-traumatic stress disorder; relationship problems; and alterations in systems of belief (Stien and Kendall, 2004; van der Kolk et al., 2007). In John's story there is evidence of cognitive, emotional, relational and physical harms. Survivors of childhood abuse often blame themselves: John might explain away the violence by saying, 'if I hadn't have woken up my dad, he wouldn't have dragged me upstairs by my feet'. Even after a childhood full of violence John describes it as normal, almost flippantly, as if his status quo was *the* status quo of parenting for the time period. The more survivors blame themselves, the more their shame increases. John might think, 'I must be a bad person' for this to happen to me. Trauma expert Judith Herman (1997) says that shame is a core impact of trauma: 'shame is a response to helplessness, the violation of bodily integrity, and the indignity suffered in the eyes of another ... to imagine that one could have done better may be more tolerable than to face the reality of utter helplessness' (pp. 53, 54). The core of a person's identity – how he/she sees himself/herself – is disturbed by trauma. Judith Herman (1997) describes this identity disruption as losing a 'basic sense of self', which in turn affects how a person relates to others (p. 52).

Trauma Affects How People Relate to Others

Attachment theory is helpful for explaining the relational impacts of trauma. Initially developed by John Bowlby, and later Mary Ainsworth, attachment theory argues that the capacity for human beings to learn to relate well with others is founded in early childhood (especially age zero to two), by the quality of relationships with caregivers (Bowlby, 1969, 1988). A secure sense of self, in relation to others, results when caregivers offer a stable base from which to explore the world (Bowlby, 1969, 1988). Insecurity and anxiety arise when a caregiver is consistently unavailable to a distressed child (Bowlby, 1969, 1988). When a caregiver is responsible for violence, as in the story of John, the child's ability to trust others is damaged. This can have lifelong impacts:

> Trauma impels people both to withdraw from close relationships and to seek them desperately. The profound disruption in basic trust, the common feelings of shame, guilt, and inferiority, and the need to avoid reminders of the trauma that might be found in social life, all foster withdrawal from close relationships. But the terror of the traumatic event intensifies the need for protective attachments. The traumatized person therefore frequently alternates between isolation and anxious clinging to others. The dialectic of trauma … results in the formation of intense, unstable relationships that fluctuate between extremes. (Herman, 1997, p. 56)

Research has consistently demonstrated that boys who witness or experience domestic violence are at greater risk of perpetrating it in future than those who do not (Narayan et al., 2013; Cunningham and Baker, 2007). From the perspective of attachment theory this makes sense. In fact, psychologists Donald Dutton and Katherine White (2012), in their extensive research on the topic of intimate partner violence, have found that the most reliable predictor of perpetration is attachment insecurity in the perpetrator.

The field of psychology has added some important texturing to the complex topic of violence. Research explains shame as being the mediating, or influencing, factor for why some people who are hurt, hurt others. Not only is attachment disrupted, victimization often leaves a survivor feeling ashamed. James Gilligan (2001), a psychiatrist who has worked with very violent offenders in the US penitentiary system, says, 'the basic psychological motive, or cause, of violent behaviour is the wish to ward off or eliminate the feeling of shame and humiliation – a feeling that is painful, and can even be intolerable and overwhelming – and replace it with the opposite, the feeling of pride' (p. 29). Violent offending is symptomatic of a deeper troubled state. It communicates something about the person who uses it. It communicates something of their life experiences, context and ultimately how they see themselves in relation to others.

In response, the criminal justice system assesses risk and incarcerates the convicted offender. Ignoring prior trauma, and adding more trauma and shame in the process of imprisonment, simply adds difficulty instead of ease to desistance. Studies have found prison to have a 'boomerang' effect – an increase in the odds of intimate partner violence post-incarceration (Dugan, 2003). Prison often reinforces some of the negative ways of relating to others that it is attempting to ameliorate. The challenge is to adopt a different perspective, a healthier way of doing justice that pays closer attention to root causes, and helps offenders heal, while not losing sight of meaningful consequences or accountability.

A Restorative Justice Framework that is Trauma-Informed

One way of bringing together the spheres of psychology and restorative justice, for offender rehabilitation, is applying a restorative justice framework that is trauma-informed. Restorative justice provides a framework for desistance, while psychological understandings of trauma can enrich it. As stated earlier, most offenders who come into conflict with the law have experienced some form of trauma in their lives, whether it is individual – like family violence or sexual abuse – or collective – like colonialism or patriarchy. Processes of desistance, in order to be more meaningful and effective, must consider trauma. In *The Little Book of Restorative Justice*, one of the founders of the restorative justice movement, Howard Zehr (2002), suggests that offenders have four needs if they are 'to assume their responsibilities, to change their behavior, to become contributing members of our communities': accountability, personal transformation, support for integration into the community and, possibly, temporary restraint (pp. 16, 17). Zehr describes each as follows:
Offenders need from justice:

1. Accountability that addresses the resulting harms, encourages empathy and responsibility, and transforms shame.
2. Encouragement to experience personal transformation, including healing for the harms that contributed to their offending behaviour, opportunities for treatment for addictions and/or other problems, [and] enhancement of personal competencies.
3. Encouragement and support for integration into the community.
4. For some, at least temporary restraint. (p. 17)

Zehr's four needs can be used as a restorative justice framework for trauma-informed rehabilitation.

Accountability

The task of desistance is moot without helping offenders understand the impacts of their actions. Restorative justice is fundamentally about responsibility-taking. What are the obligations of offenders? In other writing, I suggest it is a four-step process:

1. I did it.
2. It was wrong.

3. I will make amends.
4. I will get the support necessary to change. (Oudshoorn, 2015)

The first two points are about acknowledgement. Victims want offenders to admit that they did the crime and that it was wrong. 'I did it' casts any doubt aside that the offender is responsible for the crime. 'It was wrong' is recognition that crime hurts people and relationships. For most crimes, there are no excuses – regardless of a traumatic life history – for hurting another. Mark Yantzi (1998), a founder of the modern restorative justice movement, writes about offenders taking responsibility in *Sexual Offending and Restoration*. He claims that acknowledgement without excuses by offenders can help survivors heal. One survivor of sexual abuse, named Alexandra, who shared some of her experience in his book, says:

> I do not want to hear that my abuser couldn't help what he did because he was crazy, hurting, or whatever. I feel that these comments negate or invalidate my pain and experience. I can now look at life histories as causal factors in abuse, but I didn't want to hear about it when I was struggling to survive. I felt my abuser was being left off the hook. Yes, he had a rough life, but he still had no right to do what he did, and he is responsible for his behaviour. (p. 104)

One of the tragedies in the case of sexual abuse is that survivors are so often doubted, which compounds their trauma. Offenders need to own their behaviour to help in the healing process.

The next step is, where possible, for an offender to make amends. Sometimes there are practical ways an offender can do so – some form of restitution. Often in violent crimes, the best way is for offenders to do their utmost to put themselves in the shoes of the victim(s), to develop empathy. Alan Jenkins (2009), who has spent many years working with violent offenders, argues that an offender needs an accountability process that supports other awareness, or examining 'otherness', a movement beyond the self (p. 40). Once offenders start to understand the impact of their actions, they will realize they must change their behaviour.

A shift in consequences from the risk focus of criminal justice to the accountability of restorative justice puts an emphasis on taking responsibility. Instead of classification and containment, restorative justice, as Jenkins (2009) argues, puts a focus on the ethics and values of an offender – how the offender understands their choices in the context of who they want to be. The importance of this shift cannot be understated. A risk focus highlights deficits, everything that is wrong with a person. A move towards values and identity is a strengths-based perspective. In a compelling work, *Making Good: How Ex-convicts Reform and Rebuild Their Lives*, Shadd Maruna (2001) argues for the need for offenders to be able to reconstitute their identity in order to be able to desist from crime. He suggests that those who desist are able to 'make good', or find a 'redemption script [that] allows the person to rewrite a shameful past into a necessary prelude to a productive and worthy life' (p. 87). In his research with ex-offenders Maruna has found that what is most needed is a 'generative' script; that is, as opposed to degenerative, or narratives that contribute to breakdown, generative ones allow the ex-offender to translate experiences into ways that help others. According to Maruna (2001):

> Generative pursuits seem to address all of these needs in the lives of desisting interviewees:
>
> • Fulfilment: Generative roles can provide an alternative source of meaning and achievement in one's life.
> • Exoneration: By helping others, one relieves his or her own sense of guilt and shame.
> • Legitimacy: The penitent ex-offender who tries to persuade others not to offend is a well-known and established role in society.
> • Therapy: Helping others actually helps the ex-offender maintain his or her own reform efforts. (pp. 118, 119)

Of course, this begs the question: how can desistance practices best support this type of process?

Returning to Alan Jenkins: he claims that practitioners need to be careful about uses, or more specifically, misuses of power. Those who intervene must undergo a parallel journey with the client, measuring their own use of power to ensure they are not being overly coercive to clients. His concern is that misuses of power are violent, a violation of another's autonomy. In order for clients to cease violence they must be treated non-violently (Jenkins, 2009). As this is accomplished with offenders, Jenkins claims that the values that give rise to abusive behaviours can be challenged. Jenkins' proposed framework runs counter to the trauma of criminal justice practices like imprisonment. Fundamentally, from a restorative justice perspective, offender accountability is best fostered within a context of support. This brings me to Howard Zehr's second point about offender needs: personal transformation.

Personal Transformation

Personal transformation is about getting at the root causes of offending behaviours, by helping an offender understand 'why' they committed a crime. Trauma-informed restorative justice for rehabilitation means supporting an offender to heal from his or her own prior traumas. Trauma shapes identity and in turn influences how a person relates to others. In an autobiographical account, *So Youth Think You Know Me*, ex-offender Allan Weaver (2008) shares his life journey, from being a young offender to desisting from crime. His childhood was characterized by family violence. He describes how this left a lasting impression on him; 'The vision of my maw being beaten burned like a hot poker into my memory every day for some time afterwards as I relived every blow, every part of the horrid scene. I knew even then that my life could never be quite the same again' (pp. 34–35). Allan was disruptive in school, and later used alcohol and violence, carrying forward some of what he had experienced as a boy. The story of Allan Weaver signals how hurting people are prone to hurting others. Franciscan Priest Richard Rohr says that trauma that is not transformed is transferred. Desistance processes that support personal transformation are needed to break cycles of violence. Being trauma-informed means, first, establishing safety; second, mourning the effects of trauma; and third, promoting resilience.

After trauma, the primary task of healing is to help establish safety for the survivor (Herman, 1997). Trauma has a way of consistently surfacing, or reminding the survivor of its presence, even when it is not wanted. For example, from the fictitious story of John, he might be reminded of being dragged up the stairs every time he walks up a set of stairs, disorientating him, and causing him to lose track of where he is going. Or, John might flashback into the past every time he smells body odour because it reminds him of his father's sweaty state whenever he was beaten. John's senses might work against him, making him live in a constant state of hypervigilance: always in fear that his life is at risk, even when it is not. To work towards safety, survivors must be listened to, their stories validated. Judith Herman (1997) calls this part trauma recovery remembrance and mourning – '[i]n the second stage of recovery, the survivor tells the story of trauma. She tells it completely, in depth and in detail. This work of reconstruction actually transforms the traumatic memory, so that it can be integrated into the survivor's life' (p. 175). The process of telling allows a survivor to gain mastery over his/her story, which in turn reduces flashbacks, anxiety and fear. As the person gains control he/she is then better able to relate to others (Herman, 1997).

Restorative justice interventions have arisen in part because of a concern for better treatment of people who have committed crime. Without minimizing harm, the concern is that labelling people as 'criminals', 'offenders' or 'batterers' and only treating them as such we are instilling a sense of worthlessness in people that remains with them. According to social theorists Peter Berger and Thomas Luckmann (1966), the 'self cannot be adequately understood apart from the particular social context in which they [sic] were shaped' (p. 50). The more forceful – or harmful – the institution of punishment becomes, the more likely an offender is to reify, or become entrenched, in the symbolic language – 'batterer', 'monster', 'violent', 'perpetrator' – of his/her identity. Which is why those from a restorative justice perspective often use language like 'men who use abuse' or 'men who have perpetrated intimate partner violence'. The terms are more cumbersome, but deliberate. The intention is to create a trustworthy, respectful way of relating to an offender. In a paper produced by the Institute for Research and Innovation in Social Services titled 'How and Why People Stop Offending: Discovering Desistance', scholars Fergus McNeill, Stephen Farrall, Claire Lightowler and Shadd Maruna (2012) say about desistance and relationships: 'Desistance can only be understood in the context of human relationships; not just relationships between workers and offenders (though these are important) but also between offenders and those who matter to them' (p. 9).

By starting from a place of respecting the humanity of offenders, we can help them heal from trauma. This isn't only a humanitarian exercise, but also about community safety. When offenders are allowed to heal, communities become safer places. What I am proposing mirrors what is known about effective desistance processes. A healthy process of desistance allows for complexity, addressing both the harms that offenders have perpetrated, and ones done to them (McNeill et al., 2012). Desistance that works emphasizes an individualized process that increases the capacity of individual offenders to develop personal competencies, through a strengths-based approach (Maruna and LeBel, 2009; McNeill et al., 2012). Although a relatively new idea – bringing together psychological understandings of trauma under a restorative justice framework – others before me have made a similar proposal. In an important article in the *Dalhousie Law Journal*, titled 'Trauma-Informed Approaches to Law: Why Restorative Justice Must Understand Trauma and Psychological Coping', legal scholar Melanie Randall and psychologist Lori Haskell (2013) argue that justice responses can be improved by 'an enhanced appreciation of the complexities of human psychology' (p. 531). Randall and Haskell emphasize that justice should be done in the context of a healing relationship, one that fosters resilience in both victims and offenders:

> It is well recognized by experts in the field, that the most effective and best trauma treatments and approaches to healing trauma take a strengths-based approach to working with traumatized people, an approach which expressly draws out, identifies, and builds on people's abilities and positive attributes ... Recognizing and promoting resilience, therefore, is also a fundamental component of effective trauma-informed work. (p. 509)

Resilience is the capacity for a person to be able to deal with adversity. It is an important goal for trauma-informed desistance with individual offenders and their communities.

Community Integration

For too long, correctional systems in North America have ignored collective traumas. Rehabilitative practices can no longer be only about individual offenders. Society needs to be rehabilitated. What emerges as one adopts a trauma-informed framework of restorative justice are the issues of colonialism and racism. Whether it is embracing decolonizing practices towards Indigenous Peoples or truly acknowledging how mass incarceration has simply replaced enslavement of African American people in the USA, it is time for correctional systems to be actively involved in social justice practices. An inmate whose poverty is the primary influencing factor behind his/her criminality does not need cognitive restructuring, as a risk assessment might demand; he/she needs a job and a home.

Someone who breaks the law because of a mental health challenge, or an addiction, cannot be 'educated out of it' without the proper support. Cognitive-behavioural programming designed to address risk does nothing to honour treaties, return lands or compensate for residential school experiences of an Indigenous inmate.

Some might argue that these are problems of law – that law needs to change in order to avoid casting its net unjustly. Others might say that these are social problems – issues that governmental policy makers or non-governmental organizations should resolve. However, I would argue that since correctional systems in North America are a multi-billion dollar industry, they are not simply a basin that collects the tap water of law, or any run-off from society. Corrections are a valve, responsible for public safety by caring for offender populations. How this valve is turned will have a dramatic impact on community safety. The offending behaviour – the male violence – perpetrated by both John and his dad are indicative of a patriarchal context. Men are given permission to (mis)use their power to control others. Men are given permission to take without consent. A restorative justice ethos expands accountability from individuals also to the community.

In 'Another Push for Restorative Justice: Positive Psychology and Offender Rehabilitation', lawyer and scholar Theo Gavrielides, together with psychologist Piers Worth (2014), articulate how restorative justice primarily works at repairing relationships in communities, which secondarily helps in the rehabilitation of offenders: 'the goal of restorative justice is to repair broken relationships not offenders. The latter is a bi-product of the restorative justice approach' (p. 175). What this means is that correctional practices need to consider, if not become more seriously involved with, repairing social harms. From a restorative justice, trauma-informed framework to rehabilitation, practitioners need to be in the business of healing relationships between settler and Indigenous Peoples, between races, between rich and poor, and so on. A starting point would be to acknowledge that criminal justice systems were founded in a time of beliefs, laws and other institutions of white supremacy, and patriarchy – that the corresponding racism, sexism and violence have been blamed on the individual offender rather than on the social context. It seems to me that the normative task of those working in the field of rehabilitation should be to speak out against social ills.

Restraint

Finally, in my view, restorative justice is not necessarily opposed to incapacitation. Some people are bent on hurting themselves or others. However, how we do incapacitation or imprisonment needs to become more trauma-informed. Some researchers have begun to explore how prisons must be careful not to re-enact traumatic dynamics, and do no further harm (Miller and Najavits, 2012,). Others, like Theo Gavrielides (2014), have argued that restorative justice and incapacitation are not necessarily diametrically opposed, but share some common ground. In an article called 'Reconciling the Notions of Restorative Justice and Imprisonment', Gavrielides terms the connection between incapacitation and restorative justice as 'restorative punishment'. He contends that restorative justice, like punishment of prison, is inherently painful. As an example, Gavrielides says offenders experience restorative pain when they commit to facing the consequences of their actions. However, where restorative punishment diverges from traditional, retributive imprisonment is that pain is not for pain's sake, but instead 'aims to restore, create, construct, repair and reintegrate' (Gavrielides, 2014, p. 493).

Here, though, on the topic of restraining offenders, I must acknowledge the constraining limits of my privileges. Indeed, as someone with many social privileges – white, male, heterosexual and so on – I need to take the lead from others. Perhaps prisons are an obsolete way of doing justice, one that only perpetuates because white men, like me, have for too long been using criminal justice to control other races and marginalized communities. African American activist and scholar Angela Davis (2003), in *Are Prisons Obsolete?*, asks an important question: 'Is racism so deeply entrenched in the institution of the prison that it is not possible to eliminate one without eliminating the other?' (p. 26). Davis challenges her reader to imagine beyond prisons towards abolition. She says we get stuck as we try to think of alternatives because we are being simplistic, trying to think of only one alternative to prisons instead of adopting a broader framework. Our first step, Davis says, should 'be to let go of the desire to discover one single alternative system of punishment that would occupy the same footprint as the prison system' (p. 106).

Conclusion

Although a significant section in this chapter is occupied with a critique of the psychology of criminal conduct approach to offender rehabilitation, I am not advocating throwing out in favour of a pie-in-the-sky restorative justice framework. There is strong evidence to support some continued use of a risk-based approach. However, it is not sufficient – far from it. We can no longer ignore individual and collective traumas in offender populations. To be trauma-informed means to understand trauma, do no further harm and focus on healing, strengths and fostering resilience. To use a restorative justice framework for accountability means holding individuals responsible, allowing space for personal transformation, mobilizing the community to address the root causes of crime, and using incapacitation only where necessary. At this stage in theory development, and collecting of evidence, restorative justice is no longer pie-in-the-sky. A restorative justice framework is a worthy approach.

A number of themes emerge while examining rehabilitation from a trauma-informed perspective. I should make two of these themes more explicit. First, when doing a literature review of the data on the lived experiences of offenders, as I have done in this chapter, in particular the issues of racism, patriarchy and colonialism surface. Second, although this chapter hints at it, a multi- or interdisciplinary perspective is better than a narrow one. Further dialogue with anti-racist, feminist and decolonizing theories, among others, is needed. There is much more for folks like me to learn.

Trauma-informed desistance, using a restorative justice framework, is a better way than simply measuring and managing risk. In this chapter I first problematized the overuse of a psychology of criminal conduct – the use of risk assessment measures – to highlight how offender trauma is so often ignored in correctional practices, to the detriment of community safety. Next, I described how trauma affects a person, influencing or giving shape to criminal behaviour. Randall and Haskell (2013) explain the correlation between prior trauma and crime:

> Research has demonstrated the interconnection between histories of violence and abuse, traumatic experiences, and criminal behaviour. This does not mean that violence and abuse in life creates or causes criminality in a simplistic way, or that those who commit crime can merely "blame it on" their previous experiences. Still, it does mean that there are complex interconnections between people's life experiences, opportunities, choices and chances, and their personal histories, including trauma histories. (p. 516)

Finally, I proposed adopting a restorative justice framework for doing trauma-informed desistance. Restorative justice allows for accountability and support, while also addressing root causes.

Bibliography

Alexander, M. (2010). *The new Jim Crow: mass incarceration in the age of colorblindness*. New York: The New Press.

Anaya, J. (2014). *Report of the Special Rapporteur on the rights of indigenous peoples: the situation of indigenous peoples in Canada*. Geneva: United Nations General Assembly.

Andrews, D.A. and Bonta, J. (2010). *The psychology of criminal conduct*. New York: Routledge.

Andrews, D.A., Bonta, J. and Hoge, R.D. (1990). Classification for effective rehabilitation: rediscovering psychology. *Criminal Justice and Behavior*, *17*, 19–52.

Andrews, D.A. and Dowden, C. (2008). The Risk–Need–Responsivity model of assessment and human service in prevention and corrections: crime-prevention jurisprudence. *Canadian Journal of Criminology and Criminal Justice*, *49*(4), 439–464.

Anumba, N., DeMatteo, D. and Heilbrun, K. (2012). Social functioning, victimization, and mental health among female offenders. *Criminal Justice and Behavior*, *39*(9), 1204–1218.

Baird, C. (2009). *A question of evidence: a critique of risk assessment models used in the justice system*. Washington, DC: National Council on Crime and Delinquency.

Berger, P.L. and Luckmann, T. (1966). *The social construction of reality: a treatise in the sociology of knowledge*. New York: Anchor Books.

Bonczar, T. (2003). *Prevalence of imprisonment in the U.S. population, 1974–2001*. Washington: Bureau of Justice Statistics.

Bonta, J. (2002). Offender risk assessment: guidelines for selection and use. *Criminal Justice and Behaviour*, *29*, 355–379.

Bowlby, J. (1969). *Attachment*. London: Random House.

Bowlby, J. (1988). *A secure base: parent–child attachment and healthy human development*. London: Routledge.

Brodeur, J.-P. (1992). Cartesian penology. *Canadian Journal of Law and Jurisprudence*, *5*(1) 15–41.

Buchbinder, E. and Eisikovits, Z. (2008). Doing treatment: batterers' experience of intervention. *Children and Youth Services Review*, *30*, 616–630.

Bureau of Justice Statistics (1999). *Prior abuse reported by inmates and probationers*. Washington.

Challeen, D.A. (1986). *Making it right: a common sense approach to criminal justice*. Aberdeen: Melius Peterson Publishing Co.

Chan, W. and Rigakos, G.S. (2002). Risk, crime and gender. *British Journal of Criminology*, *42*, 743–761.

Chancer, L. and Donovan, P. (1994). A mass psychology of punishment: crime and the futility of rationally based approaches. *Social Justice*, *21*(3), 50.

Cunningham, A. and Baker, L. (2007). *Little eyes, little ears: how violence against a mother shapes children as they grow*. London: The Centre for Children and Families in the Justice System.

Davis, A.Y. (2003). *Are prisons obsolete?* New York: Seven Stories Press.

DeVeaux, M. (2013). The trauma of the incarceration experience. *Harvard Civil Rights-Civil Liberties Law Review*, *48*, 257–277.

Dierkhising, C.B., Ko, S.J., Woods-Jaeger, B., et al. (2013). Trauma histories among justice-involved youth. *European Journal of Psychotraumatology*, *4*, 1–12.

Dugan, L. (2003). Domestic violence legislation: exploring its impact on the likelihood of domestic violence, police intervention and arrest. *Criminology and Public Policy*, *2*, 283–312.

Dutton, D.G. and White, K.R. (2012). Attachment insecurity and intimate partner violence. *Aggression and Violent Behavior*, *17*, 475–481.

Ericson, R.V. and Haggerty, K.D. (1997). *Policing and risk society*. Toronto: University of Toronto Press.

Ford, J.D., Chapman, J., Connor, D.F. and Cruise, K.R. (2012). Complex trauma and aggression in secure juvenile justice settings. *Criminal Justice and Behaviour*, *39*, 694–724.

Gavrielides, T. (2014). Reconciling the notions of restorative justice and imprisonment. *The Prison Journal*, *94*(4), 479–505.

Gavrielides, T. and Worth, P. (2014). Another push for restorative justice: positive psychology and offender rehabilitation. In M.H. Pearson (ed.), *Crime: international perspectives, socioeconomic factors and psychological implications* (pp. 161–182). New York: Nova Science Publishers.

Gilligan, J. (2001). *Preventing violence*. New York: Thames & Hudson.

Hannah-Moffat, K. and Shaw, M. (2001). Situation risqué: le risqué et les services correctionnels au Canada. *Criminologie, 34*, 47–72.

Hartney, C. and Vuong, L. (2009). *Created equal: racial and ethnic disparities in the U.S. criminal justice system*. New York: National Council on Crime and Delinquency.

Herman, J.L. (1997). *Trauma and recovery: the aftermath of violence – from domestic abuse to political terror*. New York: Basic Books.

Jenkins, A. (2009). *Becoming ethical: a parallel, political journey with men who have abused*. Lyme Regis: Russell House Publishing.

Jenkins, A. (2011). Becoming resilient: overturning common sense – part 1. *The Australian and New Zealand Journal of Family Therapy, 32*(1), 33–42.

Johnston, N. (2004). The world's most influential prison: success or failure. *The Prison Journal, 84*(4), 20–40.

Liebling, A. and Maruna, S. (2005). *The effects of imprisonment*. New York: Routledge.

Maruna, S. (2001). *Making good: how ex-convicts reform and rebuild their lives*. Washington: American Psychological Association.

Maruna, S. and LeBel, T.P. (2009). Strengths-based approaches to reentry: extra mileage toward reintegration and destigmatization. *Japanese Journal of Sociological Criminology, 34*, 59–81.

McNeill, F., Farrall, S., Lightowler, C. and Maruna, S. (2012). How and why people stop offending: discovering desistance. *Insights: Evidence Summaries to Support Social Services in Scotland, 15*, 1–12.

Miller, N.A. and Najavits, L.M. (2012). Creating trauma-informed correctional care: a balance of goals and environment. *European Journal of Psychotraumatology, 3*, 1.

Munch, C. (2012). *Youth correctional statistics in Canada – 2010/2011*. Ottawa: Statistics Canada. Retrieved from http://www.statcan.gc.ca/pub/85-002-x/201 2001/article/11716-eng.htm#a4.

Nafekh, M. and Motiuk, L.L. (2002). *Statistical Information on Recidivism – Revised 1 (SIR-R1) Scale: a psychometric examination*. Ottawa: Research Branch, Correctional Service of Canada.

Narayan, A.J., Englund, M.M. and Egeland, B. (2013). Developmental timing and continuity of exposure to interparental violence and externalizing behavior as prospective predictors of dating violence. *Development and Psychopathology, 25*, 973–990.

Olver, M.E., Stockdale, K.C. and Wormith, J.S. (2009). Risk assessment with young offenders: a meta-analysis of three assessment measures. *Criminal Justice and Behavior, 36*, 329–353.

Oudshoorn, J. (2015). *Trauma-informed youth justice in Canada: a new framework toward a kinder future*. Toronto: Canadian Scholars Press.

Pratt, J. (2001). Dangerosite, risqué et technologies du pouvoir. *Criminologie*, *34*, 101–121.

Randall, M. and Haskell, L. (2013). Trauma-informed approaches to law: why restorative justice must understand trauma and psychological coping. *Dalhousie Law Journal*, *36*, 501–533.

Rauscher, F. (2012). Kant's social and political philosophy. In E.N. Zalta (ed.), *The Stanford encyclopedia of philosophy*. Stanford: Stanford University.

Robert, D. (2001). Transformations récentes de la législation fédérale sur la mise en liberté sous condition au Canada. Une lecture à la lumière des écrits sur la notion de risque. *Criminologie*, *34*, 71–99.

Rothman, D.J. (1980). *Conscience and convenience: the asylum and its alternatives in progressive America*. Boston: Little, Brown and Company.

Sapers, H. (2013). Annual report of the Office of the Correctional Investigator – 2012/2013. Ottawa: Office of the Correctional Investigator. Retrieved from http://www.oci-bec.gc.ca/cnt/rpt/annrpt/annrpt20122013-eng.aspx#sIV.

Sentencing Project, The. (2014). *Facts about prisons and people in prisons*. Washington.

Serin, R.C., Gobeil, R., Hanby, L.J. and Lloyd, C.D. (2012). Evidence-based practice in corrections: entry points for improvements in case-based decisions. *Corrections Today*, *74*(1), 81.

Shields, R. (2013). *Mental health and criminal justice policy framework*. Toronto: Centre for Addiction and Mental Health.

Silver, E. and Miller, L.L. (2002). A cautionary note on the use of actuarial risk assessment tools for social control. *Crime & Delinquency*, *48*(1), 138–161.

Stien, P.T. and Kendall, J. (2004). *Psychological trauma and the developing brain: neurologically based interventions for troubled children*. New York: Routledge.

van der Kolk, B.A., McFarlane, A.C. and Weisaeth, L. (2007). *Traumatic stress: the effects of overwhelming experience on mind, body, and society*. New York: Guilford Press.

Vandergoot, M. (2006). *Justice for young offenders: their needs, our responses*. Saskatoon: Purich Publishing.

Vieraitis, L.M., Kovandzic, T.V. and Marvell, T.B. (2007). The criminogenic effects of imprisonment: evidence from state panel data, 1974–2002. *Criminology & Public Policy*, *6*, 589–622.

Weaver, A. (2008). *So you think you know me*. Hook: Waterside Press.

Weeks, R. and Widom, C.S. (1998). Self-reports of early childhood victimization among incarcerated adult male felons. *Journal of Interpersonal Violence*, *13*(3), 346–361.

Yantzi, M. (1998). *Sexual offending and restoration*. Waterloo: Herald Press.

Zehr, H. (1990). *Changing lenses: a new focus for crime and justice*. Scottdale: Herald Press.

Zehr, H. (2001). *Transcending: reflections of crime victims*. Intercourse, PA: Good Books.

Zehr, H. (2002). *The little book of restorative justice*. Intercourse, PA: Good Books.

Zinger, I. (2004). Actuarial risk assessment and human rights: a commentary. *Canadian Journal of Criminology and Criminal Justice*, *46*(5), 607–620.

Chapter 10
Challenging Power Dynamics in Restorative Justice

Mikhail Lyubansky and Elaine Shpungin[1]

Modern societies are plagued by differential access to human rights and 'justice' created by the intersections of group membership and social status. At its heart, the modern restorative justice (RJ) movement aims to address some of these inequities by giving voice, power and choice back to the communities in which the crime or painful conflict took place (for example, Christie, 1977). However, we contend that most modern RJ practices inadvertently mirror and exacerbate existing power dynamics, and, in some instances, even create new artificial power hierarchies that were not previously present. We further contend that, although they exert both subtle and explicit influences on RJ processes and outcomes, power dynamics have mostly been under-studied, under-discussed and under-appreciated by the restorative movement.

In this chapter, we first describe the ways these power dynamics manifest at three ecological levels:[2] (a) societal attitudes and beliefs, such as implicit racial biases (macro-level); (b) restorative systems, such as the 'victim–offender' paradigm (exo-level); and (c) restorative processes, such as participant disempowerment (micro-level). We then offer strategies and recommendations that can help counterbalance these power dynamics at multiple levels of the system. We approach this work as both academic psychologists[3] and RJ practitioners[4] with facilitation experience in various contexts including university residence halls, intentional communities, academic departments, the juvenile detention centre, schools, churches and families.

---

1 The two authors contributed equally to this work.

2 These ecological levels are dynamic and interactive, and power dynamics manifesting at any level affect the others. Similarly, each of the recommended strategies, while being nested in a specific level, is understood to affect power dynamics at multiple levels.

3 In addition to restorative justice, our academic interests include racial justice (Mikhail) and community psychology (Elaine).

4 We both facilitate a community-based restorative process developed in the Brazilian favelas by Dominic Barter and associates called Restorative Circles. See http://www.restorativecircles.org.

Power Dynamics within Society: Implicit and Explicit Biases

Power dynamics within society are created when individuals with structural power hold (and therefore act upon) *explicit and/or implicit biases* based on *group-level characteristics*, such as race, gender, ethnicity, immigration status, socioeconomic class, caste, religion, sexual orientation, age and disability. These rays of social location are not unidirectional but intersect in complex ways (for example, gay, Christian, female, professor) with some intersections being differentially salient in diverse global and local contexts (for example, Nash, 2008). As will be discussed below, the power dynamics created by this intersectionality are both ubiquitous and covert. It is thus our contention that unless individuals explicitly attend to the privileges associated with their group status, the power dynamics resulting from the intersectional identities will create tears of inequity in the fabric of restorative justice. Below, the examples of social status and racial status are used to illustrate the point.

Explicit Bias: Social Status

Explicit racism is increasingly taboo, but it is still normative and socially acceptable in many communities, especially at the intersection of gender, age and poverty, as is readily evident in the increasingly frequent usage of 'thugs' to refer to young, black males living in poverty. More saliently, it is common for individuals to hold shared beliefs about which groups of people in the community deserve more respect and deference. For instance, in many communities around the world, it is an explicit value that adults (parents, teachers) and elders are to be treated differently than children and adolescents. Similarly, for many people, professional status within the community (for example, mechanic versus professor), or within a specific organization (for example, doctor versus nurse), carries unquestioned rules around deference and respect that may show up in social manners, language and habitual differential treatment.

   In a restorative process, this may exhibit itself, for instance, as men asserting power over women, or adults asserting power over young people. Wadhwa (forthcoming), writing about the school context, describes multiple examples, including a circle of 19 high school students in which boys outnumbered girls two to one. In this circle, the author is an *adult participant* and the facilitator is a youth.

> I continue to hear a lot of crosstalk among the boys. Lincoln says, "I was so hungry in the middle of the night!" When I turn toward the boys, I see Romero making a gesture toward his friends; he flits his tongue in and out between two fingers shaped in a V, a reference to oral sex on a woman. I get the piece and say, "Even though people think words don't impact people, they definitely do. And actions also impact people". I ponder whether to derail a conversation from a talk about race to what I've just seen. My decision to speak up about the

sexual gesture is fraught; was I perpetuating a youth-adult dynamic in which I called upon my power as a grown up to essentially discipline him for his action? "Romero, I just saw what you did and it really grosses me out". Lois, traditionally one of the more vocal females in circle, says, "I saw you too". It takes him a minute to understand what I'm referring to and then he starts laughing, covering his mouth. He says, "Oh! I didn't know". Lois whispers to Monica, "We should do a circle on sexism".

This example shows the complexity of intersectionality. The facilitator, the boys and the affected girls are all adolescents. The adult is a participant who can exert her age-related power to advocate for the girls, at the risk of silencing or reprimanding the boys. While the focus of this example is the intersection of age and gender, such dynamics can also occur along other previously discussed lines (for example, race, ethnicity, religion). Because Wadhwa is aware of these dynamics, she navigates them with caution and awareness. When those with structural power are not aware of the weight of their words and actions, they can inadvertently affect the extent to which the process is restorative for all. For now, we simply point out the way power dynamics may play out between participants. Later, we will discuss how the restorative system, and facilitator biases, also play important roles in such interactions.

Implicit Bias: Race

Implicit bias refers to bias in judgement that operates without intentional control and typically without conscious awareness. Because of its salience in the US context in which we are based, and because of the preponderance of data regarding racial inequities (see Lyubansky and Hunter, 2014, for review), we use racial status in the USA to illustrate how one kind of implicit bias may operate in one particular global context. We invite readers to use this example to examine dynamics that are likely to be present within their own community and national context.

In the USA (and other global contexts) individuals who are perceived to be white enjoy many unearned benefits related to employment, education, medicine, housing, the legal system and financial resources (McIntosh, 1998). Multiple studies have shown that perceptions of race significantly affect the unconscious behaviour of police officers, attorneys, jurors and judges, as well as health care providers, school staff, landlords, salespersons and many other professionals (Staats, 2014). This difference even shows up in studies in which concocted résumés, or emails to professors, are identical except for the presence of an ethnic sounding versus Caucasian sounding name (for example, Bertrand and Mullainathan, 2003). In all these cases, the perception of *non-whiteness* creates barriers to obtaining home loans, decreases chances of an interview and negatively affects treatment by teachers, professors and doctors. In the legal sphere, being black or Latino increases one's chances of being searched, arrested, accidentally shot and imprisoned, even in laboratory studies (for example, Sadler et al., 2012; Correll et al., 2002).

Importantly, the findings suggest that, while some are indeed overtly bigoted and prejudicial, most behave this way unintentionally, based on implicit biases of which they are not aware (Staats, 2014). The findings are so pervasive, so consistent and so robust that Dasgupta (2013) suggests that everyone is vulnerable, regardless of his/her good intentions.

Despite this reality (or perhaps because of it), the past decade has seen the rise of the so-called 'colour-blind' ideology (Apfelbaum et al., 2012). This philosophy asserts that the most moral and effective response to racial inequities is to 'not see colour' – that is, to treat all people the same, regardless of their race or ethnicity.

The colour-blind approach, while appearing just, actually serves to deny the racial reality of US life. To use a metaphor, not seeing colour is akin to treating the results of all contestants in a race in the same way at the finish line, even though some competitors had to carry heavy gear and jump over more obstacles, received less help along the way or started the race at a further distance (Lyubansky and Hunter, 2014).

Notably, the negative effects of colour-blindness on both those endorsing the ideology and on members of racial minority groups are well documented. For example, Burkard and Knox (2004) found that psychotherapists' level of colour-blindness was inversely related to their capacity for empathy with black clients, but not white clients, while Plaut et al. (2009) found that dominant-group members' colour-blindness had a negative impact on their work colleagues' psychological engagement with the job.

Power Dynamics within the RJ System: Unquestioned Paradigms

Victims and Offenders

Differentiation of needs
The most invisible and insidious power dynamic present in the vast majority of restorative practices is based on a 'core' RJ principle: that victims and offenders play fundamentally different roles, and therefore, have fundamentally different needs in a restorative process. For instance, Zehr (2002) explains that because victims are *violated*, they need: (a) information from the offender about what happened; (b) the opportunity to tell and retell their story; (c) empowerment through ownership of the process; and (d) restitution and vindication through reparative actions by the offender. On the other hand, because offenders do the violating, they need to: (a) take responsibility for their actions, express empathy,

make amends; (b) address issues of competency, personal healing and community integration; and (c) address issues of future community safety.[5]

While this magical combination (information sharing, empowerment, harm reduction, accountability, empathy, community reintegration, reparation and safety) is undoubtedly the driving force behind the well-documented positive outcomes associated with restorative justice (for example, Sherman and Strang, 2007), the parsing of these needs by victim versus offender unintentionally mirrors and exacerbates the power dynamics found in the outside world, distracting from the act that needs restoration and reducing restorative outcomes for all (Gavrielides, 2013). This is because both victimhood and offenderhood are fluid concepts that are: (a) socially constructed by culture, media and impacted stakeholders; (b) artificially assigned by gatekeepers based on limited legal definitions of crime; (c) muddled by contextual factors (for example, domestic violence) and systemic inequities (for example, unequal arrest rates for certain groups); and (d) often shared by multiple parties in a conflict (Shpungin, 2014). As a result, multiple people in a restorative process usually experience both victimhood and offenderhood and, consequently, the need for safety, empowerment and information, on the one hand, and healing, self-responsibility, and self-accountability, on the other.

Fluidity of needs
Numerous cases studies from the media, the RJ literature and our own Restorative Circles (RC) practice illustrate the inherent risks of assigning *a priori* victim–offender roles and *systematically* treating individuals differently based on these. As just one example, one of our Restorative Circles revealed that the legal system's designated offender (a young man who had fatally shot another young man) was experiencing: (a) realistically founded fears for his life, via retaliation by the brothers and cousins of the deceased; and (b) significant unaddressed trauma and grief caused by the accidental firing of the gun that resulted in the death of his close friend.

Thus, in addition to his need to take responsibility, make amends and integrate back into his neighbourhood and school, the 'offender' also had a clear need to 'tell and retell' his story, remain safe from future harm and experience some sense of empowerment in what had turned out to be a nightmare situation in his young life. At the same time, the deceased man's brother, who was seen by the justice system as the 'victim', had needs that are generally associated with those we regard as 'offenders'. These included taking responsibility for his leadership in the revenge plan, which could have potentially led to a cycle of violence and multiple incarcerations that would affect the community at multiple levels, as well as co-creating (with the 'offender) a new restorative plan: a memorial poster for the deceased. This is just one of multiple examples where 'offenders' experience

---

5　It is important to note here that Zehr's RJ formulation also includes the presence of the community, which holds needs related to both victimization and co-responsibility, making their roles more fluid and complex.

victimhood and 'victims', if given the chance along with community members, benefit from the opportunity to explore self-responsibility, accountability, reparation and the multi-directionality of conflict or violence in the relationship.

Gatekeepers and Facilitators

Many restorative systems are designed in such a way that those with structural power (for example, school officials, law enforcement personnel, prosecuting attorney) have the right to: (a) determine whether or not a restorative process will occur; and (b) formally assign to individuals the labels of 'offender' and 'victim' (see the next section). At the same time, both gatekeepers[6] and facilitators are more likely to come from backgrounds of relative privilege in terms of education, financial resources, gender, race, caste, ethnicity and other group-level variables. In other words, gatekeepers and facilitators do not typically represent, demographically speaking, those they 'serve'. As such, they are more likely to hold colour-blind ideologies that can negatively affect their gatekeeping and facilitation.

Finally, because implicit bias is almost a 'universal virus', gatekeepers and facilitators are likely to be influenced by unintentional beliefs and prejudices about certain groups. For gatekeepers, this is likely to affect their decisions about who can and cannot appropriately engage in – and benefit from – restorative practices. It therefore follows that courts, schools and organizations may unintentionally create structures in which restorative processes are more likely to be offered to individuals from certain ethnic, racial, religious or gender groups. On the facilitation side, implicit biases may affect how facilitators interact with participants in both preparation meetings and within the restorative justice process.

Just as importantly, however, the very concept of needing professional gatekeepers and facilitators show an implicit and unquestioned bias within our RJ system. It is true that the restorative justice processes, not unlike formal justice processes, require resources of time, education (of facilitators) and space. However, it does not naturally follow that professional gatekeepers are the best judges of how these resources ought to be spent, and on whom. As a frequent example used by Dominic Barter, access to police officers, ambulances and fire fighters was significantly less equitable before the introduction of the 'universal emergency telephone number'.[7] Would it not better reflect the values of empowerment, voice and choice inherent in the restorative justice movement if

---

6   In this context, 'gatekeepers' refer to all individuals who are not directly involved in the conflict but have the structural power and authority to determine whether a particular act will be responded to restoratively. While this power sometimes resides with the facilitators, more often it is held by school disciplinarians, work supervisors or, if the act is criminal in nature, the various parts of the criminal justice system.

7   The first universal emergency number (999) was introduced in London in 1937, though it took many decades for infrastructure to catch up to this invention around the globe.

any participant in the system could press a button to initiate a restorative process – without permission and access from someone in structural power? Similarly, how much more restorative might justice be if facilitators came from all walks of life and represented the communities using the process?

Power Dynamics within the RJ Process: Facilitation and Participation

Facilitation

As we discussed earlier, factors such as racial status and victim–offender labels create power dynamics among restorative process stakeholders.[8] Here we want to zoom in on aspects of the facilitation itself. Facilitators hold power in the process by virtue of their facilitation role. That is, facilitators are often given explicit power to direct who is speaking, when, how and how much. This creates a dialectic – a tension between two seemingly opposing approaches to addressing power in RJ. On the one hand, facilitators may use their power to balance out pre-existing inequities between participants. On the other hand, by using their power this way, facilitators may mirror or exacerbate existing power dynamics, or create new ones. For instance, facilitators may use their power to 'equalize' air-time among participants. Facilitators may also choose to step in when, in their judgement, the participants are behaving in ways that seem to be 'disruptive', pejorative, sexist, homophobic, or racist. McDonald (2012) argues that such use of power ensures that the RJ process is free of tyranny. However, it can also exacerbate the power dynamics present between facilitators and participants, especially since facilitators are more likely to come from sectors of society with more structural power, especially in school settings where facilitation is often done by adults who may also be vested with other authority.

In addition, personality differences and other interpersonal power dynamics (see the next section) may also lead facilitators to want to assert their own power in order to bring the dialogue back to a more constructive form or otherwise support connection and truth-telling. Finally, facilitators may have more experience than participants in understanding which types of agreements are more likely to be restorative and may be tempted to lend their wisdom to others. Though all of these may, at times, create more restorative outcomes, they also undermine participant agency and efficacy, potentially creating a narrative that the participants lack the skills or desire to work through the conflict on their own.

---

8   In this context, 'stakeholders' refers both to those participating in the restorative process and those impacted by the conflict and its outcomes.

Participation

The last type of power dynamics we want to discuss is the power associated with RJ participants holding different occupational and/or familial roles. These include teachers and students, parents and children, supervisors and supervisees and a variety of other ways in which structural and interpersonal power is evidently dissimilar among participants. In our own facilitation, we have frequently observed parents, teachers and bosses insist on being heard without (in our evaluation) being open to hearing and being impacted by the words and experiences of others. While it is certainly the case that no restorative process can guarantee such openness, there are two strategies that we believe can create conditions for it to occur: community involvement and participant preparation.

Below we present strategies for restoratively addressing the various power dynamics associated with the three ecological levels explored in the chapter. These recommendations are distilled from our knowledge of restorative justice theory, principles and practices as well as our understanding of how power, oppression and privilege operate in a variety of domains. Most importantly, these strategies are ones we have explored both through our own RC practice and through multiple discussions with Dominic Barter, the founder of RC.

Countering Power Dynamics Based on Societal Biases: Cultural Competence

While there are only a few things that can be done to affect the way that colour-blindness, explicit prejudice and implicit bias operate *between participants* in a restorative justice process,[9] there is much we can do to balance out these power dynamics as they manifest themselves in RJ gatekeeping, facilitation and treatment of participants.

The notion of 'cultural competence' to describe the consciousness and communication skills necessary to work with individuals from different cultural/ racial/ethnic backgrounds (and diverging identities) has been embraced by both the helping professions and the corporate world. As psychologists, we know all too well that the academic literature on cultural competence is fraught with inconsistencies and contradictions that require further scrutiny. We also recognize that there are no objective criteria for a 'culturally competent' professional. Nevertheless, cultural competence's influence and contributions are undeniable, and the restorative justice movement would do well to adopt its insistence that

---

9   The question of how we can increase authentic (rather than tokenized) listening between participants of unequal social status is of great interest to us, and we have been experimenting with some strategies around this. However, these are beyond the scope of the current chapter.

individuals be recognized and acknowledged not only as human beings and unique individuals but also as racial, ethnic and cultural beings.

Our rationale for urging the restorative justice movement to explicitly recognize race and other differences and explicitly address the various forms of injustice is based on our recognition that, whether we want them to or not, race and other forms of difference matter in our society. Given the historical and current racial bias in the criminal justice system, a justice movement that fails to address this bias explicitly will be perceived by racially targeted groups as either uninformed, unjust, uncaring or all of the above.[10] To be sure, even colour-blind *restorative justice* is likely to be superior to the current justice system in that it's more likely to involve community members who have the cultural knowledge and experience necessary to handle the conflicts with sensitivity. However, not all communities have retained or developed this cultural knowledge, and a justice system that fails to acknowledge and take measures to address racial inequity is bound, in our opinion, to create conditions for racial inequity to continue, regardless of its good intentions to the contrary.

Facilitator Self-Awareness

A detailed description of what a 'privilege-conscious'[11] restorative justice system would look like is beyond the scope of this chapter. However, we want to propose three dimensions of competence that are often articulated in the psychotherapy/ counselling literature: '(a) awareness of own assumptions, values, biases and historical experiences; (b) understanding the worldview of culturally/ethnically/ spiritually different individuals; and (c) developing appropriate [facilitation] strategies and techniques' (Sue et al., 1998). Of these, we find the first dimension to be foundational, as empirical data show that those who are interested in justice can learn to recognize and eventually cognitively override their own prejudices and biases, including those that are implicit in nature (see Staats, 2014, for a review). Self-reflection and awareness training can support facilitators in learning how to recognize and acknowledge their privileged status, which if unseen can create unintentional harm. Similarly, by becoming more aware of how social privilege may be impacting those participating in the restorative process (for example, by interfering with responsibility-taking and making amends for unintentional harm), facilitators may be better able to create conditions for more restorative outcomes.

---

10   Gavrielides (2014) has similarly argued that if RJ doesn't pay attention to racial inequality, it will soon have to face its demise.

11   We refer here to the privileges and benefits associated with membership in dominant groups (for example, racial, gender, religious).

Facilitator Education

Though time-consuming and potentially controversial, we contend that restorative systems need to integrate this kind of self-awareness work (including of implicit bias) into formal facilitator education. Where facilitator education is less formal (for example, learned through apprenticeship), facilitators can engage these issues independently or in small groups through relevant readings, videos and discussion. What is critical here is that facilitators are introduced to the idea that 'colour-blindness' (or ethnic-, religious-, GLBTQ-, disability-, gender- or age-blindness) can be seductive but unproductive, creating unintended biases in their facilitation and contributing to pain rather than restoration for some participants.

Facilitator Multi-Partiality

Many restorative justice facilitators and circle-keepers aim for neutrality. Some even adopt a more biased, protective stance towards participants they consider most vulnerable. While the latter approach may seem, at first glance, to support the levelling of power differentials, it instead often serves to reify structural power differences. In contrast, a multi-partial approach, in which the facilitator aims to be equally allied, respectful and caring towards all participants, lets participants know that the restorative process will take place within a container in which each person will be treated, at least by the facilitator, without blame or judgement.

One strategy for increasing facilitator multi-partiality is to build short *facilitator preparation* meetings into the restorative system. In the Restorative Circles model developed by Barter in Brazil, facilitators support each other by taking turns answering the following question before facilitating either the circle itself or the preparatory meetings that precede it: 'Do you hold any ideas, thoughts, images or beliefs that may prevent you from seeing the humanity of everyone involved?' The facilitator then speaks freely about his/her worries, fears, assumptions and pre-dispositions in regard to either self or others in the process. The listener (an informed co-facilitator or colleague) listens non-judgementally without giving advice, criticism or reassurance, perhaps reflecting back the essential things being said. Similar to the non-fixing, non-rescuing approach of facilitation itself, the goal here is not therapy or problem-solving but bringing biases and worries into awareness with the goal of increased multi-partiality.

Countering Power Dynamics Based in RJ Structures: Procedural Fairness

The goal of procedural fairness is not equal treatment but treatment that is fair and transparent. In the context of restorative justice, this means: (a) treating all participants with respect and dignity; (b) guaranteeing that like cases are treated alike; and (c) ensuring that all those directly affected have a voice in the process (Maiese, 2004).

To these ends, it is our contention that the unquestioned paradigm that victims and offenders have orthogonal needs based on their roles vis-à-vis the conflict limits rather than enhances the benefit to all parties. It provides a dualistic frame that restrains the dialogue and constricts perceptions about what is possible. Starting with a clean slate and letting the information about needs and harms emerge through open questions is likely to take the process to a deeper level. We also contend that the needs of all participants can be better met with a paradigm shift that calls for *standardizing systemic components* of the process while simultaneously *increasing customized supports*. Rather than being contradictory, these two concepts are like twin pillars holding up the restorative platform, which predictably becomes unstable if either pillar is given short shrift.

Standardized Procedures

In many contemporary restorative practices, the *identified offenders* are often asked, both in the preparation and restorative conferences, to talk about how their actions have *impacted others*, while the remaining participants are asked to speak about how *they have been impacted*. In contrast, we believe that it is important to standardize the questions and procedures used in the preparation and restorative meetings, while, at the same time, addressing participants' individual needs, which may include language interpretation, age-related supports, disability accommodations and individualized safety plans in order to increase safety, clarity and buy-in for all participants, regardless of their status or role in the conflict.

Our experience shows that when we ask all participants the same question (for example, 'What is important to you about what happened?' or 'What do you want Person X to know?') the restorative process is more likely to include multiple narratives about co-responsibility as well as co-victimization. As Shpungin (2014) noted, the European Union's victim-centred movement provides an excellent blueprint for individualized supports and accommodations that increase meaningful (as opposed to tokenized) participation in restorative practices. However, these individualized accommodations would address power and privilege much more effectively if they were actually offered to participants based on individual need, regardless of their identified role in the process.

Individualized Supports

At the same time, when power discrepancies are evident, facilitators or circle-keepers may need to support those with less structural power in order to create conditions that maximize both participation and restoration. For example, those who fear harm or retaliation may benefit from the presence and participation of advocates, support persons, written agreements concerning future legal actions and safety accommodations. Examples of such accommodations include having the restorative meeting via teleconference from another room or location or even placing limits on certain people's participation (for example, Braithwaite and

Daly, 1994). It is important to note here that it is not necessarily clear, before preparation meetings begin, which parties will feel a lack of safety (that is, it could be the identified victim or the offender who fears physical attack from others; it could be the family member or partner of either the official victim or offender who feels most traumatized by the event). Ideally, the menu of possible supports and constraints would have been established previously by a community process, making such supports easy to invoke and, if necessary, tweak, to accommodate a particular case.

To summarize, restorative justice has always taken pride in the way it shifts the focus of the process from 'Who violated which rule and how should we punish them?' to 'What harm was done and how do we repair it?' By labelling offenders, victims and community members ahead of time, we find ourselves still operating, in part, through the 'who violated?' lens. By eradicating this concept more fully from our vocabulary[12] and restorative processes and allowing the restorative process itself to co-create and co-discover the most fitting narrative about harm, impact and restorative action, we simply take this core restorative justice value to its natural conclusion.

Participant Preparation

Earlier, we briefly described some ways that facilitators might prepare themselves and each other. Here we want to focus on the preparatory work with the participants. This is a big topic and our intention is only to discuss those aspects that we believe can support participants in listening to and being impacted by others' experiences. In this context, we take the position that 'empathy begats empathy'. Thus, by providing an empathic presence to all participants during the many preparatory meetings leading up to the restorative process, facilitators not only help participants become more clear about what matters to them and what they want to say when everyone is brought together, but also provide a sense of being heard, understood and accepted without judgement. Though sometimes time-consuming – empathy tends to be in short supply in our world – this kind of presence can relieve some of the internal pain and thus make room for the experiences and perceptions of others.

---

12   To help facilitators track participants vis à vis a specific act of harm, RJ practices can adopt new vocabulary, like "author" and "receiver" (Lyubansky and Barter, 2011). These would not be synonyms for offender and victim but new language that reflects the paradigm shift that we are suggesting.

Countering Power Dynamics Based in the Process:
For the People by the People

System Co-Creation

We believe that when people have a say in what their restorative process looks like, especially if they come from disenfranchised or marginalized groups, they are more likely to participate in the process in a meaningful way and sustain the gains made in the process. Given the realities of painful conflict and the demands of modern life, most communities are likely to adopt a restorative practice from another community or school (rather than co-creating one from scratch), based on word of mouth, seeming fit or local knowledge. However, theoretically sound and effective such a borrowed practice might be, it will be stronger still when those who are most likely to use it get to make meaningful modifications so that the process better fits their specific circumstances and needs. This is analogous to modifying the rules of UNO[13] to accommodate the needs of younger players or the preferences of a particular group. Having a voice in decisions about facilitation, guidelines and process can make a restorative process more powerful and more empowering for community members, while also countering the often well-intentioned, top-down tendency of professionals and helpers to deliver ready-made products.

Non-Rescuing

In a similar vein, we recommend that systems examine the extent to which facilitators are inadvertently doing much of the restorative work for the participants, rather than creating conditions that allow participants to do it themselves. The idea of participant empowerment is woven into the spirit of restorative justice, which aims to do justice 'with those affected, rather than for them, or to them'. Even our language reflects our hopes for how restorative justice is different from other processes. The word 'facilitator' stems from Latin *facilis*, to make easier, while 'keeper', as in circle-keeper, is a caretaker, custodian or guardian of something. However, in practice, facilitators are often seduced into cajoling, reassuring, advising, fixing and leading, in both preparation and restorative meetings, turning themselves into restorative 'directors' (Old Latin for *governor* and *guide*), 'coaches' (originating in the concept of *tutoring*) and rescuers (*to drive out or remove*). While these heroic actions may result in gratitude and a glowing sense of accomplishment, they diminish the potential of the process to create conditions in which the participants themselves struggle with the tough questions of power, co-responsibility and restorative actions. As McDonald (2012) says:

> Facilitation is not only about technique. However to be a good facilitator technique is critical. A facilitator should work hard not to be noticed by the

---

13   A card game also known, in some parts of the world, as Mau-Mau or FLAPS.

participants. The role is not designed for people who want to rescue others, or for facilitators who want to be the centre of attention. In fact it's the exact opposite ... When we facilitate a process that delivers justice through participation, equality, deliberation and non-tyranny, we enable a group affected by a crime to understand better what has happened and why it took place. The group also gets to learn more about how they and others have been affected by what's happened and eventually to determine what to do, if anything, to make things better ...

Community Involvement

Painful conflict is not only about the unmet needs of the involved individuals but also represents unmet community and system needs (Barter, 2014). In this way, it is not just those directly involved in a particular conflict who benefit from a restorative process but also those who have been impacted by what happened, as well as those who might get entangled in similar (or different) conflicts in the future. By ensuring that the community is fully represented rather than excluded or tokenized, we create conditions for greater accountability, wider sharing of power and responsibility and deeper reintegration into community for those who did harm. In addition, we also create conditions for understanding systemic as well as interpersonal harm and, therefore, for creating not only interpersonal but also systemic strategies for both restoration and prevention of future harm.

Additionally, as Braithwaite (2002) pointed out, though only a few people may have been involved in committing a crime, many more often have the power to prevent it. Thus, in the corporate world, superiors can use their structural power to put an end to harmful practices by subordinates, subordinates can exert their influence through whistle-blowing, and business partners, auditors, regulators and consultants can create conditions for socially responsible behaviour by refusing to collude in (and by reporting) unethical practices. The inclusion of all these parties in the restorative process widens the scope of responsibility and, in so doing, limits the ability of any particularly powerful actor (for example, a corporate CEO) to shape the outcome to his/her will. Similarly, restorative dialogues and subsequent restorative actions following a drunk driving incident could include loved ones, drinking buddies and even the bar staff to minimize the possibility that the usually young, male driver will minimize the incident and not show sufficient motivation to change (Braithwaite, 2002).

In regards to power dynamics, the extent to which a restorative process can achieve more restorative outcomes may be improved by allowing those who are directly involved to create their own invitation lists of community members, once again minimizing the power of gatekeepers to determine who will be present. As each participant is invited, he/she is asked, in turn, to identify and invite others who need to be present for the process to be more fully restorative. This snowball invitation method creates a Venn diagram of invitees, with overlapping areas containing individuals that many people invite, and critical non-overlapping areas containing important voices and supports which were invited by only one or two other participants.

Such a list may eventually include people who were directly and indirectly impacted by the events, people who helped create the conditions (even if inadvertently) for what occurred, advocates and support persons, and others affected by the systemic nature of conflict (for example, neighbours, organizational staff). Although McDonald (2012) does not explicitly address the presence of support persons such as translators and mentors, he speaks eloquently to the importance of wide participation in ensuring a more democratic process:

> Of the four conditions necessary to deliver deliberative democracy, participation remains one of the most difficult for facilitators to translate into practice. There are very few crimes committed which do not affect a wide system of relationships: the victim, the offender, family members, extended family, friends, neighbours, work colleagues, community workers, drug or alcohol counsellors and police officers. Take the Restorative Justice Conference mentioned in the opening paragraph. Thirty five participants attended and participated and that number could have stretched to many more. For facilitators, the more participants involved, the more likely it is that the participants will engage with others, learn how deeply each other has been affected and provide ideas to respond to the hurt and harm, while considering ways to prevent future harm. Sadly for most programs, this number of participants would be the exception rather than the rule. Our sense is that facilitators often decide not to include a wide group of people. I believe this is much more about the facilitator's anxiety at not being able to control a larger group of people, than it is about people not wanting to attend.

Open Access and Facilitation

Finally, to fully uphold its claim that restorative justice is a justice done *with* those who are directly involved, it is necessary for RJ to become an open-access, open-facilitation system. That means that RJ needs to move away from the concept of gatekeeping with all possible haste. In other words, any member of a community in which restorative justice is an option needs to be able to initiate the process by using a 'universal restorative justice number'. This may look different in each community, ranging from writing to a predetermined email address that can be accessed by more than one person to putting a note in a cardboard box. The important thing is that there is an unbiased way to initiate a restorative process that does not require anyone's permission or consent.

In a similar vein, facilitators and others associated with the community's restorative system need to be representative of the community itself in regard to race, gender, education and other characteristics that are valued by the community. Thus, in a high school with a school-wide restorative system, the RJ facilitators/circle-keepers would ideally include teachers, administrators and diverse staff (for example, bus-drivers, custodians). Just as importantly, facilitators would also include students (a) from all grade levels; (b) in both remedial and college-bound tracks; (c) with and without a history of disciplinary problems; and (d) who more or less proportionally resemble the student body demographically.

Notably, in the psychotherapy literature, decades of research (see Christensen and Jacobson, 1994) have shown that treatments delivered by trained community volunteers (paraprofessionals) consistently have outcomes that match or surpass treatment delivered by licensed psychotherapists. Although not typical, there are RJ systems in which those who are most vulnerable and most affected by conflict (for example, students in a school, inmates in a prison, families in a working-class neighbourhood) facilitate restorative processes within their own 'community'. As an example, in Houston, USA, high school teacher Anita Wadhwa taught students with the worst discipline records to be circle-keepers, attracting accolades for the positive and empowering outcomes, and grant support to share this approach through the Houston Restorative Justice Collaboration. Similarly, the award-winning Restorative Circles process (see Gillinson et al., 2010) involves all members of a community in facilitation, as well as participation in restorative practices.

Conclusion

Because addressing power dynamics in a restorative system typically requires us to acknowledge and confront (and possibly share) our own power, there is substantial psychological resistance that must be overcome. As restorative justice becomes increasingly mainstream, there will be corresponding increasing pressure to either ignore or replicate existing power hierarchies. How the restorative justice movement responds to this pressure will go a long way in determining whether restorative justice will be a truly revolutionary force for justice or just a slightly less punitive version of what we've been doing all along.

In its ideal form, restorative justice is a community response. As such, restorative efforts require collaboration with a wide range of allies, including those with divergent worldviews and ideologies and both those with and without the trappings of structural power. It is appealing to distance ourselves from those who embrace punitive and retributive strategies and dismiss their efforts as misguided or even unenlightened. It is easy, as well, to avoid conflicting ideologies (for example, regarding the victim–offender paradigm) within the restorative movement, which is itself ideologically diverse. It is certainly tempting to avoid the racialized dimensions of justice on the grounds that they are too controversial or too deeply entrenched. Such conflict avoidance might be logical in a right–wrong, win–lose paradigm but is at odds with restorative principles, which urge us to move towards conflict with the goals of understanding it and finding ways to move forward that work for all involved. Such collaborations are only possible if those who identify with the restorative movement are themselves willing to move towards conflict restoratively. In our view, doing so is essential both to achieving sustainable social justice outcomes and to 'walking the walk' with integrity as we propel the restorative revolution forward.

Bibliography

Apfelbaum, E.P., Norton, M.I. and Sommers, S.R. (2012). Racial color blindness emergence, practice, and implications. *Current Directions in Psychological Science*, *21*(3), 205–209.

Barter, D. (2014). A two-day exploration of nonviolence with Dominic Barter and Kit Miller. Ashland, OR.

Bertrand, M. and Mullainathan, S. (2003). *Are Emily and Greg more employable than Lakisha and Jamal? A field experiment on labor market discrimination* (No. w9873). Cambridge, MA: National Bureau of Economic Research.

Braithwaite, J. (2002). *Restorative justice and responsive regulation*. Oxford: Oxford University Press.

Braithwaite, J. and Daly, K. (1994). Masculinities, violence and communitarian control. In T. Newburn and E. Stanko (eds), *Just boys doing business? Men, masculinities and crime* (pp. 189–213). London: Routledge.

Burkard, A.W. and Knox, S. (2004). Effect of therapist color-blindness on empathy and attributions in cross-cultural counseling. *Journal of Counseling Psychology*, *51*(4), 387.

Christensen, A. and Jacobson, N.S. (1994). Who (or what) can do psychotherapy: the status and challenge of nonprofessional therapies. *Psychological Science*, *5*(1), 8–14.

Christie, N. (1977). Conflicts as property. *British Journal of Criminology*, *17*(1), 1–15.

Correll, J., Park, B., Judd, C.M. and Wittenbrink, B. (2002). The police officer's dilemma: using ethnicity to disambiguate potentially threatening individuals. *Journal of Personality and Social Psychology*, *83*(6), 1314–1329.

Dasgupta, N. (2013). Implicit attitudes and beliefs adapt to situations: a decade of research on the malleability of implicit prejudice, stereotypes, and the self-concept. *Advances in Experimental Social Psychology*, *47*, 233–279.

Gavrielides, T. (2013). Restorative pain: a new vision of punishment. In T. Gavrielides and V. Artinopoulou (eds), *Reconstructing restorative justice philosophy* (pp. 311–337). Farnham: Ashgate Publishing.

Gavrielides T. (2014). Bringing race telations into the restorative justice debate. *Journal of Black Studies*, *45*(3), 216–246.

Gillinson, S., Horne, M. and Baeck, P. (2010). *Radical efficiency: different, better, lower cost public services*. London: NESTA.

Lyubansky, M. and Barter, D. (2011). A restorative approach to interpersonal racial conflict. *Peace Review: A Journal of Social Justice*, *23*(1), 37–44.

Lyubansky, M. and Hunter, C.D. (2014). Toward racial justice. In E. Mustakova-Possardt, M. Lyubansky, M. Basseches and J. Oxenberg (eds), *Toward a socially responsible psychology for a global era* (pp. 183–205). New York: Springer.

Maiese, M. (2004). Procedural justice. In G. Burgess and H. Burgess (eds), *Beyond intractability*. Conflict Information Consortium, University of Colorado, Boulder. Posted: January 2004. http://www.beyondintractability.org/essay/pro cedural-justice.

McDonald, J. (2012). Best practice in restorative justice conference facilitation: some big ideas. In J. Bolitho, J. Bruce and G. Mason (eds), *Restorative justice: adults and emerging practice* (pp. 156–172). Sydney: Institute of Criminology Press.

McIntosh, P. (1998). White privilege: unpacking the invisible knapsack. *Race, Class, and Gender in the United States: An Integrated Study*, *4*, 165–169.

Morris, A. (2002). Critiquing the critics: a brief response to critics of restorative justice. *British Journal of Criminology*, *42*(3), 596–615.

Nash, J.C. (2008). Re-thinking intersectionality. *Feminist Review*, *89*(1), 1–15.

Plaut, V.C., Thomas, K.M. and Goren, M.J. (2009). Is multiculturalism or color blindness better for minorities? *Psychological Science*, *20*(4), 444–446.

Sadler, M.S., Correll, J., Park, B. and Judd, C.M. (2012). The world is not black and white: racial bias in the decision to shoot in a multiethnic context. *Journal of Social Issues*, *68*(2), 286–313.

Sherman, L.W. and Strang, H. (2007). *Restorative justice: the evidence* (p. 4). London: Smith Institute.

Shpungin (2014). The fluidity of victimhood. In T. Gavrielides (ed.), *A victim-led criminal justice system: addressing the paradox* (pp. 21–40). London: Independent Academic Research Studies (IARS) Publications.

Staats, C. (2014). *State of the science: implicit bias review.* Columbus: Kirwan Institute for the Study of Race and Ethnicity.

Sue, D.W., Carter, R.T., Casas, J.M., et al. (1998). *Multicultural counseling competencies: individual and organizational development.* Multicultural Aspects of Counseling Series, No. 11. Thousand Oaks: SAGE.

Wadhwa, A. (forthcoming). *Restorative justice in urban schools: disrupting the school-to-prison pipeline.* Abingdon: Routledge.

Zehr, H. (2002). *The little book of restorative justice* (Vol. 266). Intercourse, PA: Good Books.

PART III:
New Research

Chapter 11

The Psychology of Restorative Justice: Creating the Inner and Outer Space for Change – An Observation of Restorative Justice Meetings

Piers Worth, Theo Gavrielides, Matthew Smith,
Andriana Ntziadima and Ioanna Gouseti

Introduction

Restorative justice (RJ) is one of the most studied practices of criminal justice, and yet it is often far from being used in the way that its proponents hope (Braithwaite, 2002; Gavrielides and Artinopoulou, 2014; Shapland et al., 2006). The truth is that we are still learning how to do RJ well. For instance, we know that RJ works, but our knowledge of *why* and/or *when* it works, from a psychological perspective, is limited (Gavrielides and Worth, 2013).

This chapter represents an attempt by a group of criminologists, legal theorists and psychologists to bridge this knowledge gap via interdisciplinary working. We aim to show how and why an interdisciplinary approach to RJ is important, by sending a message that criminologists, psychologists, lawyers and other scholars can work together to produce new knowledge about RJ as a topic of scientific inquiry and push the barriers of RJ as a criminal justice practice.

In particular, we will use our separate perspectives to ask what is happening within different RJ processes as a means to explore RJ theory and practice. From a positive psychology perspective, which seeks to foster well-being in communities and individuals (see inter alia Seligman and Csikszentmihalyi, 2000; Worthington and Wade, 1999), we develop an approach to RJ through the lens of the Good Lives Model (GLM; see Ward and Brown, 2004; Ward et al., 2007).

The GLM approaches offender rehabilitation, premised on the idea that reoffending can be reduced by building capabilities and strengths. This is because individuals, according to the GLM, break the law while attempting to achieve some valued goals in their life; the goal seeking is legitimate, but the way it manifests itself happens to be harmful. So, the aim of the criminal justice interventions should be to help offenders improve their social functioning rather than exclude them from society through incarceration (ibid.).

The chapter is part of a larger project supported by Buckinghamshire New University aiming to test the contribution of positive psychology for the theoretical development of RJ as well as the design, evaluation and delivery of its practices (Gavrielides and Worth, 2013). The chapter draws upon qualitative data from fieldwork that was carried out in 2013–2014. By bringing positive psychology into the RJ debate, the larger project may be able to generate a much needed normative and practical direction for improved implementation of RJ, including minimizing the risks associated with its delivery as well as increasing the positive effects that we know it can have on victims, offenders and the community (Gavrielides and Worth, 2013).

We accept from the outset that in the investigation of social justice processes there are no undeniable truths. The very term 'restorative justice' remains contested (Gavrielides, 2008). Gavrielides (2008) explains that the many definitions of RJ tend to be divided into two wider groups in its extensive literature. The first places emphasis on the various types of restorative process, while the second highlights restorative outcomes. There are also the wider, value-based definitions in which RJ is regarded as 'an *ethos* with practical goals, among which is *to restore harm* by including affected parties in a (direct or indirect) *encounter* and a process of understanding through voluntary and honest dialogue' (Gavrielides, 2007, p. 139). For Braithwaite (1999, 2002) and McCold (2006) the principles underlying this 'ethos' are: victim reparation, offender responsibility and communities of care.

We are at a critical point in the development of RJ in the UK. The rising costs of incarceration and the failure of the criminal justice system to keep communities safe lead reformists and policy makers to search for alternatives. For example, according to the Offender Management Caseload Statistics, in 2009, the UK had 151 prisoners per 100,000 population, the second highest rate in Western Europe, below Spain (Ministry of Justice, 2010b). In England and Wales, the prison population was forecast to rise to 94,000 before the 2015 general election (Berman, 2010, 2013). These failings are at an annual cost of £10 billion (National Audit Office, 2010). In July 2015, the prison population was 84,985 (Ministry of Justice, 2015).

Arguably, the biggest development is said to be the passing of the Crime and Courts Act in 2013 (Ministry of Justice, 2013b). Part 2, 'Deferring the passing of sentence to allow for restorative justice', provides for the diversion of adult cases to a RJ practice at the pre-sentence stage. The Act was enacted in December 2013 and since April 2014 courts have had the power to defer the passing of a sentence, provided that all parties agree (that is, both the offender and the victim). The Act does not specify the types of cases or the profile of offenders. It does not specify the type of restorative practices either. It merely encourages judges to consider restorative practices, while it requires that anyone practising RJ must have regard to the guidance that is issued by the Secretary of State.

It is reasonable to assume that this increase of interest in RJ will have direct impact on criminal justice services. For example, as part of its commissioning intentions for 2013–2014, the National Offender Management Service (NOMS), the key governmental body funding probation services in England and Wales, set out a specific intention for both prisons and probation trusts to continue to develop sustainable capacity and capability to deliver effective face-to-face victim–offender conferencing, working with partners.

The commitment to RJ is also evident at the international level. For example, the EU and the Council of Europe have issued a number of relevant recommendations, and have a significant number of publications in the field of RJ. The range of topics covered in these documents is wide, including the role of victims in the criminal proceedings, the process of mediation, and the state's assistance to victims (see Committee of Ministers of the Council of Europe, 1985, 1987; 26th Conference of European Ministers of Justice, 2005; European Union, 2001; European Parliament and Council of the European Union, 2012).

In our work on this project to increase knowledge and understanding of RJ, we moved to observe it openly, in action. We start with the premise that the path towards offender rehabilitation and desistance is a rather complex one (Farrall and Calverley, 2005; Maruna, 2001; Maruna et al., 2004). Research is divided among those who argue that the focus should be placed on the management and reduction of offenders 'criminogenic needs' (Bonta and Andrews, 2007), and those who adopt a more positive approach to offenders' treatment by focusing on the relationship between risk management and good lives (Ward and Brown, 2004). In any case, criminological and psychological scholarship has made apparent that rehabilitation is more likely to be achieved through interventions that equip individuals with tools that can carry on a fulfilling life rather than focus on punishment (Gavrielides, 2007; Ward and Maruna, 2007).

The opportunity to observe RJ at work for research purposes is understandably rare, for both ethical and practical reasons – that is, in order not to intrude upon a sensitive and personal process. The main objective of the research project was to ask, as open observers, what we see within the different RJ processes, and in particular the psychological dynamic present in these RJ meetings – that is, this research show how an interdisciplinary approach to understanding RJ and its potential and risks is important. The various contributions were aiming to challenge the RJ movement by helping it to think outside the box and by sending a message that criminologists, psychologists, lawyers and so on can all work together to push the barriers of RJ. Analysing our data through an interdisciplinary lens, we aimed to show how RJ theory and practice can be improved by combining knowledge from different fields. In the following sections, we present the methodology of our study, its key objectives and findings, and the main conclusions that are derived from this research.

Methodology

The current analysis draws upon qualitative data from three observations. The first consisted of RJ meetings between victims and offenders, organized by the

Mediation, Negotiation and Arbitration Centre (MNAC) of the Central University of Chile. The remaining two consisted of offender-focused pre-release educational and change interventions run by two UK registered charities – namely, the Silence the Violence (STV) programme of Khulisa UK[1] and the Restore programme of The Forgiveness Project.[2] Our data capture different types of qualitative techniques of data collection and analysis as well as different typologies of RJ processes. We also note that we are observing processes taking place in different sociocultural contexts and in different languages.

The opportunity for observation within these contexts falls within the principles of ethnography as a research method (Atkinson et al., 2004). The intention is to explore the nature of social phenomena and human experiences within these settings. The observational focus has been open and unstructured, with the objective of making interpretations of the psychological dynamic witnessed (Atkinson and Hammersley, 1994, p. 284). The rationale for observation as a research method is that the relationships, the shared meaning and the conflicts, which are generated through social interaction, become meaningful as one looks at them at close range (Goffman, 1963).

The methods that we employed draw on multi-modal ethnography (Dicks et al., 2006), and include both non-participant observation and participant observation as the main methods of data collection and analysis (DeWalt and DeWalt, 2010; Jorgensen, 1989). The former was used in the case of the MNAC of the Central University of Chile, which involves analysis of recorded RJ mediation, while the later was used in the STV programme of Khulisa and the Restore programme of The Forgiveness Project, which involve the researchers' attendance of RJ conferences. Permission to act as observers was gained from the managers or management boards of the aforementioned organizations, for which ethical approval was sought and gained via the University Ethics Committee of Buckinghamshire New University.

The research team comprised two researchers who acted as participant-observers (Ioanna Gouseti with the Khulisa programme; Andriana Ntziadima with The Forgiveness Project), and two academic psychologists (Piers Worth and Matthew Smith). The project was facilitated and co-ordinated by Theo Gavrielides and funded by Bucks New University. Preparation and training for the participant observers was facilitated by PW, who also provided support for the observers during and after the observations.

Following the typologies of the membership roles of the participant observers as developed by Gold (1958) and Adler and Adler (1987), we were 'active member researchers' in that we were involved in the group's central activities, but we were not fully engaged (see also Gold, 1997). This does not apply to the case of the MNAC of the Central University of Chile, which involves analysis of secondary data. In the cases where collection of primary data was involved (that is, in the RJ

---

1   http://www.khulisa.co.uk/silence-violence/.

2   http://theforgivenessproject.com/programmes/restore/.

meetings held by Khulisa and The Forgiveness Project) written permission was asked by the RJ conferences' participants, who were informed about the identity of the observers prior to the programme and gave their consent for the researcher's presence and participation.

The field notes of the observers included briefings from the facilitators, chronological descriptions of the meetings and events, and subsequent reflections, and interpretations of the experiences (Emerson et al., 2011). In addition, there was a lengthy 'de-brief' meeting between the two participant observers (AN and IG) and the two psychologists (PW and MS) to review the experiences of the former. A transcript of this meeting also comprised data used.

Data analysis was thematic. Thematic analysis is considered as one of the foundational methods of exploring qualitative data, and customarily involves six steps: familiarization with data; generating initial codes; searching for themes; reviewing themes; defining and naming themes; writing up the outcome (Braun and Clarke, 2006, p. 87). While it can be used inductively or deductively, in this instance focus was inductive, reflecting the research intention of the project, letting the experiences be viewed openly to bring forward possible understanding and learning.

As regards the processes of RJ that are analysed, we had the chance to observe both 'fully restorative' processes, involving the participation of offenders, victims and the community, and 'partially' restorative processes, involving one or two of these parties (McCold and Wachtel, 2003). In particular, in the case of the MNAC of the Central University of Chile, the meetings included the offenders, the victims and, on one occasion, family members. The Khulisa's Silence the Violence programme focused on offenders; while the Restore programme of The Forgiveness Project included offenders, surrogate victims and prison staff.

The nature of the RJ practices (such as conferences, circles, family group decision) that are included in our observations also varies (see Morris and Maxwell, 2001; Morse and Maxwell, 2001; Pranis et al., 2003). On the one hand, the meetings of the Mediation, Negotiation and Arbitration Centre of the Central University of Chile fall more into the category of mediation, where the process is more structured and the main aim is to deal with the consequences of the crime and find the best way to repair the harm (McCold, 2006). On the other hand, the meetings of both the Khulisa's STV and The Forgiveness Project's Restore fall more into the category of conferences, where the participants share stories and offer personal perspectives, aiming to provide support, resolve conflicts and develop relationships (Morris and Maxwell, 2001).

In the following paragraphs, we provide a brief description of the three organizations that carry out the RJ practices, which we had the chance to observe.[3]

---

3   We would like to express our thanks to the three organizations for granting access for this research, and to the participants who formed part of the observations themselves.

Mediation, Negotiation and Arbitration Centre, Central University of Chile

The Mediation, Negotiation and Arbitration Centre (MNAC) of the Central University of Chile conducts mediation between offenders and victims when referred by the criminal justice system (CJS), and as a potential alternative to court imposed action. As such, its work may divert court cases from a sentencing outcome as provided by Chile's penal code.

Data provided by the MNAC consisted of two videoed case sessions, provided with a translation into English via subtitles. These video-recordings, lasting 80 minutes and 86 minutes respectively, allowed us to act as non-participant observers to the mediation meetings. Both cases included a defendant and a complainant, and the mediation sessions were facilitated by two female trained mediators.

In one case, relating to the theft of a laptop computer, the complainant was a female law student (aged 19) and the defendant was a fellow male law student (aged 21). In the second case, in which the complaint related to failure to provide goods that had already been paid for, the complainant was a male psychologist (aged 36) and the defendant was a male film student (aged 20). In each case, the recordings were of all four meetings that comprised the mediation (offender alone; victim alone; victim and offender together; final meeting in which an agreed outcome is discussed and recorded).

Khulisa (UK): Silence the Violence Programme

Khulisa UK is a charity registered in England and Wales that has organized programmes of offender rehabilitation and RJ since 2009. Khulisa UK is an independent part of Khulisa Social Solutions, one of the leading providers of similar programmes in South Africa. The emphasis within the observed programme – Silence the Violence – is placed on the insights and skills that could enhance the ability of an offender to develop alternatives to criminal behaviour, thereby desisting from crime and improving their social interaction.

The fieldwork took place in a Category C Prison of young male offenders in spring 2014. The participants of the RJ programme were four prisoners, aged 18–22, the two facilitators and one observer from our research team (IG). The meetings lasted five hours per day, and included a morning session, followed by a lunch break and an afternoon session.

Silence the Violence (STV) involves group work and one-to-one meetings. The programme focuses on social learning, cognitive behaviour, pro-social behaviour changes, self-awareness and pro-social identity. The programme draws upon the Good Lives Model, which approaches offending as a behaviour that is related to a lack of internal and/or external challenges and difficulties, instead of a criminal reaction or a personal tendency (Ward et al., 2007).

The programme involves 10 modules of two to three hours' duration in facilitated group sessions, over a five-day period, and is followed by individual sessions between each offender, the programme facilitators and the offender's probation supervisor. The emphasis of the post-programme meetings is placed on the offender's needs, and post-release matters, such as housing, employment and family.

The Forgiveness Project: Restore

The Forgiveness Project is a UK-based charity with a mission 'to create dialogue about forgiveness and promote understanding through awareness, understanding and transformation'. To achieve its charitable mission The Forgiveness Project utilizes real stories of forgiveness and reconciliation from both victims and perpetrators of crime as a tool to facilitate conflict resolution, behavioural change and rehabilitation. At the heart of The Forgiveness Project is the Restore programme, which has been delivered over 150 times to prison and probation institutions in England and Wales over the past 10 years. Restore is an offender-focused intervention programme that aims to promote the understanding that everyone has a potential to change. The programme is co-facilitated by a lead facilitator, a survivor and/or ex-offender using personal stories to encourage offenders to reflect on their own experiences and offending behaviour.

The observed programme took place in an adult male and young offenders' prison located in South Wales, UK, in March 2014. The programme unfolded over two and a half days, split over five sessions, which took place in the mornings and afternoons. There were 27 participants, co-facilitated by a lead facilitator, a trained ex-offender and a survivor. The latter two both used their own personal life stories to encourage prisoners to reflect on their own experiences and offending behaviour with a view to changing their perspectives and taking responsibility for their acts.

Findings

The content of the three observations is very different, given the differences in the observation context. Findings relating to each intervention are therefore described separately, before some common themes from across all three contexts are highlighted.

The Mediation, Negotiation and Arbitration Centre, Chile:
Offender–Victim Mediation

As noted earlier, the mediation undertaken comprised four separate meetings. The first with the offender alone; the second with the victim, alone; the third, with the victim and offender in which initial mediation is attempted; and the fourth in which an agreed outcome is discussed and recorded for the CJS.

What follows is an attempt to summarize what was seen across all four of these meetings in the video-recorded cases.

Creating psychological space
Each meeting – the individual meeting with the offender and victim separately, and then the joint meeting – opens with an explanation of the purpose of the meeting and how it will be conducted. This may appear simple, or organized. However, it is fundamental to what will be achieved. It is made clear each person will be given an opportunity to speak and to be heard. This appears to create the psychological space and the safety in which to work through something difficult. The mediators hold to that process, and help and make participants stay within it.

The 'tone' of voice and 'being' (of the mediators)
The mediators create this space and work in a way that sounds gentle, respectful and firm. By creating this and doing so in an open and respectful manner, both sides are respected and become a full and accepted part of the interaction. The 'tone' is central.

Listening to the experience – summarizing the experience
With a way of working established, the mediators then listen to the experience. They give each person, alone initially and then together, time to speak. They explore and clarify what the offender or victim says where necessary, and what they felt and experienced. The mediators were able to gently and respectfully get the offender to admit and accept parts of his background and behaviour, more than he had admitted to or described previously. It was evident the mediators knew more about his background than they disclosed and as a result pressed him to face the whole of his experiences and behaviour. He did not appear willing to do that at the beginning of the session.

   The mediators then summarize what they have been told by the person. They do so in detail and in a gentle tone. This tells the contributor they have been heard and respected. We infer it communicates an acceptance of the person, which is crucial psychologically (whether offender or victim) to help him/her act and change. However, when the victim and offender hear the mediators summarizing and understanding their behaviour and experience it also changes something. By hearing the words it is as if the experience has reality in the world. The words provide acceptance, respect and 'form' to the experience, feelings and behaviour.

Signs of anxiety, stress or fear
The meetings are complex and sensitive. It is human and natural for individuals to feel anxiety, stress or fear in situations such as these. Signs of these could be observed through changes in body posture on behalf of the offender. For example, the crossing of arms, backing away, breaking eye contact and looking down and away might all be interpreted as ways of showing some form of stress or anxiety. The victim appeared to be struggling with the option of punishment or some form of restitution. We infer this showed initially in very one-sided arm movements, yet when he decided to move towards a solution, his whole body moved and engaged.

Applying pressure, gaining a resolution

Mediation appears to balance the goals of some kind of restitution alongside possible punishment. The two goals were potentially at variance. Gaining one might not achieve the other. For example, in one of the cases, one of the mediators pressed the victim to consider whether punishment and the courts were helpful to him given the extent to which restitution might be essential to his business progress. This might be interpreted as a pressure that might help or make the victim decide what he most wanted or needed.

The mediation also made both parties pause for a few days after being heard, and think for themselves about how to find a helpful way forward. This places responsibility on individuals to use their own judgment and creativity to find a solution, and to find it with the other party. It places them in a situation, in the best of ways, where they have to come together to resolve things. By giving them time to think, we speculated that the offender may have proposed a more generous solution and restitution than might have occurred beforehand.

Khulisa's Silence the Violence (STV)

The following paragraphs summarize the STV programme through the key topics that are discussed during the five days of the intervention. Despite the descriptive nature of these data, we do acknowledge the 'active processes of interpretation and sense-making' that are involved in their collection and analysis (Emerson et al., 2011).

Creating an opening

The programme begins with a briefing for participants regarding its origins and aims, and an exploration of what they hope to gain from taking part. Most of the participants' hopes pertain to their families. The introductory part involves short 'warm-up' games. For example, one striking in its simplicity yet powerful in its effect enables *all* participants, facilitators and offenders to talk from a place of *similarity* between them, not difference. This opens up the possibility of communication that follows. The structure of the programme is also presented at this stage, along with its principles, including mutual respect and confidentiality.

Violence awareness

This is the first theme on which the programme focuses, and is the core subject that is covered in the first two days. It aims to sensitize participants to the nature of violence, its origins, manifestations and consequences.

The activities of this phase are of two main types: first, circles of discussion, where the participants express their ideas and beliefs about the meaning of violence, its different types, possible reactions to violence, feelings related to violent behaviour and victimization, and other topics, such as the cycle of violence; second, circles of sharing, where the participants discuss primary or vicarious experiences of violence from the standpoint of the perpetrator and/or the victim. Overall, the activities draw upon the idea that violence is not necessarily a personality trait, and open perspectives for choices of change.

Echoing criminological and psychological research findings, these activities aim to show that violence is a behavioural reaction that is associated with individual states, environmental factors and societal parameters (Farrington, 1989; Loeber and Stouthamer-Loeber, 1998; Loeber and Ahonen, 2014). To convey this idea and encourage the participants to share views on the sensitive topic of violence, the implicit nature of some of the activities is 'symbolic', they take the form of games and creative activities. This sensitivity in approach is crucial, especially when it comes to people who have been assigned the 'label' of the 'violent criminal' through their conviction and incarceration (Chiricos et al., 1972; Goffman, 1963; Pager et al., 2009).

One of the key topics of discussion of this phase pertains to the cycle of violence, and centres around the idea that violent behaviour might be habitual – that is, learned and thus reversible (see Maruna and King, 2004). It prompts a way of thinking about violence that associates it with behaviour rather than personality. The former taps more into one's actions, which are manifestations of not only personality characteristics, but also their interplay with the wider context, and thus are more prone to change.

Experiences of violence

The programme aims to 'silence' the potential triggers of violent reactions, which might be quite common when one has been exposed to violence, and through this has developed a sense of tolerance to its manifestations. Importantly, criminological research has shown that interpersonal violence does relate to individuals' commitment to values that reflect a wider subculture of violence (Felson et al., 1994; Wolfgang and Ferracuti, 1982).

Here, the activities are again mainly of a 'creative' character, such as drawing, and are followed by circles of discussion. This practice is based on the idea that having, say, a drawing as a starting point of discussions about sensitive topics, such as violent victimization, will encourage people to open up and share such experiences more easily and in a less painful way, as the facilitators explained. These activities are followed by discussions about positive experiences to counterbalance the negative emotions that might be triggered by talking about unpleasant experiences.

Along with the more attitudinal activities of the previous phase, STV thus generates an environment of violence awareness and sensitization that includes both cognitive and affective elements.

Power relations

STV looks at violence not only as an attitude and experience, but also as an element of social interaction. Through different types of activities, such as poem reading and the screening of a documentary about gang crime in the USA, the programme aims to show that violent behaviour not only affects the perpetrator and the victim of violence, but also the society in general, by damaging people's relationships and their well-being.

The negative effects of violence on social interaction are discussed in STV through the notions of *inferiority, superiority* and *equality*. This approach to violence draws upon criminological work that examines the associations between structural factors, such as economic inequality, social exclusion, social cohesion, social control and violent behaviour (Kramer, 2000; Morenoff et al., 2001; Wilkinson, 2004).

This is considered to be an important approach to the 'determinants' of violence. It is likely that STV participants have experienced violence from both a 'superior' perspective (for example, as perpetrators of crime in relation to their victims) and an 'inferior' perspective (for example, as young, poor and unemployed prisoners). Showing this contradiction that is intrinsic to experiences of violence, STV aims to highlight the importance of equality as a prerequisite for the prevention of violence.

The association between violence and inequality is further explored and discussed through the screening of a documentary film that presents the life of members of criminal gangs, their victims and the wider community. The screening acts as a 'mirror' that aims to give some perspective to the participants' personal experiences, thoughts and feelings that are related to violence. This creates a possibility for developing a third-person perspective to familiar experiences that are related to violence, its causes and effects, and thus help develop a more general understanding of these phenomena.

Making amends

The process of making amends is the next topic discussed through activities of sharing personal experiences of and ideas about the process of apologizing. The main aim of these activities is then to familiarize the participants with the actual stages of the process, and encourage them to work more on those that they find particularly difficult or painful.

The discussions rely on both retrospective and prospective mindsets. On the one hand, the discussion focuses on past experiences, where the participants did not apologize for a wrongdoing and they have regretted it. On the other hand, the discussion focuses on situations for which, and people to whom, participants would like to apologize in the future. The circle of sharing is followed by a more general discussion about the identification of the steps that comprise the process of making amends, including acceptance of the wrongdoing, self-exploration of its causes and development of communication with the 'victim'.

Appreciation

The last phase of the STV includes symbolic activities, such as poetry readings, discussions about future plans and a circle of sharing final thoughts. The activities aim to raise participants' awareness of their accomplishments during the programme, the knowledge acquired and the relationships that have been built.

Emphasis is put on the ability to change patterns of behaviour and develop positive ways of perceiving the world, and on the key role that trust and confidence in oneself and important others play in the process of personal development.

The next step pertains to the 'graduation ceremony', where the participants are awarded their 'graduation' certificates. This is followed by an 'appreciation activity'. First, all the parties involved in STV write on a piece of paper a few words of appreciation about everyone else in the programme, and then each participant is encouraged to read aloud the comments written for them. It is a powerful process where participants often find it difficult to listen to positive things about themselves, and have the opportunity to appreciate the importance of receiving positive feedback and appreciation. Our inference is that the participants' difficulty to accept positive comments about themselves stems from the internalization of negative attitudes of others towards themselves that they might have experienced during their lives, along with the negativity inherent in the prison environment,. In the words of one participant after the activity, 'I won't lie to you; it has been so long that I haven't heard anything positive about myself that it was hard to read all these kind words. Thank you'.

Apart from the five-day programme, STV includes post-programme meetings at two phases: first, meetings with each of the participants and the facilitators, which serve as a follow-up to the group meetings; second, meetings with each of the participants, the facilitators and their probation supervisors, where their current state in prison is discussed, along with ways forward. Participants are also informed about the post-release mentoring programme that Khulisa UK offers.

The Forgiveness Project: Restore

The observed programme took place over five sessions across two and a half days. Sessions covered the following themes: development of empathy and understanding of the impact of participants' criminal behaviour, exploration of the notion of forgiveness, understanding of the motives that led to the offending behaviour, building emotional awareness and self-esteem, taking responsibility of their own future and making amends.

The primary intervention, psychologically, comes from the stories told by a victim and an offender. Heard by participants, through listening, what occurs is an ability to identify with both stories, to identify with others, and in turn to start questioning their own story – early steps to re-story their views and lives. There is the paradox of great simplicity and power in this approach through the fundamental medium that we all relate to – story. As the process is to a large extent 'passive' in nature (i.e., listening), we noted with interest a level of nervousness and tension in participants that unfolded or showed itself in different ways.

Empathy
The Restore Programme emphasizes and focuses on the development of empathy as a tool for further exploration and understanding of participants' criminal behaviour

and its impact on their victim and society. Empathy is usually defined as an active effort to understand another person's perception of an interpersonal event by adopting the other person's perspective and leaving aside judgments that relate to one's own experiences (Malcolm and Greenberg, 2000). Participants are introduced to the notion of empathy and induced into this state by being exposed to real life stories told by their protagonists. The process involves three stages: sharing of the life stories from a victim who has reconciled with the past, an ex-offender who walked out of criminal life, and lastly, sharing of the stories of the participants within the group. The stories that were shared were very powerful with strong messages around empathy, forgiveness and restoration, revealing always very sensitive and personal aspects of the journey of their protagonists.

At first the participants had the opportunity to hear directly from a victim of a violent and extreme crime and follow her in her journey to reconcile and come to terms with the pain and the trauma that had been caused to her by her perpetrators. The victim's story was extremely powerful and involved her ordeal, her emotions and her coping mechanisms. It was evident her openness and honest sharing captured the attention, feelings and the imagination of the group who were listening to the story in absolute silence. Listening to a story that at first sight was not related to their own criminal activities, participants moved out of their own interpersonal experiences and followed the experiences, emotional pain and journey towards reconstruction of the self of another individual.

What was evident was that participants reflected on their own experiences, leaving aside the label of being the 'victim' or the 'offender'. Their role was clearly that of neutral observer. The process revealed an interesting and profound pattern of self – identification with both the victim and the offender. The participants seemed to understand the fine line between the two and reflect on their own experiences. What we were witnessing was the capacity of the 'offender' or prisoners to step away from the labelling they have, and we give them, and to meet in a shared understanding of human experience.

The path towards empathy and understanding was also paved via the narrative of the ex-offender who had successfully managed to turn his life around. The narrative was centred around the notion that life is the outcome of individuals' choices and that all individuals have the potential to 'become who they truly are'. This prompted the participants to think about their own lives, their experiences, their expectations, but also their opportunities to make decisions that could affect their lives and the lives of those around them. Although the ex-offender's story was presented as a 'success story', which prompted positive and optimistic thinking, the complexities and the difficulties that would hinder the process were explicit and the final choice would be dependent on their own decisions.

The sharing of the life stories created a safe space of mutual trust and respect between facilitators and participants. Some participants reported that they felt privileged to be able to listen to those extremely powerful personal experiences that both victim and ex-offender shared with them.

The space of mutual respect and trust that was created opened the way for the participants to revisit their own narratives and share with the group their personal life stories. To support the exploration of their life over time, portrayed as a 'time line', the facilitators provided all participants with various types of crayons, pencils and post-it notes and encouraged them to present their time lines in any way they felt comfortable. Initially the drawings revealed that most of the participants defined themselves around the crime they committed or the reasons and the situations that led to the crime. However, with the support of the facilitator almost everyone moved beyond the event that led to imprisonment and looked at the bigger picture of their life. The time lines brought to the fore more similarities and connections than differences, proving that dialogue and sharing can bring a common ground to the surface.

By sharing their personal narratives the participants identified similarities within their own stories, but also managed to single out events that triggered certain behaviours. Thus, reflection on their life, or 'time line', was not only an opportunity for self-reflection, but also an integral part of a learning process that enabled them to develop a degree of meaning and to further understand and interpret their motives behind behaviours (McAdams, 2006).

At this point special mention should be made of the active participation of the two members of prison staff in the programme who were involved in the discussions and shared their personal stories on equal terms. Staff participation added another layer in the interpretation of the dynamics of the relationship between the self and the other. The explicit hierarchical nature of these types of relationships (between prison officer and inmate) was shifted in this exploration, enabling both parties to obtain a fresh perspective that moved from the personal experience to the experience of the other and vice versa. One participant noted how connected he felt with a staff member's story and added that he never thought that he could find so many things in common with one of the prison officers.

From empathy to forgiveness

Taking empathy as the first step towards forgiveness, the Restore programme explores further the concept of forgiveness and its potential role in the lives of individuals. For the victim, who has reconciled with her own past and achieved restoration, her story is crucial in triggering the initial thoughts and reactions around forgiveness. The process of forgiveness as a construction of a new narrative or view of the self and the other (Rowe et al., 1989) is revealed through the victim's story. Forgiveness, for her, is presented as a path towards restoration and internal peace, involving the process of exploring herself and the other (the perpetrator) and attempting to understand and find closure.

Through the personal story, forgiveness is perceived as choice with the potential to bring closure and restoration. Through open and honest dialogue, an exploration of the potential directions of forgiveness takes place that ranges from forgiveness of the self to forgiveness of the perpetrators and expected or hoped-for forgiveness from the victims. Every personal story seems to shed light in a different direction but all the stories together form a mosaic of harm, pain, revenge, guilt, shame, revenge and reparation/restitution where forgiveness emerges as the invisible thread that can potentially break the cycle.

Accountability and making amends
Following the development of empathy and the exploration of forgiveness, the programme focuses on supporting participants in becoming accountable for their own choices and behaviours as well as for the harm that these behaviours have caused. Here the emphasis is not placed on individual cases but on the development of a deeper understanding of the meaning of their apology. The participants are presented with a short documentary of the life of a notorious criminal who was offered the opportunity to meet with one of his victims, who accepted it, and the encounter changed his live. The documentary was used as a prompt to introduce participants to the concept of RJ. This rather sensitive situation, in which participants are called on to make an apology, is further approached though interactive role play, where participants become the victim and they are asked to question their motives, thoughts and reasons behind their criminal activity. Through role play the participants have once again the opportunity to broaden their thinking and incorporate the feelings and emotions of the other in their thought process. As a result, to make amends is not just a matter of a possibly empty apology but the outcome of a deep thought process that involves the main aspects of empathy.

The development of empathy, the understanding of forgiveness and the role of accountability and voluntary effort for restoration have a common element, i.e., a shift in the way that the self and the other are perceived. This process is characterized by a broad perspective, self-reflection and the awareness of emotion (Pennebaker et al., 1990). In turn, self-awareness and self-reflection enhance the understanding of the self and the motives behind practices and enable the individual to define his/her identity by facing his/her actions and their impacts on the self and on the other and holding him/her responsible and accountable for them.

Rewards
The programme closes in a very positive and powerful way. Participants receive certificates for their participation to the programme and are applauded by facilitators and co-participants for their courage, efforts and bravery to open up, share their experiences and connect with others by following their journeys. The process of certification can be seen as highly symbolic as participants see the process as a journey with a start, middle and end. Following the certification process participants are asked to briefly mention their future plans and whether they would be interested in finding out more about RJ practices and potentially meet their victims. One of the participants said that he would feel privileged if his victim wanted to meet him.

The journey from empathy to forgiveness and accountability was completed with the choice of a word that summarized the feelings and the thoughts of the participants during the final three days; among the key words that were chosen by the participants were the following: *hope – success – faith – empowerment – positive thinking – forgiveness – perseverance determination – change.*

Common Themes across the Observations

Despite the differences that are apparent in the examples described above, four core common themes emerge across the three observations. Beyond these themes, we recognize that each of the observed RJ interventions has different origins and distinct objectives, albeit driven by common principles, including repair of harm, respect to dignity and diversity, individuals' autonomy and confidentiality. Given that the majority of participants in each programme were offenders, the following comments are primarily directed to the offender. These themes are: (a) beliefs and perspectives about the offender; (b) the anxiety that the offender (and the victim) bring into the RJ process; (c) a psychological space that enables inner and outer openness, exploration and learning; (d) the speed of apparent insight and change.

Core Theme 1: The Beliefs and Perspectives about the Offender

The beliefs and perspectives we bring to justice, and RJ, shape everything that follows. In each of the observations, it was evident that the observers, however 'open' their research intentions were, brought personal preconceptions and expectations to the process about the nature of the 'offenders' (see Alvesson and Sköldberg, 2009). In hindsight, we could assume, despite the professional backgrounds of the observers, that these are formed and shaped by the norms, expectations and discourses that occur within our society about crime and the criminal.

The existence of these preconceptions, and how they were then questioned, was one of the earliest pieces of experience and data that emerged. For example, to quote one of the observers in a de-brief meeting between the research team, 'you are in a room with thirty people that you feel like, they're offenders, not ex-offenders, they're offenders, they're participants in a course in prison and you come in and you are from a different world ... and you suddenly see all these connections, not only between them, but between them and you. This is thrown in your face, basically, and makes you change your life approach ... A lot of things change, about how you feel about the world and your stereotypes ... I could connect ... We are not different. I saw it there in practice. That we are sharing thoughts and feelings, that we are the same'.

The ability to experience this connection with the 'offender' and to see them as more than a criminal calls into question the clear-cut distinctions that society often draws (for example, in media images of crime and political discourse about crime) between the law-abiding citizen and the criminal (Becker, 1973; Chiricos et al., 1972; Maruna et al., 2004). This creates further questions at the policy level: Can a criminal be perceived in a way that her/his identity is not absorbed by the criminal act? Can these other features of a criminal's identity (rather than the criminal act) be the focus of initiatives to prevent reoffending? If the answer is yes, then there are fundamental changes that need to be made in the official responses and public attitudes to crime. We see this as fundamentally reflective of perspectives embedded in the Good Lives Model (Ward and Brown, 2004; Ward et al., 2007). We argue that RJ can contribute to such changes in that it approaches crime not only as a violation of the criminal law, but also as a wound in human relationships.

Core Theme 2: The Anxiety Associated with the RJ Process

In all of the observations, we saw the offenders entering into the meetings in a state of tension and anxiety. Our interpretation is that where someone is negatively labelled at the level of identity for their wrongdoing, and then is brought into an environment intended to explore what has happened, the sense of anxiety and 'difference' is, initially at least, strengthened. The level of this is, to us, an ethical issue in the conduct of RJ and needs identification in the training of practitioners and the delivery of the process to guard against harm We also saw, however, that when the participants realized that in the programme's context they are not seen solely through the lens of their criminal act, but of wider potential, the psychological space and movement, inner and outer, towards acceptance, empathy and positivity became possible.

Core Theme 3: Creating a Psychological Space that
Enables an Offender to Open, Explore and Learn

In all three observations, the context of the meetings was structured in a way that brought individuals into relationship. In the case of MNAC mediation meetings, there were two mediators who set down a clear set of rules that framed the process by which individuals would be heard. They made a 'space', which implies respect and acceptance, for someone to talk, and they summarized and checked understanding as they went. This is not 'soft' or easy; the mediators summarized, questioned and pushed, however gently, for greater understanding to emerge.

While the STV programme is different in many respects, the very early interaction between the facilitators and the participants, in which the former illustrated simply and without threat the commonality and similarity between the participants as ordinary people, also breaks open a capacity for communication and change. Moreover, the educational exercises that are carried out throughout the programme illustrate a fast and stunning capacity for the offenders to gain insight and knowledge, and thus self-appreciation.

The Forgiveness Project's Restore programme has a different approach, but again it takes people to new perceptions. The use of 'stories' is a fundamental medium through which we understand our worlds and ourselves. The offender-participants hear the stories of a 'victim' and an 'ex-offender'. They do so 'passively', through listening, but the results are far from passive. Through hearing stories that they can relate to and share understandings with, the barriers and differences come down.

We argue that the common thread to the three observations was the creation of a quality of psychological space in order to help participants come to terms with the criminal act, and stop internalizing the label of the 'criminal'. Put psychologically, the offenders are often negatively labelled at the level of identity. Therefore, if their crime is their identity, then there is not much room for change. To the contrary, if we say that the crime is an unacceptable behaviour, but one's identity has more to it than the crime, then we are seeing offenders as people and not just as criminals. When that was recognized and psychological space was made for it, the offenders in each observation moved, gained insight and learned at a pace that was startling to those involved in this project.

Core Theme 4: The Speed of Apparent Insight and Change

In psychological terms, the core 'event' within each programme is simple, skilful and profound, and it involves creating space where someone can be respected, say what they need to say, be heard, know they have been heard, and learn from having been heard. Importantly, an integral part of the process is the 'recognition' and respect to all the parties that are involved, which constitutes potentially a form of 'healing'. When that happens it is possible for the participants to 'meet' as human beings, and work towards a resolution. It also allows them to draw on their own creativity to resolve and heal a situation.

In one of the meetings observed from the MNAC, for instance, we saw an offender finding ways of making restitution, and offering additional work and support to the victim. In Khulisa's STV, it was observed that the ability to see the similarities and commonalities between the participants led to rapid open discussions about the nature, sources and causes of violence. In the Restore programme, we observed how the opportunity to hear the story of another person prompted levels of insight that made sense, for some, of experiences that had run over previous years.

The success reflects the skill, care and humanity of the mediators and facilitators, and their willingness to extend this to the other people involved. The RJ context, and the educational nature of the process, creates a space where people can develop holistic perspectives of themselves and others. This in turn might help create the resolution and healing for the victim.

These insights reflect the work of Carl Rogers (for example, Rogers, 1961). Rogers argued that if you create an environment based on certain characteristics of behaviour, where one person offers acceptance, respect and care to another person, while at the same time being themselves, the other person will inevitably change and grow.

Concluding Comments

This research project constitutes a rare opportunity to observe different types of RJ in action, from an open and interdisciplinary perspective. We acknowledge the project was a snapshot and brief insight into three separate and different interventions. However, the emergence of the core themes common to each is a notable insight worthy of further research and consideration.

Drawing upon positive psychology and criminological research, the analysis highlighted how the beliefs we hold about an offender influence the capacity for RJ and even rehabilitation to be effective. In order for RJ to work, a psychological space was created which allowed the offenders to be more than their offence, to be seen as a 'larger' or fuller person than their crime alone. In this space we saw individuals display insight, understanding, movement and a willingness to be more than their stereotype and their crime.

At the same time we saw the anxiety about the process impacted the offender, and we advocate that this must be acknowledged and managed in some way. The prison-based programmes create insight and change, and then return the offenders to an environment where one participant said, 'If you show vulnerability you are finished' (see Gavrielides, 2007; Liebmann and Braithwaite, 1999; Shapland, 2008). Given the priority placed on RJ and the knowledge that exists about its effectiveness, we also advocate as a result of this observation that consideration be given to how the potential changes within the offender may be sustained and supported after the RJ intervention.

Lives of individuals are linked and connected through invisible threads that consist of emotions, thoughts, experiences and actions. We believe we witnessed individuals, in a space of acceptance, come into relationship and display the emotions of empathy, acceptance and self-acceptance, forgiveness and hope. These interconnected invisible threads will further allow the development of both empathy and perspective. Indeed, rehabilitation is a rather complex concept but any steps towards it should encompass the journey of the individual and opportunities to self-identification, 'self-empathy' and self-forgiveness. These are opportunities that the criminal justice system typically fails to provide and address.

When we reach this perspective, RJ and views of rehabilitation overlap: these assumptions are found in the Good Lives Model (Ward and Brown, 2004; Ward et al., 2007). As mentioned earlier, this model views any of us, the offender included, as able to work and move towards our freely chosen goals, and in a manner or way of living that assumes 'certain freedom and well-being goods' (Laws and Ward, 2011, p. 177). The model sees us within a 'moral community' and sharing, as human beings, a capacity for free choice, even if offenders may need to face some restrictions within this. If we believe this about human beings generally, then in turn it influences the perceptions of and manner of behaviour towards others.

If RJ has this capacity for change, and the creation of psychological space based on certain values forms part of the power within it, then this in turn would need to be reflected in the training of RJ practitioners. The role of the wider society, however, remains crucial. If society works on the basis that those who commit crimes are criminals at the level of identity, then the aforementioned power of RJ is doomed to diminish. For this process of labelling serves to further justify and excuse all the 'unofficial sentences' that the offenders often experience.

A reduction in rates of reoffending, and an increase in rehabilitation, are desired and essential goals for modern societies. The current research indicates that there is more to offenders than their criminal behaviour, and in this small sample, when 'met' as a whole person, the speed and capacity for change was staggering to us. As researchers and practitioners we advocate further interdisciplinary case studies of this nature to test and expand these ideas.

Bibliography

26th Conference of European Ministers of Justice (2005). *Resolution No 2 on The Social Mission of the Criminal Justice System – Restorative Justice*. Helsinki.

Adler, P.A. and Adler, P. (1987). *Membership roles in field research*. Newbury Park, CA: Sage Publications.

Alvesson, M. and Sköldberg, K. (2009). *Reflexive methodology: new vistas for qualitative research*. London: SAGE.

Atkinson, P., Delamont, S. and Coffey, A. (2004). *Key themes in qualitative research: continuities and changes*. Walnut Creek: Rowman AltaMira Press.

Atkinson, P. and Hammersley, M. (1994). Ethnography and participant observation. In N.K. Denzin and Y.S. Lincoln (eds), *Handbook of qualitative research* (pp. 248–261). Thousand Oaks: SAGE.

Becker, S.H. (1973). *Outsiders: studies in the sociology of deviance*. New York: Free Press.

Berman, G. (2010). Prison population statistics. London: House of Commons Library.

Berman, G. (2013). Prison population statistics. London: House of Commons Library. Retrieved from http://www.antoniocasella.eu/nume/Berman_2013.pdf.

Bonta, J. and Andrews, D. (2007). Risk-need-responsivity model for offender assessment and rehabilitation. *Rehabilitation, 22*. Retrieved from https://cpoc.memberclicks.net/assets/Realignment/risk_need_2007–06_e.pdf.

Braithwaite, J. (1999). Restorative justice: assessing optimistic and pessimistic accounts. *Crime and Justice, 25*, 1–27.

Braithwaite, J. (2002). *Restorative justice and responsive regulation*. Oxford: Oxford University Press.

Braun, V. and Clarke, V. (2006). Using thematic analysis in psychology. *Qualitative Research in Psychology, 3*(2), 77–101. Retrieved from http://www.tandfonline.com/doi/abs/10.1191/1478088706qp063oa#.VMz5Pa0D1Kw.mendeley.

Chiricos, T.G., Jackson, P.D. and Waldo, G.P. (1972). *Inequality in the Imposition of a Criminal Label, 19*(4), 553–572.

Committee of Ministers of the Council of Europe (1985). *Recommendation No. R (85) 11 of the Committee of Ministers to member states on the position of the victim in the framework of criminal law and procedure. 387th meeting of the Ministers' Deputies*. Strasbourg.

Committee of Ministers of the Council of Europe (1987). *Recommendation No. R (87) 21 of the Committee of Ministers to member states on assistance to victims and the prevention of victimisation. 410th meeting of the Ministers' Deputies*. Strasbourg.

DeWalt, K.M. and DeWalt, B.R. (2010). *Participant observation: a guide for fieldworkers*. Walnut Creek: AltaMira Press.

Dicks, B., Soyinka, B. and Coffey, A. (2006). Multimodal ethnography. *Qualitative Research*, 6(1), 77–96.

Emerson, R., Fretz, R.I. and Shaw, L.L. (2011). *Writing ethnographic fieldnotes* (2nd edn). Chicago and London: University of Chicago Press.

European Parliament and Council of the European Union (2012). Directive 2012/29/EU of the European Parliament and of the Council of 25 October 2012 establishing minimum standards on the rights, support and protection of victims of crime, and replacing Council Framework Decision 2001/220/JHA. *Official Journal of the European Union, L 315* (April 2011), 57–73.

European Union (2001). *Council Framework Decision of 15 March 2001 on the standing of victims in criminal proceedings* (pp. 1–4). Brussels.

Farrall, S. and Calverley, A. (2006). *Understanding desistance from crime*. Maidenhead: Open University Press and McGraw-Hill Education.

Farrington, D.P. (1989). Early predictors of adolescent aggression and adult violence. *Violence and Victims*, 4(2), 79–100.

Felson, R.B., Liska, A.E., South, S.J. and McNulty, T.L. (1994). The subculture of violence and delinquency: individual vs. school context effects. *Social Forces*, 73, 155–173. doi:10.1093/sf/73.1.155.

Gavrielides, T. (2007). *Restorative justice theory and practice: addressing the discrepancy.* Helsinki: HEUNI.

Gavrielides, T. (2008). Restorative justice – the perplexing concept: conceptual fault-lines and power battles within the restorative justice movement. *Criminology and Criminal Justice*, 8(2), 165–183.

Gavrielides, T. and Artinopoulou, V. (2014). *Reconstructing restorative justice philosophy*. Farnham: Ashgate Publishing.

Gavrielides, T. and Worth, P. (2013). Another push for restorative justice: positive psychology and offender rehabilitation. In M.H. Pearson (ed.), *Crime: international perspectives, socioeconomic factors and psychological implications* (pp. 161–182). New York: Nova Science Publishers.

Goffman, E. (1963). *Stigma*. London: Penguin.

Gold, R. (1958). Roles in sociological field observation. *Social Forces*, 36, 17–213.

Gold, R.L. (1997). The ethnographic method in sociology. *Qualitative Inquiry*, 3, 388–402. doi:10.1177/107780049700300402.

Greene, D. (2013). Repeat performance: is restorative justice another good reform gone bad? *Contemporary Justice Review, 16*(3), 359–390. doi:10.1080/10282 580.2013.828912.

Jorgensen, D.L. (1989). *Participant observation: a methodology for human studies.* New York: SAGE.

Kauffman, K. (2000). Chile's revamped criminal justice system. *The Summit: Georgetown Journal of International Law, 40*(1), 25–47.

Kramer, R.C. (2000). Poverty, inequality, and youth violence. *The Annals of the American Academy of Political and Social Science, 567,* 123–139.

Laws, D.R. and Ward, T. (2011). *Desistance from sex offending: alternatives to throwing away the keys.* New York: Guilford Press.

Liebmann, M. and Braithwaite, S. (1999). *Restorative justice in custodial settings: report for the Restorative Justice Working Group in Northern Ireland.*

Loeber, R. and Ahonen, L. (2014). What are the policy implications of our knowledge on serious, violent, and chronic offenders? *Criminology & Public Policy, 13*(1), 117–125. doi:10.1111/1745-9133.12072.

Loeber, R. and Stouthamer-Loeber, M. (1998). Development of juvenile aggression and violence. Some common misconceptions and controversies. *American Psychologist, 53*(2), 242–259. doi:10.1037/0003-066X.53.2.242.

Malcolm, W.M. and Greenberg, L.S. (2000). Forgiveness as a process of change in individual psychotherapy. In M.E. McCullough, K.I. Pargament and C.E. Thoresen (eds), *Forgiveness: theory, research, and practice* (pp. 179–202). New York: Guilford Press.

Maruna, S. (2001). Defining desistance. In *Making good: how ex-convicts reform and rebuild their lives* (pp. 19–35). Washington: American Psychological Association.

Maruna, S. and King, A. (2004). Public opinion and community penalties. In A. Bottoms, S. Rex and G. Robinson (eds), *Alternatives to prison: options for an insecure society* (pp. 83–112). Cullompton: Willan.

Maruna, S., Lebel, T.P., Mitchell, N. and Naples, M. (2004). Pygmalion in the reintegration process: desistance from crime through the looking glass. *Psychology, Crime & Law, 10*(3), 271–281. doi:10.1080/106831604100016 62762.

McAdams, D.P. (2006). The problem of narrative coherence. *Journal of Constructivist Psychology, 19*(2), 109–125. doi:10.1080/10720530500508720.

McCold, P. (2006). The recent history of restorative justice: mediation, circles, and conferencing. In D. Sullivan and L. Tifft (eds), *Handbook of restorative justice: a global perspective* (pp. 23–51). New York: Routledge.

McCold, P. and Wachtel, T. (2003). *In pursuit of paradigm: a theory of restorative justice.* Paper presented at the XIII World Congress of Criminology, Rio de Janeiro, Brazil. Retrieved from http://www.iirp.edu/iirpWebsites/web/uploads/article_pdfs/paradigm.pdf.

Ministry of Justice (2010a). *Breaking the cycle: effective punishment, rehabilitation and sentencing of offenders. Rehabilitation* (p. 96). The Stationery Office.

Retrieved from http://www.justice.gov.uk/consultations/docs/breaking-the-cyc
le.pdf.

Ministry of Justice (2010b). *Offender management caseload statistics 2009: an overview of the main findings.* Ministry of Justice, statistics bulletin (July).

Ministry of Justice (2012a). *Referral orders and youth offender panels guidance for the courts, youth offending teams and youth offender panels.*

Ministry of Justice (2012b). *Restorative justice action plan for the criminal justice system.*

Ministry of Justice (2013a). *Code of practice for victims of crime.* London: The Stationery Office.

Ministry of Justice (2013b). *Crime and Courts Act 2013.*

Ministry of Justice (2015). *Population bulletin: weekly 24 July 2015.* Available at: https://www.gov.uk/government/statistics/prison-population-figures-2015.

Morenoff, J.D., Sampson, R.J. and Raudenbush, S.W. (2001). Neighborhood inequality, collective efficacy, and the spacial dynamics of urban violence. *Criminology*, *39*(3), 517–559. Retrieved from http://search.ebscohost.com/login.aspx?direct=trueanddb=sihandAN=5101427andsite=ehost-live.

Morris, A. and Maxwell, G. (2001). Restorative conferencing. In G. Bazemore and M. Schiff (eds), *Restorative community justice: repairing harm and transforming communities* (pp. 173–197). Cincinnati: Anderson Publishing Co.

Morse, A. and Maxwell, G. (2001). *Restorative justice for juveniles: conferencing, mediation and circles.* Oxford: Hart.

National Audit Office (2010). *Managing offenders on short custodial sentences.* London: The Stationery Office.

Pager, D., Western, B. and Sugie, N. (2009). Sequencing disadvantage: barriers to employment facing young black and white men with criminal records. *The Annals of the American Academy of Political and Social Science*, *623*(1), 195–213. doi:10.1177/0002716208330793.

Pennebaker, J.W., Czajka, J.A., Cropanzano, R., et al. (1990). Levels of thinking. *Personality and Social Psychology Bulletin*, *16*(4), 743–757.

Pranis, K., Stuart, B. and Wedge, M. (2003). *Peacemaking circles: from crime to community.* St Paul: Living Justice Press.

Rogers, C. (1961). *On becoming a person.* Boston: Houghton Mifflin.

Rowe, J.O., Halling, S., Davies, E., et al. (1989). The psychology of forgiving another: a dialogal research approach. In R.S. Valle and S. Halling (eds), *Existential-phenomenological perspectives in psychology: exploring the breadth of human experience* (pp. 233–244). New York: Plenum.

Seligman, M.E.P. and Csikszentmihalyi, M. (2000). Positive psychology: an introduction. *American Psychologist*, *55*(1), 5–14.

Shapland, J. (2008). Restorative justice and prisons. Presentation to the Commission on English Prisons Today, 7 November 2008.

Shapland, J., Atkinson, A., Atkinson, A., et al. (2006). Situating restorative justice within criminal justice. *Theoretical Criminology*, *10*(4), 505–532.

Ward, T. and Brown, M. (2004). The good lives model and conceptual issues in offender rehabilitation. *Psychology, Crime & Law, 10*(3), 243–257. doi:10.10 80/10683160410001662744.

Ward, T., Mann, R.E. and Gannon, T.A. (2007). The good lives model of offender rehabilitation: clinical implications. *Aggression and Violent Behavior, 12*(1), 87–107. doi:10.1016/j.avb.2006.03.004.

Ward, T. and Maruna, S. (2007). *Rehabilitation*. London: Routledge.

Wilkinson, R. (2004). Why is violence more common where inequality is greater? *Annals of the New York Academy of Sciences, 1036*, 1–12. doi:10.1196/ann als.1330.001.

Wolfgang, M. and Ferracuti, F. (1982). *The subculture of violence: towards an integrated theory in criminology*. Beverly Hills: SAGE.

Worthington, E.L.J. and Wade, N.G. (1999). The psychology of unforgiveness and forgiveness and implications for clinical practice. *Journal of Social and Clinical Psychology, 18*(4), 385–418. doi:10.1521/jscp.1999.18.4.385.

Chapter 12

Positive Psychology as a Contribution to Rehabilitation in Restorative Justice Systems: Analysis of Two Cases of Penal Mediation in Chile

Isabel González Ramírez, María Soledad Fuentealba Martínez and
Samuel Malamud Herrera

Introduction

In their own ways, common law and civil law criminal justice systems have shown a permanent adaptation to new criminal justice policy tendencies, mainly due to the observation that the imposition of sentence, the creation of new criminal offences and the prison system do not effectively reduce crime nor rehabilitate the offender, merely responding in the same way to conflicts of sufficient heterogeneity (Zaffaroni, 1998; Varona Martínez, 1998; Bergalli, 2003).

Chile has not lagged behind in this process. As a result of a deep context of modernization, the current Chilean criminal procedure has arisen from the reform efforts that began over 20 years ago in South America, passing through an inquisitorial penal system to an accusatory (oral and public) one, incorporating the 'opportunity principle', which means 'the faculty bestowed upon the prosecutor to not initiate, or to suspend, interrupt, or cease the course of a criminal prosecution, when ulterior motives of social utility or criminal-political reasons demand it' (Horvitz and López, 2002, p. 48) and some new institutions such as alternative forms of conflict resolution as diversionary mechanisms.

An example of this adaptation has been the incorporation into the criminal justice system of restorative justice mechanisms such as penal mediation and other instruments that enable the effective participation of those directly involved in the offence, including the supportive community. Despite this, such mechanisms appear to be only marginally used in programmes that are far from widespread.

With this in mind, this chapter explores, from the perspective of positive psychology, the contribution of restorative justice and penal mediation to the criminal justice system. To do this, the document presents the analytical process developed in two penal mediation cases, whose conflicts were treated at the Centre for Mediation, Negotiation and Arbitration of the Central University of Chile, through an agreement with the Public Prosecution Office. One of these offences consisted in a less serious injury and the other in a misappropriation of a computer, both of which formally ended by reparative agreements, which are an alternative to trial, contemplated in the Chilean criminal procedure.

Penal Mediation as a Manifestation of Restorative Justice

In Chile, the incorporation of the principle of opportunity, which means – in a broad sense – 'the power given to the persecutor authority to not initiate, to suspend, discontinue or terminate the course of a criminal prosecution, when such a decision is based on social utility or criminal policy reasons' (Horvitz and López, 2002, p. 48), has allowed the use of alternatives to oral trial, along with other means of diversion, such as temporary file and the power not to investigate.

The situation is part of the attempt by the government to use criteria that aim towards the efficiency of the criminal justice system, allowing auto-compositional mechanisms in public prosecution (Horvitz and López, 2002), which give a greater role to the victim in the process of resolving the conflict.

The alternatives outlets can be defined as 'conflict resolution mechanisms, which allow the parties to reach agreements in order to avoid settling problems in the penal system' (Jiménez et al., 2004, p. 32).These alternative mechanisms, which can take the form of reparative agreements, conditional suspension of the proceedings and/or the principle of opportunity – in a strict sense– incorporate some restorative values (Díaz, 2010). However, to say that the Chilean criminal justice system includes restorative justice elements, these outputs must play a much more important role than the current one. Such a system must include collaborative mechanisms that enable a comprehensive treatment of the conflict, effective reparation to the victim and reintegration of the victim and offender into the community (Van Ness and Strong, 1997).

The manifestations of restorative justice in Chile have focused almost exclusively on penal mediation. This practice differs from conferencing and circles which include the participation of family and other members of the community, and are common in countries such as Canada, New Zealand, England and the USA (McCold and Wachtell, 2012). This difference can be explained –in part – by the lack of a gregarious culture of the people and the weakness of community interaction among Chilean institutions (Díaz, 2010).

When we refer in this chapter to 'restorative justice' of which there is no single or definitive definition, we will use the one provided by Gavrielides (2007), considered one of the most comprehensive: 'restorative justice is an ethos with practical goals, among which is to restore the harm done by including all affected parties in a process of understanding through voluntary and honest dialogue, and by adopting a fresh approach to conflicts and their control, retaining at the same time certain rehabilitative goals' (p. 119).

Notwithstanding that studies on penal mediation in Chile show a positive evaluation of this mechanism among its operators and users, the absence of an express legal regulation referred to collaborative mechanisms, as a valid means for achieving agreements as an alternative to trial, has prevented this or other restorative forms from being used as a widespread mechanism in the criminal justice procedure (González and Fuentealba, 2013). Undoubtedly, the lack of these mechanisms has prevented the existence of restorative solutions in alternative outlets, preventing such outlets operate with the active participation of the parties or to offer a variety of solutions to criminal conflict according to their nature and gravity.

Additionally, the lack of formalization of mediation, and its incipient use in Chile, has hindered the development of further studies on the subject, especially studies which systematize qualitatively and quantitatively the few experiences.

This has prevented a comprehensive model of penal mediation at a national level, implemented so far only in pilot programmes, which follow protocols from other legislative realities or some methodologies used in other areas of legal conflicts (that is, family mediation).

Despite this not very favourable scenario, the advantages of mediation as a pathway for resolving legal disputes versus criminal trial and eventual conviction are manifold. Most significantly, mediation is a quick and effective solution to the criminal conflict, which can be applied early, close to the commission of the wrongful act, as a diversionary mechanism adopted in the formal indictment hearing.

With penal mediation, the process of stigmatization of the offender does not occur; it reduces the possibility of detention pending investigation and provides opportunities for the offender to have access to an alternative measure orientated towards his/her reintegration into the community, allowing him/her to avoid a criminal record (Braithwaite, 1997).

Moreover, based on statistics compiled by The National Prison Service (*Gendarmería de Chile*), we can see that offenders who have been cleared through these alternative solutions do not exhibit levels of recidivism higher than 10 per cent, whereas offenders who have served their sentence in prison exhibit levels of over 60 per cent (Biblioteca del Congreso Nacional de Chile, 2007).

Reparative agreements constitute the formal legal institution by which penal mediation finds a more adequate place in Chile. Reparative agreements, a form of alternative outcomes, can be defined as the voluntary and informed agreement between the victim and the offender under which the latter is obliged to repair the damaging effects caused by the offence to the victim, in those cases related to crimes that affect property, less serious injuries or reckless offences, where there is no public prevalent interest in the prosecution of these offences (Horvitz and López, 2002). Also, prior formalization of the investigation by the prosecutor is required, as well as the approval of the supervising judge, who must summon all participants to a hearing, as provided in Article 241 of the criminal procedure law.

The criminal effects of reparative agreements are, as provided in Article 242 of the criminal procedure law, that once the obligations have been fulfilled by the accused or guaranteed in some form, the court will grant definitive stay of the proceedings, which will extinguish all or part of the criminal responsibility of the accused.

Although initially the reparative agreements were projected as a leading solution to an economic reparation to the victim, in practice there have been new types of reparation introduced within them, especially through processes of penal mediation, such as asking for a public apology in the case of offenders and establishing obligations intended to overcome the vulnerability of the accused (that is, health problems, labour or education) (Jiménez et al., 2004). According to a study by Jiménez et al. (2004), the most frequent form of reparation within reparative agreements is monetary compensation (78 per cent of the cases), followed by undergoing treatment (11 per cent of the cases) and apologizing to the victim (10 per cent of the cases). Agreements are satisfied in 96 per cent of the cases.

Penal mediation allows the diversification of reparation in order to make it accessible to people without resources, promoting the institutionalization of formulas such as public apologies, community service and contributions to charities. This mechanism provides material and symbolic benefits, distinguishing penalty from reparation, linking the latter to the actual harm caused to the victim in a process in which the confrontation of damages and accountability are two key aspects (Zárate Campos, 2002).

The Model of Penal Mediation in Chile

In Chile, penal mediation pilots have been implemented since 1998, linked to universities, the public prosecution office, the SEMANE (National Service for the Protection of Minors) and legal aid services.

Moreover, the experience of legal aid services (Corporación de Asistencia Judicial), which pioneered the incorporation of mediation in Chile, has allowed them, since 2005, to refocus their attention from the family law field to other conflict areas such as community and criminal conflicts. This effort was supported through training and research carried out by the Chilean Ministry of Justice through the United Nations Development and Cooperation Programme, in the years 2006 to 2012 (Ramírez and Pavlic, 2011).

In this regard, the Ministry of Justice, in 2005, created a National Network of Access to Justice, through collaboration between public and private entities. This network was in charge of the coordination of a thematic panel centred on penal mediation, and had the mission of analysing the international experiences and making some proposals for improvements and implementation.

Despite these advances, it could not be argued that penal mediation is consolidated in our criminal justice system. From a study conducted by the Centre of Mediation, Negotiation and Arbitration of the Central University of Chile (CMNA) (González and Fuentealba, 2013), three challenges were identified: first, generating massive awareness and socialization instruments are required, targeting both the citizens and the practitioners; second, expanding the presence of criminal mediation centres throughout the country, so that these are not isolated initiatives, as has happened so far; third, the need for developing a model of penal mediation, which contains a detailed action protocol, spread among actors in the system and replicated by mediation centres across the country, improving the quality of service. This model has to be evaluated during its implementation and thereafter periodically, according to Cohen and Franco (1993), in order to detect the difficulties that exist in its programming, management and control, and to allow them to be corrected.

To promote the strengthening and recognition of mediation, the CMNA has conducted a series of activities in the area of teaching, research and mediation of criminal conflicts in agreement with certain public prosecutors' offices. The theory of positive psychology promises new arguments to promote the expansion of restorative practices. This theoretical perspective is presented as a new support for an indispensable mechanism that has not yet reached its potential in a society whose penal system has diversified little.

Positive Psychology and Penal Mediation

Positive psychology raises a number of foundations on which the therapeutic work is based from this clinical model, demonstrating a significant relationship with the approaches of restorative justice restorative justice and penal mediation. In relation to this, a brief introduction is presented, about the rise and current status of positive psychology, as a recent field within the discipline of human behaviour.

The beginnings of this discipline dates back to Carl Rogers (1961), who argues that the change in attitude of the conflicted person is not caused by the guidelines given by the helper, but rather as a result of his/her attitudes and feelings, allowing for people to open mutually to each other, analyse problems from another angle, and be interested in alternative solutions to the conflict that can contribute to an agreement.

Among the various definitions of positive psychology, we follow the one delivered by Sheldon and King (2001), who understood it as 'the scientific study of natural forces and human virtues, a discipline that asks what is the nature of the effective operation of human beings, focusing on their potentials, motives and capacities' (p. 216).

From 2002, through studies of positive emotions, from theorists such as Seligman (2002), Fredrickson (2009) and Csikszentmihalyi (2009), among others, scholars began to conceive psychology as a discipline aimed at regulating positive emotions, delivering a paradigm opposed to the traditional one, which is focused on the disease, but at the same time complementary to traditional psychology.

Through the implementation of the three basic pillars of positive psychology: subjective experience, positive characteristics of people (strengths and virtues), and positive institutions and communities; is that the processes of penal mediation would give the parties in a conflict the possibility to move from the different factors that allow subjects to withstand adversity (Almedon and Glandon, 2012) and enjoy resources that promote welfare, with the consequent benefits in psychological, social and communitarian terms (Fredrickson, 2009).

So, in each stage of the process of penal mediation, considering also the techniques used by the mediator, it is possible to observe the behaviours of the parties from the perspective of positive psychology, and see the benefits of face-to-face encounters in the light of this discipline.

The contributions of positive psychology are that it gives meaning to and provides a higher level of understanding of the processes of accountability, forgiveness and repentance that take place in mediation processes (Mayumi, and Willis, 2011). These values are also shared by restorative justice and the Good Lives Model (GLM) perspective, which is a model for the offender's rehabilitation and which, due to its holistic nature, addresses the limitations of the traditional approach of risk management.

This model explains delinquent behaviour as the desire of the offender to obtain a valuable gain in his/her life. However, due to environmental and individual deficiencies and weaknesses, the behaviour is expressed in a damaging and antisocial way. In this way, the GLM, developed by Ward and Stewart (2003), discusses the motivational role which basic needs perform in personal fulfilment, such as friendship, affections, creative activities, positive sexual satisfaction and a stimulating intellectual environment. These needs should be a priority consideration in the treatment of offenders, particularly young offenders. Thus, the GLM becomes a strategy based on the construction of capacities and strengths of offenders, which are key for their rehabilitation, reducing the risk of recidivism, as well as contributing to the fulfilment of pro-social behaviour.

Finally, this model establishes that there are a series of goals that people search for in life, such as health and physical security, loving relationships and friendships, mental peace, happiness and pleasure, being good at what one does (sports, work), having knowledge in areas of interest, having control of one's own life, finding meaning in life, being part of a group of people, and being creative (Ward and Maruna, 2007). The problem is that the means to obtain these goals are not always adequate and in several cases are accomplished by antisocial behaviour.

From another perspective, mediation incorporates four dogmatic principles: voluntariness of the parties involved, confidentiality, impartiality and neutrality of the mediator. Furthermore, the procedure is based on several stages: legitimacy of the mediation process, openness or exploration of conflict, conflict management and resolution (Suares, 1996).

In order to prove that positive psychology is not only compatible with the goals of restorative justice and the principles of mediation but also gives them sustenance and support (Gavrielides and Worth, 2014), in the following section two penal mediation cases are analysed in the light of positive psychology.

Two Case Studies of Penal Mediation Analysed

The methodology used for the analysis of the cases studied consisted first in the selection of cases received by the CMNA.

Always part of mediation processes is the requirement to obtain the parties' consent to be videotaped and observed – as well as the need to safeguard the principle of confidentiality. In this case the parties gave their consent to be videotaped after they had been informed of the goals of the study and assured that their names and other identification data would be kept confidential and that the data obtained would be used only for the purposes of the study.

The infrastructure used for filming and observing both mediation sessions was the *Gessel room* of the CMNA, which is specially prepared to allow for the observation of mediation processes and consists of two separate environments divided by one-sided glass, provided with audio and video equipment.

Two psychologists, who are also mediators, observed the videotapes, registering in writing all the parties' physical and verbal signs, their proxemics and gestures, as well as writing down the main aspects of positive psychology on the basis of the 'Observation Guide' (provided by Dr Theo Gavrielides within the context of the project 'The Positive Psychology of Restorative Justice').

The observational process was undertaken considering each of the mediation stages above-mentioned, and was strengthened by the experience in penal mediation of both psychologists, as well as their skills as clinical psychologists in identifying discourse indicators, paralinguistic or non-verbal communication.

After the written registration of what was observed, an analysis of the semantic content was attempted (Pérez Serrano, 2002, p. 144), giving marks to those terms that were repeated most often in the parties' discourse. This then allowed the mediators to assign categories and decodify the subjects' discourse, on the basis of a comparison between the marks assigned and the topics contained in the 'Observation Guide'. The first case ('Mauricio/Juan Pablo') corresponds to a penal mediation process, conducted between Mauricio and Juan Pablo, protagonists of a conflict caused by physical aggression by Juan Pablo towards Mauricio, as a result of a contract breach by Juan Pablo (a young student of audio-visual communication), in the completion of work entrusted by Mauricio (director of a youth centre). This aggression led to a criminal complaint, for the offence of less serious injuries, established in article 399° of the Chilean Penal Code.

The second case ('Isabel/Alberto') corresponds to a conflict between Isabel and Alberto, university fellows and friends. Alberto, the offender in the dispute, gave a computer that was given on loan to him by Isabel to third parties as part of a payment for a debt previously acquired. This resulted in a criminal complaint for the crime of misappropriation, punishable under the article 470 No. 1 of the Chilean Penal Code.

From the two cases systematized by the research team of the CMNA, it can be established some correlation: that each of the characteristics stages of the mediation process, with its techniques and objectives, are consistent with each

234 *The Psychology of Restorative Justice*

of the pillars on which positive psychology rests. Both, positive psychology and penal mediation, value the restoration of the harm done, repentance of the offender, forgiveness and restoration of the relationship, all of which, in turn, moves them closer to the concept of therapeutic justice, which has impacted various incipient theories of justice. From the correlation stated above, restorative justice and positive psychology, acquires empirical elements, which provide greater strength to these approaches.

In both of these cases, it is possible to identify the purposes of each stage of the mediation process, and how they engage in turn with key aspects of positive psychology.

From the start, in both cases, perceptions of the conflicts were rather negative' (something that is not denied by positive psychology, which considers both positive and negative aspects in human functioning), situation which is viewed in the theory of collaborative conflict resolution, as a 'primacy' or 'preponderance' of the positions of the parties.

The postures are generally rigid and represent personal desires of each of the parties involved in the conflict, implying emotions and cognitive representations as worries, pain, anger and other emotions (Suares, 1996). From the treatment of the conflict through language and communication, the mediator, as well as the 'positive' therapist, can access the interests of the parties towards the resolution of the conflict, considering the 'why questions' of possible solutions to the conflict. This, understood from mediation, are the so-called 'interests' of the parties who participate in this collaborative space (Suares, 1996).

Also, these positions are understood from positive psychology as the *world's beliefs* that bring the parties to the mediation table, where a major change is seen in the beliefs and values that each gives to interpersonal relationships, particularly with regard to the trust or distrust that represents the world for each of them, in terms of security or insecurity to manage his/her own life.

In the first case mentioned above ('Mauricio/Juan Pablo'), the peculiarity lies in the previous existence of a friendship between them, as well as between Mauricio and the mother of the young Juan Pablo. These peculiarities generated rigid positions, caused by disappointment of the adult and a feel of being misunderstood by the youth.

Besides that, it is possible to identify *world beliefs* altered after the occurrence of the crime, particularly in the mental representations of the victim, which are negative, disappointing and painful, with the consequent desire to punish the offender at the expense of participating in a collaborative process.

On the other hand, in the second case systematized ('Isabel/Alberto') –in a similar way – it is possible to appreciate rigid positions where the need for retributive justice by the victim prevails; in addition the *world beliefs* take the form of a hostile place and getting full of distrust. At the same time, the emotional level is important, where the friendship between the two subjects has suffered a significant break, leaving the victim with feelings of disappointment, pain and rage.

Both cases can be analysed through positive psychology and penal mediation, in that there is a need to move from rigid positions or from negative beliefs about the world towards a collaborative approach focused on the potentials of each of the parties, to facilitate the process of forgiveness and restoration of the damage done beyond material reparation.

Thus, from the techniques used by the penal mediator in the opening or exploring phase of the conflict, based on communication, it is possible to explore these positions, so that the subjects themselves can discover that under these positions there are 'interests' and 'needs' which can be satisfied through a collaborative perspective and a psychological process of empathy and mutual understanding.

Mediation uses opening techniques (Suares, 1996), those set out in different interrogative ways (questions of various types) and affirmatively (returning what has been verbalized by the parties, with certain filters). Thus, open questions,[1] closed questions,[2] clarifying questions,[3] reflective questions,[4] summary[5] and paraphrase[6] techniques were applied, all of which allow exploration of the negative beliefs about the world. These techniques consider the interests of each person, as well as common interests and the need to satisfy them both and repair the damage caused by the offence. They also consider the restoration of friendship, in order to modify their perceptions and restore the feelings that existed in each of them before the offense was committed.

In addition, the techniques described from this partially restorative mechanism coincide with aspects of Peterson and Seligman's (2004) model of 24 human strengths, where virtues like wisdom and knowledge, formed by aspects like judgement, critical thinking and open-mindedness are those that are addressed from communication between subjects, focusing on strengthening and consistency between these virtues and the real needs of the parties to positively address this conflict.

This process of transformation between positions, interests and needs is seen in both cases, where the offender and victim go through a process whereby they

---

1   An interrogative technique that involves asking questions in such a way that subjects deliver expanded answers and abundant information.

2   An interrogative technique aimed at obtaining accurate and specific information from the subjects, such as details of dates, people involved and so on.

3   An interrogative technique formulated with the aim of encouraging responses in subjects through providing information or verbalization of their positions, in the most concrete and specific way possible.

4   An interrogative technique that aims to generate reflection, by individuals, on other possible perspectives on the conflict and its consequences for others involved.

5   An affirmative technique that gives account, synthetically, of what has been addressed in each session, integrating advances in the positions of the parties and the contributions of each of them, for the construction of a new definition about the conflict, allowing later the protagonism and collaboration of both parties in possible solutions.

6   An affirmative technique that aims to return to individuals what was verbalized by each of them, but without negative connotations.

reflect, analyse and move from the initial rigid, punitive and lack of accountability positions towards shared interests and needs that go beyond the criminal act itself, such as friendship, the maintenance of the emotional bond, forgiveness and gratitude. Reflections that arises from the interventions of the mediator who conducts communication processes, as a neutral agent, without being able to suggest or recommend alternative solutions to the parties.

Then, from the stage of conflict management, it is possible to appreciate and relate other relevant aspects of the 24 strengths model (Peterson and Seligman, 2004), such as the value of courage, integrated by strengths such as honesty and authenticity, which effectively are appreciated as a result of the intervention of the mediator through the techniques mostly used in this stage of treating the conflict. The 24 strengths model aims to breakdown and subsequent reorganization of conflict, where the parties work on mutual recognition.

Both the Mauricio/Juan Pablo case and the Isabel/Alberto case illustrate how offender and victim begin to acquire the skills to understand and consider *the other's perspective* (according to Maturana (1994), a *legitimate other*) through the use of communication techniques, such as: circular questions, positive connotation and legitimacy of the parties themselves. All of them, from positive psychology, would facilitate the attainment of the virtue *value/courage* starting from the authenticity and honesty and the virtue of *love and humanity*, where aspects such as generosity, emotional, personal and social intelligence are strengthened and installed in mutual mental representations of the participants, who are then able to deconstruct the conflict, initially seen from personal positions, to restructure it and see the individual interests and mutual needs, and recognize and validate the other's story.

Although the achievement of each of the virtues from positive psychology and the stages and objectives of penal mediation demands of the subjects significant mental and symbolic capacities, it is the task of the mediator, as a driver of the process, to activate these mental processes from the adaptability of the subjects' adversity (Calhoun and Tedeschi, 1999 achieving, which has been defined as post-traumatic personal growth, where building resilience play a fundamental role in this task.

Regarding this purpose, neuroscience – defined as the group of sciences whose object of research is the nervous system, with a particular interest in how brain activity relates to behaviour and learning (Kandel et al., 1997) – plays a fundamental role in explaining and justifying how subjects initially focused on rigid and unique positions are able to move towards shared visions, empathic and strengthened, in regard of the same conflict situation.

This discipline attempts to study the nervous system from the perspective of the functioning of neurons and the behaviour, proposing explanations about the individuality of human behaviour on the basis of the functioning of nervous cells, influenced by the environment, including the behaviour of other human beings (Kandel et al., 1997).

In this way, it is possible to justify how positive emotions broaden the repertoire of thoughts and actions, facilitating generativity and flexibility (Fredrickson, 1998), which is an important stage of the conflict resolution process in mediation, or to generate alternative solutions, which are observed in both of the cases analysed.

Also, from neuroscience (discipline presented as the biological basis of positive psychology), we see how emotions produce physiologically pleasant feelings that people seek; emotions that in addition biologically shape our behaviour, from the so called *mirror neurons* (Goleman, 2006), performing functions such as 'reading' other people's emotions, 'reading' their intentions and understanding the implications of what someone does as well as imitating other people's actions.

Thus, the operation and activation of these neurons not only occurs in the interaction between the subjects participating in mediation, but also between them and the mediator who leads the process, which coincides with the human communication basis, where mediation techniques, such as 'legitimation', lead to the activation and function of mirror neurons, resulting in objectively observable and measurable indicators, such as the verbalization of this mutual recognition.

To achieve this process of mutual recognition an adequate management by the mediator is essential, through various communication techniques that promote the expression of gratitude (Emmons, 2007) by the individuals. This concept is understood from positive psychology as the recognition of goodness in the lives of people, which is a reflective awareness of the generosity of another person who has incurred some personal cost in order to contribute to the personal welfare of the subject.

At the moment that the parties recognize each other in mediation, validation of the virtues contained in this discipline would be recognized, and simultaneously, the achievement of the restoration of the damage caused by the offender, the recognition of the victim as a subject entitled with rights and responsible for their rehabilitation, as well as the appropriate and consistent reintegration of the offender in their immediate and wider community, understood as society in a more abstract sense.

The expression of gratitude is observed in both cases, where in particular the victim gradually acquires the ability to understand the positions and reasons why the offender for having committed the offence, a expression that requires the ability to perceive the conflict from a different angle, which is possible due to the empathy developed in both parties as a result of the mediation process.

It is at this point that the parties are willing to forgive, something that was observed in each of the victims in both cases. Furthermore was observed the offenders' ability to express regret, to request forgiveness from the victim and to generate alternative solutions, compatible what is achievable by the offender, but geared towards the satisfaction of the victim, orientated towards the restoration of the relationship and of the offence committed. In relation to this, it is worth noting that among the aspects analysed in each of the cases, forgiveness and gratitude appeared were the most prominent ones.

In relation to the first aspect, it was possible to observe in the mediation process of Mauricio/Juan Pablo that, in the case of the victim, he was more prompt to show signs of forgiveness for others. This situation was observed in the development of the narrative of the victim, mainly in his posture and body language. At first he proved uncooperative with the stance of the offender, but then he opens up to a more kinaesthetic and emotional harmony. That connection allows them to achieve forgiveness for one another. In spite of this, the victim does not establish a connection to his own possible responsibility in the treatment of the conflict.

With regard to the offender, despite the offender acknowledging at first the damage he did to the other (the victim) by assuming a disposition to repair the material damage, it is during the mediation process that the offender starts to resonate with the victim's feelings. This lets the offender understand the experiences of the victim, which in turn enables the offender to offer proposals that might achieve forgiveness and compensation for the emotional damage caused. Furthermore, at the beginning of the process, the offender exteriorizes his guilt, which reveals a locus of external control. However, once the communication process is over and the victim hears the narrative of the offender, the latter is able to recognize and assume his responsibility and move the locus of control towards one of internal characteristics. Thus, he is able to collaborate in a solution that achieves forgiveness from both the victim and himself. At that point, the offender manifests calmness and personal satisfaction.

In parallel, and regarding 'forgiveness' it was observed in the case of Isabel/Alberto that with regard to the victim,the process of a future forgiveness progressively develops once she listens to and observes that the offender shows communicational and affective elements that denote repentance. She also deliberates on a higher value-like friendship. After the offender goes through a process of self-accountability, the victim is able to consider it as an important factor to analyse how compensation might be of use for her.

The development of a dialogue with the victim indicates a change in her posture and body language, from an uncompromising response to the offender's position to a better affective and kinaesthetic harmony. This allows her to start conceiving the possibility of forgiving her counterpart in the future after she has expressed the emotional pain she suffered. On the other hand, it is difficult to distinguish any self-blame by her in a meaningful way, as the victim does not present an acknowledgement of self-accountability that would allow her to victimize herself.

With regard to the offender, it is possible from the beginning to identify, through his narrative and affects, indicators of a feeling of guilt. However, the offender becomes capable during the process of appraising the damage done to himself by the offence, and in particular, the damage to his professional career. Moreover, he recognizes the damage done to his personal development, as the consequences of his acts interfere with the possibility of maintaining values such as solidarity and trust on the establishment of social relationships. This caused an emotional shift towards the development and manifestation of concrete actions to obtain forgiveness from both the victim and himself. At the time forgiveness is achieved, it is possible to tell how the offender puts his emotions to rest, and takes control of the compensation proposals in order to fulfil the victim's needs.

Finally, in relation to the second prominent aspect of 'gratitude', in the case of Mauricio/Juan Pablo it is effectively possible to determine signs of the communication of Mauricio's feelings and thoughts, which are expressed with a negatively colour. Notwithstanding, when the process of forgiveness and acknowledgement of the other is started, the victim shows satisfaction for the level of communication reached. He then manifests the benefits he perceives from the mediation process, as an opportunity useful to tell the story of what he experienced during this conflict. He also perceives benefits from the solution and compensation achieved.

At first, the communication of emotions is focused on the victim's own feelings of victimization, on the verbalization of the damage done and on the demand for compensation, without thinking about the possibility of forgiveness for the offender. Afterwards, and once he visualizes feelings of empathy and understanding for the offender, the victim is able to analyse in depth his own thoughts and feelings by considering the position of the other, as well as the reasons for which the crime was committed.

In the case of the offender, from the beginning he demonstrates signs of regret. However, it is difficult for him to understand the situation from the point of view of the other by comprehending the harm experienced by the victim. At the end of the meeting, the offender is capable not only of regretting the material harm done, but also the emotional damage caused to the victim. He also starts to consider aspects missed before, which can only be evaluated once he has actively listened to the thoughts and feelings expressed by the victim and listened to the victim's perspective of the facts. Finally, the offender is capable of positively evaluating the process and appreciating the opportunity to look at the conflict beyond the mere material damage done, by having an insight into his behaviour and its reach and consequences for others – in this particular case, the victim.

In the same vein, in the Isabel/Alberto case, with regard to the aspect of 'gratitude', it is effectively possible to determine signs of the communication of Alberto's feelings and thoughts, which are expressed with a negatively colour. Notwithstanding, when the process of forgiveness and acknowledgement of the other is started, the victim shows satisfaction for the level of communication reached, because she feels understood by the offender. This makes the verbalization of how beneficial the process has been to her much easier, when she sees it as an opportunity to express what she went through because of the conflict, to reprimand the offender in the context of her feelings and mutual trust, and to demand a solution to repair the damage done.

At the beginning, the communication of feelings is focused on the expression of the anger and rage caused by the offender, as he was the cause of the breakdown of trust and solidarity essential to friendship. Notwithstanding, after the emotional contention process is carried out by the mediators, the process of circularization of the conflict among the parties helps the victim to perceive the empathy and understanding felt by the offender. This understanding lets her deepen her feelings and thoughts by including her counterpart's perception of the conflict and the reasons he had to commit the offence.

Furthermore, in the case of the offender, it was observed that despite him showing signs of regret from the start, as was previously stated, he has difficulty completely understanding the situation from the point of view of the other. He does not fully consider the damage done to the victim, in particular to the feelings that existed between them. As the meeting develops, the offender becomes capable of not only regretting the material damage done by him, but also of giving the importance of the damage done to the bond between them as a result of the conflict. This bond is a central element that must be repaired if he wishes to re-establish a relationship and to regain the victim's trust. He finally realizes that a point of agreement can be reached more easily by an approach of such nature.

Finally, the offender is able to appreciate and positively evaluate the opportunity to look at the conflict beyond the material damage done and the expectations he had already assumed the victim would fulfil. He obtains an insight into his behaviour and the consequences it has had on others – in this particular case, the victim.

Conclusions

Certainly, the bond and relationship between restorative justice and positive psychology is highly significant. This is so especially with regard to the coherence between the principles and techniques used in one of the mechanisms of restorative justice – penal mediation – and those postulated by theorists of positive psychology. Issues like forgiveness, restoration and subsequent reintegration are clearly identifiable in both processes, considering the notion of therapeutic justice, by an approach where the parties involved in a criminal conflict assume responsibility for solving the conflict, unlike more traditional approaches in which the state assumes direct responsibility for punishing the offender, thereby distancing the victim from the process.

Thus, positive psychology fulfils parameters to investigate how it is possible to supplement aspects of the traditional psychology paradigm – based on negative emotions seen as synonymous with sickness – with those aspects which address and focus on people's strengths and virtues,inherent to the human being to achieve a welfare state and greater happiness.

Thereby it is possible to appreciate to what extent restorative justice processes that encourage face-to-face meetings between offender and victim, through the conduct of an impartial third party called a mediator, facilitate the development and maintenance of collaborative behaviours, such as becoming aware of mutual recognition, the ability to ask for and grant forgiveness, and the possibility of expressing gratitude and coming to a consensus; in doing so, rigid attitudes are sacrificed for a shared vision of the conflict.

This is possible through the application of techniques based on communication that activate cognitive processes in participants in the process, allowing synchronous activation of intrapsychic processes (reflection and insight) around the shared visions of the same conflict, which in the initial stages of the process were perceived by the parties in a personal and unalterable way.

It is this transformation in both communication and interaction which gives empirical and scientific support to the important link between both disciplines, and, increasingly and systemically, invites research initiatives to continue to develop about aspects as restorative justice and positive psychology.

To sum up, the observation points suggested in the 'Observation Guide' could certainly be connected to the theory behind positive psychology and its new approach to human beings and their achievements, as detailed below.

The starting point for both victim and offender is their beliefs about the world; it is the analysis of the event that brings them together. Their beliefs about the world, their optimism or pessimism for the world or themselves; their ability to be resilient, empathetic; their ability to forgive, the need to be of service to something bigger, the pressing need to look after interpersonal relationships: all of these will be determined by how each of the involved parties deal with the conflict during the criminal mediation process.

The point in the analysis regarding the 'meaning' and the 'new narrative' signals the importance of developing the skills identified by positive psychology, such as the development of empathy, resilience and optimism. They are key to the configuration of the new meaning and the development of a new narrative during the process of criminal mediation. The possibility to listen to each other, to understand each other's motives and feelings of fear, anger and impotence are the only way to allow a resignification of the facts as they occurred for each party. Resignification will make possible the change in the relationship between the parties.

Forgiveness, another point in the analysis, either for the other or for oneself – victim and offender respectively – is an element that, when present, allow the opportunity for both actors to advance the process towards a new platform of analysis. Thus, by overcoming the situation, they bring unforeseen benefits to each other. The ability to forgive and to receive forgiveness by experiencing positive emotions allows the involvement of human values and virtues of a higher scale. By giving people the opportunity to contribute to their spiritual and personal development, it is possible to consider this process as part of a post-traumatic growth motivated by the event on each part.

Gratitude is equally capable of connecting to supreme values as it can bring out of the best in human beings. Likewise, it is established that it is invaluable to the development of rehabilitation and withdrawal from the criminal process.

Finally, we believe that it is of the utmost importance for the processes of restoration and rehabilitation to focus on the actors' strengths and to emphasize them. This is the only way to achieve real change, and a definite and sustained distance between the offender and the criminal world –and in turn, a genuine restoration of the victim's broken rights.

Bibliography

Almedon, A. and Glandon, D. (2012). Resilience is not the absence of PTSD any more than health is the absence of disease. *Journal of Loss and Trauma*, *12*(2), 127–143.

Bergalli, R. (2003). Las funciones del sistema penal en el estado constitucional de derecho social y democrático: perspectivas socio-jurídicas. In R. Bergalli (ed.), *Sistema penal y problema social*. Valencia: Tirant lo Blanch.

Biblioteca del Congreso Nacional de Chile (2007). *Historia de la Ley del Código Procesal Penal: Segundo Informe de la Comisión de Constitución, Legislación, Justicia y Reglamento del Senado*. Boletín No. 4321-07. Retrieved from www.senado.cl.

Braithwaite, J. (1997). *Crime, shame and reintegration*. Cambridge: Cambridge University Press.

Calhoun, L.G. and Tedeschi, R.G. (1999). *Facilitating post-traumatic growth: a clinician's guide*. London: Lawrence Erlbaum Associates.

Cohen, E. and Franco, R. (1993). *Evaluación de proyectos sociales*. Madrid: Siglo XXI.

Csikszentmihalyi, M. (2009). *Fluir (Flow). Una psicología de la felicidad*. Barcelona: Kairós de Bolsillo.

Díaz, A. (2010). La experiencia de la mediación penal en Chile. *Política Criminal*, *5*(9), 1–67.

Emmons, R. (2007). ¡Gracias! De cómo la gratitud *puede hacerte feliz*. Madrid: Ediciones B.

Fredrickson, B. (1998). What good are positive emotions? *Review of General Psychology*, *2*(3), 300–319.

Fredrickson, B. (2009). *Positivity: top-notch research reveals the 3 to 1 ratio that will change your life*. New York: Three Rivers Press.

Gavrielides, T. (2007). *Restorative justice theory and practice: addressing the discrepancy*. Helsinki: HEUNI.

Gavrielides, T. and Worth, P. (2014). Another push for restorative justice: positive psychology and offender rehabilitation'. In M.H. Pearson (ed.), *Crime: international perspectives, socioeconomic factors and psychological implications* (pp. 161–182). New York: Nova Science Publishers.

Goleman, D. (2006). *La inteligencia social: Las nuevas ciencias para mejorar las relaciones humanas*. México D.F.: Planeta.

González, I. and Fuentealba, M.S. (2013). Mediación penal como mecanismo de justicia restaurativa en Chile. *Revista Chilena de Derecho y Ciencia Política, Universidad Católica de Temuco*, *4*(3), 175–210.

Horvitz, M.I. and López, J. (2002). *Derecho procesal penal chileno* (2 vols). Santiago: Editorial Jurídica de Chile.

Jiménez, M.A. et al. (2004). *Estudio exploratorio sobre las medidas cautelares y salidas alternativas en el nuevo proceso penal*. Santiago: CESOP Universidad Central de Chile.

Kandel, E.R., Schwartz, J.H. and Jessell, T.M. (1997). *Neurociencia y conducta*. Madrid: Prentice Hall.

Maturana, H. (1994). *El sentido de lo humano*. Santiago: Dolmen.

Maturana, H. (2006). El sentido de lo humano y la mediación. Ministerio de Justicia (ed.), *Foro Iberoamericano de Justicia Restaurativa y Colaborativa* (22–30). Santiago, Chile.

Mayumi, P. and Willis, G. (2011). The Good Lives model in practice: offence pathways and case management. *European Journal of Probation, University of Bucharest*, *3*(2), 4–28. Retrieved from http://www.ejprob.ro/uploads_ro/730/The_Good_Lives_Model_in_Practice.pdf.

McCold, P. and Wachtel, T. (2012). En busca de un paradigma: una teoría sobre justicia restaurativa. Paper presented at the XIII World Congress of Criminology, 10–15 August 2003, Río de Janeiro, Brazil. Retrieved from http://www.iirp.edu/article_detail.php?article_id=NTYx.

Pérez Serrano, G. (2002). *Investigación cualitativa. Retos e interrogantes. II Técnicas y análisis de datos* (3rd edn). Madrid: La muralla S.A.

Peterson, C. and Seligman, M.P. (2004). *Character strengths and virtues: a handbook and classification*. Oxford: Oxford University Press.

Ramírez, M.C. and Pavlic, C. (2011). *Justicia Restaurativa desde la óptica del Ministerio Público chileno; Justicia Restaurativa desde la óptica de la defensoría Penal Pública*. AGCI (ed.), Santiago: Editorial EquipoAGCI.

Rogers, C. (1961). *El proceso de convertirse en persona*. Buenos Aires: Paidós.

Seligman, M. (2002). *La auténtica felicidad*. Barcelona: Sello Zeta Bolsillo.

Sheldon, K.M., and King, L. (2001). Why positive psychology is necessary. *American Psychologist*, *56*(3), 216–217. Retrieved from http://web.missouri.edu/~sheldonk/pdfarticles/AP01.pdf.

Suares, M. (1996). *Mediación, conducción de disputas, comunicación y técnicas*. Argentina: Paidós.

Van Ness, D. and Strong, K.H. (1997). *Restoring justice*. Cincinnati: Anderson Publishing.

Varona Martínez, G. (1998). *La mediación reparadora como estrategia del control social, una perspectiva criminológica*. Granada: Comares.

Ward, T. and Maruna, S. (2007). *Rehabilitation: beyond the risk assessment paradigm*. London: Routledge.

Ward, T. and Stewart, C. (2003). Criminogenic needs and human needs: a theoretical critique. *Psychology, Crime and Law*, *9*(3), 125–43.

Zaffaroni, E.R. (1998). *En búsqueda de las penas perdidas*. Buenos Aires: Ediar.

Zárate Campos, M. (2002). Comentarios de los acuerdos reparatorios: algunos comentarios a partir de las nociones de reparación y negociación. *Revista de Derecho y Humanidades, Universidad de Chile*, *9*, 125–146. Santiago: University of Chile.

PART IV:
Concluding Thoughts

Chapter 13

The Sceptic and the Believer:
The Psychology of Restorative Justice

Theo Gavrielides

Psychologizing Oneself: Psychologizing Restorative Justice

There can be no doubt that over the past 30 years the field of restorative justice has made incredible progress. Since its revival in the 1970s (Gavrielides, 2011a), the restorative justice notion (whether in theory or practice) has been the subject of volumes of writings and the focus of billions of investments by governments, international bodies[1] and philanthropists. Dating as far back as 2005, Van Ness recorded approximately 100 countries that utilize restorative justice (2005), while in 2011 Gavrielides identified 23 different types of prison-based restorative justice programmes in at least 84 countries (2011b, pp. 35–37). Umbreit (2008) estimated that there are over 300 victim–offender mediation programmes just in the USA and over 700 in Europe.

It is hard to map restorative justice; the reasons are mainly due to its fluid and community-led nature. It can be a hidden practice in a small neighbourhood or a mainstream approach for an entire prison. It can also be the manner in which we treat our children, or the way in which we approach our relationships more generally. In my years of researching restorative justice within the criminal justice field, I have tried to remain objective about its promises, claims, failures, successes and aspirations. I have expressed my frustration with attempts to compare it with what is not (Gavrielides, 2013), while calling for the end of definitions (Gavrielides and Artinopoulou, 2013). On many occasions, I have written: 'The focus of researchers should not be on the superiority of restorative justice, but on the development of its processes and principles' (Gavrielides 2007, 2008). It is with this objective in mind that I approached the topic of this book.

I still think there is a long way to go before we can safely claim that we know how to do restorative justice well. Pilots need to continue, especially in relation to grey areas of practice such as domestic violence, hate crimes and other complex

---

1 See, for instance, 'Mediation in Penal Matters' – Council of Europe 1999 Recommendation No. R(99) and 'Establishing Minimum Standards on the Rights, Support and Protection of Victims of Crime', EU Directive 2011/0129. At the international level, as early as 2002, the United Nations (UN) issued UN Resolution E/CN.15/2002/L.2/Rev.1 'Basic Principles on the Use of Restorative Justice Programmes in Criminal Matters'.

cases. The extant research on restorative justice has indeed helped me to address many of my questions, particularly in relation to what restorative justice cannot do for rehabilitation and the criminal justice system. The many policies that governments and international bodies have introduced to mainstream restorative justice have also guided me to understand the true drivers of social policy. Finally, they have helped me identify where the true origins and strengths of restorative justice lie.[2] More importantly, research with practitioners, victims and offenders has given us a flavour of what this 'magic of restorative justice' truly is. This is not the space to repeat these learnings.

My focus here is on one question: where does restorative justice fit as an academic discipline and as a field of study? By extension, if we are to study, analyse, improve, criticize and develop restorative justice, who should we be looking at? Sociologists, criminologists, lawyers, psychologists, neuroscientists, educators, philosophers, historians? Is it time to be talking about a restorative justice discipline?

This question prompted me to take on a new editorial challenge by bringing together different disciplines in one volume to debate restorative justice. I hoped that by bringing these different viewpoints together, I would once again push the barriers of restorative justice. What helped this plan were my recent projects with psychologists. In 2013, I was fortunate to receive a grant from Buckinghamshire New University where I serve as a visiting professor. In partnership with Dr Piers Worth, the head of the Academic Department of Psychology, we completed a programme (2013–2015) looking at the application of positive psychology in restorative justice. The initial findings appeared in a joint publication (Gavrielides and Worth, 2014), while the fieldwork results appear in Chapter 12 of this volume. Furthermore, my interactions with neuroscientists such as Dr Daniel Reisel, as well as my discussions with psychologists such as Dr Mikhail Lyubansky and new training that I received on attachment and brain development, opened new areas of investigation that I had never considered before.

In this concluding chapter, I reach down into my own psychology and emotions to understand where I personally sit with regard to the advancement of restorative justice through fields such as those found in applied sciences. To this end, I looked back at all the contributions to develop a critical review of a multi-disciplinary nature. A disclaimer that must be made is that I have no training in psychology, neurology, psychotherapy or the like. I must also disclose my natural bias towards a philosophical interpretation of the world, its beauty, pain and meanings. In the past, I have attempted to analyse, understand, criticize and deepen restorative justice through normative, theoretical and philosophical thinking (for example, Gavrielides, 2005, 2013). Here, I attempt to do justice to the diverse and multi-disciplinary accounts that have been developed by this volume's international authors.

---

2   See 'The McDonaldisation of a Community-born and Community-led Ethos': http://iars.org.uk/content/mcdonaldisation-rj (retrieved February 2015).

In my attempt to write this concluding chapter, I felt like a split personality in need for a psychotherapist. While, on the one hand, I am a sceptic of multi-disciplinary approaches, particularly those involving applied sciences, on the other, I am a great believer of multi-disciplinarity as a way of answering persistent questions in academia and practice. This chapter investigates the reasons behind my scepticism as it acts as a record of my inner thoughts and fears as they emerge while I psychologize myself.

Similarly to other disciplines, restorative justice is faced with a number of disagreements relating to definition, normative and empirical promises (for example, see Gavrielides, 2008; Johnstone and van Ness, 2011). By this, I do not mean that agreement must be reached for every single aspect of restorative justice theory and practice. In fact, occasional confusion should be expected with relatively untested concepts that are trying to find their place within our complex, modern societies (Gavrielides, 2007; Gavrielides and Artinopoulou, 2013). Disagreements are also part of creative thinking. Without friction there is no fire; and without fire there is no creation. What I am referring to here is a shared denominator for the restorative justice identity.

Here, in my attempt to research and identify the restorative justice barometer, I called for chapters that would unravel the dynamics, powers, weaknesses and peculiarities of restorative justice from the perspectives of various disciplines. As a result, this volume brought together positioning theory (Chapter 1), social psychology (Chapter 2), neuroscience (Chapter 3), affect script psychology (Chapter 4), sociology (Chapter 5), forensic mental health (Chapter 6), political sciences (Chapter 7), psychology (chapters 8, 9 and 10) and positive psychology (chapters 11 and 12).

I can now conclude that the answer to my central question lies in understanding the psychology of restorative justice. Not psychology *for* restorative justice, but the actual psychology *of* restorative justice. Hence the title of this book.

This, of course, raises a series of complex questions of a multi-disciplinary nature. To understand the psychology of restorative justice itself, we must look into the power structures of the restorative justice movement, the very psychology, motivations and emotions of the practitioners who implement it as well as the drivers of its theoreticians and researchers. Furthermore, we must look at the strengths and weakness of our own communities that are called to participate as parties in restorative justice. Their own biases, hunger for power and control, fears and hopes are as crucial. Also relevant is the psychology and the dynamics between those it aims to reach – that is, victims and offenders. Equally important is understanding those who are funding restorative justice as well as the policy makers and the politicians who have the power to bring it into a system. These are critical matters that cannot be ignored as we move with confidence into the future.

The chapters in this volume have touched on all these aspects, which I will call the ingredients of understanding the true psychology of restorative justice. In fact, many authors of this volume have warned that if we continue to ignore the psychology of restorative justice and its related dangers, then we may soon be faced with the demise of the restorative justice movement. This concluding chapter looks back at these contributions while engaging in a debate between my sceptic and believer selves. My claims and conclusions in this chapter are drawn principally from the evidence and arguments developed by the volume's authors. They are an amalgamation of the interdisciplinary arguments that were put forward as well as of my own thoughts and feelings. I conclude with a call for a move towards an independent restorative justice discipline that does not ignore its own psychology and the learning that we can take from it through the tools supplied by sciences.

The Believer

Applied disciplines, and with them psychology, involve the scientific study of mental functions and human behaviours. Psychology, in particular, aims to understand individuals and groups by establishing general principles and researching specific cases. To this end, psychologists employ an array of techniques in order to explain our mental functions and social behaviour. Psychology may extend to physiological, biological and sociological spheres, while many psychologists will often see themselves as social, behavioural or cognitive scientists.

Merely the word 'science' should make restorative justice proponents jump for joy, as the prospect of a potential relationship between science and restorative justice could instil credibility to the restorative justice movement. Looking at the various critiques of restorative justice, Acorn (2004), for instance, has written that the commitment of the rule of law 'to consistency, predictability, precision, and universal application continue[s] to have compelling and even essential connections to any sane and workable notion of justice. Thus, the restorative aspiration to divorce justice from reciprocal infliction of suffering, along with its faith in context super-sensitivity … caused me considerable anxiety' (p. 122). Some have accused Acorn of doing damage to restorative justice, accusing her of being fundamentally wrong about her dismissal of restorative justice (for example, see Archibald, 2005). The truth is that Acorn represents the mainstream legal mind that sees restorative justice as an arbitrary practice. I may not necessarily agree with Acorn, but I have warned the restorative justice movement that if it does not learn to listen to concerns that come from a long experience of practising the law, then the chances of moving restorative justice out of the shadows will continue to be slim (Gavrielides, 2015a). The call of science, and in particular applied sciences and psychology, to evaluate, measure, understand and explain to restorativists (whether theoreticians, researchers, policy makers or practitioners) the dynamics that tend to develop within the room of restoration is thus exciting.

There is another reason why bringing restorative justice into the science sphere is invigorating. Pavlich (2005) has spoken of a paradox in restorative justice. He points out that although restorative justice claims to be offering a distinctive alternative to criminal justice, it assumes a place within an existing system and the very framework and mentality that it aims to challenge. He asks what sort of alternative to state power and monopoly restorative justice offers, if it is provided through the law and via existing court and other criminal justice processes. He uses Foucault's concept of 'governmentalities' to explore dominant conceptions of the victim in 'restorative governmentalities' while considering how these seek to govern subjects through the notions of the empowered victim. Pavlich identifies two problems. First, '[t]he claim to empower victims as victims is problematic when one considers that by definition the victim is a disempowered identity' (p. 45). Second, 'the expectations that victims can eventually transcend that identity by translating harm into need is incongruous' (p. 46). The process of victim empowerment in restorative justice is then unpacked within the context of the exiting power structures that dominate us all. Therefore, understanding the societal context, as well as the power structures within which restorative justice is mainstream, appears to be a critical question for its future and legitimacy.

I have spoken of a similar paradox in the context of equalities and race equality (Gavrielides, 2014). Restorative justice was reborn with a promise to provide a better sense and experience of justice, especially for those who are let down the most by the criminal justice system. And yet, despite well-evidenced disproportionality and race inequality issues within criminal justice institutions, restorative justice research and practice within the context of race are almost non-existent. Is there more to be learned about the psychology and the hidden biases of restorative justice theoreticians and authors? Furthermore, restorative justice practices promise an alternative and more personalized vision of 'the other'. And yet, how is it possible to provide this personalized vision of justice and individual treatment of each individual's circumstances, if we do not have the tools to understand them? How is it possible to break out of the vicious circle of overt and hidden biases of restorative practice, if we are not equipped to understand the psychology of the societal and organizational context within which restorative justice is applied? With great fear but with a sense of responsibility, I warned that if restorative justice continues to ignore the challenges raised within a race equality context, the power structures inherent within our current structural framework of criminal justice will lead to its demise.

For all the above reasons, I was excited to read the contributions in this volume, advocating in favour of a multi-disciplinary approach including the use of psychology. Maglione (Chapter 1) explains that an interdisciplinary socio-psychological field can offer a much needed understanding and development for restorative justice. He believes that this can be achieved at both normative and empirical levels, and that restorative justice is 'nothing but a range, more or less fluid, of discourses'. Restorative practices, he claims, are conversational processes within and through which the content (subject positions, storylines) of those societal discourses is reproduced and reshaped. Therefore, understanding restorative justice as a discursive field where we can establish the conditions for the formation of different positions, common elements, overlaps and tensions is the only way we can really distinguish it from the traditional criminal justice system. By extension, the understanding of the subject positions and dynamics can have social effects, which can then again be interpreted and controlled through the multi-disciplinary approach of positioning theory. This also includes the unfolding of the power relationships that take place between restorative justice practitioners. Maglione goes as far as saying that positioning theory can actually help restorative justice handle these power relationships which many (Gavrielides, 2013, 2014; Pavlich, 2005) have warned may have catastrophic consequences. 'Positioning theory can help to devise understandings of restorative justice which aim at unleashing its transformative and inclusive potential, providing awareness of the limitations and risks that restorative discourses and practices might embody'.

My enthusiasm increased when I read Reisel's work who is an expert in neuroscience (Chapter 3). There, he presents new and ground-breaking research with offenders that he claims represents a paradigm shift in biology. He reminds us that '[u]ntil recently, different forms of determinism have clouded the study of human behaviour'. Reductionist scientists claim that our biology and social functioning are determined by our genes. Psychodynamic theory has also claimed that personality and mood are ordained by our upbringing and unresolved conflicts from childhood. Similarly, systems theory professes the idea that genes interact with environment to produce personality characteristics and moods. Cognitive theory is also highly regarded, which states that feelings are produced by stories (that is, explanations) that we give to our experience.

However, Reisel argues that epigenetics, the study of how the DNA code is read, can allow an individual, including offenders, to pick up adaptations without the need for natural selection. Unlike genes, epigenetic mechanisms are potentially reversible. With this in mind, Reisel claims that restorative justice can rewire the brain sufficiently to prevent future crime. Surely, after reading this, one can only be a believer of multi-disciplinarity for the benefit of restorative justice. It also appears that applied sciences, psychology and neurology may have a prominent role to play in redefining a more positivist restorative justice. In Reisel's terms:

> [a] deeper understanding of the neuroscience of restorative justice would also be invaluable in helping us design more effective restorative intervention … we now have over a century of data on what makes learning more or less efficient. These insights can now be harnessed in helping us understand how to optimize preparatory work prior to conferencing, as well as the importance of follow-up and support.

Preston's work (Chapter 4) appraised similar developments in neuroscience, education and psychology in advancing the evidence behind restorative practices and social and emotional learning. She claims that these multi-disciplinary advances provide us with a greater understanding of the psychological theory that indeed underpins the restorative approach. Preston goes as far as saying that psychology '[can help] us to develop a stronger, more explicit framework in which to support people to manage conflict and harm, and build positive affect and healthy relationships'. Her conclusion spoke directly to me: 'It is encouraging to see the development of this cross-discipline research [this volume], which will continue to help us gain a better understanding of how and why restorative practice works'. I started to see what I have been missing in the past so many years of my studies of restorative justice.

Drennan et al.'s work in implementing restorative justice practice in a forensic mental health service in the UK provided me with much empirical evidence (Chapter 6) of the need for interdisciplinarity. By definition, restorative justice must involve all affected parties in a voluntary and conscious dialogue where responsibility taking and negotiation take place. Drennan et al. conclude that 'restorative practices could make a powerful contribution to the development of insight and emotional understanding in offenders with serious mental health challenges'. However, in the same breathe they go on to say that we must be careful not to prioritize the recovery needs of the wrongdoer while neglecting the primary moral and ethical requirements of prioritizing the restoration of the victim. This warning took me back to my original concerns of looking at restorative justice as a clinical process that can interpret and correct human behaviour.

Kashyap's analysis of humiliation as it impacts on our mental and emotional state of being (Chapter 7) enhanced my questioning around balancing the idealism of restorative justice and its potential to scientifically interpret our existence. Her work also addressed some of my concerns around power and its impact on the structural and environmental prerequisites of restorative justice. She argues that power is an important element in the relationship between the humiliated and the humiliator. It generates violence and victimization not only between two individuals, but also within societies. Humiliation, she says, is not merely an emotion but a social practice that is embedded in national and political discourses. Understanding these multi-dimensions of humiliation as they impact on restorative justice can only be achieved through a combination of discourses.

Walker's case study about people imprisoned for crimes that they did not commit (Chapter 8) helped me make the connections between the restorative practice of circles and psychology. It also raised a series of new questions, such as where does group therapy end and where do restorative justice circles begin? Looking at innocent incarcerated people and their families, she claims that circles can help them heal for their suffering caused both by harmful behaviours and from the loss of their loved one to prison and absence in their daily lives. Walker's arguments made me ask whether restorative justice circle is another form of group therapy. If the answer is yes, then a further question was raised and that is whether psychology is trying to claim justice territory. As a trained lawyer, this question made me feel anxious.

I continued looking for answers to my aforementioned question in the remaining papers. Of special significance to the objectives of the volume are the two empirical chapters, 11 and 12. Worth et al. (Chapter 11) and Ramírez et al. (Chapter 12) conducted new qualitative research specifically for the purposes of this volume using the tools of psychology and positive psychology to measure, understand and challenge restorative justice. With much gratitude and excitement, I welcomed these unique contributions.

Worth et al. used observation and interviews to collect data on selected restorative justice interventions. Subsequently, using their background as psychologists and social scientists they analysed what they saw as objectively as possible. They argue that in order for restorative justice to work, a psychological space must be created which allows offenders to be more than their offence, to be seen as a larger or fuller person than their crime alone. They explain, 'In this space we saw individuals display insight, understanding, movement and a willingness to be more than their stereotype and their crime'. They then advise us that through their eyes as psychologists, they also saw the impact of anxiety about the restorative justice process impacting the offender. They advocate that this must be acknowledged and managed if restorative justice is to be effective. Worth et al. made me think how much more we can learn by using applied sciences as learning tools for restorative justice. It also made me realize where the relationship between restorative justice and psychology should end – it was finally becoming clearer to me that psychology and applied sciences are just a tool for learning.

Ramírez et al. then presented their new research with two penal cases that they used as case studies for their chapter. The findings affirmed my aforementioned conclusion. They explain that while using the tools of positive psychology, they were able to map the feelings, emotions and belief systems of the participants and through this knowledge understand the potential and contribution of the restorative justice meetings that took place for the penal cases they studied. They explain that the parties' beliefs about the world, their optimism or pessimism, their ability to be resilient and empathetic and their willingness to forgive must be determined through the way they deal with the given conflict during restorative justice. This measurement can be achieved through the tool of psychology.

The Sceptic

I now turn to understanding my sceptic self. In their attempt to unravel the contribution of applied disciplines and the value of interdisciplinarity, Van de Vyver et al. (Chapter 2) examine restorative justice through a hybrid of social and psychological lens. Through their analysis, they attempt to show why a social psychologically informed approach is relevant for future research and policy strategy for restorative justice. They draw on the psychology intergroup relations, dehumanization and social exclusion to challenge restorative justice. Their analysis confirmed my scepticism of treating applied approaches to restorative justice as more than just measurement tools for its encounters. Their empirical study reminds us of a harsh reality that must be acknowledged in the implementation of restorative justice:

People do not apply human rights, justice and fairness equally to all outgroups in society ... Our review and conceptual framework identified that society and its agents are likely to be biased and selective in offering restorative justice, thereby limiting its potential to promote constructive change. Empirical evidence shows that people are more willing to support restorative justice for ingroup members.

How fair is restorative justice, if the societal context within which it is applied makes it a luxury entitlement for selected groups? More importantly, if psychology, neuroscience and the applied sciences are all about the individual, then what role do they have in addressing this societal caveat that may indeed bring restorative justice to its knees?

The argument of equality and of a consistent, transparent and proportionate implementation of restorative justice was further explored in Oudshoorn's work on individual and collective trauma (Chapter 9). He explains that psychology can be useful in helping us to understand the significance of individual trauma as a cause for criminality, but also as a vehicle for changing offending behaviour. 'Trauma-informed desistance, using a restorative justice framework, is a better way than simply measuring and managing risk', he says. However, the fact that within our societies we experience a collective trauma caused by inequalities and power structures (e.g. colonialism), a mere practical and scientific approach to resolving conflict will not do. The need to combine various approaches to progress justice and criminal justice is obvious. However, like Oudshoorn I believe that the caveats created by the context within which justice practices are applied place value-based approaches in realms beyond science and into the world of spiritual learning and belonging.

My scepticism of the role of applied sciences for restorative justice grew stronger as I read Artinopoulou's work (Chapter 5). She argues us that psychology and the related applied disciplines focus on understanding and correcting the individual. All this is good, but justice as a value extends far beyond the 'you' and 'I'. She concludes that the recent trend to introduce neuro and psy (Ψ) approaches to the way we do and deliver justice redefines the values of equity, restoration, transformation, punishment, and crime prevention. She warns us, 'Neuro-turn in this context is critical for imposing – through the neo-Darwinianism – an *a-moral*, *a-historical* and *a-cultural* perspective in explaining the human/social/criminal behaviour. Restorative justice has to include the multiple social and structural inequalities in its debate and not focus only on individuals per se'. She goes on to say:

> Thus, the possible warning for restorative justice is not the "Ψ" discourse itself and what it represents. It is rather the individualization that leads to the neglection of structures and the marginalization of social policies. Furthermore, it is the risk of restorative justice to lose its democratic character and its "ethos", according to Gavrielides' (2007) definition, and to align with the neoliberal ideologies.

Reminding me of the definition I coined through the testaments of practitioners was a wake-up call. Can 'ethos' be subject to science?

Lyubansky and Shpungin's analysis of what they call 'the unacknowledged power of power dynamics in restorative justice' (Chapter 10) was conclusive for my scepticism. In its ideal form, restorative justice is a community response, they say. This expects us to endorse a range of ideologies and methodologies often found through an interdisciplinary journey. The various tools found within diverse disciples should be welcomed and used with discretion. Their work also looks at the dynamics of the practitioners and researchers who make the restorative justice movement. They perform what I described above: a psychology for restorative justice. After analysing the power structures of the restorative justice movement as well as the context within restorative justice operates, they conclude that the conflicts within the movement as well as the overt and hidden biases, weaknesses and power dynamics reveal a field much in need of understanding itself. They add: 'How the restorative justice movement responds to this pressure will go a long way in determining whether restorative justice will be a truly revolutionary force for justice or just a slightly less punitive version of what we've been doing all along'.

Back to Justice

In the introduction of this concluding chapter, I stated my objective. I set off on a journey to psychologise myself and while doing so I spotted my co-existing sceptic and believer selves. Looking back at the volume's contributions, and without any psychology training, with relief I can now say that I am as healthy in mind as I am in spirit. My sceptic and believer selves suddenly merged into one as I realized that my questioning around the role of sciences, applied sciences, psychologists, neuroscientists, biologists and others was misplaced.

Justice, and with it restorative justice, is a value not for psychological, biological and neurological treatment. It is a virtue beyond our scientific reach and minds. It is central to our existence and interconnecteness. I asked who we should be looking at if we are to understand and progress restorative justice. Looking at the contributions in this volume, the answer becomes clear: at ourselves. This is the true power of restorative justice; a power so strong that it is capable of collapsing the power structures that surround us.

Of course, this conclusion should not be read as a dismissal of the role and contribution of psychology, positive psychology and other sciences. These can all serve as tools for evaluation and observation. They can also serve in helping us channel and safeguard this power within, and what surrounds it. As noted by a number of authors in this volume, understanding the psychology of restorative justice and managing the related powers is crucial for the future. I was particularly alarmed by Lyubansky and Shpungin's warning that the most invisible and insidious power dynamic that they have experienced while practising restorative justice reaches deep down into one of the core values of restorative justice. That is the belief that victims and offenders play fundamentally different roles in restorative practice, and thus have different needs that must be respected. This resonated with me as I remembered Sphungin's (2014) work on the fluidity of victimhood. Similarly, in their chapter, Lyubanksy and Sphungin say that 'victimhood and offenderhood are fluid concepts that are: (a) socially constructed by culture, media and impacted stakeholders; (b) artificially assigned by gatekeepers based on limited legal definitions of crime; (c) muddled by contextual factors … and systemic inequities; and (d) often shared by multiple parties in a conflict (Shpungin, 2014)'. I agree with the authors that as restorative justice becomes more and more popular among politicians, funders and policy makers, and as we see it developing through top-down structures of control, the power dynamics and risks will become even more prominent. While science should be used as a tool for understanding and controlling these powers, we must remember that the underlying values and norms making the restorative justice notion exist beyond scientific interpretation. These lie within our collective and individual ethos, hearts and communities.

And community is the missing word here. How can individually focused disciplines claim a prominent role in the delivery of the virtue of justice? It is in the very DNA of restorative justice to depend on the existence of others. Let's start by looking at what is to be restored. Zehr (1990) sees harm as a 'wound in human relationships' and an action that 'creates an obligation to restore and repair' (p. 33). In the restorative justice paradigm, '[c]rime is fundamentally a violation of people and interpersonal relationships' (Zehr and Mika, 1998, p. 47), a conflict not between the individual and the state, but between individuals. This understanding of crime transcends the burden of the criminal process, introducing a new target: the restoration of the relationship between victims and offenders, and offenders and their communities. As Zehr (1990) puts it, restorative justice understanding of crime 'creates an obligation to make things right' (p. 35). A question that follows from this is what created this relationship that restorative justice aims to restore?

Restorative justice assumes the existence of what I called a 'social liaison' that bonds individuals in a relationship of respect for others' rights and freedoms (Gavrielides, 2005). Restorative justice assumes that this liaison has always been with us, because it is innately human. We cannot see it, but we can feel it in moments of danger, or of extreme happiness. Individuals are not really strangers, and that is why victim and offender are not enemies. The pre-existence of this social liaison that restorative justice aims to restore elevates its practices and values to spheres that are beyond science.

To understand this better, we resort to the teachings of Collectivists. In Barnes' (1991) words, Collectivists' 'oddities and accidents may be individual and independent, their movements and machinations largely self-determined, but in their essence they are necessarily bound to others; for all are adjuncts and elements of a larger whole' (p. 1). Alexander Pope, at the end of the first Epistle of the 'Essay on Man' said: 'each of us, like any other natural object, is a part of the universe; it is folly to deny the fact – and folly to wish it changed … for our good is determined and our moral comportment should be governed by our partial statues in the universal All' (Mack, 1950, p. 2). On the other hand, each of us is not only a part, but also a system or a whole. We are what Barnes (1988) calls 'partial whole'. We are parts of a greater whole, and again wholes with parts of our own. Marcus Aurelius' work 'Meditations' (Rutherford, 1989) is said to be the closest ancient parallel to Pope's views (Barnes, 1991, pp. 1–23). He insisted that we are a part (μέρος) of Nature (φύσις), or of the universe (κόσμος), or of Fate (ειμαρμένη). He said that we stand to the universe as our hands and feet stand to our bodies and that, as with organic parts, we have mutually interdependent functions and activities, working together (συνεργούσιν) to a common end; a common good. In other words, 'we are interdependent parts of an organized whole, and our mutual dependencies determine our nature and our function' (Barnes, 1991, p. 7).

What restorative justice takes from these philosophies is their central feature of interdependency, determination and self-assurance through the realization of the existence of others. This reality creates the social liaison which connects individuals, and which might be broken if a crime occurs. This liaison is once again not susceptive to psychological treatment.

Barnes (1991) said: 'Systems, or integral wholes, are wholes which have (at least) one special sort of partition. This is characterized by the fact that its members are united by a special relation (or set of relations); they form a family. Families are defined in terms of binary relations' (p. 13). The broken social liaison, or what Barnes called the 'special relation', between individuals and individuals and their community is the focus of restoration.

In restorative justice, victim and offender are treated as free individuals, responsible for their actions and decisions. They are not strangers, but related because of the 'social liaison' that connects them. It does not matter whether they have met before or not. What is important is that they live in the same environment; let it be social or legal. As free individuals, both have rights that need to be respected and protected. They also have obligations (Braithwaite, 2002), which include restoring the balance that the harm has disturbed in the community. Therefore, what restorative justice calls on them to do is to restore the broken liaison that used to bond them. To this end, the experience of pain is welcomed and justified.

Under this matrix, victim and offender are seen as two sides of the same coin. The offender is not dealt with as a parasite of society, but as 'one of us'. Offenders distort the social liaison, but this does not make them our enemy. On the contrary, their actions are seen as an opportunity to prevent greater evils, 'to confront crime with a grace that transforms human lives to paths of love and giving' (Braithwaite, 1999, p. 2).

Restorative justice makes one more assumption. It takes individuals to be dependent on their communities; their lives gain meaning from the aggregation, and their happiness is linked to the existence of the aggregation that witnesses it. The existence of community is a prerequisite for the liaison that relates individuals. The community strives to instil a sense in individuals to respect and protect the liaison. It attempts this by keeping a liaison between itself and the individual; not a liaison of control and power, but of care. The liaison is also based on the recognition that I am impacted by you, and you are impacted by me. Therefore, the imposition of state-inflicted punishment is irrelevant. A central belief in the restorative thought is that 'it is wiser to strengthen our relationship with offenders rather than weaken it' by segregating and ostracizing them (Johnstone, 2001, p. 13). That is why 'it makes sense to show them that we care about them' (p. 13). Accordingly, 'offenders are provided opportunities and encouragement to understand the harm they have caused to others, and develop plans for taking appropriate responsibility. Voluntary participation is maximised; coercion and exclusion are minimised' (Zehr and Mika, 1998, p. 51).

There Is Room for Everyone in Restorative Justice

I dare to conclude that restorative justice must be developed as an independent field of study and as a discipline that transcends science. I will also humbly add that as a researcher, I welcome the potential relationship between restorative justice and science. However, it does not excite me as much as the relationship that must be deepened between the restorative justice practice and theory, including philosophy. Many authors in this volume warned not to ignore the psychology of restorative justice. They also warned scientists not to insist on claiming something so unattainable as the notion of justice – a notion that is ingrained in the hearts of the aboriginal, indigenous, religious, African, Hellenic and ancient civilizations that have been practising it for centuries.

In a recent book review of *The Psychology of Emotion in Restorative Practice*, I expressed similar concerns to Kelly and Thorsborne (Gavrielides, 2015). Their starting point is that '[h]uman beings are neurobiological entities before they become psychological, social and ethical beings'. They proceed to build their arguments around the theory of affect script psychology (ASP). Kelly and Thorsborne go so far as to say that researchers failed 'to fully grasp the depth and consequences of the biological and evolutionary insights provided by ASP ... nor had any other theoretician ... developed any significant unifying theory for restorative justice' (Kelly and Thorsborne, 2014, p. 18). With much regret, I therefore wrote:

> The book's insistence on viewing individuals only as biological entities is problematic in providing a holistic vision of restorative justice. The Collectivists, Utilitarians, Communitarians and many normative theorists including Mill, Bentham, Hegel, Foucault and Descartes as well as religious and spiritual leaders would be turning in their graves if a book insisted that our inter-connections and relationships are the results of us being neurobiological entities. (Gavrielides, 2015b, p. 2)

The answers as to why our interconnectedness exists, why it can be broken and how it can be restored may exist in realms beyond neuroscience and psychology. Applied sciences approaches should work alongside other normative, spiritual, cultural, historical and philosophical understandings of restorative justice. I hope that this book has taken the first step in helping us achieve a truly interdisciplinary dialogue for restorative justice.

With courage, I will conclude that restorative justice lives beyond the realms of criminology, social sciences, applied sciences and the like. In our attempt to understand, serve and apply it, various tools should become available. Here, there is plenty of room for everyone including psychologists, neuroscientists, sociologists, criminologists and so on. However, it is pretentious to believe that applied sciences alone can give the clarity and meaning that we have been looking for in restorative justice. Restorative justice must be treated as an autonomous field of study that can be explored and developed through a multi-disciplinary approach. Its strong ethical foundations, as well as the need to use the power within to control and fight the power structures that could bring its demise, are what make it a special field. I welcome this challenge and call on the restorative justice movement to focus its energy on developing its emerging, independent field rather than continue to justify it through superiority dialogues and by comparing it with what isn't.

Bibliography

Acorn, A. (2004). Compulsory compassion: justice, fellow-feeling, and the restorative encounter. In A. Acorn (ed.), *Compulsory compassion: a critique of restorative justice* (pp. 120–160). Vancouver: University of British Columbia Press.

Archibald, B. (2005). Why restorative justice is not compulsory compassion: Annalise Acorn's labour of love lost [A review of *Compulsory compassion: a critique of restorative justice*, Annalise E. Acorn (Vancouver: University of British Columbia Press, 2004)], *Alberta Law Review*, 42(3).

Barnes, J. (1988). Bits and pieces. In J. Barnes and M. Mignucci (eds), *Matter and metaphysics* (pp. 223–294), Naples: Bibliopolis.

Barnes, J. (1991). Partial wholes. In J. Paul (ed.), *Ethics, politics, and human nature* (pp. 1–23). Oxford: Basil Blackwell.

Braithwaite, J. (1999). *Restorative justice: assessing optimistic and pessimistic accounts* Crime and Justice: A Review of Research, vol. 25, edited by Michael Tonry (pp. 1–127) Chicago, IL: University of Chicago Press.

Braithwaite, J. (2002). *Restorative justice and responsive regulation.* New York: Oxford University Press.

Gavrielides, T. (2005). Some meta-theoretical questions for restorative justice. *Ratio Juris*, 18(1), 84–106.

Gavrielides, T. (2007). *Restorative justice theory and practice: addressing the discrepancy*, Helsinki: HEUNI.

Gavrielides, T. (2008). Restorative justice: the perplexing concept. Conceptual fault lines and power battles within the restorative justice movement. *Criminology and Criminal Justice Journal, 8*(2), 165–183.

Gavrielides, T. (2011a). Restorative practices: from the early societies to the 1970s. *Internet Journal of Criminology*, ISSN 2045-6743.

Gavrielides, T. (2011b). *Restorative justice and the secure estate: alternatives for young people in custody.* London: IARS Publications.

Gavrielides, T. (2013). Restorative pain: a new vision of punishment. In T. Gavrielides and V. Artinopoulou (eds), *Reconstructing restorative justice philosophy* (pp. 311–337). Farnham: Ashgate Publishing.

Gavrielides T. (2014). Bringing race relations into the restorative justice debate. *Journal of Black Studies, 45*(3), 216–246.

Gavrielides, T. (2015a). *Restorative justice.* The Library of Essays on Justice. Farnham: Ashgate Publishing.

Gavrielides, T. (2015b). Review of *The psychology of emotion in restorative practice* by Vernon C. Kelly and Margaret Thorsborne (London: Jessica Kingsley Publishers, 2014).

Gavrielides, T. and Artinopoulou, V. (2013). *Reconstructing the restorative justice philosophy.* Farnham: Ashgate Publishing.

Gavrielides, T. and Worth, P. (2014). Another push for restorative justice: positive psychology and offender rehabilitation. In M.H. Pearson (ed.), *Crime: international perspectives, socioeconomic factors and psychological implications* (pp. 161–182). New York: Nova Science Publishers.

Johnstone, G. (2001). *Restorative justice: ideas, values, debates.* Cullompton: Willan Publishing.

Johnstone, G. and van Ness, D. (2011). *Handbook of restorative justice.* Cullompton: Willan Publishing.

Mack, M. (1950). *The poems of Alexander Pope III.* London: Methuen.

Pavlich, G. (2005). Victims of restorative governmentalities. In G. Pavlich (ed.), *Governing paradoxes of restorative justice* (pp. 43–65). London: Glasshouse Press.

Rutherford, R. (1989). *The meditations of Marcus Aurelius: a study.* Oxford: Clarendon Press.

Shpungin, E. (2014). The fluidity of victimhood. In T. Gavrielides (ed.), *A victim-led criminal justice system: addressing the paradox.* London: IARS Publications.

Umbreit, M.S. (2008). Criminal and juvenile mediation in the United States. In Scalfati (ed.), *Developments in juvenile justice.* Rome: Italian Ministry of Justice.

Van Ness, D. (2005). An overview of restorative justice around the world. Paper presented to the Eleventh United Nations Congress on Crime Prevention and Criminal Justice, Bangkok, Thailand.

Zehr, H. (1990). *Changing lenses: a new focus for crime and justice.* Scottdale and Waterloo: Herald Press.

Zehr, H. and Mika, H. (1998). Fundamental concepts of restorative justice. *Contemporary Justice Review*, *1*, 47–55.

Index